Todd G. Morrison, PhD
Bruce W. Whitehead
Editors

Male Sex Work:
A Business Doing Pleasure

Male Sex Work: A Business Doing Pleasure has been co-published simultaneously as *Journal of Homosexuality*, Volume 53, Numbers 1/2 2007.

Pre-publication
REVIEWS,
COMMENTARIES,
EVALUATIONS . . .

"**A** much needed text on the male sex trade. . . . A fascinating yet sober look at the tapestry of individuals within this understudied area, including those 'tricking' on the street or bars, paid escorts (including those advertising on the Internet), strip club dancers, and individuals performing in pornography. The book debunks typical myths surrounding the topic and players, and illustrates both the struggles and successes of individuals within this business. Complex relationship dynamics and cares are revealed, as are reasons for entering and departing the trade. Multiple-city perspectives are presented from the U.S., as are international perspectives from countries including Australia, Canada, and the Dominican Republic. I HIGHLY RECOMMEND THIS BOOK . . . . SHOULD BE CONSIDERED BY ANYONE WORKING WITH THIS DIVERSE POPULATION."

William D. Marelich, PhD
Associate Professor of Psychology
California State University, Fullerton

More pre-publication
REVIEWS, COMMENTARIES, EVALUATIONS . . .

"Todd Morrison and Bruce Whitehead have, like all good sex workers, 'given us our money's worth.' From informal interviews to more formal ethnographic studies, they and their worthy contributors have all widened our perceptions of male sex work and the issues that shape it in articles that are well-written, scholarly yet accessible. Beginning with a look at those paradigms that have guided the research heretofore, they then move into addressing issues of power and control—worker to worker and worker to client—the construction of sexuality, stigma and its effects, racial politics, and the question of authenticity. Of special interest is Jeffrey Escoffier's essay on career trajectories, highlighting some of the porn 'stars' of yesteryear many of us 'knew' and 'loved.' For those researchers brave enough to excavate this terrain, THIS BOOK IS INDISPENSABLE."

Andrew R. Gottlieb, PhD
Author of *Out of the Twilight: Fathers of Gay Men Speak* and *Sons Talk About Their Gay Fathers: Life Curves;* Editor of *Side by Side: On Having a Gay or Lesbian Sibling* and Co-Editor of *Interventions with Families of Gay, Lesbian, Bisexual, and Transgender People: From the Inside Out*

The Haworth Press, Inc.

www.HaworthPress.com

Male Sex Work:
A Business Doing Pleasure

Male Sex Work: A Business Doing Pleasure has been co-published simultaneously as *Journal of Homosexuality*, Volume 53, Numbers 1/2 2007.

Monographs from the *Journal of Homosexuality*®

For additional information on these and other Haworth Press titles, including descriptions, tables of contents, reviews, and prices, use the QuickSearch catalog at http://www.HaworthPress.com.

1. *Homosexuality and the Law,* edtied by Donald C. Knutson, JD (Vol. 5, No. 1/2, 1979). *Leading law professors and practicing lawyers address the important legal issues and court decisions relevant to male and female homosexuality–criminal punishment for gay sex acts, employment discrimination, child custody, gay organizational rights, and more.*

2. *The Gay Past: A Collection of Historical Essays,* edited by Salvatore J. Licata, PhD, and Robert P. Petersen (Vol. 6, No. 1/2, 1980). *"Scholarly and excellent. Its authority is impeccable, and its treatment of this neglected area exemplary." (Choice)*

3. *Philosophy and Homosexuality,* edtied by Noretta Koertge, PhD (Vol. 6, No. 4, 1981). *"An interesting, thought-provoking book, well worth reading as a corrective to much of the research literature on homosexuality." (Australian Journal of Sex, Marriage & Family)*

4. *A Guide to Psychotherapy with Gay and Lesbian Clients,* edited by John C. Gonsiorek, PhD (Vol. 7, No. 2/3, 1982). *"A book that seeks to create affirmative psychotherapeutic models. . . . The contributors' credentials and experiences are impressive and extensive. . . . To say this book is needed by all doing therapy with gay or lesbian clients is an understatement." (The Advocate)*

5. *Gay and Sober: Directions for Counseling and Therapy,* edited by Thomas O. Ziebold, PhD, and John E. Mongeon (d. 1994) (Vol. 7, No. 4, 1982). *"A good book, easy to read, and free from jargon and prejudices. It is a research-oriented, academic work which deals with special problems posed by being an alcoholic and at the same time being gay. Even those whose work does not involve specifically working with the gay population will find this an interesting book." (Alcohol & Alcoholism)*

6. *Literary Visions of Homosexuality,* edited by Stuart Kellogg, PhD (Vol. 8, No. 3/4, 1983). *"An important book. Gay sensibility has never been given such a boost." (The Advocate)*

7. *Homosexuality, Masculinity, and Femininity,* edited by Michael W. Ross, PhD (Vol. 9, No. 1, 1983). *"A useful addition to the literature in both gender roles and sexual preference . . . it raises a number of questions which deserve further exploration." (Family Relations)*

8. *Origins of Sexuality and Homosexuality,* edited by John P. DeCecco, PhD, and Michael G. Shively, MA (Vol. 9, No. 2/3, 1984). *"Raises fundamentally important questions about the variable usage of the concept 'identity' in theory development and research. It is important reading for scholars who use that concept, regardless of any interest they may have in the specific topic of homosexuality." (The Journal of Nerves and Mental Disease)*

9. *Gay Personality and Sexual Labeling,* edited by John P. DeCecco, PhD (Vol. 9, No. 4, 1984). *Some of the best minds in sexual liberation take a hard look at how homosexuality is still defined and viewed by established schools of thought and propose fascinating and often controversial ideas on the true nature of the gay personality and identity.*

10. *Bashers, Baiters, and Bigots: Homophobia in America Society,* edited by John P. De Cecco, PhD (Vol. 10, No. 1/2, 1984). *"Breaks ground in helping to make the study of homophobia a science." (Contemporary Psychiatry)*

11. *Two Lives to Lead: Bisexuality in Men and Women,* edited by Fritz Klein, MD, and Timothy J. Wolf, PhD (Vol. 11, No. 1/2, 1985). *"The editors have brought together a formidable array of new data challenging old stereotypes about a very important human phenomenon. . . . A milestone in furthering our knowledge about sexual orientation." (David P. McWhirter, Co-author, The Male Couple)*

12. ***The Many Faces of Homosexuality: Anthropological Approaches to Homosexual Behavior,*** edited by Evelyn Blackwood, PhD (cand.) (Vol. 11, No. 3/4, 1986). *"A fascinating account of homosexuality during various historical periods and in non-Western cultures." (SIECUS Report)*

13. ***Historical, Literary, and Erotic Aspects of Lesbianism,*** edited by Monika Kehoe, PhD (Vol. 12, No. 3/4, 1986). *"Fascinating. . . . Even though this entire volume is serious scholarship penned by degreed writers, most of it is vital, accessible, and thoroughly readable even to the casual student of lesbian history." (Lambda Rising)*

14. ***Gay Life in Dutch Society,*** edited by A. X. van Naerssen, PhD (Vol. 13, No. 2/3, 1987). *"Valuable not just for its insightful analysis of the evolution of gay rights in The Netherlands, but also for the lessons that can be extracted by our own society from the Dutch tradition of tolerance for homosexuals." (The San Francisco Chronicle)*

15. ***Integrated Identity for Gay Men and Lesbians: Psychotherapeutic Approaches for Emotional Well-Being,*** edited by Eli Coleman, PhD (Vol. 14, No. 1/2, 1987). *"An invaluable tool. . . . This is an extremely useful book for the clinician seeking better ways to understand gay and lesbian patients." (Hospital and Community Psychiatry)*

16. ***The Treatment of Homosexuals with Mental Disorders,*** edited by Michael W. Ross, PhD (Vol. 15, No. 1/2, 1988). *"One of the more objective, scientific collections of articles concerning the mental health of gays and lesbians. . . . Extraordinarily thoughtful. . . . New thoughts about treatments. Vital viewpoints." (The Book Reader)*

17. ***The Pursuit of Sodomy: Male Homosexuality in Renaissance and Enlightenment Europe,*** edited by Kent Gerard, PhD, and Gert Hekma, PhD (Vol. 16, No. 1/2, 1989). *"Presenting a wealth of information in a compact form, this book should be welcomed by anyone with an interest in this period in European history or in the precursors to modern concepts of homosexuality." (The Canadian Journal of Human Sexuality)*

18. ***Lesbians Over 60 Speak for Themselves,*** edited by Monika Kehoe, PhD (Vol. 16, No. 3/4, 1989). *"A pioneering book examining the social, economical, physical, sexual, and emotional lives of aging lesbians." (Feminist Bookstore News)*

19. ***Gay and Lesbian Youth,*** edited by Gilbert Herdt, PhD (Vol. 17, No. 1/2/3/4, 1989). *"Provides a much-needed compilation of research dealing with homosexuality and adolescents." (GLTF Newsletter)*

20. ***Homosexuality and the Family,*** edited by Frederick W. Bozett, PhD (Vol. 18, No. 1/2, 1989). *"Enlightening and answers a host of questions about the effects of homosexuality upon family members and the family as a unit." (Ambush Magazine)*

21. ***Homosexuality and Religion,*** edited by Richard Hasbany, PhD (Vol. 18, No. 3/4, 1990). *"A welcome resource that provides historical and contemporary views on many issues involving religious life and homosexuality." (Journal of Sex Education and Therapy)*

22. ***Love Letters Between a Certain Late Nobleman and the Famous Mr. Wilson,*** edited by Michael S. Kimmel, PhD (Vol. 19, No. 2, 1990). *"An intriguing book about homosexuality in 18th-Century England. Many details of the period, such as meeting places, coded language, and 'camping' are all covered in the book. If you're a history buff, you'll enjoy this one." (Prime Timers)*

23. ***Male Intergenerational Intimacy: Historical, Socio-Psychological, and Legal Perspectives,*** edited by Theo G. M. Sandfort, PhD, Edward Brongersma, JD, and A. X. van Naerssen, PhD (Vol. 20, No. 1/2, 1991). *"The most important book on the subject since Tom O'Carroll's 1980 Paedophilia: The Radical Case." (The North American Man/Boy Love Association Bulletin, May 1991)*

24. ***Gay Midlife and Maturity: Crises, Opportunities, and Fulfillment,*** edited by John Alan Lee, PhD (Vol. 20, No. 3/4, 1991). *"The insight into gay aging is amazing, accurate, and much-needed. . . . A real contribution to the older gay community." (Prime Timers)*

25. ***Gay People, Sex, and the Media,*** edited by Michelle A. Wolf, PhD, and Alfred P. Kielwasser, MA (Vol. 21, No. 1/2, 1991). *"Altogether, the kind of research anthology which is useful to many disciplines in gay studies. Good stuff!" (Communique)*

26. *Homosexuality and Male Bonding in Pre-Nazi Germany: The Youth Movement, the Gay Movement, and Male Bonding Before Hitler's Rise: Original Transcripts from* **Der Eigene,** *the First Gay Journal in the World,* edited by Harry Oosterhuis, PhD, and Hubert Kennedy, PhD (Vol. 22, No. 1/2, 1992). *"Provide[s] insight into the early gay movement, particularly in its relation to the various political currents in pre-World War II Germany." (Lambda Book Report)*

27. *Coming Out of the Classroom Closet: Gay and Lesbian Students, Teachers, and Curricula,* edited by Karen M. Harbeck, PhD, JD, Recipient of Lesbian and Gay Educators Award by the American Educational Research Association's Lesbian and Gay Studies Special Interest Group (AREA) (Vol. 22, No. 3/4, 1992). *"Presents recent research about gay and lesbian students and teachers and the school system in which they function." (Contemporary Psychology)*

28. *Homosexuality in Renaissance and Enlightenment England: Literary Representations in Historical Context,* edited by Claude J. Summers, PhD (Vol. 23, No. 1/2, 1992). *"It is remarkable among studies in this field in its depth of scholarship and variety of approaches and is accessible." (Chronique)*

29. *Gay and Lesbian Studies,* edited by Henry L. Minton, PhD (Vol. 24, No. 1/2, 1993). *"The volume's essays provide insight into the field's remarkable accomplishments and future goals." (Lambda Book Report)*

30. *If You Seduce a Straight Person, Can You Make Them Gay? Issues in Biological Essentialism versus Social Constructionism in Gay and Lesbian Identities,* edited by John P. DeCecco, PhD, and John P. Elia, MA, PhD (cand.) (Vol. 24, No. 3/4, 1993). *"You'll find this alternative view of the age old question to be one that will become the subject of many conversations to come. Thought-provoking to say the least!" (Prime Timers)*

31. *Gay Studies from the French Cultures: Voices from France, Belgium, Brazil, Canada, and the Netherlands,* edited by Rommel Mendès-Leite, PhD, and Pierre-Olivier de Busscher, PhD (cand.) (Vol. 25, No. 1/2/3, 1993). *"The first book that allows an English-speaking world to have a comprehensive look at the principal trends in gay studies in France and French-speaking countries." (André Bèjin, PhD, Directeur, de Recherche au Centre National de la Recherche Scientifique [CNRS], Paris)*

32. *Critical Essays: Gay and Lesbian Writers of Color,* edited by Emmanuel S. Nelson, PhD (Vol. 26, No. 2/3, 1993). *"A much-needed book, sparkling with stirring perceptions and resonating with depth. . . . The anthology not only breaks new ground, it also attempts to heal wounds inflicted by our oppressed pasts." (Lambda)*

33. *Gay and Lesbian Studies in Art History,* edited by Whitney Davis, PhD (Vol. 27, No. 1/2, 1994). *"Informed, challenging . . . never dull. . . . Contributors take risks and, within the restrictions of scholarly publishing, find new ways to use materials already available or examine topics never previously explored." (Lambda Book Report)*

34. *Gay Ethics: Controversies in Outing, Civil Rights, and Sexual Science,* edited by Timothy F. Murphy, PhD (Vol. 27, No. 3/4, 1994). *"The contributors bring the traditional tools of ethics and political philosophy to bear in a clear and forceful way on issues surrounding the rights of homosexuals." (David L. Hull, Dressler Professor in the Humanities, Department of Philosophy, Northwestern University)*

35. *Sex, Cells, and Same-Sex Desire: The Biology of Sexual Preference,* edited by John P. DeCecco, PhD, and David Allen Parker, MA (Vol. 28, No. 1/2/3/4, 1995). *"A stellar compilation of chapters examining the most important evidence underlying theories on the biological basis of human sexual orientation." (MGW)*

36. *Gay Men and the Sexual History of the Political Left,* edited by Gert Hekma, PhD, Harry Oosterhuis, PhD, and James Steakley, PhD (Vol. 29, No. 2/3/4, 1995). *"Contributors delve into the contours of a long-forgotten history, bringing to light new historical data and fresh insight. . . . An excellent account of the tense historical relationship between the political left and gay liberation." (People's Voice)*

37. *Gays, Lesbians, and Consumer Behavior: Theory, Practice, and Research Issues in Marketing,* edited by Daniel L. Wardlow, PhD (Vol. 31, No. 1/2, 1996). *"For those scholars,*

market researchers, and marketing managers who are considering marketing to the gay and lesbian community, this book should be on their required reading list." (Mississippi Voice)

38. **Activism and Marginalization in the AIDS Crisis,** edited by Michael A. Hallett, PhD (Vol. 32, No. 3/4, 1997). *Shows readers how the advent of HIV-disease has brought into question the utility of certain forms of "activism" as they relate to understanding and fighting the social impacts of disease.*

39. **Reclaiming the Sacred: The Bible in Gay and Lesbian Culture,** edited by Raymond-Jean Frontain, PhD (Vol. 33, No. 3/4, 1997). *"Finely wrought, sharply focused, daring, and always dignified. . . . In chapter after chapter, the Bible is shown to be a more sympathetic and humane book in its attitudes toward homosexuality than usually thought and a challenge equally to the straight and gay moral imagination." (Joseph Wittreich, PhD, Distinguished Professor of English, The Graduate School, The City University of New York)*

40. **Gay and Lesbian Literature Since World War II: History and Memory,** edited by Sonya L. Jones, PhD (Vol. 34, No. 3/4, 1998). *"The authors of these essays manage to gracefully incorporate the latest insights of feminist, postmodernist, and queer theory into solidly grounded readings . . . challenging and moving, informed by the passion that prompts both readers and critics into deeper inquiry." (Diane Griffin Growder, PhD, Professor of French and Women's Studies, Cornell College, Mt. Vernon, Iowa)*

41. **Scandinavian Homosexualities: Essays on Gay and Lesbian Studies,** edited by Jan Löfström, PhD (Vol. 35, No. 3/4, 1998). *"Everybody interested in the formation of lesbian and gay identities and their interaction with the sociopolitical can find something to suit their taste in this volume." (Judith Schuyf, PhD, Assistant Professor of Lesbian and Gay Studies, Center for Gay and Lesbian Studies, Utrecht University, The Netherlands)*

42. **Multicultural Queer: Australian Narratives,** edited by Peter A. Jackson, PhD, and Gerard Sullivan, PhD (Vol. 36, No. 3/4, 1999). *Shares the way that people from ethnic minorities in Australia (those who are not of Anglo-Celtic background) view homosexuality, their experiences as homosexual men and women, and their feelings about the lesbian and gay community.*

43. **The Ideal Gay Man: The Story of Der Kreis,** by Hubert Kennedy, PhD (Vol. 38, No. 1/2, 1999). *"Very profound. . . . Excellent insight into the problems of the early fight for homosexual emancipation in Europe and in the USA. . . . The ideal gay man (high-mindedness, purity, cleanness), as he was imagined by the editor of 'Der Kreis,' is delineated by the fascinating quotations out of the published erotic stories." (Wolfgang Breidert, PhD, Academic Director, Institute of Philosophy, University Karlsruhe, Germany)*

44. **Gay Community Survival in the New Millennium,** edited by Michael R. Botnick, PhD (cand.) (Vol. 38, No. 4, 2000). *Examines the notion of community from several different perspectives focusing on the imagined, the structural, and the emotive. You will explore a theoretical overview and you will peek into the moral discourses that frame "gay community," the rift between HIV-positive and HIV-negative gay men, and how Israeli gays seek their place in the public sphere.*

45. **Queer Asian Cinema: Shadows in the Shade,** edited by Andrew Grossman, MA (Vol. 39, No. 3/4, 2000). *"An extremely rich tapestry of detailed ethnographies and state-of-the-art theorizing. . . . Not only is this a landmark record of queer Asia, but it will certainly also be a seminal, contributive challenge to gender and sexuality studies in general." (Dédé Oetomo, PhD, Coordinator of the Indonesian organization GAYa NUSANTARA: Adjunct Reader in Linguistics and Anthropology, School of Social Sciences, Universitas Airlangga, Surabaya, Indonesia)*

46. **Gay and Lesbian Asia: Culture, Identity, Community,** edited by Gerard Sullivan, PhD, and Peter A. Jackson, PhD (Vol. 40, No. 3/4, 2001). *"Superb. . . . Covers a happily wide range of styles . . . will appeal to both students and educated fans." (Gary Morris, Editor/Publisher, Bright Lights Film Journal)*

47. **Homosexuality in French History and Culture,** edited by Jeffrey Merrick and Michael Sibalis (Vol. 41, No. 3/4, 2001). *"Fascinating. . . . Merrick and Sibalis bring together historians, literary scholars, and political activists from both sides of the Atlantic to examine same-sex sexuality in the past and present." (Bryant T. Ragan, PhD, Associate Professor of History, Fordham University, New York City)*

48. **The Drag King Anthology,** edited by Donna Jean Troka, PhD (cand.), Kathleen LeBesco, PhD, and Jean Bobby Noble, PhD (Vol. 43, No. 3/4, 2002). *"All university courses on masculinity*

should use this book . . . challenges preconceptions through the empirical richness of direct experience. The contributors and editors have worked together to produce cultural analysis that enhances our perception of the dynamic uncertainty of gendered experience." (Sally R. Munt. DPhil. Subject Chair. Media Studies, University of Sussex)

49. **Icelandic Lives: The Queer Experience,** edited by Voon Chin Phua (Vol. 44, No. 2, 2002). *"The first of its kind, this book shows the emergence of gay and lesbian visibility through the biographical narratives of a dozen Icelanders. Through their lives can be seen a small nation's transition, in just a few decades, from a pervasive silence concealing its queer citizens to widespread acknowledgment characterized by some of the most progressive laws in the world." (Barry D. Adam, PhD, University Professor, Department of Sociology & Anthropology, University of Windsor, Ontario, Canada)*

50. **Gay Bathhouses and Public Health Policy,** edited by William J. Woods, PhD, and Diane Binson, PhD (Vol. 44, No. 3/4, 2003). *"Important. . . . Long overdue. . . . A unique and valuable contribution to the social science and public health literature. The inclusion of detailed historical descriptions of public policy debates about the place of bathhouses in urban gay communities, together with summaries of the legal controversies about bathhouses, insightful examinations of patrons' behaviors and reviews of successful programs for HIV/STD education and testing programs in bathhouses provides. A well rounded and informative overview." (Richard Tewksbury, PhD, Professor of Justice Administration, University of Louisville)*

51. **Queer Theory and Communication: From Disciplining Queers to Queering the Discipline(s),** edited by Gust A. Yep, PhD, Karen E. Lovaas, PhD, and John P. Elia, PhD (Vol. 45, No. 2/3/4, 2003). *"Sheds light on how sexual orientation and identity are socially produced–and how they can be challenged and changed–through everyday practices and institutional activities, as well as academic research and teaching. . . . Illuminates the theoretical and practical significance of queer theory–not only as a specific area of inquiry, but also as a productive challenge to the heteronormativity of mainstream communication theory, research, and pedagogy." (Julia T. Wood, PhD, Lineberger Professor of Humanities, Professor of Communication Studies, The University of North Carolina at Chapel Hill)*

52. **The Drag Queen Anthology: The Absolutely Fabulous but Flawlessly Customary World of Female Impersonators,** edited by Steven P. Schacht, PhD, with Lisa Underwood (Vol. 46, No. 3/4, 2004). *"Indispensable. . . . For more than a decade, Steven P. Schacht has been one of the social sciences' most reliable guides to the world of drag queens and female impersonators. . . . This book assembles an impressive cast of scholars who are as theoretically astute, methodologically careful, and conceptually playful as the drag queens themselves." (Michael Kimmel, author of* The Gendered Society; *Professor of Sociology, SUNY Stony Brook)*

53. **Eclectic Views on Gay Male Pornography: Pornucopia,** edited by Todd G. Morrison, PhD (Vol. 47, No. 3/4, 2004). *"An instant classic. . . . Lively and readable." (Jerry Zientara, EdD, Librarian, Institute for Advanced Study of Human Sexuality)*

54. **Sexuality and Human Rights: A Global Overview,** edited by Helmut Graupner, JD, and Philip Tahmindjis, BA, LLB, LLM, SJD (Vol. 48, No. 3/4, 2005). *"An important resource for anybody concerned about the status of legal protection for the human rights of sexual minorities, especially for those concerned with attaining a comparative perspective. The chapters are all of high quality and are written in a straightforward manner that will be accessible to the non-specialist while containing much detail of interest to specialists in the area." (Arthur S. Leonard, JD, Professor of Law, New York Law School)*

55. **Same-Sex Desire and Love in Greco-Roman Antiquity and in the Classical Tradition of the West,** edited by Beert C. Verstraete and Vernon Provencal (Vol. 49, No. 3/4, 2005)."*This wide-ranging collection engages with the existing scholarship in the history of sexuality and the uses of the classical tradition and opens up exciting new areas of study. The book is an important addition to queer theory." (Stephen Guy-Bray, PhD, Associate Professor, University of British Columbia)*

56. **Sadomasochism: Powerful Pleasures,** edited by Peggy J. Kleinplatz, PhD, and Charles Moser, PhD, MD (Vol. 50, No. 2/3, 2006). *"I would advise anyone interested in doing research on this topic or trying to understand this severely stigmatized behavior to begin with this collection." (Vern L. Bullough, PhD, DSci, RN, Visiting Professor Emeritus, State University of New York; Editor of* Before Stonewall: Activists for Gay and Lesbian Rights in Historical Context)

57. *Current Issues in Lesbian, Gay, Bisexual, and Transgender Health*, edited by Jay Harcourt, MPH (Vol. 51, No. 1, 2006). *"A fine addition to our knowledge of LGBT youth adults. The chapter by Dr. Case and her colleagues gives us a wonderful study that supports the addition of sexual orientation to the demographic questions within research studies. Dr. Koh and Dr. Ross's work exploring mental health issues by sexual orientation is also very important." (Suzanne L. Dibble, RN, DNSc, Professor and Co-Director, Lesbian Health Research Center, University of California at San Francisco)*

58. *Sodomites and Urnings: Homosexual Representations in Classic German Journals*, edited and translated by Michael A. Lombardi-Nash, PhD (Vol. 51 Suppl. 1, 2006). *"These classic articles are a reminder that the homosexual liberation movement existed long before Stonewall. Especially interesting to me was Karoly Maria Kertbeny's 1868 letter to Karl Heinrich Ulrichs, which raises theoretical and tactical questions that are still pertinent. A 1909 poem by Magnus Hirschfeld,* Three German Graves in a Distant Land, *is informative and moving." (John Lauritsen, Independent Scholar, Author of* A Freethinker's Primer of Male Love, *and co-author of* The Early Homosexual Rights Movement (1864-1935), *(1974/ Revised Second Edition 1995)*

59. *LGBT Studies and Queer Theory: New Conflicts, Collaborations, and Contested Terrain*, edited by Karen E. Lovaas, PhD, John P. Elia, PhD, and Gust A. Yep, PhD (Vol. 52, No. 1/2, 2006). *"Most useful for readers who do not know much about these disciplines. The more specific articles focus on how the tensions between lesbian and gay studies and queer theory translate into various arenas of life. The reader can choose all or specific areas of interest to explore how they are enlightened by the views of these disciplines and the critiques of queer theory." (Ski Hunter, MSW, PhD, Professor, School of Social Work, University of Texas at Arlington)*

60. *Male Sex Work: A Business Doing Pleasure*, edited by Todd G. Morrison, PhD, and Bruce W. Whitehead (Vol. 53, No. 1/2, 2007). *A straightforward look at what really goes in the clubs, on the Internet, and behind the scenes of the gay sex industry.*

Published by

Harrington Park Press®, 10 Alice Street, Binghamton, NY 13904-1580 USA

Harrington Park Press® is an imprint of The Haworth Press, Inc., 10 Alice Street, Binghamton, NY 13904-1580 USA.

Male Sex Work: A Business Doing Pleasure has been co-published simultaneously as *Journal of Homosexuality*, Volume 53, Numbers 1/2 2007.

© 2007 by The Haworth Press, Inc. All rights reserved. No part of this work may be reproduced or utilized in any form or by any means, electronic or mechanical, including photocopying, microfilm and recording, or by any information storage and retrieval system, without permission in writing from the publisher. Printed in the United States of America.

The development, preparation, and publication of this work has been undertaken with great care. However, the publisher, employees, editors, and agents of The Haworth Press and all imprints of The Haworth Press, Inc., including The Haworth Medical Press® and Pharmaceutical Products Press®, are not responsible for any errors contained herein or for consequences that may ensue from use of materials or information contained in this work. With regard to case studies, identities and circumstances of individuals discussed herein have been changed to protect confidentiality. Any resemblance to actual persons, living or dead, is entirely coincidental.

The Haworth Press is committed to the dissemination of ideas and information according to the highest standards of intellectual freedom and the free exchange of ideas. Statements made and opinions expressed in this publication do not necessarily reflect the views of the Publisher, Directors, management, or staff of The Haworth Press, Inc., or an endorsement by them.

Cover artwork by Yvon Goulet: frontcover, *Greed*; back cover, *Hitchhiker*. Used by permission of the artist.

Library of Congress Cataloging-in-Publication Data

Male sex work : a business doing pleasure / Todd G. Morrison, Bruce W. Whitehead, editors.
    p. cm.
"Co-published simultaneously as Journal of Homosexuality, Volume 53, Numbers 1/2 2007."
    Includes bibliographical references and index.
    ISBN-13: 978-1-56023-726-6 (hard cover : alk. paper)
    ISBN-13: 978-1-56023-727-3 (soft cover : alk. paper)
    1. Male prostitution. 2. Male prostitutes. I. Morrison, Todd G. II. Whitehead, Bruce W. III. Journal of homosexuality.
    HQ117.M27 2007
    306.74'3–dc22
                                  2007032810

Male Sex Work:
A Business Doing Pleasure

Todd G. Morrison, PhD
Bruce W. Whitehead
Editors

Male Sex Work: A Business Doing Pleasure has been co-published simultaneously as *Journal of Homosexuality*, Volume 53, Numbers 1/2 2007.

The Haworth Press, Inc.

www.HaworthPress.com

ALL HAWORTH BOOKS AND JOURNALS
ARE PRINTED ON CERTIFIED
ACID-FREE PAPER

The HAWORTH PRESS Inc.

Abstracting, Indexing & Outward Linking

PRINT *and* ELECTRONIC BOOKS & JOURNALS

This section provides you with a list of major indexing & abstracting services and other tools for bibliographic access. That is to say, each service began covering this periodical during the year noted in the right column. Most Websites which are listed below have indicated that they will either post, disseminate, compile, archive, cite or alert their own Website users with research-based content from this work. (This list is as current as the copyright date of this publication.)

Abstracting, Website/Indexing Coverage . . . . Year When Coverage Began

- ****Academic Search Premier (EBSCO)****
  <http://search.ebscohost.com> 2007
- ****Chemical Abstracts Service**** *<http://www.cas.org>* 1982
- ****CINAHL (Cumulative Index to Nursing & Allied Health Literature) (EBSCO)**** *<http://www.cinahl.com>* 1985
- ****CINAHL Plus (EBSCO)**** *<http://search.ebscohost.com>* 2006
- ****INSPEC (The Institution of Engineering and Technology)**** *<http://www.iee.org.uk/publish/>* 2002
- ****LISA: Library and Information Science Abstracts (ProQuest CSA)**** *<http://www.csa.com/factsheets/list-set-c.php>* 1990
- ****MasterFILE Premier (EBSCO)**** *<http://search.ebscohost.com>* 2006
- ****ProQuest Academic Research Library (ProQuest CSA)**** *<http://www.proquest.com>* 2006
- ****Research Library (ProQuest CSA)**** *<http://www.proquest.com>* . . . 2006
- *Academic Search Alumni Edition (EBSCO)* *<http://search.ebscohost.com>* 2007
- *Academic Search Complete (EBSCO)* *<http://search.ebscohost.com>* . . . . *
- *Academic Search Elite (EBSCO)* *<http://search.ebscohost.com>* . . . 1993

(continued)

- *Academic Source Premier (EBSCO) <http://search.ebscohost.com>*... 2007
- *Advanced Polymers Abstracts (Cambridge Scientific Abstracts)*
  <http://www.csa.com/factsheets/ema-polymers-set-c.php> 2006
- *Aluminium Industry Abstracts (Cambridge Scientific Abstracts)*
  <http://www.csa.com/factsheets/aia-set-c.php> 2006
- *Biomeditaties (Biomedical Information of the Dutch*
  Library Association) <http://www.nvb-online.nl>............. 2006
- *Cabell's Directory of Publishing Opportunities*
  in Educational Technology & Library Science
  <http://www.cabells.com> 2006
- *Cambridge Scientific Abstracts <http://www.csa.com>* 2006
- *Ceramic Abstracts (Cambridge Scientific Abstracts)*
  <http://www.csa.com/factsheets/wca-set-c.php>.............. 2006
- *Composites Industry Abstracts (Cambridge Scientific Abstracts)*
  <http://www.csa.com/factsheets/ema-composites-set-c.php> 2006
- *Computer & Control Abstracts (INSPEC–The Institution*
  of Engineering and Technology)
  <http://www.iee.org.uk/publish/> 2006
- *Computer and Information Systems Abstracts (Cambridge*
  Scientific Abstracts)
  <http://www.csa.com/factsheets/computer-set-c.php> 2004
- *Corrosion Abstracts (Cambridge Scientific Abstracts)*
  <http://www.csa.com/factsheets/corrosion-set-c.php> 2006
- *CSA Engineering Research Database (Cambridge Scientific Abstracts)*
  <http://www.csa.com/factsheets/engineering-set-c.php> 2006
- *CSA High Technology Research Database With Aerospace*
  (Cambridge Scientific Abstracts)
  <http://www.csa.com/factsheets/hightech-set-c.php>.......... 2006
- *CSA Technology Research Database (Cambridge Scientific Abstracts)*
  <http://www.csa.com/factsheets/techresearch-set-c.php> 2006
- *CSA/ASCE Civil Engineering Abstracts (Cambridge Scientific*
  Abstracts) <http://www.csa.com/factsheets/civil-set-c.php> 2006
- *Current Abstracts (EBSCO) <http://search.ebscohost.com>* 2007
- *Current Citations Express (EBSCO) <http://search.ebscohost.com>*... 2007
- *EBSCOhost Electronic Journals Service (EJS)*
  <http://search.ebscohost.com> 2001
- *Education Research Complete (EBSCO)*
  <http://search.ebscohost.com> 2006

(continued)

- *Education Research Index (EBSCO) <http://search.ebscohost.com>* .. 2007
- *Electrical & Electronics Abstracts (INSPEC–The Institution of Engineering and Technology) <http://www.iee.org.uk/publish/>* 2006
- *Electronic Collections Online (OCLC) <http://www.oclc.org/electroniccollections/>* 2006
- *Electronics and Communications Abstracts (Cambridge Scientific Abstracts) <http://www.csa.com/factsheets/electronics-set-c.php>* 2006
- *Elsevier Eflow-l>* 2006
- *Elsevier Scopus <http://www.info.scopus.com>* 2002
- *EMCare(Elsevier) <http://www.elsevier.com>* 2006
- *Engineered Materials Abstracts (Cambridge Scientific Abstracts) <http://www.csa.com/factsheets/emaclust-set-c.php>* .. 2006
- *Foods Adlibra* .... *
- *Google <http://www.google.com>* 2004
- *Google Scholar <http://scholar.google.com>* 2004
- *Handbook of Latin American Studies* 1992
- *Haworth Document Delivery Center <http://www.HaworthPress.com/journals/dds.asp>* 2004
- *HealthSTAR (Ovid)>* 2006
- *Hein's Legal Periodical Checklist: Index to Periodical Articles Pertaining to Law <http://www.wshein.com>* 1989
- *(IBR) International Bibliography of Book Reviews on the Humanities and Social Sciences (Thomson) <http://www.saur.de>* 2006
- *(IBZ) International Bibliography of Periodical Literature on the Humanities and Social Sciences (Thomson) <http://www.saur.de>* 1993
- *Index Guide to College Journals* 1999
- *Index to Periodical Articles Related to Law <http://www.law.utexas.edu>* 1990
- *Information Reports & Bibliographies* 1992
- *Informed Librarian, The <http://www.informedlibrarian.com>* 1993
- *INIST-CNRS <http://www.inist.fr>* 1992
- *Internationale Bibliographie der geistes- und sozialwissenschaftlichen Zeitschriftenliteratur ... See IBZ <http://www.saur.de>* 1996

(continued)

- *Journal of Academic Librarianship: Guide to Professional Literature, The* 1992
- *JournalSeek <http://www.journalseek.net>* 2006
- *Konyvtari Figyelo (Library Review)* 1995
- *Legal Information Management Index (LIMI) <http://www.legalinformationservices.com>* 2007
- *Library Literature & Information Science Index / Full Text (H.W. Wilson) <http://www.hwwilson.com>* 1989
- *Library Reference Center (EBSCO) <http://search.ebscohost.com>* .. 2007
- *Library, Information Science & Technology Abstracts (EBSCO) <http://search.ebscohost.com>* 2006
- *Library, Information Science & Technology Abstracts with Full Text (EBSCO) <http://search.ebscohost.com>* 2007
- *Links@Ovid (via CrossRef targeted DOI links) <http://www.ovid.com>* 2005
- *MasterFILE Elite (EBSCO) <http://search.ebscohost.com>* 2007
- *MasterFILE Select (EBSCO) <http://search.ebscohost.com>* 2007
- *Materials Business File (Cambridge Scientific Abstracts) <http://www.csa.com/factsheets/mbf-set-c.php>* 2006
- *Materials Research Database with METADEX (Cambridge Scientific Abstracts) <http://www.csa.com/factsheets/materials-set-c.php>* 2006
- *Mechanical & Transportation Engineering Abstracts (Cambridge Scientific Abstracts) <http://www.csa.com/factsheets/mechtrans-set-c.php>* 2006
- *METADEX (Cambridge Scientific Abstracts) <http://www.csa.com/factsheets/metadex-set-c.php>* 2006
- *NewJour (Electronic Journals & Newsletters) <http://gort.ucsd.edu/newjour/>* 2006
- *OCLC ArticleFirst <http://www.oclc.org/services/databases/>* 2006
- *Ovid Linksolver (OpenURL link resolver via CrossRef targeted DOI links) <http://www.linksolver.com>* 2005
- *Physics Abstracts (INSPEC–The Institution of Engineering and Technology) <http://www.iee.org.uk/publish/>* 2006
- *Platinum Periodicals (ProQuest) <http://www.proquest.com>* 2006
- *ProQuest CSA <http://www.proquest.com>* 2007
- *ProQuest Discovery (ProQuest CSA) <http://www.proquest.com>* .. 2006

(continued)

- *ProQuest 5000 International (ProQuest CSA)*
  <http://www.proquest.com>..............................2006
- *Referativnyi Zhurnal (Abstracts Journal of the All-Russian
  Institute of Scientific and Technical Information–in Russian)*
  <http://www.viniti.ru>...................................1986
- *ScienceDirect Navigator (Elsevier)*
  <http://www.info.sciencedirect.com>....................2002
- *Scopus (See instead Elsevier Scopus) <http://www.info.scopus.com>*..2002
- *Social Care Online (formerly CareData) <http://www.elsc.org.uk>*...2003
- *Social Sciences Module (ProQuest CSA)*
  <http://www.proquest.com>..............................2006
- *Solid State and Superconductivity Abstracts
  (Cambridge Scientific Abstracts)*
  <http://www.csa.com/factsheets/solid-state-set-c.php>.........2006
- *Subject Index to Literature on Electronic Sources of Information*
  <http://library2.usask.ca/~dworacze/SUB_INT.HTM>........1990
- *SwetsWise <http://www.swets.com>*..........................2001
- *TOC Premier (EBSCO) <http://search.ebscohost.com>*..........2007
- *WilsonWeb <http://vnweb.hwwilsonweb.com/hww/Journals/>*.....2005

Bibliographic Access

- *Cabell's Directory of Publishing Opportunities in Educational
  Curriculum and Methods <http://www.cabells.com/>*
- *Magazines for Libraries (Katz)*
- *MediaFinder <http://www.mediafinder.com/>*
- *Ulrich's Periodicals Directory: The Global Source for Periodicals
  Information Since 1932 <http://www.bowkerlink.com>*

*Special Bibliographic Notes related to special journal issues
(separates) and indexing/abstracting:*

- indexing/abstracting services in this list will also cover material in any "separate" that is co-published simultaneously with Haworth's special thematic journal issue or DocuSerial. Indexing/abstracting usually covers material at the article/chapter level.
- monographic co-editions are intended for either non-subscribers or libraries which intend to purchase a second copy for their circulating collections.
- monographic co-editions are reported to all jobbers/wholesalers/approval plans. The source journal is listed as the "series" to assist the prevention of duplicate purchasing in the same manner utilized for books-in-series.
- to facilitate user/access services all indexing/abstracting services are encouraged to utilize the co-indexing entry note indicated at the bottom of the first page of each article/chapter/contribution.
- this is intended to assist a library user of any reference tool (whether print, electronic, online, or CD-ROM) to locate the monographic version if the library has purchased this version but not a subscription to the source journal.
- individual articles/chapters in any Haworth publication are also available through the Haworth Document Delivery Service (HDDS).

As part of
Haworth's
continuing
commitment
to better serve
our library
patrons,
we are
proud to
be working
with the
following
electronic
services:

AGGREGATOR SERVICES

EBSCOhost

Ingenta

J-Gate

Minerva

OCLC FirstSearch

Oxmill

SwetsWise

FirstSearch

Oxmill Publishing

SwetsWise

LINK RESOLVER SERVICES

1Cate (Openly Informatics)

ChemPort
(American Chemical Society)

CrossRef

Gold Rush (Coalliance)

LinkOut (PubMed)

LINKplus (Atypon)

LinkSolver (Ovid)

LinkSource with A-to-Z (EBSCO)

Resource Linker (Ulrich)

SerialsSolutions (ProQuest)

SFX (Ex Libris)

Sirsi Resolver (SirsiDynix)

Tour (TDnet)

Vlink (Extensity, formerly Geac)

WebBridge (Innovative Interfaces)

ChemPort

Gold Rush

LinkOut.
LINKING TO A WORLD OF RESOURCES

atypon

LinkSolver

ULRICH'S
RESOURCE LINKER

SerialsSolutions

S·F·X

SirsiDynix

UR

extensity

WebBridge

ABOUT THE EDITORS

Todd G. Morrison, PhD, a social psychologist at the National University of Ireland, Galway, conducts research on male body image, media, sex work, and homonegativity. He is editor of *Eclectic views on gay male pornography: Pornucopia* (2004, Harrington Park Press) and has published in a number of peer-reviewed journals including *Psychology of Men and Masculinity, Sexuality & Culture, Adolescence, Journal of Social Psychology,* and *Canadian Journal of Human Sexuality.* He is founder and past-chair of the Canadian Psychological Association's Section on Sexual Orientation and Gender Identity Issues (SOGII).

Bruce W. Whitehead, BA, is an independent scholar. His research interests include sex work, gay men's conscious decision to engage in condomless sexual behaviour (i.e., barebacking), gay pornography, and identity formation among sexual minorities. His research has been published in *Journal of Homosexuality* and *Journal of Psychology and Human Sexuality.*

Male Sex Work:
A Business Doing Pleasure

CONTENTS

Foreword   xix
    Benjamin Scuglia

Acknowledgments   xxi

INTRODUCTION

"It's a Business Doing Pleasure with You": An Interdisciplinary
    Reader on Male Sex Work   1
    Todd G. Morrison, PhD
    Bruce W. Whitehead

ON THE STREETS

Male Prostitution: Pathology, Paradigms and Progress
    in Research   7
    David S. Bimbi, PhD (candidate)

Sex and the Unspoken in Male Street Prostitution   37
    Kerwin Kaye, PhD (candidate)

Exploring the Interpersonal Relationships in Street-Based Male
    Sex Work: Results from an Australian Qualitative Study   75
    David Leary, MCouns, PhD (candidate)
    Victor Minichiello, PhD

IN THE CLUBS

Power and Control in Gay Strip Clubs   111
    Joseph R. G. DeMarco

Alienation of Sexuality in Male Erotic Dancing   129

David M. Boden, JD, PhD

The Closing of *Atlantis*   153
   Jonathan David Jackson

ON THE NET AND BEYOND

Porn Star/Stripper/Escort: Economic and Sexual Dynamics
   in a Sex Work Career   173
   Jeffrey Escoffier

"Nobody's Ever Going to Make a Fag *Pretty Woman*":
   Stigma Awareness and the Putative Effects of Stigma
   Among a Sample of Canadian Male Sex Workers   201
   Todd G. Morrison, PhD
   Bruce W. Whitehead

Looking Beyond HIV: Eliciting Individual and Community
   Needs of Male Internet Escorts   219
   Jeffrey T. Parsons, PhD
   Juline A. Koken, PhD (candidate)
   David S. Bimbi, PhD (candidate)

'Western Union Daddies' and Their Quest for Authenticity:
   An Ethnographic Study of the Dominican Gay Sex
   Tourism Industry   241
   Mark B. Padilla, PhD, MPH

CONCLUSION

Musings on Male Sex Work: A "Virtual" Discussion   277
   Rebecca L. Harriman, PhD (candidate)
   Barry Johnston, MA (candidate)
   Paula M. Kenny, MA

Index   319

Foreword

Casey Donovan, Al Parker, Joey Stefano. The "Holy Trinity" of
Stryker, Ryker, and Idol (no first names are needed). Rod Barry, Dean
Phoenix, Matthew Rush. Porn "stars" all, and members of an industry
whose influence is felt throughout gay culture and popular culture at
large. To wit: the sleek, buffed Falcon Studios aesthetic has permeated
fashion photography to such a degree that tanned, hairless perfection
has become celebrated as the male ideal. Without Falcon "Exclusives,"
there would be no metrosexuality.

And yet, the culture and evolution of sex workers from porn stars to
strippers and beyond, has remained frustratingly under-examined. Not
any longer. The esteemed essayists between these covers travel from
Vancouver to New York, Los Angeles to the Dominican Republic, and
explore a compelling range of topics. "Male Sex Work: A Business Doing Pleasure" is a thoroughly rich and absorbing book.

Benjamin Scuglia

[Haworth co-indexing entry note]: "Foreword." Scuglia, Benjamin. Co-published simultaneously in
Journal of Homosexuality (The Haworth Press, Inc.) Vol. 53, No. 1/2, 2007, p. xxxi; and: *Male Sex Work: A
Business Doing Pleasure* (ed: Todd G. Morrison, and Bruce W. Whitehead) The Haworth Press, Inc., 2007,
p. xxi. Single or multiple copies of this article are available for a fee from The Haworth Document Delivery
Service [1-800-HAWORTH, 9:00 a.m. - 5:00 p.m. (EST). E-mail address: docdelivery@ haworthpress.com].

Available online at http://jh.haworthpress.com
© 2007 by The Haworth Press, Inc. All rights reserved.

Acknowledgements

A gaggle, a passel, a bushel (repetition becomes us) of individuals were instrumental in the completion of this book. Given that we were unable to provide them with any form of remuneration (beyond gratitude and our inimitable snaggletoothed grins), their contributions are especially praiseworthy. We would like to thank the people whose writings appear in this volume: David S. Bimbi, David M. Boden, Joseph R. G. DeMarco, Jeffrey Escoffier, Rebecca Harriman, Jonathan David Jackson, Barry Johnston, Kerwin Kaye, Paula Kenny, Juline A. Koken, David Leary, Victor Minichiello, Mark B. Padilla, Jeffrey T. Parsons, and Benjamin Scuglia. We appreciated their patience with the review process and their willingness to respond to a never-ending parade of queries. As well, we are grateful to the "silent stars" of the academic industry; namely, those who expend considerable time and effort serving as reviewers. For this book, the individuals in question were Anomi Bearden, Melanie A. Morrison, Ian Stewart, and Diarmuid Verrier. A hearty "thank you" also is extended to Paula Kenny (who spent countless hours proofreading various manuscripts), Dr. John DeCecco (whose support and encouragement made this book possible), Yvon Goulet (for the arresting art work that appears on the cover), and JoEllen A. Morrison (for unconditional support). Finally, in a heretofore unknown display of modesty, we will refrain from issuing our greatest proclamation of gratitude to ourselves. What we will (and, indeed, must say) is that, although various individuals assisted with the creation of this book, as editors, we bear responsibility for any errors or problematic elements detected by readers.

On a personal note, Bruce would like to acknowledge the following individuals:

I would like to thank my parents (Grant Whitehead Sr., Ken Cornell, and Judie Cornell) for reasons too numerous to list. Equal amounts of gratitude are extended to Jerome Prieur and Andrew McDonald for different but equivalent reasons. I also would like to acknowledge the efforts, actions, and resistance posed by pioneers of pornography and sexual work, and all those who have labored under the stigma of their occupations while making the dialogue about sex work public, personal, and political. To those writers, researchers, and "unrepentant whores," I express my sincerest gratitude. As well, I would like to thank the men who participated in this research for their time, candor, and introspection. My primary gratitude, however, is extended to Dr. Todd G. Morrison for myriad reasons. If you require clarification, Todd, then feel free to e-mail me. And lastly, because I can, I would like to thank Zak Spears. Just because.

Being a naturally reserved person, Todd will say only the following:

Enumerating the different ways in which various people made this book possible would be time-consuming not to mention exhausting (a state, that, as an academic–I am conditioned to avoid). Therefore, in the interests of brevity, I will simply say: "You helped one or both of us! Now what do you want–a medal?" Finally, and just because I CAN, I am thanking: Chic, Joan Crawford, Bette Davis, Doris Day, Geraldine Page, the Pointer Sisters, Diana Ross, Sister Sledge, Barbara Streisand, the Weather Girls and, yes, Shelley Winters for countless hours of non-masturbatory fun.

INTRODUCTION

"It's a Business Doing Pleasure with You": An Interdisciplinary Reader on Male Sex Work

Todd G. Morrison, PhD
Bruce W. Whitehead

The male sex industry has been likened to Pandora's Box, albeit one "which, until recently, few researchers have been willing to unlock" (Browne & Minichiello, 1996, p. 30).[1] Assuming this industry possesses a scintilla of interest to at least some academics, one must grapple with the following question: Why have scholars displayed an unwillingness to conduct research on this topic? A number of explanations have been forwarded in an effort to address this query. For example, Davies and Feldman (1997) assert that the multiple marginalities of male sex workers are responsible for the scant attention they have received from social scientists. Specifically, these authors maintain:

> [male sex work is] marginal to two phenomena that are themselves peripheral to academic interest: prostitution and homosexuality. But, more than that, it is the potential of male homosexual prostitution

[Haworth co-indexing entry note]: ""It's a Business Doing Pleasure with You": An Interdisciplinary Reader on Male Sex Work." Morrison, Todd G., and Bruce W. Whitehead. Co-published simultaneously in *Journal of Homosexuality* (The Haworth Press, Inc.) Vol. 53, No. 1/2, 2007, pp. 1-6; and: *Male Sex Work: A Business Doing Pleasure* (ed: Todd G. Morrison and Bruce W. Whitehead) The Haworth Press, Inc., 2007, pp. 1-6. Single or multiple copies of this article are available for a fee from The Haworth Document Delivery Service [1-800-HAWORTH, 9:00 a.m. - 5:00 p.m. (EST). E-mail address: docdelivery@haworthpress.com].

Available online at http://jh.haworthpress.com
© 2007 by The Haworth Press, Inc. All rights reserved.
doi:10.1300/J082v53n01_01

1

to contradict current orthodoxies that guarantees its academic invisibility...Because it involves a contract between two men [it] confounds those who regard [female] prostitution as a simple reversal of gender inequality. Because, in some cases, the punter [i.e., client] pays for the orgasm of the prostitute, it challenges those who would reduce prostitution to a form of consumer capitalism: mere payment for pleasure; and because it exists at all in the era of gay liberation, it embarrasses those who extol the revolutionary egalitarianism of the gay community. (p. 30)

Browne and Minichiello (1996) identify other deterrents including the absence of compelling theoretical frameworks that may be used to "explain" male sex work; the practical difficulties inherent in studying clandestine populations; and the dearth of funding for this type of research. While the aforementioned make intuitive sense, we believe that *personal* factors also may serve to dissuade some individuals from investigating the male sex industry. Given the exaltation of "empirical rigor" in the social sciences, some academics may be concerned that work in this area will be labelled trivial and unimportant; that they may be perceived as "wasting their time" on a topic that is "sensationalistic" and "socially irrelevant." As well, individuals may harbor the legitimate fear that expressing scholarly interest in male sex work will be dismissed as justificatory window-dressing; as an attempt to conceal prurience[2] or social activism (the latter being evident in simplistic "sex work as liberation" and "sex work as oppression" rhetoric).[3]

Despite these obstacles, research has been conducted on the male sex industry. Unfortunately, it has been fairly myopic in scope, with most contemporary studies focusing on prostitution and safer sex (e.g., Allman & Myers, 1999; Bloor, McKeganey, Finlay, & Barnard, 1992; Boles & Elifson, 1994; Browne & Minichiello, 1995; Elifson, Boles, & Sweat, 1993; Estep, Waldorf, & Marotta, 1992; Joffe & Dockrell, 1995; Marino, Browne, & Minichiello, 2000; Markos, Wade, & Walzman, 1994; Miller, Klotz, & Eckholdt, 1998; Minichiello et al., 2000; Weinberg, Worth, & Williams, 2001). More recently, studies have been published that target different categories of prostitute, and move beyond the discourses of disease transmission and psychopathology (e.g., Parsons, Koken, & Bimbi, 2004; Uy, Parsons, Bimbi, Koken, & Halkitis, 2004). Although these efforts to present a more heterogeneous view of prostitution are commendable, their emphasis remains firmly on one category of sex work.

The purpose of the current volume is to offer a more comprehensive view of the male sex industry, which we have defined broadly as any occupation designed to provide sexual arousal to consumers.[4] Thus, there are several papers focusing on strippers and pornographic performers/models as well as entries examining understudied categories of prostitution such as Internet escorts and men who target sex tourists.

Organizing articles by "theme" runs the risk of simplification. However, despite this potential problem, we felt that a majority of the contributors' work could be accurately reflected by one of the following three categories: "On the Streets," "In the Clubs," and "On the Net and Beyond."

As one might imagine, "On the Streets" focuses on street-based prostitution, which is the category of sex work most commonly studied by social scientists. The articles contained in this section differ from traditional investigations of street prostitutes in two important ways. First, they do not focus on this type of sex worker as a "[vector] of disease transmission" (Parsons et al., 2004, p. 1021) and, thus, do not concern themselves with the topics of safer sex and sexually transmitted infections (STIs). Second, none of these articles are characterized by attempts to construct oft-times prefatory taxonomies of the "sorts of men most likely to ..." Instead, this section begins with David S. Bimbi's article, "Male prostitution: Pathology, paradigms, and progress in research." In this literature review, the author identifies four discourses that have surrounded male prostitutes as objects of study. He contends that the replacement of one discourse by another occurred in concert with the scientific community's changing view of homosexuality, and identifies the fourth, and most current discourse (prostitute as professional), as embracing a more positive view of sex work. The next article, written by Kerwin Kaye, is entitled, "Sex and the unspoken in male street prostitution." The author challenges the hegemonic representation of male street prostitutes as young, drug dependent, economically desperate, and abused. As well, he delineates some of the social conditions framing the experience of street prostitution and identifies ways in which these conditions are similar to those experienced by other street-based populations. The final article in this section is David Leary and Victor Minichiello's, "Exploring the interpersonal relationships in street-based male sex work: Results from an Australian qualitative study." Here the authors examine the relational dynamics of a small sample of male street prostitutes, and the ways in which those dynamics change as a function of participants' involvement with and–in some cases–departure from, the sex trade.

Male strippers are the focus of the second section of this volume, which is entitled "In the Clubs." Although some might assume that this form of sex work involves little more than possessing the willingness to remove one's clothes, both Joseph R. G. DeMarco's "Power and control in gay strip clubs" and David M. Boden's "Alienation of sexuality in male erotic dancing" detail performers' complex perceptions of what they do for a living. The various relationships that may operate between customer and performer also are outlined. In Jonathan David Jackson's article, "The closing of *Atlantis*," the racial politics of erotic dancing and, by extension, the male sex industry in general are explored. Based on informal interviews and the author's personal experience in a now-defunct Maryland strip club, Jonathan David Jackson examines black Americans' experience with an industry that caters to, and promotes, the white male as an ideal.

Four articles constitute "On the Net and Beyond," the third, and final, collection of articles. In "Porn star/stripper/escort: Economic and sexual dynamics in a sex work career," Jeffrey Escoffier contends that performers in gay male pornography are subject to a "retrogressive dynamic" whereby their earning potential and status typically diminish the longer they remain in the industry. The author identifies several ways of combating this inevitable decline, one of which is to pursue complementary forms of sex work such as stripping and escorting. Todd G. Morrison and Bruce W. Whitehead's "'Nobody's ever going to make a fag *Pretty Woman*': Stigma awareness and the putative effects of stigma among a sample of Canadian male sex workers" and Jeffrey T. Parsons, Juline A. Koken, and David S. Bimbi's "Looking beyond HIV: Eliciting individual and community needs of male Internet escorts" examine groups of male prostitutes that, until recently, have been largely ignored by researchers; namely, those who work for escort agencies and those who advertise on the Internet. Both articles underscore the need to acknowledge the diversity that exists among male prostitutes as well as the importance of recognizing that findings obtained with street-based prostitutes are not necessarily applicable to those working in other venues. This section concludes with Mark B. Padilla's "'Western Union Daddies' and their quest for authenticity: An ethnographic study of the Dominican gay sex tourism industry." In this article, the author outlines some of the ways in which clients and prostitutes attempt to construct an "authentic" relationship and, in so doing, hide its instrumentality. Also explored are the ways in which these demonstrations of authenticity may conflict with Dominican sex workers' conceptions of masculinity.

Finally, Rebecca L. Harriman, Barry Johnston, and Paula M. Kenny *Harriman, Johnston & Kenny* provide a "conversational" chapter detailing contributors' informal responses to nine questions concerning male prostitution. This article illustrates the multifarious ways in which ostensibly "like-minded" individuals perceive this complex element of the male sex industry.

NOTES

1. This statement may be overly optimistic as it suggests that–at the very least–researchers acknowledge the existence of the male sex industry. Perhaps a more accurate version would read: The male sex industry is akin to Pandora's Box, albeit one which remains hidden to most scholars.

2. A critical question is why do social scientists feel compelled to provide a "high-brow" rationale for their "academic" investigation of topics concerning sexuality? Is the utility of sexological research compromised by the admission that one finds the topic in question sexually exciting?

3. The possibility also exists that some individuals are reluctant to study the male sex industry because they fear the "backlash" that may occur when one embraces a non-pejorative view of sex work.

4. Although this definition could include aspects of the industry that target women as consumers, the articles in this volume focus exclusively on male sex workers providing services to male customers.

REFERENCES

Allman, D., & Myers, T. (1999). Male sex work and HIV/AIDS in Canada. In P. Aggleton (Ed.), *Men who sell sex: International perspectives on male prostitution and HIV/AIDS* (pp. 61-81). Philadelphia, PA: Temple University Press.

Bloor, M. J., McKeganey, N. P., Finlay, A., & Barnard, M. A. (1992). The inappropriate-ness of psycho-social models of risk behavior for understanding HIV-related risk practices among Glasgow male prostitutes. *AIDS Care, 4,* 131-137.

Boles, J., & Elifson, K. W. (1994). Sexual identity and HIV: The male prostitute. *The Journal of Sex Research, 31,* 39-46.

Browne, J., & Minichiello, V. (1995). The social meanings behind male sex work: Implications for sexual interactions. *British Journal of Sociology, 46,* 598-622.

Browne, J., & Minichiello, V. (1996). Research directions in male sex work. *Journal of Homosexuality, 31*(4), 29-56.

Davies, P., & Feldman, R. (1997). Prostitute men now. In G. Scambler & A. Scambler (Eds.), *Rethinking prostitution: Purchasing sex in the 1990s* (pp. 29-53). New York, NY: Routledge.

Elifson, K. W., Boles, J., & Sweat, M. (1993). Risk factors associated with HIV infection among male prostitutes. *American Journal of Public Health, 83,* 79-83.

Estep, R., Waldorf, D., & Marotta, T. (1992). Sexual behavior of male prostitutes. In J. Huber & B. E. Schneider (Eds.), *The social context of AIDS* (pp. 95-112). Newbury Park, CA: Sage.

Joffe, H., & Dockrell, J. E. (1995). Safer sex: Lessons from the male sex industry. *Journal of Community & Applied Social Psychology, 5*, 333-346.

Marino, R., Browne, J., & Minichiello, V. (2000). An instrument to measure safer sex strategies used by male sex workers. *Archives of Sexual Behavior, 29*, 217-228.

Markos, A. R., Wade, A. A. H., & Walzman, M. (1994). The adolescent male prostitute and sexually transmitted diseases, HIV, and AIDS. *Journal of Adolescence, 17*, 123-130.

Miller, R. L., Klotz, D., & Eckholdt, H. M. (1998). HIV prevention with male prostitutes and patrons of hustler bars: Replication of an HIV prevention intervention. *American Journal of Community Psychology, 26*, 97-131.

Minichiello, V., Marino, R., Browne, J., Jamieson, M., Peterson, K., Reuter, B., & Robinson, K. (2000). Commercial sex between men: A prospective diary-based study. *Journal of Sex Research, 37*, 151-160.

Parsons, J. T., Koken, J. A., & Bimbi, D. S. (2004). The use of the Internet by gay and bisexual male escorts: Sex workers as sex educators. *AIDS Care, 16*, 1021-1035.

Uy, J. M., Parsons, J. T., Bimbi, D. S., Koken, J. A., & Halkitis, P. N. (2004). Gay and bisexual male escorts who advertise on the Internet: Understanding reasons for and effect of involvement in commercial sex. *International Journal of Men's Health, 3*, 11-26.

Weinberg, M. S., Worth, H., & Williams, C. J. (2001). Men sex workers and other men who have sex with men: How do their HIV risks compare in New Zealand? *Archives of Sexual Behavior, 30*, 273-286.

doi:10.1300/J082v53n01_01

ON THE STREETS

Male Prostitution:
Pathology, Paradigms
and Progress in Research

David S. Bimbi, PhD (candidate)

City University of New York

SUMMARY. The body of research on male sex workers (MSWs) in the social science literature has evolved concurrently with the research that de-pathologized homosexuality. Unfortunately, the majority of studies focusing on MSWs have been dominated by paradigms that dehumanize

David S. Bimbi is a doctoral student at the Graduate Center, City University of New York, and The Center for HIV Educational Studies and Training (CHEST), Hunter College, City University of New York.

Mr. Bimbi has worked in the field of behavioral HIV research since 1996. He is currently finishing his dissertation on male sex workers. The author wishes to thank his mentors, Dr. Jeffrey Parsons and Dr. Vita Rabinowitz, for their support and feedback; the reviewers for their constructive comments; the outstanding librarians and archivists who assisted in locating some difficult to find primary sources cited in this article; and lastly, friends and acquaintances in sex work who encouraged him to undertake this area of research. Correspondence may be addressed to David S. Bimbi, Center for HIV/AIDS Educational Studies and Training, 250 West 26th Street, Suite 300, New York, NY, 10001.

[Haworth co-indexing entry note]: "Male Prostitution: Pathology, Paradigms and Progress in Research." Bimbi, David S. Co-published simultaneously in *Journal of Homosexuality* (The Haworth Press, Inc.) Vol. 53, No. 1/2, 2007, pp. 7-35; and: *Male Sex Work: A Business Doing Pleasure* (ed: Todd G. Morrison and Bruce W. Whitehead) The Haworth Press, Inc., 2007, pp. 7-35. Single or multiple copies of this article are available for a fee from The Haworth Document Delivery Service [1-800- HAWORTH, 9:00 a.m. - 5:00 p.m. (EST). E-mail address: docdelivery@haworthpress.com].

Available online at http://jh.haworthpress.com
© 2007 by The Haworth Press, Inc. All rights reserved.
doi:10.1300/J082v53n01_02

7

the researched. Psychopathology, social deviance and, with the advent of HIV, MSWs as "vectors of disease," framed research questions. Further, many researchers have focused on typologies of MSWs, reporting respective associated characteristics. However, the knowledge gained by past research was often a product of the places MSWs were sampled; social scientists relied heavily on street MSWs, although other places and venues for sex work existed. What has been learned through this narrow focus has often been generalized to all men engaged in sex work resulting in stigmatization, stereotyping, and demonization. In the past decade, two important developments related to the field of sex work have been introduced. First, researchers have embraced a new paradigm that respects MSWs' personal motivations for sex work. Dominant among these motivations is the view of sex work as a job and, hence, a valid source of income. Second, the Internet has emerged as a new venue for sex work; a venue to which researchers are just beginning to turn their gaze. doi:10.1300/J082v53n01_02 *[Article copies available for a fee from The Haworth Document Delivery Service: 1-800-HAWORTH. E-mail address: <docdelivery@haworthpress.com> Website: <http://www.HaworthPress.com> © 2007 by The Haworth Press, Inc. All rights reserved.]*

KEYWORDS. Male sex work, research, psychopathology, deviance, Internet

PARADIGMS, PROBLEMS, AND PROGRESS IN RESEARCH ON MALE SEX WORKERS

Many people in western cultures are familiar with the euphemism "the world's oldest profession." Typically, the picture that emerges in the mind's eye is that of a female prostitute (Van der Poel, 1992). However, recorded history has documented that the world's oldest profession also has been practiced by males as well since the time of the Romans and Greeks up through Victorian England, and to the present (Perkins & Bennett, 1997). Scott (2003) observes that early scientific, medical, criminal, and religious works were focused on female sex workers and their role in spreading sexually transmitted diseases. Passing notice was made of male sex workers (MSWs) but they were not examined in depth.

Academic publications have examined male prostitution retrospectively utilizing historical sources (Kaye, 2003; Weeks, 1981), but a similar examination within the social sciences has not been conducted. Further, when male prostitution has been studied scientifically, researchers may have had their "objectivity" influenced by prevailing cultural attitudes toward homosexuality (Kaye, 2003; Weeks, 1981).

Published findings have been sensationalistic and often narrowly focused (Robinson & Davies, 1991) and, as a result, have further stigmatized male prostitutes who also must contend with the stigma of homosexuality (as the vast majority provide sexual services to other males) (Weeks, 1981). Hoffman (1972) suggests that researchers have lost compassion for their fellow human beings and often view male prostitutes as "exotic" members of a subculture or "as merely objects of study" (p. 17). Luckenbill (1984) comments that, "for the most part, researchers have examined the causes of male prostitution, the types of male prostitutes, their sexual identification, and the means for treating them" (p. 338). Lastly, the term prostitution has become so laden with stigma that contemporary researchers, such as Vanwesenbeeck (2001), have abandoned the term, opting instead for the expression *sex work* to describe any practice that involves the exchange of money for human sexual behavior such as direct sexual activities; sexual stimulation, as in the case of erotic dancers; and sexual performance in adult erotic photography and videography.

Similarly, specific to the case of male sex workers, the vernacular term *hustler* has developed negative connotations and is actually derived from the Dutch word for "turning something over and shaking the coins out" (White, 2003). In the *Joy of Gay Sex,* a book written by gay men for gay men, Silverstein and Picano (2003) reinforce this connotation by stating that the term sex worker is simply a politically correct term for hustler. The authors also present the "characteristics" of male sex workers, which are given without citations or discussion of any published data. In this otherwise sex affirmative reference book, assumptions are made about male sex workers that may stigmatize them *within* the gay community.

In one of the first social science publications on the topic of male sex work, a case study was presented in which the individual is described as psychopathic (Freyhan, 1947). Soon after, MSWs were described as delinquent youths in need of help (Reiss, 1961). The delinquency paradigm of male sex work was prevalent in the literature from Reiss' first publication into the 1980s when reports of different motivations for engaging in sex work began to appear (Luckenbill, 1985; Weisburg, 1985). Van der Poel (1992) concludes that the literature on male sex work has often been based on a cause-cure assumption and typically relies on samples that are formed after involvement with the police, different public agencies, and/or social service organizations, with which the researchers themselves are associated.

In the early 1990s, the delinquency paradigm gave way to a focus on disease, as had been the case for more than a century of research into female sex work (Scott, 2003). The emergence of the human immunodeficiency virus (HIV) and the behaviors related to its spread, specifically injection drug use and homosexual sex, facilitated this shift. Injection drug use was not addressed in terms of the harm it may pose to the sex worker himself, but only as a transmission route for HIV. Investigators began publishing research on injection drug-use among MSWs, HIV prevalence among MSWs, and unsafe sex among MSWs. This created a new paradigm of male sex work: "vector of transmission for HIV infection," a description which first appeared in the title of an article by Morse, Simon, Osofsky, Balson and Gaumer (1991). Heading into the 1990s, the a priori hypotheses for research questions into male sex work were thus: MSWs had psychological problems and backgrounds that contributed to delinquency; they abused illicit substances; and engaged in sexual activities that fostered the spread of HIV.

The historical context of the past 40 years of publications on male sex work shaped this paradigm. Research into male sex work as well as homosexuality began to enter scientific publication and discourse simultaneously. Kaye (2003) suggests that this intersection first emerged culturally at the turn of the century when the increasing prevalence of gay men offering working class men money for sex led to societal prohibitions on all homosexual activity and persons.

Up until the 1980s, the vast majority of research on MSWs was composed of samples of self-identified or presumed heterosexuals. As researchers started to explore new recruitment strategies, diverse samples of MSWs began to appear in the literature. Ironically, it was the advent of HIV that led to the reappearance of gay men in samples of MSWs. The inclusion of gay men also uncovered a new paradigm: engaging in sex as a legitimate source of income. Further, researchers began to present sex work as a rational vocation by focusing on the legal and socio-political aspects of the industry (Browne & Minichiello, 1996a; Minichiello, Marino, Browne, & Jamieson, 1999).

Tiby (2003) states that because police focus on the streets, this one particular form of sex work has come to constitute how all MSWs are perceived. Van der Poel (1992) offers a much stronger critique, suggesting that the design of the sample(s) has often amounted to fabrication of results due to researchers not addressing flaws in methodology and issues of generalizability. It is doubtful that much of the early research on MSWs would be approved as ethically and scientifically sound under contemporary standards. Further, Van der Poel (1992) concludes that male prostitution has a dangerous reputation precisely because researchers have selected young males from the "fringes of the world of prostitution" and that the young men sampled have been "renounced by the profession" or have never been part of it (p. 272). Salamon (1989) argues that the role of the escort and the activities of the escort agency have remained unclear because the focus has been on street prostitution.

It has become obvious that the body of research on male sex work over the last half a century demonstrates how paradigms of male sex work within the social sciences emerged from specific samples of MSWs, research designs, and a priori assumptions. The purpose of this article is to review the published research which conveys the paradigmatic shifts that have occurred as a result of changing methods and approaches to social scientific inquiry into male sex work. Further, this article will reveal that previous paradigms have been neither supplanted nor replaced; however, a less narrow and ultimately deeper understanding of the phenomenon of male sex work has emerged as researchers expanded their focus and, at times, permitted MSWs to express their opinions regarding their involvement in sex work.

THE FIRST PARADIGM EMERGES:
MSWS ARE PSYCHOPATHOLOGICAL

During the 1940s, homosexuality as a mental illness was the paradigm held by psychologists and psychiatrists. It was in this context that the first two academic publications on male sex work in the United States appeared in 1947. A case report by Freyhan (1947) describes the subject as a young man arrested for soliciting other men for sex near a naval base while dressed in a U.S. Navy uniform. The man then was institutionalized and came to the attention of the author who describes him as mentally dull and egocentric and reports that the young man expressed no guilt or shame about his sexual attraction to men. He was diagnosed as psychopathic and a lobotomy (the preferred treatment for homosexuality at the time) was recommended as an appropriate course of action. Homosexuality, but not prostitution, was the problem to be addressed.

That same year, Butts (1947) reported on a convenience sample of young, street-based MSWs who were never aware that they were part of a research study. Butts (1947) observed 128 MSWs, interviewed 38 several times and reported on a final sample of 26 (who had sufficient data for analyses). The author (Butts, 1947) describes four of these young men as "fixed inverts" (homosexuals) and refers to the sexual services provided by the sample as including "all forms of perversion" (p. 675). Regardless, he depicts the sample as "victims of circumstance" and maladjusted, unhappy boys. The young men were from low-income, overcrowded homes (but they did exhibit "good table manners" during the interviews which took place over meals paid for by the author) and spent much of their free time on the streets engaged in delinquent behaviors, such as panhandling, petty theft, and sex work. The author cautions that these were young, mostly heterosexual youths in need of intervention before they became seduced into the homosexual subculture. Clearly this argument was influenced by the dominant cultural belief that engaging in homosexual behavior would make one homosexual. Butts (1947) presents a solution to this problem: these young men should be institutionalized rather than punished, as the former might allow many of them to achieve a normal, happy, useful life. Ironically, while homosexuality was pathologized and classified as a mental disorder at this time in history, for the next several decades, the focus would not be on homosexual sex workers. "Normal" men (i.e., heterosexual men) who engaged in sex work due to purported "deviance" and the psychological correlates and consequences of sex work drove research agendas.

MSWs who acknowledged their homosexuality rarely appeared in the literature, for reasons directly related to sampling biases and the status of homosexuals during the concurrent time. Weisburg (1985) argues that early research often stated that MSWs were not homosexual and overcompensated with hyper-masculine images. In addition, Weisburg (1985) observes that homosexuality as a pathology informed most early research and, therefore, it is quite possible that researchers communicated their biased attitudes toward homosexuality to their subjects who then were less likely to admit to being gay. The trend to focus on convenience samples that were assumed to be heterosexual (or self-identified as heterosexual) continued until the 1980s when research reports sampling other places where male sex work occurred began to appear in the literature.

An early example of this trend is Reiss (1961), who utilized a convenience sample of young men incarcerated in youth institutions throughout the state of Tennessee. He reported that the young men were motivated to engage in sex work by delinquent peer norms learned on the streets. He further detailed how, as a means of protecting their heterosexual identity, the young MSWs were often threatening and, at times, violent with the older homosexual men who solicited them. It is unclear, however, if these behaviors were part of the heterosexual MSWs' erotic allure to potential clients and, therefore, exaggerated for reasons other than distancing oneself from homosexuality.

Using ethnographic methods, which did not always involve the author disclosing his status as a researcher, MacNamara (1965) observed and casually interviewed 103 MSWs on the streets in seven American cities. While never explicitly describing the sample as homosexual, MacNamara (1965) is the only researcher during this time to refute the prevailing beliefs that homosexuals as well as MSWs are psychopathological:

> [I]f we were to ignore the sexual proclivities and way of life and observe them as only teenagers . . . it would be difficult indeed to label the group pathological . . . Are they male prostitutes as a result of some neurotic, psychopathic or psychotic syndrome? Quite likely not. (p. 204)

MacNamara (1965) clearly concludes that entering into male sex work is driven by socio-economic and not psychopathological factors. However, similar to Reiss (1961), he does describe the MSWs as being from deprived family backgrounds characterized by paternal rejection, alcoholism, brutality, and poverty.

On the contrary, Ginsberg (1967) dismisses social factors and suggests that psychodynamics drive entry into sex work. As a participant observer, he studied the street sex work scene in the tenderloin district of San Francisco. He reports that he informally struck up conversations with approximately 30 MSWs and became very familiar with about 12, until a small group of "more hostile hustlers" learned of his true identity and became antagonistic. Ginsberg (1967) presents seven case histories from the sample and details at length that sexual behavior (i.e., engaging in homosexual prostitution) is different from sexual orientation as most of these men self-identified as heterosexual. Ginsberg (1967) further stresses that gay men in the neighborhood, as well as clinicians who have written informally on the topic, often strongly believe that such heterosexually identified MSWs will eventually become gay. The case histories, according to Ginsberg (1967), revealed that MSWs did not come from "broken" homes, but rather "crippled" or "muted" homes. Lastly, he concludes that psychological drives led these MSWs into sex work based upon their family histories:

> Should parental wishes be ambivalent, vague, contradictory, either
> covertly or overtly, the child may never really understand who
> he is and what is expected of him . . . If alternatives for effective
> interpersonal relations are not learned and integrated as part of the
> self, regression to, or continued attempts at communicating in,
> known secure (that is infantile) ways may be the outcome . . . To
> reduce anxiety, unhappiness, and other unpleasant symptoms, he may
> adopt an available mode of behavior to the end that his existence
> (identity) will have meaning . . . the occupation [male sex work]
> provides built in avenues to satisfy earlier inculcated affectional
> and aggressive needs (p. 180).

In other words, engaging in sex work allows MSWs to fill unsolved
needs stemming from their childhood and simultaneously permits them
to use clients as substitutes for expressing anger and resentment held
toward their parents.

In their sample of MSWs on the streets in San Francisco and Seattle,
Deisher, Eisner and Suizbacher (1969) viewed masculine gender role
presentation as an indicator of heterosexuality. The authors note the
difficulties they encountered attempting to contact young MSWs due to
their "own ineptness and lack of social skills appropriate to this particular subculture" (p. 937). With the assistance of personnel from the staff
of a social service agency, 63 MSWs were eventually interviewed. The
authors report that most of the sample were looking for work other than
prostitution, although they were characterized as being of average intel-
ligence and lacking in social and occupational skills.[1] This study also
asked participants about recreational drug use. Drug use was reported
by half of the sample; however, as this rate was lower than anticipated,
the authors suggest that participants may not have been honest about
this matter (Deisher et al., 1969). Hoffman (1972), commenting on the
research to date on adolescent MSWs, suggests the young men in previous studies were lying (or deceiving themselves) about being homosexual. Luckenbill (1984) adds that many hustlers claim only to engage in
active fellatio with clients to maintain the appearance of heterosexuality
among their peers and clients; however, their actual sexual behaviors
are unknown. Coombs (1974) compared a sample of 41 MSWs to a
group recruited from the same coffeehouse and bar in southern California. Coombs (1974) reports that MSWs had a higher frequency of early
homosexual seduction followed by a reward than the comparison group,
and then concludes that such positive reinforcement led these young
(assumed-to-be) heterosexual men into sex work. Further, Coombs

states that many of these young men exhibited personality traits such as immaturity, poor judgment, inadequate personality, hypersensitivity about rejection, and a "total unwillingness to take criticism" (p. 789). Caukins and Coombs (1976), in a subsequent publication, posit that MSWs were hostile to clients because they resented having to depend on them, which was compounded by the need of the MSW to protect his heterosexual identity, an issue first raised by Reiss (1961).

Sagarin and Jolly (1983/1997) expanded on the psychology of the heterosexual MSW. They argue that in heterosexual prostitution, the stigma is on the sex worker; in male prostitution, the stigma is on the client for his homosexual desires. They further add "there is a great degree of evidence that homosexual prostitution results in large amounts of homicide, assault, and robbery and, for that reason alone, it constitutes a social problem" (p. 25). Nonetheless, the authors discount the pathology paradigm by proposing that most acts of prostitution can be explained more clearly in economic and social terms. In addition, they suggest that the struggle to rationalize engagement in sex work could lead to pathology that was not present initially. Further, they maintain that the emergent pathology does not result from one being defined in the first instance as pathological, but rather from being defined as evil (i.e., homosexual). Similarly, Satterfield (1981) suggests that heterosexual young men who drift into same sex relationships through sex work might experience an identity crisis over their sexual orientation by late adolescence.

Price (1984) reported on a sample of 28 young MSWs recruited from a social service agency for runaways and street youth in Boston. Heterosexual MSWs in the sample are specifically described as violent and alcohol-abusing. They also are characterized as being abusive in their relationships with women. Such behaviors could be a manifestation of the issues described by Sagarin and Jolly (1983/1997) and Satterfield (1981).

Based upon the previous literature, Earls and Helene (1989) employed a quasi-experimental design in their study of street youth from eastern Canadian cities. They hypothesized that MSWs would be heterosexual and more frequently report: family backgrounds characterized by physical, emotional or sexual abuse; earlier sexual experience; early exposure to prostitution through peers; and higher levels of depression and lower levels of self-esteem. The authors employed ethnographic observations of the streets on which MSWs were known to work to verify that a potential participant was a sex worker before approaching him about the study. The authors indicated that this was a necessary step, as engaging in sex work had not been verified in previous samples other than by self-report. They recruited 50 MSWs and 50 youths (all heterosexual) from arcades to be used for comparison.

The findings were mixed. There were no significant differences between MSWs and the comparison group in reported rates of verbal and physical abuse; however, MSWs did report witnessing more violence between their parents and substance use within their immediate family. MSWs did report earlier sexual experience, but were actually exposed to sex work later than the comparison group. The assumption of heterosexuality was not supported; only one-third of the MSWs self-identified as exclusively heterosexual. Lastly, the authors found no significant differences in self-esteem, but did find that the MSWs were significantly more depressed. The authors stated that this depression might have resulted from being gay in a homophobic society, dissatisfaction with the self for being a sex worker, or as a side effect of cocaine use (MSWs reported higher rates of use than the comparison group).

Boyer 1989

Similarly, Boyer (1989) employed a quasi-experimental design in Seattle in 1980, comparing 47 young MSWs to a group of 50 delinquents. The MSWs were contacted for involvement in the study by outreach workers, probation officers, and case managers; during fieldwork by the author; and at a youth detention center (wherein those arrested for prostitution were identified and recruited for the study). Refusal rates and breakdown by recruitment source were not specified. MSWs reported significantly more physical, psychological and sexual abuse. Further, among the MSWs, 36.3% of gay youth (who comprised 51.1% of the total sample) reported sexual abuse with someone at least 10 years older than themselves compared to 14.2% of the heterosexual youth (29.8% of the sample).[2] Boyer (1989) states that prostitution continues the victimization of those who were abused sexually; however, the author offers no explanation for why sexual abuse was higher among the gay-identified participants.

Simon et al 1992

Simon, Morse, Osofsky, Balson, and Gaumer (1992) further attempted to investigate the question of personal factors in a sample of MSWs from New Orleans. Convenience sampling was utilized to recruit the MSWs with quotas set for less than 25 years old/over 25 years old, white/non-white, and injection drug user/injection drug non-user. The authors administered the Symptom Check List (SCL-90) (Derogatis, 1977), and utilized data from two published normative samples (nonpatient and patient for this measure) for comparison purposes. The MSWs' scores on the SCL-90 fell between the two other groups. The psychological symptoms the MSWs reported were personal inadequacy, dysphoria, suspiciousness, and social alienation. The authors attributed these symptoms to an understandable response to the often chaotic and dangerous environment in which they work. Similar to Earls and Helene (1989), Simon et al. (1992) reverse the argument–moving from pathological persons who pursue sex work to pathology possibly resulting from engaging in sex work.

Others have explored the "effects" of sex work on the individual. Calhoun and Weaver (1996) utilized chain referral sampling, via an informant, to recruit 18 MSWs (aged 13 to 23) in an unnamed, medium-sized, southern city during 1984. The authors suggest that the non-homosexually identified sex worker engages in stigma management (Goffman, 1963) to conceal his involvement in homosexual activities. Heterosexual MSWs will not tell others about their involvement with sex work, disguise their source of income, and restrict the time they spend on the street. However, West (1998) reports that, in the case of gay-identified MSWs, the ease at which they enter into sex work is, perhaps, due to the fact that they are already stigmatized as homosexuals so the stigma of sex work has little or no meaning. Another view of gay and bisexual MSWs managing stigma was reported by Koken, Bimbi, Parsons and Halkitis (2004). In their sample of 50 gay and bisexual MSWs in New York City (recruited through their Internet-based advertisements), many of the men in the sample did not feel stigmatized as sex workers because they believed that sex work is normative in the gay community and that for many gay men being offered money for sex is flattering and ego-boosting.

By the close of the 20th century, the pathology paradigm had evolved from being located within the sex worker to being located within sex work itself (Calhoun & Weaver, 2001; Earls & Helene, 1989; Simon et al., 1992; West, 1998). The paradigm shifted from the strictly psychological to the social psychological and began to take into account the interaction between the person and the situation (i.e., heterosexual men engaging in sex work may develop pathological symptoms due to a homosexual threat to their identity [Caukins & Coombs, 1976; Sagarin & Jolly, 1983/1997]). Unfortunately, the interaction was only examined in one venue for sex work; namely, the streets. Further, the underlying assumption of the pathology paradigm (i.e., pathological persons engage in sex work) has not been diminished by the person to situation evolution. Thus, the view of MSWs as pathological still directs much research (Roy et al., 2002; Weber et al., 2001).

THE SECOND PARADIGM:
TYPOLOGICS OF MSWS

The first scientific article singularly on the topic of male sex work appeared in Germany (Scheinmann, 1929). The article entitled "The psychology of the male coquette" described two types of MSWs. *Normal* men who temporarily engage in sex work for money during hard times and *coquettes* who are driven by psychic drives (homosexual impulses) toward sex work because they enjoy the sex and long to find a same sex relationship. This early publication gives a harbinger of the later trend of categorizing MSWs. However, due to sampling men on the streets, only one type of MSW, the delinquent (Butts, 1947; Deisher et al., 1969; Reiss, 1961) was described in the literature for several decades.[3]

Utilizing an ethnographic approach, Ross (1959) followed 2 MSWs on their working rounds for numerous hours and interviewed one additional MSW in depth. Ross (1959) describes three types of MSWs on the basis of the location of their sex work activities. The *street hustler* is usually a teen-aged boy who finds older male clients on the streets until he reaches, or appears to reach, legal age for entry into bars at which point he is called a *bar hustler*. The *callboy* does not solicit potential clients in public settings, but maintains a clientele who call him when his services are wanted. Although Ross' (1959) study appeared in an obscure publication (*The Journal of Student Research*), it was clearly influential; many later researchers would describe these categories as types and attempt to differentiate subtypes within and across categories.

Caukins and Coombs (1976) reviewed the types reported by Ross (1959) and expanded the description of callboys to include several features. Callboys are attractive in looks and physique, dependable, "well hung," sexually versatile (active and passive anal/oral sex), and willing to engage in any sexual practice for the right price. How callboys meet clients was not described in detail. Caukins and Coombs (1976) argue that a hierarchy of sex work exists, with street hustlers occupying the lowest level with the lowest pay, followed by bar hustlers, call boys and finally *kept boys*. This last type may be described best as the homosexual equivalent of a kept woman; he trades sex with one man for room, board and, perhaps, cash and gifts. This hierarchy clearly reflects a continuum based upon venue and working conditions. Street-based MSWs work outside, exposed to the elements, whereas callboys work in their own home or the client's home or hotel room. This hierarchy also is based upon perceived level of safety and income as reported by MSWs in a later study (Luckenbill, 1986). Caukins and Coombs (1976) infer that talent plays a factor in male sex work; the "best" MSWs rise through the ranks, from street hustler to, hopefully, a kept boy. This publication solidified the frame of categorizing MSWs based upon venue of sex work.

In 1973 the American Psychiatric Association declassified homosexuality as a mental disorder. At this time, gay men and lesbian women were becoming increasingly visible as a social group and a community, and gay-identified young men began "appearing" in samples of MSWs.[4] The result of sampling both heterosexual and homosexual (or bisexual) MSWs in the same studies was sexual orientation becoming the basis of description for many sub-types, some of which were not viewed as sex workers at all by researchers.

For example, Allen (1980) argues that *delinquents* engaging in prostitution on the streets are not really MSWs, but mostly heterosexual young boys from housing projects with ineffectual parents. Other researchers similarly reframe sex work engaged in by economically and socially disadvantaged youth. Van der Poel (1992) labels delinquents *pseudo-prostitutes* who engage in sex work as part of gang or group related activity. Their motivations for sex work are criminal in essence: defrauding clients, robbery, blackmail and gay bashing. Visano (1991) states that *rough trade* (violent heterosexual street-based MSWs), similar to delinquents, also are engagers in petty crime (e.g., panhandling, stealing, drugs, welfare fraud); they are not part of the world of street prostitution and only operate in it. In contrast to Allen (1980), Price (1984) argues that runaways often engage in *survival sex;* they are simply trying to earn money to take care of their basic needs. DeGraaf, Vanwesenbeeck, Van Zessen, Straver, and Visser (1994) add that engaging in sex work to support a drug habit may be viewed as another form of survival sex. The premises of the above statements raise a reflexive question. Are these young men delinquents and runaways who engage in sex work or are these sex workers from disadvantaged backgrounds and circumstances?

After Caukins and Coombs (1976) described the basic categories or types of MSWs, Allen (1980) generated typologies based upon characteristics of the sample rather than venue. Utilizing key informants for a snowball sampling strategy, Allen (1980) reported on a diverse sample of 98 MSWs from Boston (interviewed from 1974 to 1977). In addition to this change in sampling strategy, the Kinsey sexual orientation scale was administered to the participants. The result was a very detailed typology partitioned by full and part time MSWs, each of which had two subgroups.

Full time street and bar hustlers are described as gay and bisexually identified runaways. Full time callboys are those who place advertisements in gay-oriented magazines and newspapers or work for escort agencies. This group also includes kept boys, who are portrayed not as MSWs, but as houseboys available sexually for older male patrons in exchange for a place to live. For part-time MSWs, the first subgroup are described as gay-identified young men who drift in and out of sex work (on the street, bar or escort agency) as they need extra money. The second subgroup are *delinquents*, a category which Allen (1980) does not consider to be sex workers; rather, they are young men who pretend to be prostitutes in order to receive sexual gratification from their customers (via fellatio) and then steal their money.

Allen (1980) also reports that, regardless of type, most MSWs are introduced to sex work by peers, as had been reported in research using samples of delinquents (Reiss, 1961). The author contends that young gay MSWs are often *throwaways* who leave their parental home due to conflict over their sexual orientation as well as other factors such as parental substance abuse. In addition, Allen (1980) identifies a type of MSW who is hard to find as its members work mostly underground because they suffer the most harassment on the street: drag MSWs who dress as females to attract clients. Price (1984) also mentions this type of sex worker in her sample of 28 male street youth recruited from a social service agency in Boston.

Other types reported by Price (1984) are the *permanent street hustler*, described as mostly white, bisexually identified (or confused), heroin using young adults, who lead a loner lifestyle, have no stable residence, and often travel between cities for sex work. A subtype of this group is the *macho type,* who are similar to heterosexual MSWs described previously. *Straight types* are predominately white, local young men who abuse alcohol, are violent, and view themselves as superior to other MSWs because they are not homosexual. *Flirters* are early adolescents (aged 12-17), mostly minority youth still living at home and attending school, who engage in sex work to experiment with drugs and their sexuality. They engage in hustling to become part of the peer group of other very young hustlers. They are further characterized as immature, boisterous, rowdy, and less furtive than other types of MSW. From this description, these youth appear similar to delinquents described in past research; however, they are clearly homosexual.

The last two types detailed by Price (1984) are distinct from the others because they engage in sex work solitarily and do not associate with other MSWs. *Periodic hustlers* engage in sex work only as needed to provide supplemental income. They are mostly white and college-aged, although some secondary school-aged youths will engage in sex work during the summer months. The final type, *solitary hustlers*, are characterized as possessing no social skills and having long psychiatric histories. Some are psychotic and they tend to scare off most potential clients except those seeking abusive sex.

Weisburg (1985), stressing the importance of sampling and noting the varied forms of bias in earlier work (i.e., samples from institutions, small samples from only one geographic area, etc.), surveyed 79 young MSWs recruited by agency staff at social service programs across the United States. The author reports these young men came from a variety of family situations, with the only common characteristic being some form of instability in their living situation. Weisburg (1985) classified MSWs according to their self-reported motivations for engaging in sex work. *Situational* MSWs are mostly heterosexual and engage in sex work occasionally for extra cash. *Habitual* sex workers are similar to Allen's (1980) part-time delinquent type: They are heterosexual, innercity street youth who engage in other crimes such as drugs and robbery.

Weisburg (1985) also noted that young heterosexual men are more likely to engage in sex work on the street and that young gay men are more likely to engage in sex work in gay-identified spaces.[5] In gay neighborhoods, the MSWs are portrayed as older "pros" which Weisburg (1985) labeled *vocational*. These MSWs are mostly gay-identified and view sex work as their job. Lastly, *avocational* MSWs are young gay men who engage in sex work part-time to supplement their income. This type is only differentiated from the situational MSW by sexual orientation and both are similar in description to Price's (1984) periodic hustler. Weisburg (1985) noted, as did Caukins and Coombs (1976), that some MSWs in the sample ascended in the hierarchy to eventually become callboys. Although vocational and avocational MSWs reported engaging in sex work in gay-identified spaces, such as bars and streets in gay neighborhoods, they were more likely than their heterosexual counterparts to attempt to become callboys by placing advertisements in local gay publications.

Rather than assume survival sex, or sex work as part of overall delinquent behavior, Weisberg (1985) asked the participants directly about their motivations for engaging in sex work. The majority of the sample provided monetary reasons (87%); however, sex (27%) as well as fun and adventure (19%) also were mentioned. While the types of MSWs described by Weisburg (1985) may be similar in many respects to the types described by Allen (1980), this categorization scheme is based upon the MSWs' own view toward sex work and their sexual identity.

In a sample of 26 MSWs in Chicago recruited by a graduate student with contacts in the gay community, Luckenbill (1984, 1985) examined the issue of sex work venues (e.g., street, bar, etc.) and how the men entered into sex work. His primary questions were what conditions led to entry into sex work and did certain paths of entry facilitate regular involvement? The sample was mostly white, engaged in sex work in bars (although some occasionally did work for escort services), came from working class backgrounds and had not finished high school. Ten were gay, twelve bisexual and four heterosexual. None of the sample reported coercion into sex work, but two paths of entry were identified: defensive and adventurous involvement.

In the former, financial desperation was identified by 15 young men from poor and troubled homes (and who were out on their own before the age of 18). Within one to six weeks after leaving home, they encountered sex work in various ways (i.e., cruising and meeting MSWs, or being offered money by older men). Survival sex was the motivation for most; however, four viewed sex work as a superior job and source of income. Gay and bisexual young men moved into full-time sex work soon after entry because of the money and sexual pleasure it afforded and also because they perceived sex work as an acceptable occupation.

In the other path of entry, individuals took advantage of an attractive opportunity to earn money and acquire sexual satisfaction. The 11 young men in this category inadvertently made contact with their first clients (i.e., they were unknowingly in an area where MSWs congregate) and were not motivated by survival sex. Most fully expected to enjoy the sex at the time of entry, were gay-identified, and had already had same-sex experiences. Among this group, nine moved into full time sex work when they finished school or after they decided sex work was preferable to other forms of work they had tried. Those not moving into full time sex work viewed it as a good source of supplemental income. Later studies have supported these observations documenting similar routes to entry (Calhoun, 1992; Uy, Parsons, Bimbi, Koken, & Halkitis, 2004).

Reporting on a sample of MSWs from San Francisco, Waldorf, Murphy, Lauderback, Reinarman, and Marotta (1990) describe callboys as not one 'type' but several types; the only similarity being that clients contact the MSW through the phone. The subtypes include *call book men* who work by referral and a client book, *erotic masseurs*, *models* and *escorts*, as well as *porn stars* that advertise their services. Due to a sampling strategy that did not target youth (as was the case of Allen [1980]; Luckenbill [1985]; and Weisburg [1985]), the authors report that call book men are older than hustlers and have more education. Further, the authors describe the differences in family background between call book men and hustlers in terms of class, rather than family dynamics; call book men were more likely to be from middle class families. Robinson and Davies (1991) report similar characteristics among their sample of callboys in the United Kingdom. They also detail a new characteristic of callboys; specifically, half of them had disclosed to their friends that they were sex workers. Supporting the findings of Weisburg (1985), these men viewed sex work as a job they chose to take. West (1998) adds that, in addition to having higher education and viewing themselves as better than rentboys (the UK's vernacular equivalent of a hustler), they often employ legitimate business techniques, such as taking credit cards.

Based upon previous research, Van der Poel (1992) suggests there are three types of MSWs (as well as a fourth mentioned previously, *pseudo-prostitutes,* who are not viewed by the author as sex workers). The typology is based upon the intersection of two factors: socialization and criminality. *Hustlers* are characterized as loners who belong to no social groups and who, for reasons not explained, distrust other MSWs. They also engage in other criminal activities for day-to-day survival. *Occasionals,* similar to avocationals described by Weisburg (1985), engage in sex work as needed. They range from young men who consent to be paid for sex in non-sex work environments to young men, gay and straight, who will appear on the fringe sex work scene or within sex work environments in gay-identified spaces. The last type, the *professional* is described as being "part of the world of prostitution"; these individuals socialize with each other, are well informed and career-minded.

Using this typology, Van der Poel (1992) conducted ethnographic research in Amsterdam (1984-1986) which included formal interviews with 62 MSWs and informal interviews with an additional 200. Van der Poel (1992) reports that professional MSWs require social as well as sexual skills because they must operate differently depending upon the sex work venue. Professionals who occasionally seek clients on the street capitalize on being a new face on the scene. As soon as they are aware that their novelty is fading, they will move to another street location or sex work venue. Professionals employed in organized male prostitution (i.e., brothels) must possess sufficient language and social skills needed to succeed with a mostly tourist clientele.

Similar to Waldorf et al. (1990) and Robinson and Davies (1991), call boys in Amsterdam work independently by seeking clients through advertisements and are able to prolong their career past the age of thirty. Van der Poel (1992) states that professionals working as callboys are confronted with a mainly gay-identified clientele who often see the same MSW repeatedly, which may lead to one-sided emotional involvement. The professional callboy must be able to navigate such situations in order to preserve the financial nature of the relationship; otherwise, he will lose the client or acquiesce to lower fees or no fee at all. Lastly, Van der Poel (1992) describes the *top whore,* an extension of the kept boy type (Caukins & Coombs, 1976). These professional MSWs serve only the upper classes. They must possess the skills required to socialize publicly with a client who enjoys being seen in the company of an attractive young man. They are professional opportunists who find clients among the circles of the "homo-chic."

Van der Poel (1992) and earlier researchers (e.g., Allen, 1980; Caukins & Coombs, 1976; Luckenbill, 1985, 1986; Weisburg, 1985) clearly added more depth to the understanding of the phenomenon of male sex work than the previous three decades of study. Regardless of differences in the rationale behind categorizing MSWs within each sample, a fuller picture of male sex work emerged through these publications and those that followed. First, MSWs work in a variety of places and venues. Second, it appears that sex work among males is motivated by (1) overall delinquent behavior, (2) economic factors (e.g., financial hardship, desired extra income, a drug habit, etc.), (3) sexual adventure, and (4) professional choice. Third, motivation for engaging in sex work appears to vary as a function of sexual orientation. Heterosexual MSWs are primarily motivated by delinquency and survival sex. Gay and bisexual MSWs also may engage in survival sex (particularly young throwaways); however, for some of these individuals, fun and sexual pleasure were identified as salient. Lastly, many gay MSWs have a professional attitude towards sex work, regardless of how they find clients. Additionally, in the hierarchy of sex work, the lowest paying form (finding clients on the streets) is usually engaged in by heterosexual youth whereas the highest form of sex work (professional callboy) is performed by older gay males (DeGraaf et al., 1994).

Integrating the findings reported in the 1980s, Coleman (1989) proposes a theoretical model of sex work for male adolescents. Predisposing factors (i.e., early disruption of psychosexual and psychosocial development) interact with situational factors (i.e., family environment and related psychodynamic influences) which then lead to the type of sex work entered (e.g., street, bar, etc.). Improved sampling, quasi-experimental designs and the input of MSWs themselves led to the development of a theory of sex work.[6] A study to support this theory would require sampling a broad cross section of sex workers from different venues for in depth interviews. Unfortunately, such a study is yet to be reported. Perhaps, interested researchers have not found the required support (i.e., grant/university funding). While this may be very likely, historical events also shifted the research questions posed about male sex work.

THE THIRD PARADIGM:
SEX WORKERS AS VECTORS OF DISEASE

The human immunodeficiency virus (HIV) emerged as a public health threat that dramatically changed the focus of research agendas regarding MSWs and homosexuals in general. MSWs themselves were no longer of interest as persons but as a group connected to the spread of HIV. The critiques of past research went unnoticed, new findings were overlooked, and research continued as it had previously, mostly focusing on convenience samples of MSWs found on the streets. Earlier research had described only briefly the sexual practices of MSWs (e.g., heterosexual MSWs only reporting insertive fellatio), but with the advent of HIV more detailed data were collected. The literature on male sex work noticeably increased in the early 1990s with research agendas focused explicitly on HIV.

The paradigm shift to sex workers as a public health problem is most evident in an article titled "The male street prostitute: A vector for transmission of HIV infection into the heterosexual world" (Morse et al., 1991). In 1991, Morse et al. first published data on a convenience sample of 211 MSWs from the streets of New Orleans that would be the focus of many other articles (Morse & Simon, 1992; Morse, Simon, Balson, & Osofsky, 1992; Simon, Morse, Balson, Osofsky, & Gaumer, 1993; Simon et al., 1992). The sample described in these publications was reported as 20% gay-identified, 41% bisexual, and 39% heterosexual.

Of those MSWs with female sexual partners, often sex workers themselves, 74% reported not using condoms. Needle sharing was reported by 24.7%. Unprotected anal receptive sex with clients was reported by 54% and 67% reported unprotected anal insertive sex. It should be noted that 10 of 15 clients interviewed for this study reported insisting on unsafe sex with MSWs, which may partially explain these high rates of unprotected sex. Reviewing all of the articles as a whole reveals that the "vector" had three routes of transmission: female partners of heterosexual MSWs, needle-sharing partners, and, potentially, clients. Morse et al. (1992) articulate their argument about vectors of transmission as follows:

> Customers of male prostitutes most of whom described themselves as heterosexual and bisexual and who also report not using condoms with their female partners, potentially function as vector[s] of HIV transmission from male prostitutes to their female partners and into the more mainstream heterosexual population. (p. 356)

Although this publication (Morse et al., 1992) makes it clear that HIV transmission is a multifaceted phenomenon, MSWs became stigmatized as "typhoid Harrys" (Parsons, Koken, & Bimbi, 2004). A similar paradigm occurred with female sex workers in the 19th century (Scott, 2003).

It remained preeminent, despite numerous publications from 1990 to the present day reporting that MSWs, regardless of type or venue, use condoms more frequently with male clients than with their casual male sex partners (Belza et al., 2001; Bimbi & Parsons, 2005; Boles & Elifson, 1994; Davies & Feldman, 1999; Estcourt et al., 2000; Estep, Waldorf, & Marotta, 1992; Hickson, Weatherburn, Hows, & Davies, 1994; Pennbridge, Freese, & MacKenzie, 1992; Pleak & Meyer-Bahlburg, 1990; Viera de Souza et al., 2003; Weinburg, Worth, & Williams, 2001). Thus, the HIV risk among MSWs appears to be related to non-sex work factors such as casual sex (Allman & Myers, 1999; Weber et al., 2001), injection drug use (Bower, 1990; Estep et al., 1992; Waldorf & Murphy, 1990; Waldorf et al., 1990; Williams et al., 2003) and sexual compulsivity (Parsons, Bimbi, & Halkitis, 2001). Prestage (1994), commenting on gay-identified MSWs, states that research has demonstrated consistently that MSWs are well educated about HIV, perhaps due to consistent exposure to information about the disease within the gay community. Indeed, Parsons et al. (2004) report that many of the MSWs in their sample of 50 Internet-based male escorts in New York City attempted to educate their clients about the risks of unprotected sex and refused clients seeking unprotected sex (Bimbi & Parsons, 2005). However, the idea that sex work constitutes *a significant means* by which HIV is spread into the heterosexual community continues to drive many research questions and the stigmatization of MSWs continues as a result.

THE NEWEST PARADIGM: SEX AS WORK

In 1983, Sagarin and Jolly,[7] authoritatively took the position that prostitution is not a form of work. In the case of homosexual prostitution, they stated "although it is sex for pay, it almost defies description as prostitution because it is generally not pursued as an occupation" (p. 23). The authors emphasize that professionalism when applied to other fields refers to a long and often difficult period of apprenticeship, development of special skills, peer review of one's abilities, standards of entry, etc. Lastly, they suggest that based upon such criteria, "the idea of prostitution as a profession is not to be taken seriously, and much would be gained if the concept (the world's oldest profession) could be dropped out of language and thought" (p. 28).

This is in direct contrast to the view of sex work as a job reported by many MSWs (Luckenbill, 1985; Robinson & Davies, 1991; Weisburg, 1985). In addition, studies have described "professionalism" in sex work. Visano (1991) reports that gay MSWs strive to maintain a professional level of involvement with clients. Van der Poel (1992) observes that professional MSWs have a socially enforced professional code among themselves that dictated appropriate behaviors with clients and each other. These findings directly challenge the statements of Sagarin and Jolly (1983/1997) and clearly support the notion that, at least, among some gay MSWs, sex work is a profession.

While the perspective of "sex as work" was reported by MSWs in past research, it was with the publication of the text *Sex work and sex workers in Australia* (Perkins, Prestage, Sharp, & Lovejoy, 1994) that this new paradigm emerged in the social science literature. Calhoun and Weaver (1996) extend the paradigm to include the concept of rational choice. In their study, MSWs reported the benefits and costs of engaging in sex work. Benefits include financial gain, sexual pleasure, control of work schedule, and affection. Liabilities mentioned are fear of arrest, potential violence, having sex with undesirables, and not being paid for services. The authors surmise that the decision to engage in street prostitution is a complicated process that involves the weighing of the perceived benefits against the perceived risks.

The paradigm of sex as work became visible in social service agencies when various organizations across the United States convened and formed the Coalition Advocating Safer Hustling (CASH) (Boles & Elifson, 1998) with the purpose of educating MSWs about HIV. However, the MSWs involved demanded to be included in the process and had their own agenda for the organization: They wanted CASH to teach

MSWs how to be better sex workers. Due to such conflicting goals, CASH lasted only a short time. Recently, in the United Kingdom, social service providers have elicited from MSWs what they want from such agencies; many programs include helping those who choose to remain in sex work to become better sex workers (Gaffney, 2003). Additionally, men formally employed in the sex industry have created Web sites on the Internet with similar goals such as www.hookonline.org, which was founded in 1998.[8]

Contemporary researchers continue to employ the sex trade as work paradigm. Perkins and Bennett (1997) report that among MSWs in Australia, full time gay and bisexual MSWs hold professional attitudes, and self-identify as sex workers. However, the authors note that heterosexual MSWs engage in survival sex and that their concentration in particular areas of street prostitution leads to this group appearing larger than it is in actuality.

Browne and Minichiello (1996b) as well as Parsons et al. (2004) report that the MSWs in their samples develop a work orientation to separate work sex from personal sex; reject the stigma of sex work; use their bodies as a resource that allows them to capitalize on male sexual privilege; and engage in safer sex. Minichiello, Marino and Browne (2001) report that in another sample of escorts and street-based MSWs in three Australian cities, two thirds of the sample had positive attitudes about being a sex worker.

The sex as work paradigm also has led to new forms of research such as the analyses of escort advertisements (Pruitt, 2003). Cameron, Collins and Thew (1999) factor analyzed 211 print advertisements for MSWs in London in order to identify common types of marketing. Results indicated that two major marketing tactics were employed to attract clients: promoting kink services (which was associated with older MSWs and the mention of manliness) and promoting oneself as "new." The latter type often stressed youth and attractive physiques in their advertisements.

With the advent of this paradigm, the stigma associated with being a sex worker appears to be diminishing in the gay community (Weinstein, 2001; White, 2003). This is evidenced by escort Web sites throwing parties for members of the gay community to socialize with MSWs that post on the sites (Love for sale, 2004). Many publications with a gay male readership have featured how to articles on "becoming an escort" (Liberman, 2001); how the Internet has facilitated escorting (Weinstein, 2001); and how male pornography actors have legitimized sex work (Weinstein, 2002). Other publications, however, have taken a more conservative view, warning about the risks involved in sex work (Von Metzke, 2003).

FUTURE PARADIGMS

The concurrent emergence of the sex as work paradigm and the introduction of the Internet have created a new venue. This phenomenon has clearly affected male sex work. White (2003) observes anecdotally that street sex work appears to be dying out in his neighborhood: indeed, research suggests that most MSWs are now moving to the Internet (Gaffney, 2003). The MSWs interviewed by Parsons, Bimbi and Koken (2003) suggest that the Internet actually facilitates escorting. The anonymity of the Internet permits men to offer other men money for sex in non-sex work related chat rooms and Web sites. Many of the MSWs in Parsons et al.'s (2003) sample explained that they were introduced to sex work through this medium. Social service providers (Akeret et al., 2002; Terrence Higgins Trust, 2002) and police (Tiby, 2003) also report that the explosion of the Internet has hampered traditional outreach efforts to street-based MSWs.

However, the Internet as a venue for sex work has yet to be investigated fully. It is clear that within the Internet itself, male sex work occurs in many sub-venues reflecting the diversity of interaction modes available on the web. Chat-rooms, personal Web sites/homepages of sex workers, online escort agencies, bulletin boards, and escort-finder Web sites all have become part of Internet-based male sex work. Further, the proliferation of Internet use across all social classes and the many different ways in which it is utilized by MSWs may indicate that not all MSWs who use the Internet are the same. Chat-rooms and bulletin boards may be the Internet equivalents of the streets because it costs nothing other than the initial computer and Internet service, or the fee at an Internet café. Anyone with Internet access can enter a gay chat room and start to look for clients. Gaffney (2003) reports that young MSWs in London can now be found in Internet cafes and the street scene appears to be dying out. In contrast, escorts post their ads on Web-based escort finder sites for a monthly fee or maintain personal Web sites and domains which can be costly. Differences and similarities among MSWs who reach clients via the Internet have yet to be investigated and described in published social scientific research.

The other aspect of male sex work that warrants investigation is the personal sex lives of MSWs. As discussed previously, it has been reported that MSWs are less likely to use condoms with their casual partners than with their clients. It also has become clear across studies that MSWs engage in sexual risk-taking in rates higher than gay men in general (Allman & Myers, 1999; Weber et al., 2001). While researchers have explored the factors related to sexual risk with clients, factors related to sexual risk with casual partners are, for the most part, ignored completely. Clearly, two new areas of inquiry into the phenomenon of male sex work await the attention of social scientists. Paradigms have shifted and will continue to do so with cultural and historical changes. An awareness of the history of research on male sex work and its attendant problems with methods, samples, overlooked places, venues, and persons will permit more paradigms to emerge, resulting in a fuller understanding of the world of male sex work.

NOTES

1. In a later publication, Gandy and Deisher (1970) describe attempts to vocationally rehabilitate 30 of these young men through job placement and training. Successful MSWs and those described as having psychopathic personalities rejected the authors' overtures.

2. The remainder of the sample in Boyer's (1989) study self-identified as bisexual.

3. It should be noted that non-scientific sources identified other types of MSWs (Kaye, 2003).

4. Boyer (1989) suggests many young gay and bisexual MSWs engage in sex work as a means to achieve a gay identity because they lack social outlets outside of bars and clubs (which they cannot enter until they are 21). They are restricted to the streets where they can have social interactions with other young gay men, discover sex work, and enter the gay community. Earls and Helene (1989) argue that the higher prevalence of gay youth in sex work may be due to increased societal acceptance of homosexuality, leading MSWs to disclose their true sexual identity; further, they suggest there simply may be more young gay men entering sex work.

5. Visano (1991) also describes this segregation by sexual identity; gay MSWs occupy distinct territories near gay bars and baths and heterosexual MSWs wandering in were viewed with suspicion, perhaps due to fear of competition as well as violence. One gay MSW in Visano's (1991) sample reported working among straight hustlers and having to hide his homosexuality in order to avoid being beaten up.

6. Up until this time, past research was atheoretical and based upon a priori assumptions.

7. The article by Sagarin and Jolly was republished in 1997 in its original form and, thus, did not incorporate any research findings reported in the interim.

8. Hookonline has experienced problems with affordable and reliable servers willing to host the site. The site also relies on volunteer submissions to consistently update the content with new features (S. Lujtens, personal communication, March 23, 2005).

REFERENCES

Akeret, R., Hincziza, U., Vandenbroucke, B., Vriens, P., Okoliyski, M., Lukasik, R., Georgescu, M., & Kohler, D. (2002, July). *Survey about male sex work on the Internet.* Paper presented at the XIV International AIDS Conference, Barcelona, Spain.

Allen, D. M. (1980). Young male prostitutes: A psychosocial study. *Archives of Sexual Behavior, 9,* 399-426.

Allman, D., & Myers, T. (1999). Male sex work and HIV/AIDS in Canada. In P. Aggleton (Ed.), *Men who sell sex: International perspectives on male prostitution and HIV/AIDS* (pp. 61-81). Philadelphia, PA: Temple University Press.

Belza, M. J., Llacer, A., Mora, R., Morales, M., Castilla, J., & De La Fuente, L. (2001). Sociodemographic characteristics and HIV risk behavior patterns of male sex workers in Madrid, Spain. *AIDS Care, 13,* 677-682.

Bimbi, D. S., & Parsons, J. T. (2005). Barebacking among Internet-based male sex workers. *Journal of Gay and Lesbian Psychotherapy, 9,* 89-110.

Boles, J., & Elifson, K. (1994). Sexual identity and HIV: The male prostitute. *Journal of Sex Research, 31,* 39-46.

Boles, J., & Elifson, K. (1998). Out of CASH: The rise and demise of male prostitutes' rights organizations. In J. Elias, V. Elias, & G. Brewer (Eds.), *Prostitution: On whores, hustlers and johns* (pp. 267-278). New York, NY: Prometheus Books.

Bower, B. (1990). Glimpses of AIDS and male prostitution. *Science News, 138,* 390.

Boyer, D. (1989). Male prostitution and homosexual identity. *Gay and Lesbian Youth, 17,* 151-184.

Browne, J., & Minichiello, V. (1996a). Research directions in male sex work. *Journal of Homosexuality, 31,* 29-56.

Browne, J., & Minichiello, V. (1996b). The social and work context of commercial sex between men: A research note. *The Australian and New Zealand Journal of Sociology, 32,* 86-92.

Butts, W. H. (1947). Boy prostitutes of the metropolis. *Journal of Clinical Psychopathology, 8,* 673-681.

Calhoun, T. C. (1992). Male street hustling: Introduction to processes and stigma. *Sociological Spectrum, 12,* 35-52.

Calhoun, T. C., & Weaver, G. S. (1996). Rational decision making among male street prostitutes. *Deviant Behavior, 17,* 209-227.

Calhoun, T. C., & Weaver, G. S. (2001). Male prostitution. In D. L. Peck & N. A. Dolch (Eds.), *Extraordinary behavior: A case study approach to understanding social problems* (pp. 212-226). Westport, CT: Praeger.

Cameron, S., Collins, A., & Thew, N. (1999). Prostitution services: An exploratory empirical analysis. *Applied Economics, 31,* 1523-1529.

Caukins, S. E., & Coombs, N. R. (1976). The psychodynamics of male prostitution. *American Journal of Psychotherapy, 30,* 441-451.

Coleman, E. (1989). The development of male prostitution activity among gay and bisexual adolescents. *Journal of Homosexuality, 17,* 131-149.

Coombs, N. (1974). Male prostitution: A psychosocial view of behavior. *American Journal of Orthopsychiatry, 44,* 782-789.

Davies, P., & Feldman, R. (1999). Selling sex in Cardiff and London. In P. Aggleton (Ed.), *Men who sell sex: International perspectives on male prostitution and HIV/AIDS* (pp. 1-22). Philadelphia, PA: Temple University Press.

DeGraaf, R., Vanwesenbeeck, I., Van Zessen, G., Straver, C. J., & Visser, J. H. (1994). Male prostitutes and safe sex: Different settings, different risks. *AIDS Care, 6,* 277-288.

Deisher, R. W., Eisner, V., & Suizbacher, S. I. (1969). The young male prostitute. *Pediatrics, 43*, 936-941.

Derogatis, L. R. (1977). *The SCL-90: Administration, scoring and procedure manual I.* Baltimore, MD: Clinical Psychometric Research.

Earls, C. M., & Helene, D. (1989). A psychosocial study of male prostitution. *Archives of Sexual Behavior, 18*, 401-419.

Estcourt, C. S., Marks, C., Rohrsheim, R., Johnson, A. M., Donovan, B., & Mindel, A. (2000). HIV, sexually transmitted infections, and risk behaviors in male commercial sex workers in Sydney. *Sexually Transmitted Infections, 76*, 294-298.

Estep, R., Waldorf, D., & Marotta, T. (1992). Sexual behavior of male prostitutes. In J. Huber & B. E. Schneider (Eds.), *The social context of AIDS* (pp. 95-112). Thousand Oaks, CA: Sage.

Freyhan, F. A. (1947). Homosexual prostitution: A case report. *Delaware State Medical Journal, 19*, 92-94.

Gaffney, J. (2003, June). *Working together with male sex workers in London.* Paper presented at the European Network of Male Prostitution, Hamburg, Germany.

Gandy, P., & Deisher, R., (1970). Young male prostitutes: The physician's role in social rehabilitation. *Journal of the American Medical Association, 212*, 1661-1666.

Ginsberg, K. (1967). The "meat-rack": A study of the male homosexual prostitute. *American Journal of Psychotherapy, 21*, 170-185.

Goffman, E. (1963). *Stigma: Notes on the management of a spoiled identity.* New York, NY: Simon and Schuster.

Hickson, F., Weatherburn, P., Hows, J., & Davies, P. (1994). Selling safer sex: Male masseurs and escorts in the UK. In P. Aggleton, P. Davies, & G. Hart (Eds.), *AIDS: Foundations for the future* (pp. 197-209). Bristol, PA: Taylor & Francis Inc.

Hoffman, M. (1972). The male prostitute. *Sexual Behavior, 2*(8), 16-21.

Kaye, K. (2003). Male prostitution in the twentieth century: Pseudohomosexuals, hoodlum homosexuals, and exploited teens. *Journal of Homosexuality, 46*, 1-77.

Koken, J. A., Bimbi, D. S., Parsons, J. T., & Halkitis, P. N. (2004). The experience of stigma in the lives of male Internet escorts. *Journal of Psychology and Human Sexuality, 16*,13-32.

Liberman, V. (2001, Jul/Aug). Show me the money: Instinct's guide to hiring and becoming an escort. *Instinct, 4*, 36-43.

Love for sale. (2004, September 3). *HX Magazine, 678*, p. 12

Luckenbill, D. F. (1984). Dynamics of the deviant sale. *Deviant Behavior, 5*, 337-353.

Luckenbill, D. F. (1985). Entering male prostitution. *Urban Life, 14*, 131-153.

Luckenbill, D. F. (1986). Deviant career mobility: The case of male prostitutes. *Sociology, 33*, 283-296.

MacNamara, R. (1965). Male prostitution in American cities: A socioeconomic or pathological phenomenon? *American Journal of Orthopsychiatry, 35*, 204.

Minichiello, V., Marino, R., & Browne, J. (2001). Knowledge, risk perceptions and condom usage in male sex workers from three Australian cities. *AIDS Care, 13*, 387-402.

Minichiello, V., Marino, R., Browne, J., & Jamieson, M. (1999). A profile of the clients of male sex workers in three Australian cities. *Australian and New Zealand Journal of Public Health, 23*, 511-518.

Morse, E. V., & Simon, P. M. (1992). Cofactors of substance use among male street prostitutes. *Journal of Drug Issues, 22,* 977-994.

Morse, E. V., Simon, P. M., Balson, P. M., & Osofsky, H. J. (1992). Sexual behavior patterns of customers of male street prostitutes. *Archives of Sexual Behavior, 21,* 347-357.

Morse, E. V., Simon, P. M., Osofsky, H. J., Balson, P. M., & Gaumer, H. R. (1991). The male street prostitute: A vector for transmission of HIV infection into the heterosexual world. *Social Science & Medicine, 32,* 535-539.

Parsons, J. T., Bimbi, D. S., & Halkitis, P. N. (2001). Sexual compulsivity among gay/bisexual male escorts who advertise on the Internet. *Journal of Sexual Addiction and Compulsivity, 8,* 113-123.

Parsons, J. T., Bimbi, D. S., & Koken, J. A. (2003, June). *Experiences from the United States of America.* Invited address to the Central and Eastern European Group meeting of the European Network on Male Prostitution: Hamburg, Germany.

Parsons, J. T., Koken, J. A., & Bimbi, D. S. (2004). The use of the Internet by gay and bisexual male escorts: Sex workers as sex educators. *AIDS Care, 16,* 1-15.

Pennbridge, J. N., Freese, T. E., & MacKenzie, R. G. (1992). High-risk behaviors among male street youth in Hollywood, California. *AIDS Education and Prevention* (Fall Supplement), 24-33.

Perkins, R., & Bennett, G. (1997). *Being a prostitute: Prostitute women and prostitute men (2nd edition).* Sydney, AU: George Allen and Unwin.

Perkins, R., Prestage, G., Sharp, R., & Lovejoy, F. (1994). *Sex work and sex workers in Australia.* Sydney, AU: University of New South Wales Press Ltd.

Pleak, R. R., & Meyer-Bahlburg, H. F. L. (1990). Sexual behavior and AIDS knowledge of young male prostitutes in Manhattan. *Journal of Sex Research, 27,* 557-587.

Prestage, G. (1994). Male and transsexual prostitution. In R. Perkins, G. Prestage, R. Sharp, & F. Lovejoy (Eds.), *Sex work and sex workers in Australia* (pp. 174-190). Sydney, AU: University of New South Wales Press Ltd.

Price, V. (1984). Social characteristics of adolescent male prostitution. *Victimology, 9,* 211-221.

Pruitt, M. V. (2003, March). *Online boys: Male for male Internet escorts.* Paper presented at the Southern Sociological Society, New Orleans.

Reiss, A. J. (1961). The social integration of queers and peers. *Social Problems, 9,* 102-120.

Robinson, T., & Davies, P. (1991). London's homosexual male prostitutes: Power, peer groups and HIV. In P. Aggleton, P. Davies & G. Hart (Eds.), *AIDS: Responses, interventions and care* (pp. 95-110). London, UK: Falker Press.

Ross, H. L. (1959). The "hustler" in Chicago. *Journal of Student Research, 1,* 13-19.

Roy, J. L., Otis, J., Vincelette, J., Alary, M., Zunzunegui, M. V., Gaudreault, M., Remis, R. S., Lavoie, R., LeClerc, R., Masse, B., Parent, R., & Turmel, B. (2002, July). *Characteristics of omega study participants who have received money or drugs in exchange for sex.* Paper presented at the XIV International AIDS Conference, Barcelona.

Sagarin, E., & Jolly, R. W. (1983/1997). Prostitution: Profession and pathology. In L. B. Schlesinger & E. R. Revitch (Eds.), *Sexual dynamics of anti-social behavior* (pp. 9-30). Springfield, IL: Charles C Thomas.

Salamon, E. (1989). The homosexual escort agency: Deviance disavowal. *British Journal of Sociology, 40,* 1-21.

Satterfield, S. B. (1981). Clinical aspects of juvenile prostitution. *Medical Aspects of Human Sexuality, 15,* 126-132.

Scheinmann, H. (1929). The psychology of the male coquette. *Zietschrift fuer sexualwissenschaft und sexualpolitik, 16,* 206-210.

Scott, J. (2003). A prostitute's progress: Male prostitution in scientific discourse. *Social Semiotics, 13,* 179-199.

Silverstein, C., & Picano, F. (2003). *The joy of gay sex (3rd ed.).* New York, NY: Harper Collins.

Simon, P. M., Morse, E. V., Balson, P. M., Osofsky, H. J., & Gaumer, H. R. (1993). Barriers to human immunodeficiency virus related risk reduction among male street prostitutes. *Health Education Quarterly, 20,* 261-273.

Simon, P. M., Morse, E. V., Osofsky, H. J., Balson, P. M., & Gaumer, R. (1992). Psychological characteristics of a sample of male street prostitutes. *Archives of Sexual Behavior, 21,* 33-44.

Terrence Higgins Trust (2002). *Working with young male sex workers in the city of Bristol.* Terrence Higgins Trust.

Tiby, T. P. (2003). The production and reproduction of prostitution. *Journal of Scandinavian Studies in Criminology and Crime Prevention, 3,* 154-72.

Uy, J. M, Parsons, J. T., Bimbi, D. S., Koken, J. A., Halkitis, P. N. (2004). Gay and bisexual male escorts who advertise on the Internet: Understanding reasons for and effects of involvement in commercial sex. *International Journal of Men's Health, 3,* 11-26.

Van der Poel, S. (1992). Professional male prostitution: A neglected phenomenon. *Crime, Law and Social Change, 18,* 259-275.

Vanwesenbeeck, I. (2001). Another decade of social scientific work on sex work: A review of research 1990-2000. *Annual Review of Sex Research, 12,* 242-289.

Viera de Souza, C. T., Lowndes, C. M., Landman, C., Szwarcwald, F., Sutmoller, F., & Bastos, F. I. (2003). Willingness to participate in HIV vaccine trials among a sample of men who have sex with men, with and without a history of commercial sex in Rio de Janeiro, Brazil. *AIDS Care, 15,* 539-548.

Visano, L. A. (1991). The impact of age on paid sexual encounters. *Journal of Homosexuality,* 207-226.

Von Metzke, R. (2003, Spring). Sex for hire. *Xodus, 1.*

Waldorf, D., & Murphy, S. (1990). Intravenous drug use and syringe-sharing practices of call men and hustlers. In M. A. Plant (Ed.), *AIDS, drugs, and prostitution* (pp. 109-131). New York, NY: Routledge.

Waldorf, D., Murphy, S., Lauderback, D., Reinarman, C., & Marotta, T. (1990). Needle sharing among male prostitutes: Preliminary findings of the Prospero Project. *Journal of Drug Issues, 20,* 309-334.

Weber, A. E., Craib, K. J. P., Chan, K., Martindale, S., Miller, M. L., Schechter, M. T., & Hogg, R. S. (2001). Sex trade involvement and rates of human immunodeficiency virus positivity among young gay and bisexual men. *International Journal of Epidemiology, 30,* 1449-1454.

Weeks, J. (1981). Inverts, perverts, and Mary-Annes: Male prostitution and the regulation of homosexuality in England in the nineteenth and early twentieth centuries. *Journal of Homosexuality, 6,* 113-134.

Weinberg, M. S., Worth, H., & Williams, C. J. (2001). Men sex workers and other men who have sex with men: How do their HIV risks compare in New Zealand? *Archives of Sexual Behavior, 30,* 273-286.

Weinstein, S. (2001, March). Escort report: Today's high end sex professional. *OUT,* 90-95.

Weinstein, S. (2002, March 22). Special delivery: The latest on the world's oldest profession, who's buying, who's selling and why they're doing it. *HX,* 24.

Weisburg, K. D. (1985). *Children of the night: A study of adolescent prostitution.* Lexington, MA: Lexington Books.

West, D. J. (1998). Male homosexual prostitution in England. In J. Elias, V. Elias, & G. Brewer (Eds.), *Prostitution: On whores, hustlers and johns* (pp. 228-235). New York, NY: Prometheus Books.

White, D. (2003, August). The online hook. *Instinct, 6,* 46-49.

Williams, M. L., Timpson, S., Klovdal, A., Bowen, A. M., Ross, M. W., & Keel, K. B. (2003). HIV risk among a sample of drug using male sex workers. *AIDS, 17,* 1402-1404.

doi:10.1300/J082v53n01_02

Sex and the Unspoken
in Male Street Prostitution

Kerwin Kaye, PhD (candidate)

New York University

SUMMARY. Although the overwhelming majority of male prostitutes work through agencies or by placing their own ads, most studies of male prostitution focus upon young men who work on the street. Remarkably, these studies seldom identify the dynamics of poverty and street-level violence as important elements of their examination. Investigations of male sex work–few though they are–focus almost exclusively upon sexual aspects of "the life." Despite the importance of these networks in shaping the contours of street life, and often in enabling one's very survival, the primary research focus has remained on questions of sexual identity, sexual practices with clients, and sexual abuse as a causative factor. Meanwhile, studies that do examine the dynamics of male street life typically do not examine questions of prostitution or other issues related to sexuality. A dominant theme within this literature consists of specifying the social mores of the most aggressive and socially problematic participants within street society, particularly gang members and drug dealers. The dissimilar nature of these images relates directly to the political projects of the dominant culture, which, in a very general way, seeks to "rescue" (reintegrate) deviant white youth, while controlling

---

Kerwin Kaye is a PhD student in NYU's American Studies program. Correspondence may be addressed to Kerwin Kaye, 285 Mercer Street, 8th floor, New York, NY 10003 (E-mail: kab316@nyu.edu).

[Haworth co-indexing entry note]: "Sex and the Unspoken in Male Street Prostitution." Kaye, Kerwin. Co-published simultaneously in *Journal of Homosexuality* (The Haworth Press, Inc.) Vol. 53, No. 1/2, 2007, pp. 37-73; and: *Male Sex Work: A Business Doing Pleasure* (ed: Todd G. Morrison and Bruce W. Whitehead) The Haworth Press, Inc., 2007, pp. 37-73. Single or multiple copies of this article are available for a fee from The Haworth Document Delivery Service [1-800- HAWORTH, 9:00 a.m. - 5:00 p.m. (EST). E-mail address: docdelivery@haworthpress.com].

Available online at http://jh.haworthpress.com
© 2007 by The Haworth Press, Inc. All rights reserved.
doi:10.1300/J082v53n01_03

and excluding deviant youth of color. The political aim of reintegrating runaways into middle-class trajectories has the effect of authorizing certain discourses regarding their behavior on the streets, while marginalizing or completely disallowing others. This article seeks to examine and challenge these trends of representation. doi:10.1300/J082v53n01_03 *[Article copies available for a fee from The Haworth Document Delivery Service: 1-800-HAWORTH. E-mail address: <docdelivery@haworthpress.com> Website: <http://www.HaworthPress.com> © 2007 by The Haworth Press, Inc. All rights reserved.]*

KEYWORDS. Male prostitution, street life, youth homelessness, urban poverty

INTRODUCTION

Although the overwhelming majority (around 80%) of male prostitutes work through agencies or by placing their own ads (Allman, 1999; Leigh, 1994), most studies of male prostitution focus upon young men who work on the street. Remarkably, these studies seldom identify the dynamics of poverty and street-level violence as important elements of their examination. Investigations of male sex work–few though they are–tend to follow studies of female prostitutes in focusing almost exclusively upon sexual aspects of "the life." While these studies might make reference to the notion that poverty forces individuals into prostitution, they generally do not discuss the other consequences of this poverty, and the manner in which it shapes both social networks on the street and conflict within those networks.[1]

Meanwhile, studies which do examine the dynamics of male street life typically do not examine questions of prostitution or other issues related to sexuality. A dominant theme within this literature consists of specifying the social mores of the most violent participants within street society, particularly gang members and drug dealers. Many of the contemporary classics of urban ethnography such as works by Anderson (1990, 1999), Bourgois (1996), Jankowski (1991), Venkatesh (2000), Wacquant (2003), and Williams (1992) direct attention toward the most aggressively masculine men on the street. Ethnographies within this genre typically fail to document situations in which the masculine identity of young urban men is compromised, or situations in which these men act against locally hegemonic versions of masculinity, leaving only the image of the "young tough." To the limited extent that sexuality is considered within these narratives, the imagery is heterosexual and tends to reinforce an iconography of male domination, as in Anderson's (1990) analysis of black male interest in "sexual conquest," Williams' (1992) narration of male-controlled sex-for-crack exchanges, or Bourgois' (1996) description of gang rape among urban adolescents.[2] The focus upon the most macho and terrifyingly brutal aspects of street life is, perhaps, understandable given the socially problematic nature of the behaviors described, as well as the power these men exercise within the street environment. However, in the absence of more developed literature documenting the less violent aspects of urban males' lives, these masculinized ethnographies run the risk of reinforcing an image of underclass men as dangerous, hypermasculine reprobates.

Not surprisingly, there is little crossover between the literatures which explore male prostitution and those that examine the dynamics of men's life on the street. The texts do not cite one another, and even more interestingly, their various protagonists–the sexualized male prostitute victim and the hypermasculine drug-dealing gang member–do not appear together. An artificial divide exists between these two sets of writings, despite the simple facts that (a) men prostituting on the street encounter and participate in a masculine economy of violence and threat which shapes their daily interactions; (b) many men prostituting on the street form loose cliques which may engage in a variety of illegal acts; and (c) at least a few male gang members also engage in prostitution (the practice was even relatively commonplace throughout the 1950s and 60s; see Allen, 1980; Kaye, 2003; Reiss, 1987 [1961]). Mass media representations of young men on the street similarly present two divergent foci, one upon the sexualized victim status of the (white) prostitute, and another upon the non-sexualized predator status of the (non-white) gang member, drug dealer, etc. The dissimilar nature of these images relates directly to the political projects of the dominant culture, which, in a very general way, seeks to "rescue" and thereby reintegrate deviant white youth, while controlling and excluding deviant youth of color. Given the rapid ascendancy of prisons in contemporary society, it is not surprising to find that reports on "youth" in general tend to emphasize the violence of youth of color, even though actual youth crime rates are declining (Males, 1996, 1999). At the same time, the desire to rehabilitate "lost" white youth can be seen both in the state focus on providing services for (implicitly white and middle-class) runaway youth and, more generally, in the sympathetic portrayal and victim status usually accorded runaway teens. Thus, the political aim of reintegrating runaways into middle-class trajectories has the effect of authorizing certain discourses regarding male prostitution while marginalizing or completely disallowing others.

The point in identifying these divergent trends within the representation of race and gender on the street is not to suggest that the lives of male street prostitutes exactly resemble those of male gang members; that "boy prostitutes" are really "angry young men." Given the punitive treatment young men of color receive as actual or potential "gang-bangers," this could hardly be considered a useful goal. Nor is the point to suggest that male street prostitutes should not be considered sexually exploited victims, as they are most commonly portrayed within both the popular and social scientific literature. Rather, my aim is to highlight the larger political projects which inform not only portrayals created by service agencies and researchers, but also those created by male street-based sex workers themselves. Ultimately, my aim in this regard is threefold: to illuminate the tropes which have been utilized in the portrayal of male prostitution; to point toward the material and political interests which have shaped those depictions; and to bring forth imagery which has been left out by the dominant tropes.

Directing attention to questions of power and ideology draws out the important fact that hegemonic representations of male street prostitutes are not made by the street workers themselves, but by individuals who work at various service agencies; as well as by journalists and researchers who perform their work through these organizations. In shaping a particular vision of male street prostitution, service providers implicitly define their own status and role within the environment. Seen in this light, the narratives which surround male street prostitutes often are only peripherally related to the experiences and concerns of the sex workers; instead, these narratives act as a useful means through which the authors situate themselves within the social field, both within the street and especially within society as a whole.

The narratives which surround male street prostitution deploy a variety of discourses in contradictory ways in order to achieve their particular effects. One of the central questions around which the narratives cluster concerns the issue of "agency." Given the status of free choice within ethical (i.e., social) debate, it is not surprising to find heated controversy concerning the agency, or lack thereof, of participants engaged in various disputed practices (Flax, 1995). In establishing that a given population does or does not exercise agency, one makes implicit judgments regarding the status of the activities that define that group. The result of this situation makes the subjectivity of male prostitutes a contested ground of representation, with various sides attempting to "prove" that these individuals do or do not exercise agency. Consequently, male street prostitutes are most typically portrayed as being young (vulnerable/powerless/naive), drug dependent (emotionally enslaved), sexually abused (emotionally unstable and incapable), economically desperate (powerless), and white, middle-class and perhaps even straight (innocent/worthy of rescue). Alternatively, they might be portrayed as being of age (powerful) and in search of sexual excitement and community (gay and empowered). A third narrative, more noticeable in the past than today, represents male street prostitutes as being of age (powerful), Black, Latino, and/or working class (dangerous), and law-breaking (dangerous).

In their voluminous and detailed work concerning male prostitution, West and de Villiers (1993) label these three different depictions of male street prostitutes as desperate, homosexual, and dangerous. In the first, correctly identified by West and de Villiers (1993) as dominant within the academic (and social service) literature, male prostitutes are described as runaway youth who turn to prostitution as a last resort. In the second, young men are said to move into prostitution by choice, as a means of exploring their own sexual identity as developing gay men. Finally, male street prostitutes are sometimes envisioned as "amoral delinquents" who threaten and rob their clients. While West and de Villiers (1993) suggest these three types actually exist on the street, I contend that the various portrayals have as much to do with the political agenda of the authors as they do with actual street life. Each of these portrayals highlights certain facts while underplaying others, implicitly identifying its own problems and suggesting its own solutions in the process (providing services, challenging heterosexism, and facilitating incarceration, respectively). Far from being neutral descriptions, these representations of "life on the street" implicitly serve to advance various types of political claims.

For example, with male gang members and other violent street criminals, journalistic depictions commonly create support for the idea that the individuals involved are in total control of their behavior, thereby justifying the resultant punishment. On the other hand, the predominant discourse which surrounds male prostitution today actively disavows the presence of agency. While the assertion of masculine agency facilitates punitive incarceration, the denial of agency in the case of young male prostitutes accomplishes a different series of tasks: It (1) denies the relevance of the participants' experience of a given practice, (2) encourages the adoption of external evaluations of these practices, and (3) justifies control over the lives of participants, ranging from return to one's family to allegedly *protective* custody in rule-bound shelters and treatment facilities. Thus, whereas virtually none of the "non-masculine" or subordinating experiences of gang members are explored, *only* these elements are examined in most depictions of male street prostitutes.

This narrative approach runs the risk of reinforcing conservative notions of familial benevolence and of simplistically equating street life with danger. While the "normal" family is portrayed as a good place for children, the streets are seen in a uniformly negative light, a perspective that fundamentally fails to address why many youth would choose or be forced to leave their homes. The model tends to presume that good solutions are those which "restore" a normatively middle-class and family-based lifestyle. Unsurprisingly, Christian social service organizations tend to incorporate this approach more fully (see, for example, McGeady, 1994, 1996; Ritter, 1988), but academic portrayals often hold "the family" over and against "the street" as well (for further critique, see Brock, 1998). At a different level, the image of "sexually vulnerable youth" may serve to reinforce the fetishization of innocence which partially fuels the sexual market for youth (see Kincaid, 1998). Thus, both the focus on familial goodness and on young people's "innocence" are implicated in various ideological dangers.

These ideational difficulties have concrete effects in terms of the nature and distribution of services. While familial restoration or placement in a highly controlled treatment facility may serve the needs of some participants, the exclusionary focus on sexual victimization leaves many agencies unable to offer relevant assistance to participants who do not see themselves in such terms. Such representations, then, work to limit the type of help which is available to those on the street, particularly services which are based upon the potential for ongoing prostitution and participation in street life (precisely the premise of "harm reduction"). Services based upon a model of rescue also tend to result in what is informally known within the service community as "skimming": the removal of the easiest-to-serve (read: middle-class and obedient) individuals from the street, while leaving disobedient, drug-using, and otherwise "trouble-causing" individuals without significant aid. Bringing forth new representations of male street prostitution may promote alternative services which are relevant to those whose needs fall outside what is offered by most programs.

In what follows, I will present six different male street workers who, in various ways, do not fit the dominant narrative of straightforwardly "exploited youth" (or other narratives that have been identified). Following this, I will explore three themes that have been under-examined by the majority of social scientific literature on male prostitution: space and the material underpinning of street life; street relations and emotional instrumentality; and violence and the self-management of identity. My intention is to first reveal some of the tremendous diversity which exists among male street workers, and then to situate their lives within common social conditions which are often ignored.

This material is based upon nearly nine months of ethnographic fieldwork that I conducted in a West coast city in intensive but intermittent periods from mid-1999 to mid-2001. Most of this time was spent working with a small harm-reduction agency that served male street prostitutes and emphasized a harm reduction approach (i.e., it involved street outreach, running a needle exchange, preparing and serving food, distributing clothes, condoms, etc.). Through this work, I developed some manner of contact with approximately 80-100 individuals who worked on the street. Two additional weeks were spent living in a tenement hotel near the primary hustling scene. Due to constraints placed upon my research (which I write about in some detail in my thesis [2001]), I was able to conduct only a limited number of in-depth interviews, including five with current street workers, three with other individuals who had formerly worked as hustlers on the streets, three with "sugar-daddies," and four with social workers who were directly involved with local street youth. Additional information comes from numerous informal conversations I had with the director of the harm-reduction agency. I also make liberal use of three academic works that examine the nonsexual aspects of male street workers' lives: *This idle trade* by Visano (1987), *The Times Square hustler* by McNamara (1994), and *Mean streets* by Hagan and McCarthy (1998). After presenting this work, I will return briefly to the question of the political foundations which underlie representations of male street prostitution, and suggest alternative directions which may be engaged in the future.

SIX LIVES, SIX EXPERIENCES

Aaron[3] has a B.A. in journalism and works in an office as a supervisor. Thirty-seven years old, he has been working as a prostitute for the past three years. Aaron generally works by placing an escort ad in the local gay newspaper, but sometimes he works out of the bars on Polk Street, and occasionally he works directly on the street. He earns $100 per hour when working as an off-street escort, much more than the $20 charged for the quick hand-jobs and blow-jobs that are common with street work. Though he is hired by the hour, clients sometimes finish after 15 to 20 minutes, giving him an hourly wage that far exceeds the $14 per hour he makes as an office supervisor, a wage that he has come to resent since beginning sex work. He enjoys doing sex work ("I got off on them getting off on me. I was somebody's fantasy"), and compares it positively to higher status personal services, such as therapy. He dislikes the term "hustler" because "it implies dishonesty" and "There's no hustle in what I'm doing. You call me; you know what you're going to pay." Aaron wishes he could work as a prostitute full-time as it would give him more time to pursue his artistic interests, but he typically entertains only four clients a month, making the transition impossible. (During his best month, he earned $1500, but this was an anomaly.) Though clients do sometimes arrange dates well in advance, Aaron generally works by returning daily messages and seeing clients that same evening.

Despite the fact that he earns more money with clients contacted through his ad, Aaron occasionally enjoys working on the street.

> I've always wanted to be a rebel. I like to be a little scandalous and shocking . . . I think a lot of guys would every now and then like to put on our trashiest clothes and stand out on the stroll. I don't know if a woman would ever say this, but for a gay man, being a whore isn't such a big switch. It's like doing what you've always been doing and getting paid for it.

However, Aaron does not fit in well with the rest of the street scene. "I'm wearing a three hundred dollar leather jacket and carrying a credit card in my pocket. Street guys look at me like 'What the fuck are you doing here?' They almost thought I was a date." Aaron finds the street prices "ridiculous" and often works in the bars instead, though both of these venues remain secondary to his work through the newspaper. Aaron says he would work on the street and in the bars more frequently, but he fears arrest, particularly on the street. Though he has never heard of anyone being arrested in a bar, he feels that the police are more likely to arrest people working there than those who work through advertisements.

I ran into Aaron on the streets several months after our initial discussions. He had quit his job and was about to move to Los Angeles. He needed to earn some extra cash in order to make the move though, and he was working in the bars and on the streets to get the money. He was unhappy about being so low on cash, and was clearly somewhat concerned about being able to obtain enough for the move. Still, he offered no criticisms of prostitution, and instead complained about the judgmental attitudes of some other gay men: "They put me down for having sex with guys who they think look gross. But there's always something you can find that is attractive about someone. Those guys that put me down are just smug and arrogant."

Stephen began working in a male Asian massage parlor in New York City immediately after leaving home at age 18. Now 31, he describes his childhood as "difficult, but not terribly abusive." His gay identity became a major point of contention with his parents during his teen years, and he left home ready for the freedom to explore gay sex. He found a new "family" (his term) organized around gay sex work; a group of approximately 20 boys and men, mostly white and aged 16 to 25, who lived together, did drugs together, and hung out with each other on the street while working and playing (the distinction between these two activities being not entirely absolute). Trusting no one over 21 unless they were in the group, Stephen found community, support, affection, and affirmation of his gayness among his friends. Stephen did not work on the street as he was able to earn more in the massage parlor ($35-40 per trick), but even the off-street work was difficult, and he says sometimes he felt like he was working "in a sweatshop."

Unlike Aaron, Stephen did not maintain a strictly "professional" attitude toward his work. Desperate for affection and gay affirmation, he looked to his clients for these things, even following a few that he liked to their homes as an uninvited guest. At the other end of the spectrum, he occasionally rifled through the wallets of his clients, a fact that caused him to be beaten up a few times. He continued to steal, however, and learned to enlist the support of the house management by talking back to angry victims ("This guy's trying to pull something!"). Stephen says that he experienced "a lot" of scary situations, nearly getting raped once, but that his attitude (and the attitude of his friends) was overwhelmingly dismissive: "I was more worried about not being able to work with all the cuts and bruises on my face than anything else. We almost expected to get raped. It was no big deal." The group would offer support to each other in such situations, "not by processing and stuff, but just by being there. We'd take them to the hospital where they treated us like shit because we didn't have any money." Stephen notes that the police began to arrest everyone on the street at a certain point, forcing everyone into the bars. "Only those folks who couldn't get in kept the stronghold out on the street, but most found a way in despite the difficulty" (either sneaking in or via fake IDs).

Stephen says his entire life revolved around prostitution during these years. He did, however, manage to put himself through college, though the experience was "entirely alien" for him, divorced as it was from the rest of his life. His upper middle-class parents gave him money for school, which enabled him to use his earned money only for recreational commodities, particularly drugs. He readily shared his money with his street family, most of whom had significantly less access to cash. The overall lack of income in the network forced the group to live in "a lousy neighborhood" and in extremely crowded conditions. (Six people each lived in four different flats, "but people would bring friends if they needed to crash, so there were usually more like 10 to 15 people at a time.") Stephen emphasizes that he was not economically forced to do sex work, and that, despite the difficulties he encountered, he found affection and affirmation of his gay identity.

At present, Stephen continues to do sex work, though now he does elite level outcall, advertising solely through word of mouth. He earns $350 per hour, and uses the money to support his graduate studies at an upper-tier university. He says that he takes a very different attitude toward his work today, keeping it distinct and largely separate from his personal life. He stays in touch with many of his former friends, but infrequent phone calls have replaced the intense bonds that once existed.

Jeremy, a somewhat run-down looking 33-year-old, speaks at a mile a minute, and seems to be on speed most of the time. He has difficulty tracking a single topic, and our conversation wanders in and out of coherence. He's pleasant, but is prone to excitability and anger when talking about emotional topics. During these flashes, he often stands up quickly and paces for a few seconds before sitting back down. He does not seem directly threatening, but woven within his rambling tales are stories of domestic abuse with prior boyfriends. Jeremy cannot understand why one of his young lovers cried and cried after he hit him several times. He falls deeply in love with boyfriends and does not understand why things never work out, or why some people take "an attitude" toward him. Nor can he understand why some people victimize each other on the street, though he is together enough to avoid those who do (except for those he loves). He seems to feel deeply victimized by the world and, indeed, it sounds like he is on the receiving end of as much abuse as he dishes out. At times he nearly cries when relating his story, particularly in relation to boyfriends who have left him, but his emotions change quickly and flash by before any detailed self-exploration occurs.

Jeremy gets a little bit of money from his family, but he generally has little contact with them because they wish to (once again) place him in a psychiatric institution. He receives a monthly Supplemental Security Income (SSI) check for his disability, but the total amount only meets his basic expenses, so he works as a prostitute to pay for drugs and other incidentals. Given his age and appearance, he is less able to attract clients; however, he finds enough men who are willing to pay to survive financially, even with (or perhaps because of?) his erratic interpersonal mannerisms. He works most frequently in bars, but he sometimes works on the streets as well. Occasionally, he attempts to work in cruising zones that are not understood to be for prostitution, and expresses frustration at the "negative attitude" he receives when he asks people for money. Jeremy is not completely out of touch with reality–he is not subject to hallucinations and generally knows what is going on around him–but an empathic ability to understand what others might think or feel seems beyond him.

When I see Jeremy at a health clinic several months after our initial interview, he is accepting help from a conservative Christian group, and is accompanied by a woman in her early twenties. Several of his friends have expressed displeasure about his association with the group, but he appears more concerned with getting help, rather than discerning who provides it. He says that he has been off speed for three days and is still waiting to come down. He decided to quit because the paranoia was becoming too intense: He recalls standing on a street corner for a very long time, afraid to leave. I suggest he stay away from Polk Street if he wants to stay off drugs. He agrees: "There'd always be people trying to drag me back into it." Jeremy still jumps from topic to topic during our conversation, but he seems somewhat calmer and more coherent than before.

Kevin is a 16-year-old runaway who works on Polk Street in San Francisco. He left home at age 14 to escape the physical abuse of his father, and speaks with anger about the way social service agencies only allow him to stay for three days before reporting his whereabouts to his family. He knows exactly what he can get from each agency and what their rules are regarding parental notification–information that is shared amongst his peers on the street. He uses speed regularly, and his face is covered with sores resulting from compulsive, speed-induced sessions of picking at his skin. He used to be homeless; a situation that exposed him to theft and violence from other homeless youth. More generally, however, other youth acted as sources of friendship and information regarding where to sleep, where to get food, and other details pertinent to survival. One of the reasons Kevin chooses speed over other drugs (the selection of *some* drug seems predetermined) is because "We have all these great conversations about life and philosophy and stuff. When you're on heroin, all you do is sleep and wake up and then you need to get money. That's your whole life. I don't have to pay to sleep!" Like most other youth, Kevin tends to hang out with others who do the same drug, mostly due to the incompatible pace of life produced by the various substances.

At first, running away for brief periods and getting high on the street offered Kevin a sense of adventurous fun. Drawn further into street life, however, he turned to prostitution after he had left home for a longer period and became desperate for money. Kevin was deeply affected by his experience doing sex work: "I don't see how anyone with a brain can be bought and sold like a piece of meat and still think of themselves as a whole person," he offered. "It took me a long time to get over that, though I'm not through it yet. It will be there forever." While he used to be certain he was straight, Kevin is no longer so sure: "I didn't put myself in a crutch to maintain my sexuality as much as I would like.... Every time I saw some guy I felt like I was letting myself down, like I was telling myself I wasn't heterosexual any more...'cuz I started to like it sometimes."

Kevin now spends time hanging out with his friends, especially a 31-year-old named Paul who Kevin calls his sugar-daddy. "He helps me turn tricks," comments Kevin offhandedly. Though it was not entirely clear to me if Kevin and Paul have ever had sex, I find out later that Paul has a reputation for getting young kids like Kevin high and then having sex with them without a condom, despite the fact that he is HIV positive. Whatever the case, Kevin clearly likes Paul. "He is not a forceful person. He used to give me stuff all the time, almost like an infatuation I've had with girls before....I would miss hanging out with him if I ever left." Whatever adversity Kevin faces, however, he wants to make it clear that he is *not* the victim service agencies make him out to be. "I've lived my life out here, and I've lived a lot more than most people. I've had a lot of good times too."

Timothy is hard to hear over the blaring house music he has playing in his room. It's 2:00 a.m., and he is in a heavy sweat from working out and practicing martial arts. Timothy is living in the same tenement hotel as I am, but his room, unlike most of the others, is very clean and well-ordered. His bed is much nicer than the others too–it is clearly not from the hotel–and his stereo seems expensive and powerful. Knowing how paper-thin the walls are, I wonder how his neighbors can tolerate the noise, but no one seems to be coming by to complain.

When I tell Timothy about my project and ask if he might be interested in doing an interview sometime, he immediately informs me that he can't: "No way man. I'm planning to write a book about hustling my-self," he says, "so I don't want to give you all my secrets. I will tell you this, though. Psychologists don't know shit about hustling. They're reading about it in books. That's like trying to learn about swimming by reading." Having said that he won't disclose anything, Tim nevertheless proves quite talkative.[4] He tells me he is 20-years-old. He is from New York City, but left three years ago to flee probation. "You have to know how to work the police. Like if they stop me and say 'Where are you staying?' I tell them, 'At the Holiday Inn, motherfucker. D'ya want to see my key?' See, they aren't used to being talked back to, so that takes them off guard." I seriously doubt Timothy's version of events, but the whole point seems to be to appear tough and street-savvy. "See, that's a hustler," he continues, "a hustler works the street. There's a difference between hustlers and prostitutes. A hustler will, like, play a straight guy. It's like, some guy comes up and wants to do something, you have to be 'Oh, I don't know. I'm straight. I don't do that.' 'Well, how about for some extra money?' See, a hustler works the street. A prostitute will be on his belly getting fucked in all of three months, all strung out on crack." Tim-othy jumps around from topic to topic, but the common thread underly-ing each story seems to be self-promotion. "See this guy," he says, quickly flashing me a name in a computerized address book. "This guy is into some serious shit. Mafia stuff. I saw this guy in Chicago. Me and him are real tight. I could have someone killed if I needed to."

Timothy says he's been working the streets for "a long time" now. His current plan is to obtain a fake ID (cost: $300) and obtain a job at a local gay strip club in which the workers also regularly turn tricks. "I'm young, and I want to do all this before I get to be some old, crusty shit." Despite his forceful presentation of self, Timothy alludes to difficulties entailed by his choice of life: "It's great to ride fast, but still, when you crash you wish you were going 55."

Ernest, age 41, is one of the oldest street hustlers I have met. Ernest has been working the streets for years, and though it is clearly no longer his primary source of income, Ernest insists he can still obtain tricks. The point is clearly a source of pride for him, and it seems apparent that his identity as a street hustler is tied in with his sense of attractiveness and self-esteem. With his body looking somewhat ragged, both from a life on the street and regular speed use, I am unsure how much work he is actually able to obtain.

Not surprisingly, Ernest is a somewhat marginal figure within the network of street workers. Though he knows most of the people in the scene, it appears he never spends much time with them beyond passing conversations on the street. Ernest seems somewhat bitter about his iso-lation from the social scene, telling me flatly "You have to buy your friends out here, either with money or drugs. That's pretty much what people want." Ernest's one stable contact is his lover, a partner of sev-eral years with whom he lives in a nearby hotel. His lover is on disabil-ity, and the state pays Ernest a small sum to act as his caretaker. The amount is not enough to live on, so he supplements it by writing fraudu-lent checks. (I was never sure if these were stolen or forged.) He writes a check for an item of significant value, and then returns the item for cash before the store has an opportunity to find out that the check did not clear. Taking care of his lover and check fraud are Ernest's primary sources of income, but he remains committed to occasional prostitution, identifying himself more in relation to his work on the street than any-thing else.

Some of the above individuals fit into the three representational strat-egies identified by West and de Villiers (1993), while others do not. However, even individuals who more or less fit exhibit divergent traits which are not part of the standard narratives. Kevin exemplifies the im-age of the desperate runaway in many ways, yet his emphatic rejection of a victim identity poses a difficulty for service agency narratives, as does his insistence on the mutuality of the relationship with his sugar-daddy/ pimp. Stephen closely approximates the image of the gay-identified youth who has chosen prostitution as a means of establishing a gay community and gaining sexual experience with men; yet, the various difficulties he has encountered with clients (ranging from unrequited desires for a rela-tionship to confrontations over theft) are notably absent from most por-trayals of the gay prostitute. While Timothy presents himself in a manner congruent with the "dangerous delinquent," his open homosexuality would seem to give him a problematic relationship with the role of ag-gressive street tough. Seeing Timothy during one of his self-described "crashes" may render him a more vulnerable and less threatening figure.

If the three dominant narratives ignore certain elements of the lives of those who come close to fitting these categories, they render invisible those whose lives are less useful politically. Jeremy, for example, is not only older than most sex workers, but more unstable mentally. Through prostitution he finds a way to live outside of the psychiatric institutions his parents placed him in, as well as the means to participate in a life-style of casual sex and drug use which he considers enjoyable (though his opinion regarding this has shifted over time). Aaron enjoys the "slumming" aspect of his work on the street, and if the police were less of a factor, might do it more frequently. Meanwhile, Ernest's desire to embody the sexually desirable image of the "prostitute" extends beyond his social reach. While all three of these "outliers" share certain traits–they are all gay-identified and find in prostitution something of a life-style or an identity they enjoy–they also have important differences, both in the manner in which they fit into the larger milieu of street hus-tlers, and in terms of their experiences with clients.

While emphasizing the individuality of each sex worker can act as a necessary corrective to the somewhat homogenized portrayals created in the past, an unmitigated focus upon individual experience carries its own dangers. Liberal gestures toward the uniqueness of each person are inadequate if they fail to simultaneously identify structural characteris-tics within the larger social scene, problems and dynamics with which each individual must contend. Liberal notions of "uniqueness" also fail to identify patterns in the ways varying groups of individuals come to terms with these structures. In the following section, I examine three structural features of street life which are seldom discussed in the litera-ture on male prostitution. These issues are particularly important given their near invisibility within the hegemonic narrative of the "exploited teen." In some ways, what follows may seem to veer into a study of the social dynamics of male street life rather than a study of male street prostitution, but part of my point is precisely that the non-sexual aspects of male street prostitution have been ignored. In order to correct this im-balance, the literature on male prostitution must be augmented by the literature on male street life and vice versa.

SPACE AND THE MATERIAL UNDERPINNING OF STREET LIFE

Kevin needed to find a place to shoot up. He was just starting to come down from a prior hit of speed, and he wanted to find a place before he crashed. He hated shooting up outside because the cops could come by and then he'd be busted, so he walked a block off of Polk Street to a gas station that he knew of on Van Ness. If he could get in, he figured it would be a good place because the bathrooms had locks, and he could be alone. All he had to do was convince the attendant to let him in. That proved to be easy. Kevin looked pretty put-together, not homeless at all, and probably because of this, the man working at the gas station gave him the key even though he wasn't a customer.

Kevin was still fairly new to shooting up though, and the process took some time. He had been in there about three minutes when two other men came to use the bathroom. They waited for a while, but then began to grow impatient. Knocking at first, and then pounding on the door, the two became increasingly hostile in tone. "Hey! What are you doing in there? I really gotta piss!" Kevin, however, hadn't finished preparing the shot, and he wanted it fairly badly. Besides, he couldn't leave in the middle of everything, with all of his equipment in the open. The men outside grew increasingly impatient. "I think he's shooting up in there," said one of them. "Hey! Are you shooting up in there?" The two kept pounding on the door and proceeded to call over the attendant. "What you doing in there?" demanded the attendant. "You better get out now or I'm calling the cops!" Kevin finished up and started to put away his things. "All right man, I'm coming." The attendant kept banging loudly on the door. "I'm gonna call the cops right now!" Kevin managed to get all of his things together, stuffing everything into his knapsack, opening the door to three sets of hostile eyes. "Stupid punk," said one of the men. "Get the hell out of here," added the attendant. Kevin walked away without getting beaten up, and without police involvement, but he couldn't go back to that gas station, at least not when that same attendant was there.

For those living on the street without many resources, daily activity often revolves around attempting to find what is needed for survival: food, shelter, clothing, bathrooms, and, for many, drugs. The desperation of this search is reflected in the innovation individuals display in finding spaces to use and the rapidity with which such opportunities are seized upon. Many shelters and food banks, for example, find themselves having to police the activities which occur in their bathrooms lest someone begin engaging in a behavior whose illegality could threaten the agency. Similarly, public locales that have been abandoned by their owners have the potential to quickly be taken over and converted into unofficial "squats" for living in or regular "shooting galleries" where homeless drug users can inject. As homeless people do their best to creatively appropriate their physical environment, utilizing it to meet basic needs, they often find themselves in conflict with shop-owners, police, and other stewards of the local territory.

The conflict over bathrooms, as in Kevin's story, is an example. Bathrooms serve multiple purposes for many on the street, offering one of the few private spaces that homeless people are able to find. A bathroom can become a site not only for relieving oneself, but for cleaning up, turning tricks, sleeping, reorganizing one's possessions (especially hidden items such as cash, weapons, or narcotics), and injecting drugs. Conflict over these spaces is pervasive in areas where homeless people congregate. More than one of the restaurants and bars in the local area have installed buzzer systems which prevent all non-authorized access to their bathrooms, hoping, by such a measure, to take away any incentive homeless people might have to enter their premises. Most of the local merchants have opposed the installation of a public toilet in the area, arguing that the facilities will predominantly be used to shoot up and to turn tricks, and that it will draw still more homeless people to the area. As a result, many homeless people urinate in alleyways, and the sight of human feces on the street is fairly common.

In the course of his work with street hustlers, the director of the agency I worked for (Terry) found that sometimes the guys would use the agency bathroom in order to inject drugs. Terry told people the toilet was broken, and kept the door locked. Volunteers and board members were allowed to use the bathroom when no street workers were present, but they were advised not to speak of the subterfuge. Although Terry followed a policy of harm reduction, and was not ideologically opposed to the provision of spaces for "safer shooting," he was concerned that the illegal nature of the practice would threaten the agency. He also was concerned about the possibility of an overdose, a scenario which, though less likely with him present, could be used to shut down the program. Terry chose to lie about the status of the bathroom because the clients would beg and plead if they knew of its functionality, and would feel hurt if denied access. He made exceptions to the rule based on established trust with one or two individuals but, in general, he did not allow even non-drug using clients to use the bathroom. None of the volunteers, including myself, offered any criticism of Terry's policy; instead, we actively collaborated with the maneuver by not asking for the keys when clients were around.

The lack of basic amenities does not affect all male street workers equally. At the time of Kevin's difficulty at the gas station, he only prostituted sporadically, finding it too distasteful to engage in on a regular basis. Like many other runaway youth, Kevin confronted a seemingly endless series of desperate situations as he struggled to survive. However, while most of the young men who prostitute do so only when desperate (Hagan & McCarthy, 1998; West & de Villiers, 1993), Kevin's experience does not reflect the smaller number of individuals who work on a more full-time basis. Indeed, for this smaller group, sex work can provide a means through which they are able to support themselves in greater comfort than many of those around them. Timothy, for example, had never been homeless in his entire street career, at least according to his version of events. "This is the lowest I've been," he said during our discussion, gesturing to the unblemished hotel room surrounding him, "and this ain't so bad." For those who are able to prostitute successfully on a full-time basis, the work can provide a relatively stable source of income. Stephen's earnings from the massage parlor, which he pooled with his friends who worked on the streets, enabled him to live in a shared apartment. While the amount of money varied, and might seem low in relation to middle-class standards, it is a great deal more than is available through most other options on the street. Even by seeing only one to three clients a day, most sex workers are able to lead lives which are considerably easier than those who do not engage in prostitution. As an adolescent male street prostitute in Hagan and McCarthy's (1998) study explained:

> I'm a young urban professional . . . like I go out, I make some money . . . I mean I don't sit there and panhandle and get all of maybe twenty bucks a day. I get all of twenty bucks a half-hour . . . So, uhm, I'm a "yuppie" street person in a sense . . . I can afford to live, and they're literally surviving. We are all really just surviving, because none of us know how to live. All we know how to do is survive, except we [those of us in the sex trade] survive a bit easier. (ellipses in original; p. 89)

Like Timothy and Stephen, this youth's experience on the street is radically different from Kevin's early ordeals simply by virtue of his access to cash.

Furthermore, street youth who engage in prostitution sometimes obtain access to other resources which are unavailable to their non-prostitute peers. For example, they may receive invitations from older men–often known as "sugar-daddies"–who seek longer-term relationships (West & de Villiers, 1993). Many young men on the street actively desire such relationships as they offer substantial material benefits over street prostitution. As Weisberg (1985) comments, "It maximizes personal safety and financial security, and it lessens the psychological and physical demands of numerous anonymous sex partners" (p. 161). While some workers view such relationships as a threat to their independence, in general, having a sugar-daddy is seen as a prestigious accomplishment: "It is proof of one's lovability, approval, acceptance, desirability, and smart operating" (Caukins & Coombs, 1976 as cited in Weisberg, 1985, p. 161). Frequently, those with sugar-daddies will continue to supplement their income through ongoing street prostitution; however, some who form more stable relationships with their benefactors use the association as a means to leave street life altogether.

For a variety of reasons, not every individual on the streets has equal ability to engage in prostitution. As noted above, the majority of young men on the street, like Kevin, find the idea of having sex with another man personally degrading, resorting to it only during times of extreme need. Others who are more favorably inclined toward prostitution can face different types of barriers. Ernest's participation, for example, was limited by his age and relatively low "bodily capital,"[5] requiring him to rely primarily upon other activities in order to support himself. Similarly, Jeremy's age and mental difficulties restricted his access to clients. Like Ernest, Jeremy depended upon an outside source of income (his family and monthly disability check) to pay for basic necessities and used his prostitution earnings in order to purchase drugs and other incidentals.

There also are differences based on race and class-background which shape one's ability to prostitute, particularly for those who seek sugar-daddies (who are overwhelmingly white and middle-class themselves). One sugar-daddy I spoke with, while sitting in a café on Polk Street, pointed to a noticeably well-groomed young man with middle-class "Gap"-style clothing who was standing outside and appeared to be hustling. "That kid is new," he said. "He's been well-taken care of. He'll be picked up by someone real quick. He's cute, not like some of the other guys out here. . . . Most of the guys [who act as sugar-daddies] are looking for someone they can take care of, someone who can be their son." Another sugar-daddy I spoke with wanted to find "someone who won't bring too much drama into my life," and reported terminating relationships with youth who stole from him. Terry similarly noted that many of the older men "pick a kid up and take them home for as long as they can stand them," kicking out the youth when the "chaos factor" becomes too great. This preference for stability enables those youth who are most accustomed to middle-class ways of being, and whose habitus is least affected by street life and drugs, to find older men who will sponsor them, while leaving behind others who are more reliant upon the street.[6]

The conditions under which an individual engages in prostitution play a significant role in shaping his experience of sex work. While those who are relatively well-off are able to pick and choose their clientele, those who are materially desperate find themselves pressed to accept any opportunity which comes their way. Desperation exacerbates the risk these individuals feel they must take, making them significantly more likely to be arrested, to find themselves with a dangerous client, to accept extra cash for unsafe sex, or simply to have sex with someone they find exceptionally unappealing. The task of formulating these situational or "class" differences within street life has not been sufficiently explicated in prior work, which tends to treat "male street prostitutes" or "street youth" as somewhat homogeneous categories.[7]

STREET FAMILIES AND EMOTIONAL INSTRUMENTALITY

With few economic options available, male street-based sex workers are often pressed to scrutinize one another for their survival needs. Even those who are living like "street yuppies" need to obtain resources on a daily and sometimes immediate basis, leading many to adopt an instrumental approach toward other people which frequently sanctions taking advantage of others. The "hustler" prototypically embodies this relational orientation, seeking to "work the streets" by manipulating others and turning every possible situation to his benefit. Those who fail to operate this way run the risk of becoming victims, of becoming mere "prostitutes," as Timothy put it.

For those new to the street environment, the instrumentality of social life on the street can come as a shock. Unfamiliar with the rules of the street and unconnected with the street networks which offer protection, newcomers can become easy targets for muggers and con men (Bresnahan, 1995). "You can barely trust anyone out here," Kevin told me. "Most of the people on the street are just out for themselves. They'll stab you in the back. Ninety percent of them are like that. I found that out the hard way." (For similar comments, see Visano, 1987, pp. 140-141.) Older, more experienced sex workers sometimes view those who are entering the street scene for the first time as potential resources. Seeing their vulnerability, some hustlers offer assistance in orienting the newcomers to the scene. For experienced hustlers, these relationships provide access to a subordinate who can perform undesirable tasks: running errands, creating distractions while others shoplift, acting as lookouts, and carrying drugs or weapons (Visano, 1987). In referring to his own status as a "newcomer," Visano (1987) describes the power imbalances that operate within these exchanges:

> They expected immediate deference in exchange for cooperation. They would brook no challenge to their instructions. I was advised "to keep my mouth shut and just listen" even when they hurled insults at me. It was especially difficult listening to seasoned straight hustlers take great delight in elaborating sordid details about the violence they inflict on clients and various recalcitrant newcomers.

Their casual threats of violence reinforce subordination on the part of all outsiders. (p. 53)

Other hustlers approach newcomers with more kind-hearted intentions and approaches. As one experienced hustler remarked: "We is all in the same shit. You see yourself in these fish. They're scared....I'm human too. I'm tough too, but a pussy cat when I see a really young boy looking around. No place to go. They's just cruisin' for a bruisin" (Visano, 1987, pp. 135-136). Nevertheless, in almost all cases of tutelage, it is expected that the newcomer will form a relationship that materially benefits the more experienced partner, not only through the performance of subordinate tasks, but by paying a cut of his earnings as he learns how to prostitute (Hagan & McCarthy, 1998). These relationships are not entirely one-sided, however. Newcomers gain food and shelter during their critical orientation phase, and learn the skills necessary to become independent (Visano, 1987). After a few weeks of apprenticeship, newcomers typically seek to redefine their relationships and place themselves on equal footing with their teachers (Visano, 1987).

The early phases of a relationship can become a time of testing as one individual attempts to see if he can manipulate the other to his benefit. In my own work dispensing syringes, I was repeatedly asked by the young men who visited if I could give them additional syringes, despite the agency's policy that needles be traded on a one-for-one basis.[8] Terry likewise advised me not to dispense any cash as "It would change your relationship with the kids forever. You'd be just another resource and nothing else." Terry also warned me to be on guard against any attempt to obtain anything illicitly from either me or the agency. Although the majority of the young men did not attempt to steal, the possibility was sufficiently present as to necessitate increased policing on our part, as well as to produce a heightened guardedness between the sex workers themselves. (For similar comments, see McNamara, 1994.)

Within this context, the immediacy of the quest for resources gives those with better access increased social power (Visano, 1987). Ernest's comment that "You have to buy your friends out here, either with money or drugs" speaks to this situation. One of the other street-based workers, Michael (who, at 39, was one of the older hustlers) suggested an even more cynical reading: "You don't buy your friends out here, you rent them." The need to form instrumental relationships places together individuals who would not associate with one another but for material need. Kevin, for example, described one of the people he used to hang out with regularly, Tom, as "this dorky kid," adding that "he's a retard."

Nevertheless, Kevin spent a great deal of time with Tom because Tom still lived at home and used the street only as a short-term recreation activity (such youth are sometimes called "weekend warriors"–Sims, 1999). Kevin did not really like Tom, but he appreciated Tom's access to material items, including the fact that he possessed a car.

This process works in reverse as well, potentially leaving those without access to cash socially isolated. For example, Ernest noted that one of his friends had once received a full year's worth of disability checks which had been wrongly withheld. "He had a lot of friends for a while, but he spent that $7000 in one month. Those guys are gone now, and hardly any of them are going to pay him back." The social rationality of economically irrational behaviors–spending $7000 in one month, for example–was explicated by Whyte (1943) in his study of an Italian ghetto community. While a great deal of money, $7000 is not a sufficient amount to alter one's life circumstances; thus, it makes sense to obtain some social benefit from the money by spending it quickly on those with whom one wants to party. This also creates the conditions for reciprocal involvements when others come into cash, even if the majority do not entirely pay back whatever "loans" they may have received. In the case of Ernest's friend, however, the process may have backfired if those taking advantage of his bounty decided it was likely to be a one-time occurrence, and therefore failed to reciprocate.

For some, the tendency toward relational instrumentality disrupts all possibility for strong social ties. As one young man remarked: "I don't have friends. I have associates. People who I socialize with. You know, because there's people who say they want to be your friend and they turn around and stab you in the back" (Clatts, Hillman, Atillasoy, & Rees, 1999, p. 148). Among many adolescent prostitutes, the proclivity to view others primarily in terms of their immediate usefulness is mitigated by the formation of close-knit social networks. Hagan and McCarthy (1998) found that 54% of homeless youth form close social networks of several individuals which they refer to through familial terms (such as "brother"), and further suggest that many of the remaining youth form close networks which utilize a more general terminology of friendship. For such individuals, street families play an essential role in day-to-day survival on the street. As one homeless adolescent in Hagan and McCarthy's (1998) study described it:

> The way poverty on the street works, twenty bucks can go a long way. Like you can feed four people on twenty bucks, or you can feed one. It's just a kinda thing where you have to work together

and pool your resources. Like if I find a big bag of buns in the dumpster, it's better to distribute those and not just myself eat buns all week. Somebody else'll find tomatoes, and then we have tomato sandwiches. The food doesn't go bad, and you can just eat it really quick. (p. 162)

Beyond meeting material needs, street families serve important psychological functions, providing companionship and support. Stephen, for example, spoke of having "100% confidence" in his friends from the street, arguing that the intensity of street life brought them close together:

When you go through some of the things that we went through, it's like going through a war together or something. You start to feel intensely about everyone in the group. You'd just do anything for them . . . We would always be looking out for each other. Like if someone needed food or something, then we'd give it to him. Or one time I started getting too involved with drugs, and they were there for me. They confronted me, but not in a mean way, but in a way that felt good, that showed me that they cared about me.

According to Kruks (1991), director of youth services at a gay and lesbian service center in Los Angeles, "Many of these youths feel so bonded to their street family that they may have little desire to leave street life" (p. 517).

While some youth manage to establish reciprocal relations with each other, others find themselves in dependent relationships, particularly with sugar-daddies or, as noted above, with more experienced hustlers. Kevin complained about the first sugar-daddy he had, ultimately choosing the streets rather than live under the conditions that were gradually imposed:

When I first moved in with him, I didn't even realize it was for the sex. It's like, just suddenly someone is being nice to you, and you don't know why. But if you get something, you give something, I learned that for sure. So then it was OK, but like, he wanted me to stop hanging out on the street and go back to school and stuff, and I was like, "See ya later."

Yet, based upon my interviews with men who act as sugar-daddies, it seems that most relationships do not become all-encompassing. According to one middle-aged patron, one of the young men he sees shows up only about once every three or four weeks, relying upon him to provide a "landing pad" where he can recover whenever he bottoms out from extensive periods of drug use and whoring. Another patron, who himself lived in a tenement hotel, had relationships with a number of sex workers, typically seeing them briefly (a day or two at most) whenever they dropped by his room.

Kevin's involvement with his current sugar-daddy provides an exceptional case, in that Paul, the older man, was not Kevin's patron as much as his pimp, actively helping Kevin turn tricks and living off the proceeds. A second youth, a 17-year-old runaway named Nic, also reported that his 29-year-old lover, Ronald, helped him to work and shared the resulting money. These cases are notable in that the literature typically reports that pimping is not an activity which occurs with great frequency, or at all, among men (Allen, 1980; James, 1982; Weisberg, 1985; West & de Villiers, 1993). The dynamics involved in these two relationships, however, were quite different than what is described in the literature regarding men who pimp women. Both of these "pimps" (a term not utilized by the youths, nor, as far as I know, by the older men themselves) formed exclusive working relationships with the boys, and involved themselves closely in the work, helping Kevin and Nic find places to solicit and looking out for them with their clients. While Kevin described Paul both as his sugar-daddy and friend, Nic thought of Ronald as his lover. Furthermore, both Paul and Ronald were active participants in the social network of hustlers; indeed, Ronald turned tricks on his own. Both Paul and Ronald were older and more experienced than their younger partners. However, in some sense, both of the older men were peers to the boys, a situation unlike the fixed status arrangements which prototypically characterize pimp-prostitute relations between men and women. Nevertheless, Paul and Ronald did exercise some degree of control over the teens: Kevin looked to Paul for permission when I asked for an interview, and I only learned of Nic's relationship after a scene of domestic violence in which Ronald had hit Nic on the side of his head and left him bleeding. (Nic left the relationship as a result of this incident.)

The distinction between reciprocal and instrumental relations may not always be easily discernible, especially as the social fiction of reciprocity is often needed to maintain instrumentality. It is unlikely, for example, that the "dorky kid" tolerated by Kevin would have known of Kevin's genuine feelings toward him. Many hustlers similarly attempt to downplay the material basis of their interactions with clients in order not to insult them and to encourage repeat business. Older patrons may be described instrumentally as "sugar-daddies" or amatively as "lovers," but both terms may conceal mercenary impulses. Older patrons may act instrumentally toward hustlers as well, discarding one young man in favor of a newer, younger body (West & de Villiers, 1993), or forming a long-term relationship which enables the young man to come into a gay identity and obtain work off of the streets (Visano, 1987).

The discrepancy between street scenes which facilitate the formation of strongly-knit street families and others which foster a greater degree of instrumentality in social relations has a great deal to do with the level of desperation on the street. Within New York, for example, McNamara (1994) notes that those who are more desperate for money–particularly those who utilize crack regularly–are less able to form strong social bonds of reciprocal aid. While it was the older workers in my study who expressed the most cynicism regarding the possibilities for friendship on the streets–an opinion which, perhaps, related most to their marginality within the hustler networks–it seemed to me that their access to alternate sources of income allowed them to be less instrumentally focused than those who lived under conditions of near-constant desperation. It is notable, however, that even among street families that are more amatively based, the demands of the environment lead to the frequent dissolution of social ties (Hagan & McCarthy, 1998; Visano, 1987).

VIOLENCE AND THE SELF-MANAGEMENT OF IDENTITY

Given that male prostitutes tend to be young and have access to cash, it is not surprising that hustlers sometimes find themselves targeted by more physically dominating individuals who seek to take their earnings by force (Weisberg, 1985; West & de Villiers, 1993). Indeed, assaults against street-based sex workers are more common than assaults against other street youth, precisely because others recognize that prostitutes have access to cash (Hagan & McCarthy, 1998). The criminal status of prostitution makes it less possible for hustlers to rely upon the police, as does–when this is a relevant issue–their runaway status (Weisberg, 1985). Prostitutes also have to deal with potential violence from their clients, including the possibility of rape (West & de Villiers, 1993).

For those who are isolated on the streets, the fear of being assaulted results in considerable energy being expended to avoid vulnerable situations. Jeremy, for example, told me of how he had been accosted by four young men who demanded that he pay a "toll" each time he walked by. Jeremy addressed the situation by simply "laying low" and approaching the area only during the daytime, a solution he found much safer than risking a confrontation. Ernest dealt with danger by relying upon magical beliefs, once showing me the amulet he kept "for protection," a tactic which may or may not ward off would-be attackers, but does instill a degree of confidence in the situation.[9] Concern for one's safety can permeate a street worker's lived experience. As Ernest put it, "You have to watch your back out here. You never know who's going to be coming up on you. They watch you and watch you and wait until you're alone." Kevin also feared violence from others, telling me that he sometimes used speed as a way to stay awake, preferring not to make himself vulnerable by sleeping in the open at night, "so you're not just laying out there in your bag, waiting to get popped." In a study conducted by Clatts and associates (1999), a young man similarly reported that he would flee to the relative safety of prison rather than sleep on the streets: "Sometimes I would go and hop a [subway] and purposely get arrested, just so I can sit in jail and have a place to stay" (p. 144).

For youth within street cliques, the struggle to protect oneself becomes somewhat easier. Hagan and McCarthy (1998) note that concern regarding safety is the most frequently mentioned reason why street youth join families, easily outranking the desire to be socially connected to others or a desire to obtain food and other material goods. Given the concern members of street families have for safety, it is not surprising that individuals who are more vulnerable tend to join more readily than those who feel secure. Hagan and McCarthy (1998) report, for example, that female street youth are more likely to join street families than their male counterparts. Nevertheless, the longer a young male is without housing, the more likely he is to join a street family. Given that young men constitute between 63% and 80% of the population of street youths,[10] the overall number of adolescent males involved in street families exceeds the number of adolescent females.

One of the most important demands made in exchange for community participation is that members back each other up in a fight, essentially without hesitation and no matter the cause (McNamara, 1994). Without this arrangement, community members would rapidly lose their ability to protect themselves. In addition to offering protection, the group establishes other community norms. Many of these rules are the same as those that are generally abided by on the street: sharing any drugs or money one has, paying back loans, and not giving information to the police (Visano, 1987). Core members of the hustler community enforce, or attempt to enforce, occupational norms upon other workers who are new or less well integrated into the group. These rules militate against under-pricing; specify that a worker is not to approach a potential client when another hustler is already talking with him; and prevent workers from beating up "good clients" and thereby scaring them away (Allen, 1980; McNamara, 1994; West & de Villiers, 1993).[11]

The enforcement of community norms is not an automatic process, often being achieved through violence and threats of violence against those who transgress (see, for example, McNamara, 1994, p. 67). More than taking action as individuals, street-based sex workers will often attempt to mobilize others in order to render retaliatory punishment. The manner by which a sex worker will attempt to mobilize others has a great deal to do with the implicit power hierarchies within the group. The following vignette shows how these dynamics can implicate even the service agencies involved in the area.

Don started throwing punches in the dining area. The abruptness of the attack took Jeremy by surprise, even though he and Don had been getting into it verbally for about fifteen minutes. Don's pushy in-your-face attitude had angered Jeremy, the way it tended to aggravate everyone. Don was fine one-on-one, but he became aggressive when he couldn't be the center of attention. Still, people didn't usually attack one another in the middle of the agency–they need to be able to go back, for one thing. Don had a reputation for being "crazy" though, so perhaps he wasn't really thinking. Whatever the case, Don's sudden ferocity had Jeremy on the ground, and his wild swings were making sure he stayed down. Terry, who ran the hustler-focused service agency, was quick to intervene. Weighing twice as much as either of the fighting teens, Terry grabbed Don and pulled him back. The other three kids in the room moved in, physically separating the two. Don angrily struggled to free himself from Terry's grasp. "CALM DOWN, DON!" commanded Terry, but he lost his grip, and Don turned around and hit him. Don pulled the punch a little bit, uncertain at hitting this man who provided for him in so many ways, but the blow still landed with some force, squarely on the side of Terry's face.

A silence fell upon the room, just for a moment–clearly a line had been crossed. "Get out, Don!" commanded Terry. "I'm sorry, Terry," said Don. "Get out of here," Terry repeated. "Now!" Don took off, fast. Running down the stairs, he shouted back "Fuck you, Terry!" "We'll talk about this later!" offered Terry, but Don was already beyond his reach. Grabbing the door, Don slammed it shut as he left, shattering the glass, and breaking the lock. The sound echoed upstairs into the dining area. Terry looked down the stairs for a moment at the broken glass, somewhat stunned, and then turned around and headed back into the dining area. He encouraged the young men who had witnessed the altercation to leave Don alone, but also announced that Don was no longer welcome at the agency. "He's 86'd [i.e., kicked out]," he said simply, "at least for a while."

Don began to vent his rage by going on a mini-rampage through the neighborhood. The day after breaking the door, he saw Terry in a local cafe, went inside and started yelling obscenities before throwing hot coffee on Terry's shirt. Later he broke another window at a neighboring store, and was kicked out of at least one bar for causing problems. Terry decided to let the other street workers know who had broken the window, and about the coffee. They let Terry know they would give Don an "ear beating" and tell him to knock it off. Bringing group pressure to bear wasn't necessarily going to work, however, for the simple reason that it might not amount to much. "Don is no pushover. He knows a lot of people," said Michael, one of the older and more experienced hustlers. "Guys are a lot of talk. They say they'll beat someone up, but they won't do it." Michael thought about intervening with Don himself, but decided against doing anything. "He's probably too crazy to understand anyway. Even if you beat him up, it wouldn't do anything." Noting that Michael obviously feared Don's "street heat," I figured that Michael was finding a convenient rationalization to do nothing. However, I couldn't blame him either. I certainly had no desire to face Don, should he return.

Terry was in a bit of a jam. If he went to the police, he would lose the trust and respect of the guys on the street. The entire premise of Terry's work was that he was unlike the other service agencies–he would not police the guys or tell them to quit doing drugs or engaging in prostitution. If he called in the cops, he'd be seen as weak and as a traitor. He asked some of the guys to hang out in the office for a few days during dinner in case Don showed up. A few agreed, but with some grumbling. Privately, Michael told me that he didn't mind helping, "but I don't want to baby-sit."

Knowing that he could not get guys to watch his back indefinitely, Terry figured he had one trump card he could play. "If Don makes it impossible to work, I'll just shut down for a few days, and I'll let people know why." Without food or a place to get out of the rain, Terry figured that the guys would make it clear to Don that he had to back off. Thinking about the implications of this, I realized just how crucial Terry's agency was to the guys' survival. Yet without police protection, he was subject to the same logic of street violence as anyone else–a fact that tied Terry to the scene much more closely than most service agencies. The fact that so many people relied upon Terry gave him more power and leverage than most, but ultimately he had to make the same calculations of force as everyone else on the street.

In the above situation, Terry first attempted to utilize his prestige within the community in order to protect himself. When this appeared as though it might not work, he was forced to consider employing his own positional leverage–vis-à-vis a temporary interruption of services–in order to convince others to respond to his need.

In a separate instance, Ernest threatened to spread a false rumor that another street worker was a snitch in order to take revenge over some stolen drugs. Ernest felt confident in this plan, saying "That prick has screwed over so many people that the shit is bound to come back on him. All I have to do is set it in motion." In another example, a sugar-daddy I spoke with commented that when one of the guys stole something from him, he usually would be able to get it back by spreading word on the street as to what had happened. His social standing within the group as a "good client" was such that the workers were often willing to apply pressure to the person who had taken the object to return it. These interactions highlight the implicit hierarchies within the group, revealing ways in which one's high standing can offer a degree of protection from harm, while being held in comparatively low regard can make one vulnerable to false accusations.

Given that street-based sex workers are responding to a pervasive threat of violence both from casual onlookers and from within the community itself, it is not surprising that they put a great deal of energy into managing their reputation within the community. The need to maintain one's street reputation has been discussed extensively in the context of inner city life by Anderson (1999). He describes the techniques which an individual must enact in order to maintain his or her street reputation: "A person's public bearing must send the unmistakable, if sometimes subtle, message that one is capable of violence, and possibly mayhem, when the situation requires it, that one can take care of oneself" (p. 72). These patterns were clearly demonstrated within my fieldwork. Not only did the question of Don's alleged "craziness" arise in the encounter with Terry, but others worked to create the appearance of an intimidating presence. Beyond telling me about his mafia contacts, Timothy, for example, told me that he had sparred with martial arts film star Steven Seagal, and showed me a rather nasty looking throwing knife. Threatening activities have an occupational benefit as being perceived as having the *potential* for violence encourages clients to pay (Visano, 1987). Fostering an image of potential violence also helps in attracting those clients who seek dangerous-looking "real men" (Kaye, 2003).[12]

The need to create a powerful representation of self extends to the discussions that workers have with each other and the way in which they discuss life on the street. Street hustlers often portray their lives on the street as being full of adventure, excitement, and fast action (Visano, 1987). Street life is depicted within these narratives as a place for "survivors" where individuals live by their wits and enjoy their freedom, particularly their independence from parental and school authorities (Visano, 1987). Hustlers' accounts do not necessarily ignore or underplay the difficult aspects of street life, but rather glorify the difficulties involved as foils against which they can prove themselves. One street-based sex worker, for example, argues that:

> [E]ven when I froze my ass, it was fun. It's a high out here. I guess I'm like a fucking rebel. Christ, the more I last out here, the tougher I feel. That's pretty neat. All the action. (Visano, 1987, p. 115)

Even tales of childhood abuse become grist for the creation of an aggressive identity. Visano (1987) noted a tendency for hustlers to speak with him at great lengths about their abusive pasts, and queried a worker about it:

> What else have they got? They were hurt bad. Now they're smart. What it says is, "Listen Jack, I didn't take this from my old lady, so I ain't going to take it from anybody else." It makes them feel tougher. That's why. It gets them ready for anything. They'll dish it out to their tricks, even to other kids. Don't think they just talk about it to you, no way. They rap about it to their buddies, all the time. (p. 109)[13]

Notably absent from these stories are instances of being humiliated, or of being forced to do something in order to survive which makes them appear weak and vulnerable. Narratives which expose an individual as anything other than in control must, in fact, be countered at once. For example, after one adolescent sex worker teased another about seeing him sift through the garbage, the second youth very loudly proclaimed "I was *not* digging through the garbage!" This need to conceal vulnerability and maintain the appearance of power can affect one's daily strategies for survival. Another adolescent hustler told me that he refused to go to the shelter because, he emphatically said, "I am *not* homeless." Similarly, one of the sex workers in McNamara's (1994) study refused to complete his community service for a prostitution charge because he did not wish to be seen cleaning the subways, a tactic which, while preserving his status, placed him at greater risk for future imprisonment. These decisions follow a similar logic that Bourgois (1996) noted in his observations of young men who eschew the legitimate labor market in favor of dealing crack, a job which at least affords them a degree of "respect" in relation to their peers.

Also absent from the street hustlers' boastful narratives are accounts of the wide variety of innovative tactics they employ to defuse or otherwise circumvent conflict. The most obvious is the attempt to avoid others who might be dangerous, as Jeremy did when threatened by the group who demanded a "toll." Others who are unable to avoid threatening people might attempt placating strategies. For example, I witnessed one youth make a direct appeal to another (much more menacing) hustler with whom he had a conflict: "I know we don't always get along, but I want you to know that I still pray for you." Whether self-interested or not, this comment served to allay the tension which had been rising between the two. When measures such as these are unworkable, some take the option of moving to another city. Many street kids, in fact, move along a circuit from city to city, staying in one area until either they become bored or "the heat," whether from police or from others in the scene, is too great. Still others decide that the violence on the street is too prevalent, and leave altogether. Jeremy, for example, decided to quit working when his fear of others–prompted by his run-ins with a neighborhood gang and heightened by excessive speed use–mushroomed into a debilitating paranoia. Even the effort to appear intimidating and ready for violence–a tactic employed by the more powerful to ward off conflict–can be seen in this light as a paradoxical maneuver. While the approach involves the suppression of any public display of vulnerability, it exists as a tactic only in relation to an implicit recognition of possible victimization.

CONCLUSIONS

A number of insights arise from the above observations. Perhaps, most importantly, this work underscores the importance of poverty in shaping the social lives of most street-based male prostitutes, including their need to prostitute and their ability to negotiate the terms of paid sex. Although considerable diversity exists within the population, most of the participants become involved in this work because of basic economic needs. (Social factors such as a given individual's desire for gay sex or community also shape the choice of prostitution over other options.) While this observation regarding economic necessity is unsurprising, the way the exigencies of poverty both heighten the importance of peer relations and shape the contours of these relations is less discussed. This study also suggests that some older men are able to participate in limited ways within the social networks of street youth as "sugar-daddies," and that these men constitute an important (if problematic) locus of resources for some young men.

Another issue highlighted by this study involves the manner in which class and class-like elements shape the lives of street youth. Class privilege extends from one's ability to take advantage of youth services to one's ability to form successful relationships with sugar-daddies, and potentially shapes one's ability to meet casual clients as well. The ability to present a "tough" and aggressive image of self is a crucial survival skill that is class-inflected. Middle-class norms of masculinity do not generally favor demeanors which are mild; thus, the need to deploy threats and violence can work against one's ability to receive aid from social service agencies and sugar-daddies. As Bourgois (1996) documents in relation to street-level drug dealers, this process can mitigate one's ability to leave the street scene. Generally, class is a primary factor in shaping the social responses that male street prostitution receives from the state and other mainstream institutions, determining the broad outlines of policy response from the general society.

A third critical area of inquiry concerns the role of social service institutions within street life. While some research has been conducted regarding the role of welfare within recipients' lives (e.g., Edin & Lein, 1997), very little has been written about the experiences of street youth with the agencies that serve them (though see Bresnahan, 1995; Hecht, 1998; Snell, 1995). Among the youth I witnessed, it was clear that service agencies constituted a much needed, yet frustrating, source of resources. Like Kevin, many of the young men expressed anger at the way agencies refused to offer extensive services without controlling intimate aspects of their lives (fostering familial unification, demanding an end to drug use or sex work, rigidly enforced curfews, etc.). It also was clear that taking advantage of services through any necessary means–including the creation of sympathetic "victim" selves–constituted another important strategy for daily survival.

This final comment calls attention to the context in which representations of male street prostitution are made. With notable exceptions, the academic study of prostitution has focused narrowly upon sex, as if once individuals transgress the sexual norm, the only matter of any importance is the origin, significance, and (sexual) consequences of that transgression. Representations by social service agencies often extend this by focusing exclusively upon the sexual degradation of "innocent youth," thus rendering certain populations invisible, downplaying questions of prostitute agency, and ironically reinforcing their sexualization. Both academic and social service approaches tend to marginalize questions pertaining to daily life on the street, particularly the ways in which prostitute identity and the activities of prostitution intersect with other elements of street life. Meanwhile, traditional analyses of "street life" *per se* ignore figures such as the male prostitute as he fails to epitomize the macho image of the street tough. Beyond asking how male prostitutes do (and do not) differ from other men on the street, these difficulties point toward the need to devote greater attention to the gendered ideologies which inform ethnographic representation. If the politics of representation have left us with two problematic figures–the (feminized) victim runaway and the (hyper-masculinized) street thug–it seems necessary to do more than simply mix these literatures into a socially incomprehensible image of the "sexually victimized street tough." A more nuanced examination should detail previously unexamined issues, such as the way street youth sometimes present an image of powerlessness in order to exert power vis-à-vis the social service agencies, while creating an image of toughness to partially address their vulnerabilities on the street. Such an approach begins to create images which document suffering without equating it with absolute powerlessness, and which examine male street youth's propensity toward violence and "toughness" without ignoring sites of dependency and "weakness."

NOTES

1. This essay represents a revision of a chapter from my MA thesis in Anthropology at San Francisco State University (SFSU), "Boy prostitutes and street hustlers: Depicting male street prostitution" (2001). At SFSU, I thank Jim Quesada for acting as primary supervisor on what proved to be a very difficult project, and Gil Herdt for offering numerous helpful suggestions regarding my research. I also thank Niels Teunis, Steve Gabow, Peter Biella, John De Cecco, and Philippe Bourgois for their advice and assistance on this project, as well as two anonymous reviewers at the *Journal of Homosexuality* who each offered very useful suggestions. Within "the field" (a.k.a. "the real world"), I would like to thank the people who allowed me to interview and shadow them, and especially P and T, who adopted me into their lives. Special thanks also to "Terry," who gave greatly of himself and put up with many more questions from me than I ever would want to answer myself. I also thank Laurie Schaffner, Alison Luterman, Sealing Cheng, and Clare Corcoran, friends who each offered their unique

70   *MALE SEX WORK: A BUSINESS DOING PLEASURE*

insights and personal encouragement along the way. Most of all, I thank my partner, Elizabeth Bernstein, for her deeply sage advice, both emotional and intellectual; I simply could not have completed this project without her ongoing support.

2. Bourgois (1996) partially escapes this trend by discussing barrio men's experiences of subordination within the legitimate labor market, but even these are treated as paradigmatic instances in which barrio men hold to street definitions of masculine "respect" over and against the possibility of participating in the service economy. The macho identity of the primary subjects is thus reaffirmed, while the compromised identities of men who choose to engage in the gendered performances associated with service work are not carefully explored.

3. All names are pseudonyms.

4. To be clear, I obtained consent to utilize this material on a second occasion when Timothy did not seem high.

5. I derive the phrase "bodily capital" from Loic Wacquant (1995, 2003), who argues that individuals without access to symbolic capital (such as education) instead invest their energies toward the development of their body's potentialities. While Wacquant developed his analysis in relation to boxers, here I use the term to mark the way in which one's perceived attractiveness provides one with greater or lesser saleability in the sexual market. (Wacquant [2003] briefly notes this sense of the term as well.)

6. Ironically, service agencies and sugar-daddies often compete for the same youth, leaving others behind.

7. In relation to street youth, some exceptions to this general trend can be found in Kipke, Montgomery, Simon, and Iverson (1997), Raymond, Stall, and Kennedy (1999), and Sims (1999). See also Glauser (1997) for an excellent example related to street youth in the Third World. Passaro (1996) begins such an analysis in relation to gender differences among adult homeless individuals.

8. This policy was based on the precarious legalities of the needle exchange program. While technically illegal, police have indicated a willingness to tolerate these operations only if they do not "facilitate" drug abuse by introducing more needles onto the streets. Those seeking more needles, meanwhile, may have wanted them for themselves, or they may have sought extras in order to sell. At the time of my research, 1needles had a street value of $5 each.

9. Ernest hoped his amulet would help ward off police as well as attackers.

10. Janus, McCormick, Burgess, and Hartman (1987 as cited in Hagan & McCarthy, 1998) found that 63% of street youth in Toronto were male; Raymond et al. (1999) found a higher figure of 76% in San Francisco, and Clatts et al. (1999) report an even higher figure of 80% for New York City. These statistics reflect the different uses of space in which male and female runaways engage. While females and males are equally likely to have experience with running away from home, females are more likely to use shelters than males (Research Triangle Institute, 1994). For an analysis of a similar phenomenon among adults who are homeless see Passaro (1996).

11. While male street workers (particularly those with dependencies on drugs which require larger amounts of cash) occasionally threaten and steal from their clients (McNamara, 1994), there is a general recognition that this is bad for business. Therefore, only those clients who refuse to pay are typically subject to violence at the hands of sex workers (see McNamara, 1994; Visano, 1987; West & de Villiers, 1993).

12. I thank an anonymous reviewer for reminding me of this point.

13. In other contexts, stories of abuse are sometimes deployed to different effect, as when street youth utilize them as a means of making themselves appear more deserving to social service agencies (Snell, 1995; Visano, 1987). In either instance, the stories themselves might (or might not) be factual, yet the meaning given to the events is altered in such a way as to create a different identity for the narrator as street tough or victim.

REFERENCES

Allen, D. (1980). Young male prostitutes: A psychosocial study. *Archives of Sexual Behavior, 9*, 399-426.

Allman, D. (1999). *M is for Mutual, A is for Acts: Male sex work and AIDS in Canada.* Ottawa, ON: Canadian Public Health Association/Health Canada.

Anderson, E. (1990). *StreetWise: Race, class, and change in an urban community.* Chicago, IL: University of Chicago Press.

Anderson, E. (1999). *Code of the street: Decency, violence, and the moral life of the inner city.* New York, NY: W. W. Norton & Co.

Bourgois, P. (1996). *In search of respect: Selling crack in El Barrio.* Cambridge, MA: Cambridge University Press.

Bresnahan, M. (1995). Taking it to the streets: Outreach to youth in Times Square. In R. McNamara (Ed.), *Sex, scams, and street life: The sociology of New York City's Times Square* (pp. 107-116). Westport, CT: Praeger Publishers.

Brock, D. (1998). *Making work, making trouble: Prostitution as a social problem.* Toronto, ON: University of Toronto Press.

Clatts, M., Hillman, D., Atillasoy, A., & Rees, D. W. (1999). Lives in the balance: A profile of homeless youth in New York City. In J. Blustein, C. Levine, & N. Dubler (Eds.), *The adolescent alone: Decision making in health care in the United States* (pp. 139-159). Cambridge, UK: Cambridge University Press.

Edin, K., & Lein, L. (1997). *Making ends meet: How single mothers survive welfare and low-wage work.* New York, NY: Russell Sage Foundation.

Flax, J. (1995). *Disputed subjects: Essays on psychoanalysis, politics and philosophy.* New York, NY: Routledge.

Glauser, B. (1997). Street children: Deconstructing a construct. In A. James & A. Prout (Eds.), *Constructing and reconstructing childhood: Contemporary issues in the sociological study of childhood* (pp. 145-164). New York, NY: Taylor and Francis.

Hagan, J., & McCarthy, B. (1998). *Mean streets: Youth, crime and homelessness.* Cambridge, UK: Cambridge University Press.

Hecht, T. (1998). *At home in the street: Street children of Northeast Brazil.* Cambridge, UK: Cambridge University Press.

James, J. (1982). *Entrance into juvenile male prostitution.* Washington DC: National Institute of Mental Health.

Jankowski, M. S. (1991). *Islands in the street: Gangs and American urban society.* Berkeley, CA: University of California Press.

Kaye, K. (2001). *Boy prostitutes and street hustlers: Depicting male street prostitution.* Unpublished Master's thesis, San Francisco State University, San Francisco, California [listed under Kerwin Brook].

Kaye, K. (2003). Male prostitution in the Twentieth Century: Pseudo-homosexuals, hoodlum homosexuals, and exploited teens. *Journal of Homosexuality, 46*(1/2), 1-77.

Kincaid, J. (1998). *Erotic innocence: The culture of child molesting.* Durham, NC: Duke University Press.

Kipke, M., Montgomery, S., Simon, R., & Iverson, E. (1997). Substance abuse disorders among runaway and homeless youth. *Substance Use and Misuse, 32*, 965-982.

Kruks, G. (1991). Gay and lesbian homeless/street youth: Special issues and concerns. *Journal of Adolescent Health, 12*, 515-518.

Leigh, C. (1994). Prostitution in the United States: The statistics. *Gauntlet: Exploring the Limits of Free Expression, 1,* 17-19.

Males, M. (1996). *Scapegoat generation: America's war on adolescents.* Monroe, ME: Common Courage Press.

Males, M. (1999). *Framing youth: 10 myths about the next generation.* Monroe, ME: Common Courage Press.

McGeady, M. R. (1994). *"Am I going to Heaven?" Letters from the streets.* New York, NY: Covenant House.

McGeady, M. R. (1996). *Are you there, God?* New York, NY: Covenant House.

McNamara, R. (1994). *The Times Square hustler: Male prostitution in New York City.* Westwood, CT: Praeger.

Passaro, J. (1996). *The unequal homeless: Men on the streets, women in their place.* New York, NY: Routledge.

Raymond, H., Stall, R., & Kennedy, M. (1999). *Tribes in the urban streets: Tribal affiliations among street youth and high risk behaviors for HIV transmission.* Paper written for UCSF Center for AIDS Prevention and Larkin Street Youth Center.

Reiss, A., Jr. (1987 [1961]). The social integration of queers and peers. In E. Rubington & M. Weinberg (Eds.), *Deviance: The Interactionist perspective* (pp. 352-360). New York, NY: Macmillan.

Research Triangle Institute. (1994). *Youth with runaway, throwaway, and homeless experiences: Prevalence, drug use, and other at-risk behaviors.* Washington, DC: U.S. Department of Health and Human Services, Administration on Children, Youth and Families (ACYF), Family and Youth Services Bureau (FYSB).

Ritter, B. (1988). *Sometimes God has a kid's face.* New York, NY: Covenant House.

Sims, C. R. (1999). *When the streets are home: The Ministry of Presence within the theological constructs of personalism and harm reduction.* Unpublished Master's thesis, Eden Theological Seminary, St. Louise, Missouri.

Snell, C. (1995). *Young men in the street: Help-seeking behavior of young male prostitutes.* Westport, CT: Praeger.

Venkatesh, S. (2000). *American project: The rise and fall of a modern ghetto.* Cambridge, MA: Harvard University Press.

Visano, L. (1987). *This idle trade.* Concord, ON: VitaSana Books.

Wacquant, L. (1995). Pugs at work: Bodily capital and bodily labour among professional boxers. *Body and Society, 1,* 65-95.

Wacquant, L. (2003). *Body and soul: Notes of an apprentice boxer.* New York, NY: Oxford University Press.

Weisberg, D. K. (1985). *Children of the night: Adolescent prostitution in America.* Lexington, MA: Lexington Books.

West, D. J., & de Villiers, B. (1993). *Male prostitution.* Binghamton, NY: Haworth Press.

Whyte, W. F. (1943). *Street corner society.* Chicago, IL: University of Chicago Press.

Williams, T. (1992). *Crackhouse: Notes from the end of the line.* New York, NY: Penguin Press.

doi:10.1300/J082v53n01_03

Exploring the Interpersonal Relationships in Street-Based Male Sex Work: Results from an Australian Qualitative Study

David Leary, MCouns, PhD (candidate)
Victor Minichiello, PhD

University of New England

SUMMARY. While the literature on male sex work has increased significantly over the past decade, few studies examine the influence of relational dynamics in the lives of those engaged in male sex work. This qualitative study, conducted with a sample of male street sex workers in Sydney, Australia, explores how relationships color their involvement with sex work. The findings reveal the complexity of their relationships and how their interactions with others shape their engagement in sex work. The data also offer insight into how exit pathways are influenced by money and relationships that occur within this particular male sex work

David Leary is completing his PhD in the School of Health at the University of New England in Armidale, Australia. He is Director and Senior Counselor of the *Come In* Youth Resource Centre, a counseling service operating in the inner city of Sydney, Australia. His research and professional interests are focused on marginalized adolescents and young adults, psychosocial development and resilience.

Victor Minichiello, PhD, is Professor of Health in the School of Health and Dean of the Faculty of Education, Health and Professional Studies at the University of New England in Armidale, Australia. His research interests include sexual health, sexuality across the life span, public health and health promotion. Correspondence may be addressed to Dr. Vincent Minichiello, School of Health, University of New England, Armidale, New South Wales, 2351, Australia.

[Haworth co-indexing entry note]: "Exploring the Interpersonal Relationships in Street-Based Male Sex Work: Results from an Australian Qualitative Study." Leary, David and Victor Minichiello. Co-published simultaneously in *Journal of Homosexuality* (The Haworth Press, Inc.) Vol. 53, No. 1/2, 2007, pp. 75-110; and: *Male Sex Work: A Business Doing Pleasure* (ed: Todd G. Morrison and Bruce W. Whitehead) The Haworth Press, Inc., 2007, pp. 75-110. Single or multiple copies of this article are available for a fee from The Haworth Document Delivery Service [1-800-HAWORTH, 9:00 a.m. - 5:00 p.m. (EST). E-mail address: docdelivery@haworthpress.com].

Available online at http://jh.haworthpress.com
© 2007 by The Haworth Press, Inc. All rights reserved.
doi:10.1300/J082v53n01_04

setting. Implications for health policy and intervention are considered.
doi:10.1300/J082v53n01_04 *[Article copies available for a fee from The Haworth
Document Delivery Service: 1-800-HAWORTH. E-mail address: <docdelivery@
haworthpress.com> Website: <http://www.HaworthPress.com> © 2007 by The
Haworth Press, Inc. All rights reserved.]*

KEYWORDS. Male sex work, street sex culture, relationships, adolescents, prostitution

INTRODUCTION

For decades, while researchers and health practitioners began a limited focus on males involved in sex work (MSW), the popular press appeared silent (Staller, 2003). While girls were readily connected with prostitution, boys were always adventurers, and although the discourse in the print media during the 1960s and 1970s eventually turned to the theme of young males 'running away from home,' it was rarely linked to male prostitution (Fritz & Altheide, 1987). The scientific discourse on male prostitution, however, is more complex.

Past literature has considered MSW from an historical perspective (Kaye, 2003; Scott, 2003) and examined the stratification of sex workers (Caukins & Coombs, 1976; Coleman, 1989; Luckenbill, 1986; Parsons, Bimbi, & Halkitis, 2001). Various other research perspectives have been explored. These include male prostitution as an issue of identity (Boyer, 1989; Earls & David, 1989); a sociological phenomenon concerning issues of control (Gaffney & Beverley, 2001); psychopathology (Simon, Morse, Osofsky, Balson, & Gaumer, 1992); a form of deviant behavior (Luckenbill, 1984, 1986); one sequelae of an abusive childhood (Holmes & Slap, 1998); coexistent with other negative life experiences (Ratner et al., 2003); a consequence of negative events such as poverty or homelessness (Pedersen & Hegna, 2003; Zigman, 1999); a commercial encounter (Minichiello et al., 2000); a significant public health and regulation issue (Simon, Morse, Osofsky, & Balson, 1994; Sullivan, 1996); and a matter for social welfare policy and social services intervention (Cusick, 2002; Shaw & Butler, 1998).

Historically, prostitution has been associated with negative experiences (Lascaratos & Poulakou-Rebelakou, 2000) with the research around MSW dominated by an early skew towards delinquency and a later orientation towards health education in regard to HIV. While some are critical of what is perceived as an "obsession with the dark side" of adolescent experience (Ayman-Nolley & Taira, 2000, p. 42), referring to negative research representations as "moralistic and patronising" (Davies & Feldman, 1997, p. 30), it is clear that one of the dominant motifs in the research literature on young people involved in prostitution is the experience of sexual abuse (Holmes & Slap, 1998; Janus, Burgess, & McCormack, 1987; Nadon, Koverola, & Schludermann, 1998; Shaw & Butler, 1998; Zierler et al., 1991).

Coleman (1989) and others (Cusick, 2002; Luckenbill, 1985) focus on a range of psychosocial and situational variables–such as rejection by family, poverty, substance abuse, and sexual abuse–that lead to involvement in prostitution (Cates & Markley, 1992). Coleman (1989) explores a theoretical model that details a causal nexus between predisposing factors, situational factors, and eventual involvement in prostitution. From this psychological perspective, prostitution is said to be a consequence of "early disruption of psychosexual and psychosocial development" (p. 140), where "boys who have been abused as children and who are exposed to situational variables that make male prostitution activity a logical survival mechanism are individuals at high risk for developing self-destructive prostitution activities" (p. 147). Other researchers pursue a similar line of inquiry focusing on the individual psychopathology experienced by the persons involved in sex work (Coombs, 1974; El-Bassel et al., 2000; Simon et al., 1992). This more psychological examination is common in the early literature but less so in the last decade (Vanwesenbeeck, 2001) except for the area of adolescence and resilience (Kaplan, 1999; Rutter, 1985, 1987, 1993).

Although a causal connection between familial abuse, running away from home, and involvement in sex work tends to be assumed (Widom & Ames, 1994), the research evidence for such a link (i.e., abuse→ running→ prostitution) is inconsistent (Brannigan & Van Brunschot, 1997). The only reliable part of the "hypothesized relationship" is that abuse leads to running (Widom & Ames, 1994, p. 312; Widom & Kuhns, 1996). Other researchers assert that abuse causes running, which leads to immersion within a geographical and social environment where involvement in prostitution is more likely to occur (McCarthy & Hagan, 1992; Nadon et al., 1998; Rotheram-Borus et al., 1992a; Schaffer & DeBlassie, 1984).

Recent literature is dominated by a more sociological analysis emphasizing the significance of adverse situational conditions (rather than personal background factors) in the development of delinquent behavior, including prostitution (McCarthy & Hagan, 1992). However, studies still emphasize the coexistence of prostitution and a number of negative life experiences. These include homelessness and running behavior (Belza et al., 2001; Rotheram-Borus et al., 1992a); disconnectedness from family and peers (Mallett, Rosenthal, Myers, Milburn, & Rotheram-Borus, 2004); and negative economic factors such as poverty (Boles & Elifson, 1994; DeMatteo et al., 1999; Minichiello et al., 2001; Rotheram-Borus et al., 1992b; Tyler, Whitbeck, Hoyt, & Yoder, 2000).

From the early 1990s, the tenor of research changed significantly in response to the AIDS crisis. The concentration on negative psychosocial factors took on a pragmatic rather than historical perspective (de Graaf, Vanwesenbeeck, van Zessen, Straver, & Visser, 1994) with an attempt at understanding the behavior of those engaged in MSW (Parsons et al., 2001). Rather than pathologizing the past experience of the person engaged in MSW, the emphasis shifted to questions of how best to engage, inform, monitor and retain health in the face of HIV and AIDS (Rosario, Meyer-Bahlburg, Hunter, Gwadz, 1999; Rotheram-Borus et al., 1992b). While the theme of prostitution still appears in research literature on young people (Solorio, Swendeman, & Rotheram-Borus, 2003), health is the focal point, as the palpable concern is that those engaged in prostitution are at risk for contracting HIV (Boles & Elifson, 1994; Knowles, 1998; McCamish, Storer, & Carl, 2000; Minichiello et al., 2000).

Involvement with sex work is fundamentally about involvement with people, and such involvement entails relational dynamics that can be difficult for the researcher to fathom or even to define. These relationships are mercurial; a series of events and happenings that lead inevitably to different understandings of the relational dynamics involved. This article focuses on research data that provide some indication of what individuals engaged in street-based male sex work (SMSW) think about the various relationships within their lives: prior to involvement in SMSW; as they entered the SMSW environment; during their initial and ongoing experiences; and as they leave or remain engaged in SMSW.

METHOD

The main gathering point for SMSW in Sydney is known as *The Wall*, a 200 meter strip of Darlinghurst Road in an inner suburb of Sydney, bounded by a technical college, a court house, a Catholic church, a hospice, and a park. A total of 44 young males were approached for inclusion in this study, with 27 being interviewed. Three of the participants were interviewed twice. The researchers used an unstructured interview process beginning each interview with the same non-directive question regarding when the person came to the inner city of Sydney (where SMSW occurs) and their reasons for doing so. A recursive style of questioning was maintained throughout all interviews in order to maximize participants' narrative control. Questions picked up on key words, phrases, and themes that were mentioned in earlier responses. Topics that were discussed included relationships with family, peers and significant others; life events defined as positive and negative; adversity and survival; education, work and leisure; health and general wellbeing; and aspirations, emotions and intimacy.

The average age of the participants was 23 at the time of interview with the youngest being 17 years of age. The study used a combination of opportunistic, snowball and theoretical sampling (Alvesson & Sköldberg, 2000; Minichiello, Aroni, Timewell, & Alexander, 1995; Strauss & Corbin, 1998).[1] The participants were interviewed at a time and place of their convenience. Twenty-five of the participants had experienced homelessness from an early age and fourteen had experienced juvenile or adult incarceration. Twenty-two had not completed high school with seven not completing their second year of secondary schooling. Two had completed university degrees and two others had begun to attend but withdrew from university. Twenty-four of the participants had engaged in substance use. Five of the participants advised the primary author that they are HIV positive.

Participant quotes are included *verbatim*: No stylistic or grammatical editing has occurred. Participant quotes are given using an alias in order to maintain anonymity, and identifying features have been removed. Correct age at time of interview is provided with the participant's alias just prior to their first quote. The participant's alias is provided at the end of each quote along with a numeric or alphanumeric reference mark specifying the interview number followed by a forward slash and the paragraph numbers provided by QSR NVivo (Richards, 2002). The use of "a" or "b" before the paragraph number identifies whether it is the first (a) or second (b) interview.

The current study uses a qualitative research methodology employing grounded theory (Charmaz, 1995; Minichiello et al., 1995; Strauss & Corbin, 1998). A thematic analysis was carried out on the interview transcripts. Major emergent themes were explored for categories, subcategories, and the interrelationships between emergent themes, with the emphasis being on gaining a descriptive and in-depth analysis and understanding of the phenomenon of SMSW.

PRECURSOR RELATIONSHIPS AND SMSW

Relational experiences are critical in life generally. They inform and influence the directions we take. While the main thrust of this article is an examination of relational experiences within the context of SMSW, it is important to explore relational experiences occurring prior to entry into sex work. Brian (20) began leaving home at 15 years of age:

> I suppose it was, problems with myself. I was having a lot of communication breakdown, problems with my father 'cause he's deaf, well he's partially deaf and he's getting deafer.
>
> DL: Is that the main reason?
>
> I was one of the, what's the word for it, the rejects at school, so to say as well. (Brian, 12a/46-51)

A critical factor for Brian is that there appear to be multiple disconnections. As a result of his growing separation from key people and places, he began, at 15, to drift from the outer Sydney suburbs towards the inner city and to examine his growing sense of difference:

> I went to some movie festival at Bondi Beach that had a whole heap of Australian movies. They were actually pretty good if I remember correctly. And, um, I met this girl and a lot of her, she went, she grew up in Double Bay and a lot of her friends used to hang around here ... I suppose I just started hanging around with her friends, started hanging around this area, 'cause ... I was still kind of in between being at home and yeah, I was starting to get on the streets. (Brian, 12a/70-71, 91)

Disconnections, unfettered exploration, and instability often produce a level of excitement but most significantly, aimlessness and exposure to potential danger. For Brian, this gradual unraveling led him into an environment where money-making became an imperative and other negative behavior (e.g., substance use) followed:

> There were a couple of junkies that hung around the cross and hung around The Wall and stuff like that ... it was kind of a really a tight circle of friends and ... we used to go to queue-ball together, you know, and then, 'cause I was on the streets, and finding it hard to live, I started working The Wall. (Brian, 12a/114-115)

For other young males, the unraveling is more rapid and dramatic. Damien (23) was excised from his family at 13 years of age after a new partner entered his mother's life:

> I'd just been kicked out of home and sort of hanging around with, you know, people on the streets and this seemed to be the place to be, kind of thing. So, yeah, I started hanging around here [The Wall] when I was about 13. (Damien, 4/22-23)

Malcolm (18) became homeless, and eventually travelled to Kings Cross, the red-light district of Sydney.

Germaine (22) identifies that an early awareness of his own sexual identity produced conflict between him and his family, which at age 13, led him to explore a geographical area for the sake of protection:

> I heard about Oxford Street, The Wall, that protects homosexuality and I thought, yeah, that would be the place for me. There was action all the time, there was leeriness [*sic*], there was loudness, there was everything out there. Everything that a queen could possibly want but yeah, it all comes down to, it hasn't been pretty because I haven't made it to be pretty. (Germaine, 25/66-71, 75)

Some males who engage in SMSW have precursor experiences of sexual abuse. For Jack (26), this occurred when he was 15 years of age at the hands of a police officer:

> He moved into the family house. Kicked my sister out of her bedroom, he took her bedroom, put her in the hallway and he would like put on a roster like what nights he would come in, what nights he would want to play, you know, and stuff. It started away from the house and it was on a trip to Canberra I think it first started and then when we got back from Canberra it was just like in the house every second night, every night. (Jack, 26/81-86)

Not all SMSW occurs in the inner city. Dominic (22) began SMSW away from The Wall, and these and other relational events plot a causal pathway towards SMSW:

> I was doing sex work but not at The Wall. I started that, the first time was when I was about 11 or 12. The sort of opportunity arose, and, like, I got raped when I was younger, so I figured if I can make

some money off it, it's a good thing but I didn't realise 10 years
later, I would be in the same place, you know what I mean?
(Dominic, 22/146-151)

While Dominic appeared to be desensitized to sex work, and therefore was able to speak of the experience of being raped almost as an opportunity, the overriding description of this early abuse was negative,
and the impact was visible in his use of substances and his inability to
move away from sex work:

I was offered some money to do some things and so I did it ···...
[with] sort of just an acquaintance. Like a bloke down the street
that I sort of, you know, used to talk to every now and then, when I
was out skateboarding or whatever. Yeah, sort of, one thing led to
another [Dominic cries]. I try and block it out as much as possible.
Like, you know, that's why I use drugs to sort of forget about what
has happened. (Dominic, 22/208-219)

Relational abuse also can be located within the family as with Drake
(23) who, at 12 years of age, was sexually abused by his step-father.
While he attempted to reframe or ignore the impact of such a relational
breach, it was nonetheless present:

I guess, although I do have some good memories of my time growing up ... and I didn't have any sort of bad things happen. (Drake,
6/43-44)

As early as year 7 ... I was being sexually abused by my stepfather
as well. I don't see that that in itself had a great deal to do with my
life. (Drake, 6/252)

I can speak in retrospect. I can say now that the sexual abuse that I
suffered from him had a great deal to do with my alienation from
my family. OK, yeah, he was the reason I alienated myself from
my family. (Drake, 6/259-260)

Peter (32) began SMSW at 14 years of age. Violence in his early
home life had a major impact on him:

When I was young, a lot of people used to put me down, treat me,
like a lot of my mum's boyfriends used to treat me like shit. Especially my uncle when I got adopted out by him when I was about 8

... he was ... an alcoholic, he was very violent. It was good at first but then I got in trouble a little bit and he used to punish me, like hit me, with wood or [the] buckle end of the belt; stand me near the side of the tele[vision] and I used to stand there for hours and if I'd sway ... he used to come up with a cigarette and burn my fingers. Maybe something happened to him when he was young, maybe a lot of violence or maybe he was treated the same way or similar. So now that he's older and there is a little kid in the house, he is able to re-enact that. Because I think some people re-enact things like that in their lives and that's one thing I don't want to do. (Peter, 20/178-183)

Re-enactments of violence not dissimilar to that which he experienced as a child became central to Peter's way of being. The abuse and instability brought about a running from home, a movement to Kings Cross, involvement in crime, and then prostitution at 14 years of age:

But then I stopped doing it because I didn't want to get into trouble. I thought there has got to be an easier way of doing it. So some of the blokes were selling themselves and a few times it was scary but, I don't know, it's one of the things you had to do to survive, I suppose. (Peter, 20/130-135)

The precursor relationships cannot be viewed as causing Peter's involvement in sex work. However, the ongoing experience of violence and alcohol use creates a context where SMSW is more likely to occur.

Some young males engaged in SMSW have prior experiences of institutionalization. Jeffrey (26) was placed in various state institutions. Early sexualization was a core part of his childhood experience:

It would've been within the first 6 months of me going to the institution that I had been sexually approached by one of the staff there. I was 7 when that happened. I was, because my dad did it to me, I didn't really feel there was anything wrong with it, but after it, the day after, I was worse than ever in the institution. In the 6 months I'd been there, I'd settled down quite well, but the day after that, I was back to my normal self, like I was when I was a kid. (Jeffrey, 7/200-219)

The connection between his early sexualization and extra-familial abuse, and later sex work was real and clear for him:

> I probably would have ended up doing something else to make the money. I had a brief lull between 16 and 17 of working where I became a drug courier to support my drug habit. (Jeffrey, 7/283)

Beginning sex work at 16 years of age, Dennis (21) lived with his mother until he was 19. Then, after an absence of two years, he returned home while still working The Wall and the bars. Living with family is not necessarily an experience that leads to a positive life but it can be the case when other factors are present:

> I think I get lots of stuff from her like that. Like as long as I can remember she has always had two jobs and stuff like that and she has always, like, filled me [in] on, sort of, if we are ever going to be in trouble or, sort of, if we are doing well and stuff like that. Like, even when I was really young, I can always remember sort of being part of whatever was going on with her … Like, we're really good friends as well. Like, we go out together and stuff. (Dennis, 2/813-818)

Conversation within relationships, shared interests and involvements, time, and a sense of closeness are relational qualities that, where present, can lead to a personal capacity for self-and other-protection and a capacity for adaptation. These factors promote positive physical and psychological development even where adversity is present (Resnick et al., 1997).

Adaptation and positive human development are contextualized processes and depend, in part, on cognitive ability and the relationships that exist for each person. Drake employed a combination of adaptive strategies. First, a forceful denial of the importance of the events by reframing relationships:

> I just said to myself, OK, he's not my father; he is the man that is married to my mother. He's not biologically my father. So, why is he different than any other guy that I've had sex with so far? (Drake, 6/300)

His second strategy was to seek out specific people who could help him:

> She played I guess, in a way, she's not someone that I think about a great deal, or have thought about a great deal, but she played a very important role in my 2 years at [that school] and she was incredible.

She's like a figure to me of, not just like a friend sort of thing: she was more than just a counselor to me and I saw her as more than that. She was a nun and a very, sort of, ethically sound and fundamental person, you know, who was sixty something years old, and very old and set in her ways. But she was progressive I guess in her thinking, and she presented me with a lot of new ideas and concepts and new ways to deal with things and ideas: a whole lot of other things. (Drake, 6/108)

Precursor relationships to SMSW are significant. They are the place where experience (both positive and negative) is had and where adaptations do or do not occur. Early and core relational experiences matter; where helpful, they can positively influence level of exposure to negative events, the manner in which the person copes with (and adapts to) adversity and the degree to which he engages in an aimless meandering through potentially dangerous experiences.

ENGAGING THE SCENE: A RELATIONAL PERSPECTIVE

Rarely do young males simply walk up Oxford Street in Darlinghurst, head to The Wall and begin sex work. As with most relational experiences, there are introductions to be made, and there are people that help or even facilitate engagement in the scene. In order to understand the SMSW experience from the vantage of interpersonal relationships, one needs to understand the phenomenon of SMSW introductions and the relationships in which those introductions are embedded.

Richard (21) was introduced to a mix of people and events by an older male engaged in SMSW. As he indicated, it brought about things he may have wanted and needed; yet, also introduced him, unknowingly, to events that were potentially and actually hazardous:

He showed me a few of the [welfare] places ... where I had my first sort of contact outside [statutory] welfare, where I found out there's other agencies and met other people what were in my situation. So, yeah, it did help. He showed me where The Wall was, which I didn't have a clue what it was. I ran out of money. I ended up there, ended up into the drugs from that side. I couldn't say no to people when they wanted, you know, when they tried to pick me up ... I learnt to smoke pot, all that, learned speed then, yeah, so there was a lot of negative, the party life, I learnt through him. (Richard, 1/57-64)

At 14 years of age, Richard became immersed in, and identified with, a street-based culture involving, among other things, sex work. These are associations that guard against isolation and loneliness. However, the focus of the contact with peers was dominated by substance use and SMSW:

I was so off my face. It was freaky at first, but I met a lot of nice people there, what actually worked and they, you know, sort of supported me and helped me. It was like a little community, in a community, you know, if you understand. (Richard, 1/71-76)

Nick (17) also was seeking a sense of belonging and, for him, this was found with his brother Phil, who had been homeless for some time and worked The Wall:

We rang up my mother. Mum said, "Don't bother coming home, Phil, but bring your little brother back." Then Phil said, "No, if you're going to kick me out, what is to say you are not going to do it to my brother when he is a little bit older, so I'm going to keep him with me." So I stayed with Phil. At the time Phil was working The Wall, I was not. At the age of about 12 and half, after about six months of living in a hotel called Maxim Lodge we ended up, or I ended up, working. I found that I was making a quick dollar ... so I started sex work. (Nick, 23/42-43)

Jack's engagement with SMSW is set within the context of an important relationship. His partner introduced him to substance use and, at the same time, the necessary means to sustain that practice. It is a powerful relational combination of naivety, love, nurture, drugs, and prostitution:

It started with drugs. I was living in a youth hostel and my boyfriend at the time then gave me a quarter of an ounce of speed which he then had to work for and I found out he was doing sex work so it was like it was the whole ... I don't know, it was exciting because of the image put across by movies such as *Pretty Woman* and those sort of movies. Just to go there. It was like, I don't know, it was something that really cool people did, you know, the same thing with drugs and smoking. (Jack, 26/345-350)

At 13 years of age and homeless, Damien's vulnerability was more acute. With limited capacity for rational thinking, assessment, and prudent judgement, he was victimized, which began a process that eventually led to SMSW:

> What happened was I met a guy and didn't realize that he was kind of gay ... [and] we smoked heaps of cones and had a couple of lines and I didn't even know what it was. I found out later it was heroin. I ended up staying with him for a couple of months and, you know, he pretty much looked after me. He was selling heroin so he had plenty of money and whatever I wanted was there. But there was also, you know, the kind of, sexual side of it which, you know, really sort of spun me a bit. He was kind of really sneaky about it, you know, like trying to do it when I was out of it and then gradually it started, you know, became more obvious and he was more up-front about it and, you know, I was, I didn't really want it. But, you know, I was kind of stuck because ... being young and having someone there, it was sort of like a dad almost, you know, ... it was a bit of a trap. (Damien, 4/68-71, 74-75)

Damien's experience with this older person denotes *survival sex*, which is reflected in the lives of a number of the participants, including Shaun (23):

> At first it was all good, we were just sort of friends, until about two weeks later and then, yeah. It got sexual.
>
> DL: How did he start that?
>
> Just on the sly. Never really did anything, like started a week and then after that, it was everything. (Shaun, 16/194-199)

Survival sex, as described by Shaun, does not contain the intentionality that would normally characterize involvement in sex work: "You have no money [and] you've sort of got to pay rent somehow I guess, I don't know. Fear of getting kicked out type thing, nowhere to stay" (Shaun, 16/214-215). What is actually being sought in these particular relationships is the experience of being cared for and nurtured:

> The fact that it was never gonna happen. He always said that you are not here for sex and rah, rah, rah and just did it anyway. (Shaun, 16/318-319)

I guess the way that I thought about the guy, you know, and the way he kind of conned me into thinking about him. He was like a big brother or a father kind of thing and, yeah, it's hard to describe it, you know. Those sort of things shouldn't happen, you know. (Damien, 4/142-143)

The sexual gratification of the person, who is seen as a surrogate for other primary relationships, is defined by the participant as something "I have to do." Participants who experienced such encounters had no thoughts of sex work when they happened into these self-defined surrogate relationships but the connection to prostitution is clear and the transition rapid: "They [surrogates] got me into it. I wouldn't have even known about it if I hadn't gone there: that way, that path" (Shaun, 16/448-455).

While early childhood experiences matter in the development of the person, and the experience of early sexualization that is framed as abuse clearly influences the way relationships occur, those relationships more proximate to the SMSW experience (i.e., the introductory relationships) are the ones that influence the immediate pathway into, and the early experience of, SMSW.

RELATING WITHIN THE SMSW SCENE

For the person who comes to SMSW with a current background of homelessness, his first sex work experience invariably has the broader contextual backdrop of poverty, naivety, lack of information about the scene, lack of contacts, and, of course, youthfulness. Early SMSW events are difficult to fathom: The background of the person is complex; no one is completely *tabula rasa*; and the young person may possess some knowledge, understanding and contacts, even within a dominating context of naivety and marginalization.

Malcolm was 12 years of age when he arrived at Kings Cross looking to "fend" for himself:

I was approached by a mug [client]: actually I was with a guy. I'd been in Ormond [a government institution] at that time and … we did a bolt from there, and we went up the Cross. And we got up there and he introduced me to a mug. And I didn't go at that point and me and the kid that I done the bolt with split up. And I was sitting

in the main street and the mug come up to me and asked me to go
back to his place, so I did. (Malcolm, 3/112-115)

Three features dominate this first SMSW experience: youth, confusion, and a primary desire to survive:

> I didn't really know what to think. Like I didn't think that he'd like,
> hurt me or anything. I don't know.
>
> DL: When he said come back to my place and you can stay, what
> did that mean to you?
>
> Just somewhere to stay. I was young, I didn't really think like I do
> now. If someone said that to me now I would sort of know what they
> were after but back then, I didn't know. (Malcolm, 3/136-151)

At the time of this encounter, Malcolm had some knowledge and a
degree of understanding which is implied by his presence in Kings
Cross; however, neither the knowledge nor his understanding assisted
him to assess for danger:

> DL: I am interested in what you felt like after the experience.
>
> Scared more than anything; didn't know what to do: yeah, and of
> him. I was like so small and just, I don't know. He used to lock me
> in the apartment when he went out during the day and there was no
> way of me getting out. That really scared me. (Malcolm, 3/162-163,
> 172-179)

The sense of being physically and emotionally trapped within the relational encounter dominated his retrospective analysis of this first sexual experience. For Malcolm, at 12 years of age, this was the beginning
of being "passed" around from one "mug" to another:

> About 2 months, and then he became a real arsehole, so I left when
> I got the chance to. Just violent and that. I actually moved out
> down to, it was about two streets down because Max had a friend
> who had another boy who was in a flat, a two-bedroom flat. And I
> ended up moving into the flat and just went and seen Max a couple
> of times a week and he paid my rent and all that. Then we just had
> an argument and I left. I had enough of him hitting me all the time.
> (Malcolm, 3/196-203)

Raymond (26) was introduced to the scene by other 'street kids,' but this did not guarantee a safe passage into or through the SMSW experience:

> I was 16 and I was, how do you put it, manipulated by a bloke that was in his 40s and he used to buy me things and that. He introduced me to heroin and at the time I didn't know what it was and he offered it to me and … So it worried me and my body sort of got a need for that and then he sort of regarded it in a way that I woke up one morning wanting heroin and he just wouldn't give it to me. Said I was on my own. He sort of left me with a habit and I had to go on from there. Start working. (Raymond, 15/104-119)

Raymond's assessment of the SMSW scene was negative. His conclusion was that the contacts that were made were less about relating and more about money, greed and an abuse of power:

> I believe that because for a start they wouldn't go there if they didn't know what the place was about, you know, and for them to go there knowing they would be a client figure to the, you know, to the boys that are working there. They play a role in like hanging around because the boys look up to them because they've got the money. So, you know, I get the feeling, not in general, but I seem to think that a lot of other boys might have the same opinion that, you know. They used the power to get what they want, their place in society because they have got the set up and a job and all that, they use that for what they want to get out of the boy. That's wrong.
> DL: So it's about power?
> Yeah, greed, money. (Raymond, 15/128-135)

For Jason (18), the connection with the client in SMSW was perfunctory. Substance use was a minor issue and making money was the strong incentive to engage in SMSW:

> I met this guy at Kings Cross station and he offered me, at that time, I was smoking a little bit of pot but all it did was put me to sleep, so I didn't really smoke it. This guy offered me to come to, go back to his apartment and smoke some pot and earn a bit of

extra money. So I thought OK, I need money. I ended up going back there every now and then to get more money.

DL: What did going over there all the time involve?

Usually fuckin' him, getting fucked, getting sucked off. That's it basically. (Jason, 5/245-260)

Other experiences, such as thoughts that may produce emotional conflict at a psychological level, were defended against or blocked:

DL: Do you have some thoughts about that, what that was like?

Basically, I didn't think of it at the time. Focused my mind on other things: girls. Yeah. (Jason, 5/245-260)

SMSW was about money, survival and business.

Well, I can't call them mugs ... OK, you might drink out of their pockets, so to speak, but they're a client, they're a clientele, yes. I provide a service; they pay me; They're my clients. (Jason, 5/341-344)

Young males who engage in SMSW rarely discover a person who is willing to care for their needs and not cause harm; and they do not always deal with the sex work experience in a positive or self-protective manner. At 14 years of age, Peter's first SMSW experience was imbued with little capacity for self-protection:

I was drunk and I don't really remember much at all.

DL: Do you remember any of those experiences around that time?

I remember a few of them, yeah, but a lot of them I sort of blocked out because I started to get dirty on myself because I was letting people do stuff like that; letting people take advantage of me because I needed money or because I was hungry or I needed somewhere to stay and there was always a catch to it. You can stay at my place but you have to have sex with me or something like that. (Peter, 20/140-147)

At 14 years of age, Peter understood that relationships with older males are about the satisfaction of sexual needs in return for the provision of things necessary for survival. Other significant aspects of Peter, such as his moral code, were relegated to being of lesser importance because of the overriding need for the basics of existence: money, food, and shelter.

> It just wasn't me. I only did it because I needed the money or I was hungry. I needed somewhere to stay, so I had to do something to survive. I just didn't feel that it was the right thing for me to do, to give my body to someone when that's not what I wanted to do. (Peter, 20/160-163)

At 9 years of age, and living within an institutional setting, Jeffrey's initial involvement in SMSW, while 'on the run,' appears as a logical continuation of well-known relational experiences:

> When I got out of Warrawong [an institution], I ended up in a section called Acora, and I got, yeah, it's the closest I got to bloody raped, by one of the night staff. By that morning, I pissed off. I went down to St. Kilda [red light district in Melbourne]. I only had to walk maybe 10 minutes and I got picked up by about 3 or 4 different blokes. It spun me out, you know. I'd worked it out pretty quickly. Within the first 2 or 3 nights, I'd already worked out where the boys were, where we could go and hide, do our bits, and the money was quite good. The younger you are, the more you perform, the more money you got.
>
> DL: What does performance mean to you?
>
> I didn't really understand it that much at that stage. Like performance back then: practically how much they enjoyed what you gave them.
>
> DL: What did they expect you to do?
>
> Most of it was blowjobs, you know, head jobs. (Jeffrey, 7/256-267)

Not all relational encounters in the SMSW scene are connected with clients of sex work, and not all negative encounters are related to those clients. In a 'dog eat dog' environment such as The Wall, young people who do sex work also may influence the course of another young person's life at The Wall:

> DL: What would have been the worst experience you had in doing sex work?

Peter: A lot of the times I watched. I used to go and pick up boys for this guy and he used to drug them and take advantage of them. I think that was the worst thing that I did. (Peter, 20/478-480)

Other sex workers also may pose a physical threat at times:

DL: At the time that you were in Sydney and working The Wall, what did you think of all of that?
Jeffrey: I still have good memories of it. Like, I'd never had any real problems on The Wall. I've been stood over a few times but...
DL: By mugs?
Jeffrey: No, by standover boys you know, "This is my part of The Wall," you know, "Fuck off idiot." Um, I have a good reputation on the streets of Sydney for being a little bit psycho, which is probably a good thing.
DL: Is that play-acting or do you think that's real?
Jeffrey: If I feel my safety's being threatened then I do tend to go off tack a bit. I've been like that for a long time. If I go off tack, I generally go off tack for a reason. I don't just fly off the spoon out of the blue. So I don't think it's psychotic: might be drug-induced; I don't know. (Jeffrey, 7/288-299)

Sometimes the threat is a matter of posturing, an effort to claim the space and hence the clients at The Wall for oneself; at other times, the threat may precede actual violence:

Shaun: I remember the first job I did; I got rolled for it and yeah.
DL: How do you mean you got rolled for it?
Shaun: One of the other guys took all my money. Said if I didn't give it to him he was just going to cave my head in.
DL: And that was after the job or before the job?
Shaun: After. (Shaun, 16/502-511)

The threat is real and arises from the mix of passing traffic (some with aggressive louts), clients in need of sex, and needy young people, some searching for drugs:

DL: Did you ever get hurt up there?

Jack: No, never had trouble with any client that I was with ever.

DL: What about people passing by?

Jack: Yeah. Bottles thrown and eggs thrown.

DL: Threatening guys?

Jack: No, never had that. The worst thing I had [was] with sex workers. I mean I've tried to stay, as much as I was in the sex scene, I tried to, when I wasn't doing sex work, try and stay as completely as far away from it as I could. I didn't socialise with sex workers apart from the ones that I'd known before I got into it like Les and that. So I didn't make friends in the sex industry. I kept it as far out of my personal life as I could. (Jack, 26/1395-1410)

Violence, entrapment, and substance use are not the only core elements in SMSW. For Peter, who described his SMSW experience and behavior in terms of abuse and violence, there were some psychological and material positives in SMSW:

No, I met a lot of nice people. I even met a lot of gay people that were really nice, didn't want anything from me. Just wanted to help me out, take me out for dinner sometimes, just to be good company. There was a lot of people like that I met.

DL: Through sex work? You met them through working at The Wall?

Not all the time, no. Sometimes I met them if I went to the club or something like that. (Peter, 20/298-303)

Relatively positive events can lead to a reframing of SMSW. For Richard, his first experience on The Wall, at 14 years of age, was imbued with a level of understanding and, therefore, some sense of agency oriented towards sex work: "The first time I had sex up on The Wall, it was with a guy. It was really nice. [He was] a regular of most of the boys there. He was quite understanding" (Richard, 1/91-92). By being introduced to someone who "was quite understanding" rather than abusive, the event was defined as positive, and yet, the psychological and behavioral experiences were negative:

I was telling you about the drive home, you know, all my dreams were shattered; my whole world got shattered and ever since then I was just down, you know. I was just—when I was going to get my next money, where I was going to get my next drugs. They were my only sort of, you know, happiness really. (Richard, 1/343-344)

There was haphazardness in Richard's experience of SMSW. Some encounters were clearly negative; others were associated with a negative impact, while some SMSW experiences were framed as positive:

Yeah, there was quite a few of them too. There are quite a few people that actually do help you out there. I met quite a few of them. They made you feel, you know, they gave you encouragement, support, you know, mentally and physically, you know, yeah, just a shoulder to cry on, someone to listen to you. I've had many clients where, you know, they've paid for sex and copped an ear bashing from you. Do you know what I mean? Yeah, so there are quite a few out there. (Richard, 1/347-348)

Dennis started sex work by frequenting the gay bars near Oxford Street, looking for people to support a "lifestyle," and this led him to establish relationships that he eventually defined as sex work:

Probably since I was about like sort of properly about 17. But I'd sort of done it, like when I was 16 and that but I didn't realize that you could sort of get so much money for it. Like, when I first started doing it, like, I thought that, not that you just come in and rely on it for income but it just, like, if you were lucky, like, you can, like, just be in the right spot at the right time. (Dennis, 2/90-91)

In the beginning, the experience with other males was viewed as a sexual experiment. The framing of the experience as sex work was prompted by the response of the person, only later defined as a client. His initial involvement in sex work was an epiphany to Dennis:

Like, I knew the guy for a little while and like we'd never sort of done anything sexually but when we did, like, he gave me money for it and that. Like I was sort of like a little bit surprised even. (Dennis, 2/130-131)

The motivation for contact with other males was complex. There was some attraction and sex was desired; however, money, "nice places," "cool spots," and relating were also significant. At 16 years of age, there was some haphazardness and confusion, but the contact with males, within this context, was guided, focused, structured, and controlled:

> I remember going to his place and that and sort of, like I was sort of, like, I wouldn't say I was bisexual but, like, I wanted to have sex with guys anyway. You know, so it was sort of like that a bit too.
>
> DL: An attraction to him?
>
> Yeah, sort of, but at the same time I wouldn't have done it for nothing, you know. But like if it happened I wouldn't mind.
>
> DL: How old was he?
>
> He probably was about, I don't know, in his early 40s, late 30s or something. (Dennis, 2/146-155)

Dennis set about crafting the relationships into a style that satisfied both his physical and emotional needs:

> He was pretty good. Like, I still see him and that sometimes.
>
> DL: On a friendship basis or on a work basis?
>
> Sort of both. Like sometimes I go over and he doesn't want to do anything but we will go out and sort of get a pizza or something or you know, go and watch a movie and stuff ... I don't really mind going out with him socially and that now. Like the only worry for me was like what my friends would think, you know. (Dennis, 2/158-163)

The interview data provided by Dennis suggest a significant level of control and design in his sex work experience and an attempt at integration. However, there also is an ongoing awareness of the social stigma attached to sex work and, therefore, a need to maintain a separation between different elements in his life:

> DL: Who among your friends knows?
>
> This one guy, Simon, that like I used to go to school with him and I used to surf with him and that and we are really good friends, all through high school and primary school. Sort of when I started doing it, I didn't see him, like, until about a year and a half ago, like, from when I left school and so it is sort of heaps [very] good, and that, being back with him. Like it's just like it used to be. Like he

has still got all the same friends and stuff, so I've sort of like crept back into that circle of friends, and it's really good. Like, they're all sort of grown up and older and doing their own stuff and that and like most of them have probably got secrets as well, you know. So that's all right.

DL: So does Simon know?

He knows that I see guys, and that, but I don't think he thinks I do it for money but like even still it's way, way easier to sort of talk to him about it and that. Like he has a laugh you know sometimes. (Dennis, 2/164-171)

People and relationships recur as significant themes at both a material and psychological level. Family, peers, clients, friends, and lovers all come into play and balancing and integrating these often disparate experiences is a major challenge. How this occurs is a critical question, not just for psychological and physical health but also because it influences whether a person remains engaged in SMSW or seeks a pathway out.

REMAIN OR GO: PATHWAYS OUT OF SMSW

One thing is absolutely clear: There is a 'shelf life' for those males engaged in SMSW. Clients are seeking certain qualities, youthfulness being one of them. There also is a sense in the young male that such a lifestyle cannot be permanent; there is a constant awareness that exploring other options must be on the agenda. For Jules (23), part of the rationale for change was to achieve a greater integration in life:

The job screws with me socially that way and also, when I do meet people, they go, "What do you do?" and then I've either got to take the chance that they're going to be cool or I've got to lie; and there's problems with both. I'm going to be interested to see what happens working in real estate to see how that diversifies my social circle. (Jules, 18b/236-237)

Some experience a level of ambivalence about SMSW but have a different perspective on any movement away from sex work in general:

I am doing this for the money: just think about the money in my pocket. That is all I ever thought about. I've never been happy.

I've always found it to be downgrading, low and disgusting. It is. It really, really is but, as they say, if you've got it, flaunt it. I have recently just been diagnosed HIV positive, so I preferably, in my own mind, don't want to work but for the regular clients that I did use to see, and that know that I am positive. Yes, I do occasionally do the odd job here and there. But other than that I don't go up to Darlinghurst Road any more. I don't go to brothels. (Germaine, 25/122-131)

Out of financial necessity, Jules sought an alternative pathway while he continued in sex work. Formulating an alternative pathway may be relatively easy but the implementation of that new and satisfying career path can be difficult. As Jason indicates:

If I had a nice, comfortable, enjoyable job, which is hard to find these days … I'm not making excuses for myself but, yeah, I find this is easy money. It only takes, you see, the longest, a half-hour. I have anywhere from $60 to $80 in my pocket. And usually sometimes, I'm gonna need that quick money so I can say "Hey, here you go rent Nazi, here's the fuckin' rent, no more fuckin' questions." But in today's society, you need at least a Year 10 School Certificate, which I don't have, just to get a good paying job, not a bummer's job. (Jason, 5/705-706)

For Jason and Adam (21) who began sex work at age 15, SMSW was a more socially acceptable crime and finding other alternatives is difficult:

It's not a crime to go out, sell yourself, yeah. I'd rather get fucked up the arse, even though I'm basically straight, then go out and fuckin' break into cars. And I have been tempted to do that. (Jason, 5/287-288)

I have been trying desperately to start up my own business for the past, say, four months, no, almost six months I'd say. It's taking a lot of time, a lot of effort, and a lot of money that I don't have. (Adam, 14/949-956)

Some are clear about leaving SMSW because it is a bad experience and is associated with sexual identity confusion, anxiety and internal chaos:

"Yeah. I hate it. The whole homosexual thing. I'm straight. I don't want to get into it" (Shaun, 16/672-679).

Brian also described the experience of SMSW at The Wall:

Yeah, at a personal level, yeah, 'cause it's a big emotional head-fuck having to prostitute. Any sex that I have at The Wall, it's prostitution and it's a complete emotional detachment for myself, a lot of the time. I mean, I have a couple of clients that I've known for a few years now and you know, like I'm actually, there's more than just a job there. There's actually, I know them pretty well, and, you know. I suppose, like, they know me as a person as well, which is a bit spun out because they pick me up from The Wall, you know what I mean? (Brian, 12a/174-179)

Brian understood that the whole SMSW experience caused significant damage at a psychological level:

That's well, that's one thing I'm not quite sure about at the moment because you know like I said before, I think that working has really damaged my sexuality in a way.

DL: How do you think it has damaged your sexuality?

Just the whole, we talked about it the last time, detaching from yourself and I don't know, it's not a healthy thing to do that, I don't think. I think I don't know the whole working thing is just a real head-fuck, if you know what I mean. I don't know what the word for it is. Damaging is the only word that I can think of because it's violation. I mean it's not even violation but there is a violation or something. (Brian, 12b/150-163)

The desire to leave SMSW was strong but the financial necessity remains:

I'm really over it. The only reason I do it at the moment is because I have shit all money to myself at the moment. After I pay rent I've only got $100 out of my dole cheque and $100 doesn't go very far after I buy groceries and things. It's kind of, I don't know, a little bit handy through the week when I've got nothing, to be able to get a bit of money. (Brian, 12b/384-387)

There is a history for Brian of alternative activity that established different connections and was aimed at moving his life beyond sex work:

Yeah, it's definitely trying to move on. It's just trying to occupy my mind I think because like I just said, I hadn't done anything for a long time and it was really even weird just getting into the cycle of waking up at 9:30 in the morning and coming into the city and stuff, three days a week. The first couple of weeks it was a bit strange because I don't know, I just hadn't done that since I was at school. I mean I s'pose I was doing the butchering course, you know, two years ago and working for a little bit then but, I don't know, it just wasn't like what I'm doing now. I'm actually really enjoying it [the art course] because, I don't know, the people in the class are really good and the teachers are really good. (Brian, 12b/501-502)

For some males engaged in SMSW, the past is always there, almost omnipresent. Peter, for example, experienced the lasting impact of prior relationships as it was projected into current experience making survival almost impossible:

I remember there was a time when I was selling myself. I remember one bloke, I was pretty out of it and I think he had sex with me and I was trying to get away from him but I couldn't because I was only small. This was when I first started and I tried to block all that out and not worry about it. But I suppose, actually, a lot of things prey on your mind when you are young and stuff like that and I think I was very lucky I never let it all get to me. Well, I did try to commit suicide. (Peter, 20/190-191)

It was during a stint in gaol [prison] that Peter's perspective began to change:

When I first went to gaol, I think I stopped. Then when I got out, I sort of did it on and off a couple of times and stuff like that, here and there. (Peter, 20/338-344)

It took a long time for me to learn. I don't know how I really did it. I think it come to a point in my life where I had enough and I think my mind had enough, my body had enough. I think it was time to just get on with my life. I think I made a conscious decision and I think my mind and my whole body just said, "Yeah, this is it." (Peter, 20/230-231)

The search for alternative relationships began:

> I think because I want to be something in my life. I just want to be a
> normal Joe Blow. I just want to have a job. I want to have some
> money coming in every week. I want to be able to go down the
> shops. I want to be able to buy things if I want to. I want to be able
> to buy clothes. I want to go out with friends if I can. I want to be
> able to meet nice people and the job that I've got, nice people that
> work there; I get on really well with them and I think it is very hard
> to find today. I really enjoy their company. (Peter, 20/242-243)

Establishing new connections through work assisted Peter in his efforts
to move beyond SMSW:

> That is a part of the book I can close. Part of the chapter I can close.
> I've finished that, I've done that and I think I can leave that behind.
> I feel even though I did that stuff, I can feel happy with what I did
> because that was part of my life. That was a part of my life that I
> did, whether it was good or whether it wasn't good, whether I liked
> it, I didn't like it. That's a part of my life that happened and that's
> one chapter I've done and leave it at that. (Peter, 20/467-468)

For some, the motivation to leave the SMSW scene may be attributed
to the abusive relationships they encountered and/or the substance use
in which they engaged. For Jack, the decision to leave SMSW was about
identity and self-worth:

> Early this year, I did my last client early this year.
> DL: Why did you stop?
> Self respect. I sort of looked … at myself and go, I'm worth more
> than $100 or I'm worth more, my body and my emotions and all of
> that, is worth a lot more to somebody else. It's worth a lot more
> than that to me than $120 to give it to someone else for an hour.
> You know, especially when they're there and they're gone. It's
> like there is no sustaining. It's like casual sex. I can't do casual sex
> 'cause there is nothing in it for me. Like there's nothing there. It
> doesn't mean anything. So I suppose doing sex work, sort of, like I
> had that image in my head, yeah, and I suppose I look at myself
> and I think I'm worth a lot more than that. I deserve more than that.
> (Jack, 26/357-370)

The failure to attribute worth to a person beyond monetary value, and the lack of depth in relational contacts were the motivating reasons for leaving SMSW. In sex work, the relationships were "there and gone," and there was "no sustaining" contact. In contrast to those relationships was the relationship between Jack and his partner. Notwithstanding the influence of sex work on their relationship, it also was a contact where he experienced a different form of relating:

> It's different [with Padraic]. It's not like sex work at all. I mean, I know it's difficult because boundaries and stuff, with him doing massage work and having known him as a sex worker in the past. I don't want to think of him like that and I try not to look at him like that but sometimes when he's not around that is the first thing I think of. He's out doing sex work or I can't trust him as far as that goes but apart from that, sex is fine. My sex life with him is good.
>
> DL: What defines it as being good?
>
> I don't know actually. It's just, I suppose, him trying to satisfy me and my needs as well, rather than me trying to satisfy someone else all the time. It's like someone is sort of interested in me and what I want, which is good. (Jack, 26/403-410)

Dennis remained involved in MSW but made the transition to a private list of clients, thereby avoiding some of the dangers and pitfalls of SMSW. Developing such a position on sex work allowed Dennis to integrate sex work into the 'mainstream' of his life. Physical and material needs are satisfied, and clients become friends:

> I'm at the stage with these guys now where I can ring up and I don't have to do anything, I can just ask them to put money in my bank account, like now, and they'll do that. So I don't have to do it [sex work] all the time. But I sort of do anyway. Like, sometimes I'm sitting at home and I get bored and, like, I've got money and stuff but I just go and do it anyway. Like I ring up one of my clients and say can I come over and stuff like that and we go over and because, like, most of the time we do other stuff as well. Like, I sort of like to make my clients sort of multi-purpose, you know. (Dennis, 2/556-557)

While the pathways into SMSW can be tracked with some precision, remaining in or leaving SMSW is a more fluid and often less definitive phenomenon. This reality makes understanding exit pathways difficult. The desire to leave can be real and compelling, but the ability to envision and create an exit pathway is a much more complex endeavor. It is clear that the desire to remain or leave centers invariably on two pivotal points: the need for money and the quality of the relationships existing within the MSW setting. If there are viable alternatives for financial support, leaving sex work becomes a real option. If the relationships are non-sustaining, then leaving becomes imperative. Indecision is present where an exit pathway is not financially viable and/or where the established relationships are valued and perceived as indispensable.

DISCUSSION

The current study adds to a body of research that sheds light on the multifaceted phenomenon of SMSW. By recognizing that relationships are core in the lives of those males who engage in SMSW, we gain an increasingly complex picture of the person within the phenomenon. Some relationships are perceived as negative, while others are viewed in a more positive manner. There are family relationships that, whether positive or negative, seem ever-present, even in their absence. Peers and friends come and go, as do strangers, some of whom exert an influence.

The narratives of this research tell of intersecting relationships over which there are degrees of influence and in which there occur the conversations that make and form our humanity (Taylor, 1991). The 'human stuff' of the current study is an examination of the content, structures, motivations, agency, and experience of being with others along an ever developing storyline of humanity that, in this case, takes young males into a world that few see and even fewer people understand: street-based male sex work. What we see in the research is a level of chaos co-existing with order; relationships that support and those that detract from positive development; a variety of personal and social events that shift and change life's tenor and direction.

What we also observe, in all its richness, is a complexity and movement—a mercurial element to relationships and life stories—that defies explanation. Dualistic or reductionist approaches are anathema. Relationships may be simultaneously perceived as good and bad. What academics and policy-makers regard as abuse sometimes attracts contrary personal definitions, while events viewed as benign acquire new levels of understanding through an examination of individual narratives. In the end, what is most prominent in this research is that people who are often categorized—as deviant, pathological, victims of abuse and social disorders, and a health risk—get to tell their story, partly in the hope that others will refrain from providing 'explanations' and, instead, seek to understand their experience in all its richness and complexity.

Several key themes and strategies are apparent in this research. The age of the young males and their background always play a key role in how life unfolds and whether or not resilience and adaptation in the face of adversity are present in early adolescence, or absent until a later stage in life. Youthfulness (within the context of SMSW) is seen to be a risk factor for negative outcomes; however, this is not always the case. When family and other relationships contain certain positive qualities, the likelihood of damage from involvement in sex work is lessened among young males.

In the area of SMSW, the capacity for adaptation unfolds at a variety of points in the narrative but always within the context of relationships: with parents, clients, peers, friends, and lovers. It seems that the capacity for conversation in the person's early formation and life experience places him in a good position to be able to adapt under adverse conditions. He reaches out, communicates events and concerns, and support unfolds. The early experience of conversation—which implies availability, care, nurturing, and the modeling of flexible and resilient responses—appears to the individual engaged in SMSW to coexist with foresight, assessment, judgment, and an ability to think about and reflect on experience. It is these skills that can effectively alter the experience of SMSW, sometimes regardless of age. Having said that, the life of the person engaged in SMSW is more complex than simple formulaic responses indicate. While we can approach an understanding of adaptation and resilience within this world, explanation is far from possible.

The data point to the importance attached to the desire to seek and find close, supportive, and enduring relationships that guard, protect, nurture and support. It is present in all of the participants, regardless of their background experience. What is imperative to understand is the process by which each person finds these key relationships and what they do once the relationship is discovered (or not), and the consequences should it be lost. Regardless of the outcome, the common strategy to achieve a meaningful connection with others is clear and the desire perennial.

We began this article by noting that the SMSW scene is a world that attracts little attention at an academic, educational, health or welfare level. However, it is clear that this world is one that demands such attention. The question remains as to how people should intervene in this world. Some attention has been paid to galvanizing knowledge about those who engage in SMSW and this must continue. As well, efforts have focused on the health, education and welfare needs of males engaged in SMSW. However, data from the current study suggest that the area that commands greatest attention is the relational needs and experiences of these individuals. The literature around resilience, while diverse and complex, does formulate some clear ideas of what builds capacity in the face of adversity. Those engaged in SMSW need information, health and welfare services, opportunities and pathways that offer possibilities and alternatives; however, significant and functioning relational connections appear to influence outcomes more than any other efforts that are brought to bear. These relational connections are the vehicle for all other intervention efforts—education, health and welfare—and this is the area that requires most attention.

Two strategies appear to be of paramount significance at this stage. Intervention with those engaged in SMSW will always require a focus on the basics of human survival (i.e., personal health and safety, food, shelter, education, etc.). However, if these are couched only in outcome-oriented relationships, devoid of emotion, the pragmatics of those relationships will run the risk of negating the message that is seen to be the purpose of the intervention. In other words, the message (be it health or welfare) will be lost if the conversation is not couched within a relationship that matters. The vehicle for delivering the message is, perhaps, of greater significance than the message itself.

A second key strategy is implied by the first. While we train and educate those who intervene around the issues of SMSW and life 'on the street,' we fail to inculcate within their practice base the all-important capacity to relate with a level of emotion, tenderness, and care that engages the person at the level that matters to him in his life. The data are specific in this area. For example, to Drake and Jeffrey, both of whom endured great adversity, the relationships that mattered most and to which they remained attached, both in relational process and content terms, were the ones that broke the mold, offered significant emotion and tenderness, and really provided the platform for reparative action in respect to relationship-building (Lewis, 2000). What is most significant to note is that the lessons contained within those relationships appear to remain of significance, years after they were first received. The stories told by those engaged in SMSW indicate that relationships matter; they are the crux for adaptation and the development of resilience.

LIMITATIONS OF THE STUDY

While the strength of this study lay in the rich descriptions provided by the participants, it is nonetheless a study located within specific historical and social contexts. The research was initiated soon after an extensive public commission of inquiry was held into police corruption. Male sex work was a special sub-inquiry within that commission of inquiry and, as such, focused significant attention on The Wall, those engaged in SMSW and, most especially, their clients. Court proceedings resulted; young people were pressured to testify before the commission and subsequent criminal prosecutions; clients were imprisoned; and at least one senior legal figure committed suicide. SMSW changed as a result of this complex public phenomenon.

While this current study captures the SMSW experiences of a group of young males from a particular era, change has occurred, partly as a result of that commission of inquiry and greater access to mobile communication technology. Street-based sex work is now more hidden, dissipated around the city and hence a less public phenomenon. The health implications of this change also are significant. While the health risks for those engaged in SMSW have not diminished; tracking, engaging, and health screening those engaged in SMSW are significant tasks that are now more difficult. Further research will be required to analyze the impact of the commission of inquiry, and other developments, on the various participants in SMSW and to explore anew the phenomenon of street-based male sex work.

NOTE

1. Opportunistic sampling is where the researcher accesses participants as and when they become available. Snowball sampling is where the researcher uses a group with whom the researcher has made initial contact for introductions to their friends or acquaintances willing to participate in the research. Theoretical sampling is where the researcher strategically chooses participants as a result of the coding and analysis of data and based on emergent theory.

REFERENCES

Alvesson, M., & Sköldberg, K. (2000). *Reflexive methodology: New vistas for qualitative research*. London: Sage.

Ayman-Nolley, S., & Taira, L. L. (2000). Obsession with the dark side of adolescence: A decade of psychological studies. *Journal of Youth Studies, 3*, 35-48.

Belza, M. J., Llácer, A., Mora, R., Morales, M., Castilla, J., & de la Fuente, L. (2001). Sociodemographic characteristics and HIV risk behavior patterns of male sex workers in Madrid, Spain. *AIDS Care, 13*, 677-682.

Boles, J., & Elifson, K. W. (1994). Sexual identity and HIV: The male prostitute. *Journal of Sex Research, 31*, 39-46.

Boyer, D. (1989). Male prostitution and homosexual identity. *Journal of Homosexuality, 17*, 151-184.

Brannigan, A., & Van Brunschot, E. G. (1997). Youthful prostitution and child sexual trauma. *International Journal of Law and Psychiatry, 20*, 337-354.

Cates, J. A., & Markley, J. (1992). Demographic, clinical and personality variables associated with male prostitution by choice. *Adolescence, 27*, 695-706.

Caukins, S. E., & Coombs, N. R. (1976). The psychodynamics of male prostitution. *American Journal of Psychotherapy, 30*, 441-451.

Charmaz, K. (1995). Grounded theory. In J. A. Smith, R. Harré & L. Van Langenhove (Eds.), *Rethinking methods in psychology* (pp. 27-49). London, UK: Sage.

Coleman, E. (1989). The development of male prostitution activity among gay and bisexual adolescents. *Journal of Homosexuality, 17*, 131-149.

Coombs, N. R. (1974). Male prostitution: A psychosocial view of behavior. *American Journal of Orthopsychiatry, 44*, 728-789.

Cusick, L. (2002). Youth prostitution: A literature review. *Child Abuse Review, 11*, 230-251.

Davies, P., & Feldman, R. (1997). Prostitute men now. In G. Scambler & A. Scambler (Eds.), *Rethinking prostitution: Purchasing sex in the 1990s* (pp. 29-56). London, UK: Routledge.

de Graaf, R., Vanwesenbeeck, I., van Zessen, G., Straver, C. J., & Visser, J. H. (1994). Male prostitutes and safe sex: Different settings, different risks. *AIDS Care, 6*, 277-288.

DeMatteo, D., Major, C., Block, B., Coates, R., Fearon, M., Goldberg, E., King, S.M., Millson, M., O'Shaughnessy, M., & Read, S. E. (1999). Toronto street youth and HIV/AIDS: Prevalence, demographics, and risks. *Journal of Adolescent Health, 25*, 358-366.

Earls, C. M., & David, H. (1989). A psychosocial study of male prostitution. *Archives of Sexual Behavior, 18*, 401-419.

El-Bassel, N., Schilling, R. F., Gilbert, L., Faruque, S., Irwin, K. L., & Edlin, B. R. (2000). Sex trading and psychological distress in a street-based sample of low-income urban men. *Journal of Psychoactive Drugs, 32*, 259-267.

Fritz, N. J., & Altheide, D. L. (1987). The mass media and the social construction of the missing children problem. *Sociological Quarterly, 28*, 473-492.

Gaffney, J., & Beverley, K. (2001). Contextualizing the construction and social organization of the commercial male sex industry in London at the beginning of the twenty-first century. *Feminist Review, 67*, 133-141.

Holmes, W. C., & Slap, G. B. (1998). Sexual abuse of boys: Definitions, prevalence, correlates, sequelae, and management. *Journal of the American Medical Association, 280*, 1855-1862.

Janus, M. D., Burgess, A. W., & McCormack, A. (1987). Histories of sexual abuse in adolescent male runaways. *Adolescence, 22*, 405-417.

Kaplan, H. B. (1999). Towards an understanding of resilience: A critical review of definitions and models. In M. D. Glantz & J. L. Johnson (Eds.), *Resilience and development: Positive life adaptations* (pp. 17-83). New York, NY: Kluwer Academic/Plenum.

Kaye, K. (2003). Male prostitution in the twentieth century: Pseudohomosexuals, hoodlum homosexuals, and exploited teens. *Journal of Homosexuality, 46,* 1-77.

Knowles, G. J. (1998). Heroin, crack, and AIDS: Examining social change within Honolulu, Hawaii's street sex trade. *Crime, Law and Social Change, 30,* 379-397.

Lascaratos, J., & Poulakou-Rebelakou, E. (2000). Child sexual abuse: Historical cases in the Byzantine Empire (324-1453 A.D.). *Child Abuse & Neglect, 24,* 1085-1090.

Lewis, J. M. (2000). Repairing the bond in important relationships: A dynamic for personality maturation. *American Journal of Psychiatry, 157,* 1375-1378.

Luckenbill, D. F. (1984). Dynamics of the deviant sale. *Deviant Behavior, 5,* 337-353.

Luckenbill, D. F. (1985). Entering male prostitution. *Urban Life, 14,* 131-153.

Luckenbill, D. F. (1986). Deviant career mobility: The case of male prostitutes. *Social Problems, 33,* 283-296.

Mallett, S., Rosenthal, D., Myers, P., Milburn, N., & Rotheram-Borus, M. J. (2004). Practicing homelessness: A typology approach to young people's daily routines. *Journal of Adolescence, 27,* 337-349.

McCamish, M., Storer, G., & Carl, G. (2000). Refocusing HIV/AIDS interventions in Thailand: The case for male sex workers and other homosexually active men. *Culture, Health & Sexuality, 2,* 167-182.

McCarthy, B., & Hagan, J. (1992). Mean streets: The theoretical significance of situational delinquency among homeless youth. *American Journal of Sociology, 98,* 597-627.

Minichiello, V., Aroni, R., Timewell, E., & Alexander, L. (1995). *In-depth interviewing: Principles, techniques, analysis (2nd ed.).* Melbourne, AU: Addison Wesley Longman.

Minichiello, V., MariZo, R., Browne, J., Jamieson, M., Peterson, K., Reuter, B., & Robinson, K. (2000). Commercial sex between men: A prospective diary-based study. *Journal of Sex Research, 37,* 151-160.

Minichiello, V., MariZo, R., Browne, J., Jamieson, M., Peterson, K., Reuter, B., & Robinson, K. (2001). Male sex workers in three Australian cities: Socio-demographic and sex work characteristics. *Journal of Homosexuality, 42,* 29-51.

Nadon, S. M., Koverola, C., & Schludermann, E. H. (1998). Antecedents to prostitution: Childhood victimization. *Journal of Interpersonal Violence, 13,* 206-221.

Parsons, J. T., Bimbi, D. S., & Halkitis, P. N. (2001). Sexual compulsivity among gay/bisexual male escorts who advertise on the internet. *Sexual Addiction & Compulsivity, 8,* 101-112.

Pedersen, W., & Hegna, K. (2003). Children and adolescents who sell sex: A community study. *Social Science & Medicine, 56,* 135-147.

Ratner, P. A., Johnson, J. L., Shoveller, J. A., Chan, K., Martindale, S. L., Schilder, A. J., Botnick, M.R., & Hogg, R.S. (2003). Non-consensual sex experienced by men who have sex with men: Prevalence and association with mental health. *Patient Education and Counseling, 49,* 67-74.

Resnick, M. D., Bearman, P. S., Blum, R. W., Bauman, K. E., Harris, K. M., Jones, J., Tabor, T., Beuhring, R. E., Sievins, M., Shew, M. I., Bearinger, L. H., & Udry, J. R.

(1997). Protecting adolescents from harm: Findings from the national longitudinal study on adolescent health. *Journal of the American Medical Association, 278,* 823-832.

Richards, T. (2002). *NVivo qualitative data analysis program (Version 2.0.161).* Melbourne, AU: QSR International Pty.

Rosario, M., Meyer-Bahlburg, H. F. L., Hunter, J., & Gwadz, M. (1999). Sexual risk behaviors of gay, lesbian, and bisexual youths in New York City: Prevalence and correlates. *AIDS Education and Prevention, 11,* 476-496.

Rotheram-Borus, M. J., Meyer-Bahlburg, H. F. L., Koopman, C., Rosario, M., Exner, T. M., Henderson, R., Matthieu, M., & Gruen, R.S. (1992a). Lifetime sexual behaviors among runaway males and females. *Journal of Sex Research, 29,* 15-29.

Rotheram-Borus, M. J., Meyer-Bahlburg, H. F., Rosario, M., Koopman, C., Haignere, C. S., Exner, T. M., Matthieu, M., Henderson, R., & Gruen, R. S. (1992b). Lifetime sexual behaviors among predominantly minority male runaways and gay/bisexual adolescents in New York City. *AIDS Education and Prevention, 4,* 34-42.

Rutter, M. (1985). Resilience in the face of adversity: Protective factors and resilience to psychiatric disorder. *British Journal of Psychiatry, 147,* 598-611.

Rutter, M. (1987). Psycho-social resilience and protective mechanisms. *American Journal of Orthopsychiatry, 57,* 316-331.

Rutter, M. (1993). Resilience: Some conceptual considerations. *Journal of Adolescent Health, 14,* 626-631.

Schaffer, B., & DeBlassie, R. R. (1984). Adolescent prostitution. *Adolescence, 19,* 687-696.

Scott, J. (2003). A prostitute's progress: Male prostitution in scientific discourse. *Social Semiotics, 13,* 179-199.

Shaw, I., & Butler, I. (1998). Understanding young people and prostitution: A foundation for practice? *British Journal of Social Work, 28,* 177-196.

Simon, P. M., Morse, E. V., Osofsky, H. J., & Balson, P. M. (1994). HIV and young male street prostitutes: A brief report. *Journal of Adolescence, 17,* 193-197.

Simon, P. M., Morse, E. V., Osofsky, H. J., Balson, P. M., & Gaumer, H. R. (1992). Psychological characteristics of a sample of male street prostitutes. *Archives of Sexual Behavior, 21,* 33-44.

Solorio, R., Swendeman, D., & Rotheram-Borus, M. J. (2003). Risk among young gay and bisexual men living with HIV. *AIDS Education and Prevention, 15,* 80-89.

Staller, K. M. (2003). Constructing the runaway youth problem: Boy adventurers to girl prostitutes, 1960-1978. *Journal of Communication, 53,* 330-346.

Strauss, A. L., & Corbin, J. (1998). *Basics of qualitative research: Techniques and procedures for developing grounded theory (2nd ed.).* Newbury Park, CA: Sage.

Sullivan, T. R. (1996). The challenge of HIV prevention among high-risk adolescents. *Health and Social Work, 21,* 58-66.

Taylor, C. (1991). The dialogical self. In D. R. Hiley, J. F. Bohman, & R. Shusterman (Eds.), *The interpretative turn: Philosophy, science, culture* (pp. 304-314). Ithica, NY: Cornell University Press.

Tyler, K. A., Whitbeck, L. B., Hoyt, D. R., & Yoder, K. A. (2000). Predictors of self-reported sexually transmitted diseases among homeless and runaway adolescents. *Journal of Sex Research, 37,* 369-377.

Vanwesenbeeck, I. (2001). Another decade of social scientific work on sex work: A review of research 1990-2000. *Annual Review of Sex Research, 12,* 242-289.

Widom, C. S., & Ames, M. A. (1994). Criminal consequences of childhood sexual victimization. *Child Abuse & Neglect, 18,* 303-318.

Widom, C. S., & Kuhns, J. B. (1996). Childhood victimization and subsequent risk for promiscuity, prostitution, and teenage pregnancy: A prospective study. *American Journal of Public Health, 86,* 1607-1612.

Zierler, S., Feingold, L., Laufer, D., Velentgas, P., Kantrowitz-Gordon, I., & Mayer, K. (1991). Adult survivors of childhood sexual abuse and subsequent risk of HIV infection. *American Journal of Public Health, 81,* 572-575.

Zigman, M. (1999). Under the law: Teen prostitution in Kensington. *Critique of Anthropology, 19,* 193-201.

doi:10.1300/J082v53n01_04

IN THE CLUBS

Power and Control in Gay Strip Clubs .

Joseph R. G. DeMarco

Philadelphia and Montréal

SUMMARY. The gay strip club is a place in which more than displays of male beauty take place. The mix of customers, performers, liquor, and nudity results in fascinating dynamics. Of interest in this article are the power relationships and issues of control played out both among and between strippers and customers. Based on extensive participant

---

Joseph R. G. DeMarco lives and writes in Philadelphia and Montréal and has been a correspondent for the *Advocate, In Touch,* and the *New York Native.* As well, he has been the editor for the *Weekly Gazette, New Gay Life,* and *Il Don Gennaro.* His work has appeared in gay papers around the country including the Philadelphia Gay News (PGN) and the Boston Gay Community News. In 1983, his article, "Gay racism," was awarded the prize for excellence in feature writing by the Gay Press Association and was anthologized in *Black men, white men* (Gay Sunshine Press), *Men's lives* (Macmillan), and *We are everywhere* (Routledge). Several of his stories have been anthologized in *Quickies, Quickies 2* and *Quickies 3* (Arsenal Pulp Press) and in *Men seeking men* (Painted Leaf Press). He is currently the editor of Mysterical-E (www.mystericale.com) and the Lavender Raven (www.lavenderraven.com), and is concentrating on completing the first novel in his mystery series. His Web site is www.josephdemarco.com. Correspondence may be addressed to Joseph R. G. DeMarco, 496 N. 19th Street, Philadelphia., PA, 19130, United States (E-mail: joseph@josephdemarco.com).

[Haworth co-indexing entry note]: "Power and Control in Gay Strip Clubs." DeMarco, Joseph R. G. Co-published simultaneously in *Journal of Homosexuality* (The Haworth Press, Inc.) Vol. 53, No. 1/2, 2007, pp. 111-127; and: *Male Sex Work: A Business Doing Pleasure* (ed: Todd G. Morrison and Bruce W. Whitehead) The Haworth Press, Inc., 2007, pp. 111-127. Single or multiple copies of this article are available for a fee from The Haworth Document Delivery Service [1-800-HAWORTH, 9:00 a.m. - 5:00 p.m. (EST). E-mail address: docdelivery@haworthpress.com].

Available online at http://jh.haworthpress.com
© 2007 by The Haworth Press, Inc. All rights reserved.
doi:10.1300/J082v53n01_05

observation conducted in eight cities and numerous bars/clubs and including more than 150 in-depth interviews, this article concerns just one aspect of the world of male strippers who perform for men. doi:10.1300/J082v53n01_05 *[Article copies available for a fee from The Haworth Document Delivery Service: 1-800-HAWORTH. E-mail address: <docdelivery @haworthpress.com> Website: <http://www.HaworthPress.com> © 2007 by The Haworth Press, Inc. All rights reserved.]*

KEYWORDS. Male strippers, gay strip bars, erotic labor, power

INTRODUCTION

The strip club is a place of special allure. On the surface, it appears to be all sex and fluff. Desire and money swirl together making a heady cocktail; minor sexual intimacy is traded for dollars, or so it would appear. No one can deny the strong sexual appeal of these places. In fact, more and more bars and clubs feature dancers of some sort–mostly of the unclothed sort. It's good for business; it brings in the crowds and livens up the atmosphere. Many of us have seen what goes on–or we think we have seen what goes on. Upon closer investigation, one begins to understand that the ostensible sexual activity is not all that is taking place in the strip club, particularly the gay strip club.

There is a dearth of literature specific to men who strip. A few exceptions include *The full monty handbook* (1997), an anonymously written, tongue-in-cheek book of humorous tips on how to strip and *Chippendales: The naked truth* (Kline & Bice, 1998), a dramatized biography of a heterosexual member of the Chippendales corps who was fired after engaging in excessive drug, alcohol, and sex abuse. The majority of literature has concentrated on women, who dominate the industry. Among them: *Behind the g-string* (Scott, 1996), which analyzes the world of female strippers; *G-strings and sympathy* (Frank, 2002), one woman's look at her life as a stripper; *Stripping in time* (Jarrett, 1997), which is a history of female burlesque/stripping and concentrates on historical figures; *Bare: On women, dancing, sex, and power* (Eaves, 2002), a look back at one woman's career in stripping; and *Revelations* (Dragu & Harrison, 1988), which is a book of essays and recollections by two women, one of whom is a former stripper.

Male strippers are spoken about in the sociological literature only briefly. For example, Tewksbury (1994) has written on the workings of a male strip troupe and on the male stripper as working against gender roles (1993). However, for the most part, men are studied largely as prostitutes and porn stars. Books on male prostitution, such as *Male order* (Gibson, 1995), *Male prostitution* (West & de Villiers, 1993), and *The Times Square hustler* (McNamara, 1994) exist alongside biographical works on gay porn stars such as *Wonder bread and ecstasy* (Isherwood, 1996) and *Autopornography* (O'Hara, 1997).

Male strippers,[1] in general, and men who strip for men, in particular, are largely ignored or are treated as inconsequential entertainment. The focus of this article, power dynamics in the all-male strip club, is based upon research completed for a book about the world of men who strip for men, and attempts to address some of the gaps in the literature.

METHOD

This study is based on participant observation work in 24 strip clubs/ bars located in eight cities. The clubs visited ranged from the more open and liberal such as those in Montréal and Washington, D.C. to the more restrictive (e.g., Philadelphia) as well as bars/clubs in twilight categories that find ways around the law or skate on its edge such as some in New York, Chicago, and West Palm Beach. One-hundred and sixty interviews were privately conducted. These took place with club workers as well as a variety of male strippers from beginners to those who have retired. These strippers worked not only in the cities mentioned but also in other cities around the country and the world. Finally, additional casual interviews were conducted with customers and club employees.

THE IMPORTANCE OF POWER

Strip clubs hold an ambiguous position even in the minds of many people who consider themselves liberal. There appears to be an attraction/ repulsion dichotomy at work. Individuals may want to see performers for prurient reasons, yet they may experience guilt if they feel they are objectifying others, and/or shame if they have been conditioned to think that these places and the people who work in or frequent them belong to the pornographic underbelly of the community. While there can be no doubt that such places are part of the sexual demimonde of the gay community, there is much of social scientific interest in these places and the people who appear in them.

One complex point is the idea of power, its uses and the competition for it among strippers and customers alike. An occupational analysis of male strippers naturally leads to a question about power dynamics in gay strip clubs because, as Foucault has said, "Power is everywhere ..." (Aldrich & Wotherspoon, 2001).

Definitions and discussions of power vary. However, using Weber (1993) as a referent point, I define power as having the capacity to exercise control or possessing the ability to get others to accede to one's will for the purpose of gaining control of scarce resources. Without something to be gained, there is no need to exercise power; indeed, there is no power relationship. Who has the power in the strip bar? How do strippers view the idea of power vis-à-vis other strippers and patrons? Over the course of my research, it became evident that power games were being played consciously and subconsciously. In reviewing the material collected, it became clear that power, in its many forms, was more important than one might at first suspect.

What is it that shapes these games or struggles? Three main elements seem paramount. Strippers and customers, of course, are the principals without whom nothing would happen. But the third variable is the venue which includes not only the physical setting (e.g., performance area) but also the house rules and the external laws governing such places.

There is a wide variety of strip clubs across the country, from the mundane to the exotic. Governed by differing state/provincial laws and shaped by personal taste or the strictures of space, each venue makes accommodations with the world around it and to the customers whom it is committed to serving and pleasing. By far the most interesting places are those in which interaction between customers and dancers is permitted even if the contact is minimal.

As noted by DeMarco (2002), bars which feature strippers fall into several types. There are establishments where strippers perform on the bar; where performances take place on a stage; where strippers dance on both a stage and the bar; and where strippers dance on the floor, level with the customers. This latter type is the least common. Some bars (which can fall into any of the other categories) also offer lap dancing areas set apart from the rest of the house by curtains or walls. In all these types of places, physical contact is high. Some dancers, like Derrick, a New York stripper, like bar dancing best. "I love being on a bar. I love being close to customers. That's when you make your tips. I don't like the stage setting. It's just too weird for me," he reports. Jeff echoes this, "You can be right there and the customers tip well." In their love of being close to the patrons, they are representative of a large group of male strippers.

However, not every stripper is so inclined because bar dancing comes with its own problems. "On the bar you have to be so fucking careful," Aldo, a Philadelphia stripper commented:

> Knocking over drinks is a big thing. They expanded the bar at the 247 [a defunct Philadelphia club] and that helped. But I was usually pretty good. I didn't spill a lot of drinks. It took a lot of effort because after I had three Purple Hooters [an alcoholic drink consisting of vodka, raspberry liqueur, and lemon-lime flavored soda] and it was late and hot and I was tired, it was like 'Uh-oh.'

Thom, another Philadelphian said, "After I kicked over the third drink of the night, I felt like going home."

But there are more serious problems with this type of club. Falls, broken glass, and excessively forward customers are all part of the bar dancing scene. For example, Kurt reported:

> I've fallen off a couple of times because it was slippery. One time a customer caught me and put me back. Another time I just fell off and disappeared and it was like, where is he? I returned after a little while and finished the set even though I was hurt.

Similarly, Konane, a New Yorker, said that he "stepped off a bar and onto a bottle and didn't realize it. The bottle broke and I went down and it scratched half my leg."

Then there are the customers who take liberties or present a danger to the strippers. "Customers are always trying to put their fingers where they don't belong, like up my ass. And for a dollar! They expect a lot for a dollar," Jon complained. I observed a situation in which a rather oddly behaved customer forced himself on a dancer while the dancer was in a vulnerable stance atop a bar. From a squatting position, the dancer leaped from the bar and slapped the customer hard in the face because, as he reported later, the man had tried to insert his finger into the dancer's anus. Kurt reports worse:

> I had just gotten off the bar and another dancer had taken over the set. I don't remember how or why it happened but there was a customer and a bottle of beer. The guy smashed the bottle against the bar and hit the dancer with it. He got him right in the eye.

Dancing on bars, lap dancing, table dancing–all are formats in which dancers and customers are in direct contact. It is this contact which allows the power dynamics between the two groups to become increasingly visible.

Power can be exercised in many ways. In gay strip clubs, the power of male beauty to draw customers and have them spend money is obvious. What should be equally apparent are the struggles or games arising from strippers vying for the money of customers and those stemming from customers competing for access to the bodies and, perhaps more importantly, the attention of the strippers. This kind of intimate (both physical and non-physical) contact is available in bars and clubs in which strippers and customers interact physically. Establishments which have strippers working atop bars, moving about the floor area, and doing lap dances or private shows are the places where the power aspect of the stripper-customer interaction is most evident. Certainly, even in a setting where strippers/dancers are merely decorative and out of the reach of customers, these handsome young men exert power over patrons by virtue of their physical appearance which enables them to draw the looks of their intended audience. However, for the purposes of this article, these are not the interactions which interest me, especially since these dancers were almost always unaware of specific customers, and customers never approached them.

Though strippers in every type of setting were interviewed, those who performed in the most interactive venues are the ones discussed in this article. Not considered here are the traveling *Chippendales*-type shows which usually emphasize production values over customer/dancer contact. Such entertainment extravaganzas serve a purpose, not least of which is their importance in normalizing the idea of male stripping as something good and acceptable. However, they do not necessarily cater to the same audiences or needs as dancers appearing in gay bars and gay strip clubs.

POWER AND SCARCE RESOURCES

Power appears to be an interesting element in gay strip clubs because it is inextricably entwined with the male gender role. In heterosexual clubs, the power differential appears to be the same as in the world at large–men feel they have control over the females who seem to be performing for their pleasure (Wood, 1998). In gay clubs, where men perform for men, I have observed that the power struggle is wholly different.

Sometimes subtle, sometimes overt, this struggle is always in evidence. In the strip club, however, the dancer cannot appear locked in battle. He is, after all, performing and is employed to please the customer. It is his job to make the customer satisfied, within limits, and to enhance the popularity of the club. Dancers are acutely aware of this and also are cognizant that they need to keep the upper hand when it comes to control. That, too, is part of their job–creating a performance which draws in the audience, yet keeps them at bay.

What resources are to be had in a strip club? Two stand out: money and attention. From the stripper's point of view, the tension is centered on being able to elicit money from customers as well as being financially competitive with the other dancers. The customer may also have an agenda. As I have observed, and as Frank (2002) points out with regard to heterosexual establishments, not all customers are similarly motivated to enter a strip club. Some hang back and just watch, satisfied with the display of male beauty. Some will watch, then tentatively place money in the stripper's g-string or sock and quickly retreat to the dim recesses of the bar to become a watcher again. For others, full engagement with the venue, the strippers, and what they have to offer, is the goal. These are the players of most interest in this article. From the vantage point of these customers, the goal is to see as much of the stripper as one can, to have as much access to the stripper's body as possible, and to garner as much attention from the stripper as is feasible. While the idea of attention may seem ephemeral and a less likely goal, nevertheless, for some customers, it is equally important as the ability to see and touch the dancers. Based on my observations, customers define attention as having strippers spend more time with them than with other customers (which includes slightly wider touching privileges as well as hugging and holding); being granted the aura of friendship with strippers and getting to know them on a personal basis complete with access to (sometimes accurate, often not) personal information; and, finally, being accepted as part of the strip bar in-group. Some customers will go to great lengths to cultivate this "in-crowd" appearance by giving lavish tips or buying drinks for strippers. Some will go so far as one customer, observed in a Florida bar, who permitted the strippers and the MC to treat him in what appeared to be a demeaning way (e.g., tossing objects at his head and placing him in awkward positions). This customer seemed to be enjoying what would have been humiliation for others–all for the "reward" of having strippers spend time with him, throw their arms around him and give him "buddy" hugs, occasionally rub up against him suggestively, whisper to him in knowing ways, and make him seem part of the show, part of the scene to which others were only spectators. Some customers were observed looking on in apparent envy while others seemed unimpressed. Though this particular incident occurred at a bar in Florida, I have observed the same phenomenon in other places.

In addition to providing limited access to their bodies and the attention desired by some customers, strippers work at making their customers feel special, even desirable. Goffman's (1959) work on self-presentation in daily life is telling when applied to the strip performance and makes some aspects of this "drama" understandable. As James, a Philadelphia dancer said, "It's my job to make him think my attention is only on him, my eyes are on him. I try to make him feel like I want him, like I'm attracted to him." These comments were echoed by most of the men I interviewed. They view themselves as performers and part of the performance is to excite the customer, to give him a fantasy and to get tips. Since the dancers are considered attractive and desirable, the intensity of their performance may increase, and may be reflected in their potential to earn money.

There are other resources, other sources of power and even a kind of authority, resident in the strip club setting. For the performers, one of these resources lies in being "the best of the desirable" (i.e., the stripper who is better than all the others, who is more desirable than his fellow workers). For the customer, it is being "the chief object of attention" (i.e., the customer who can command the attention of dancers in more intimate ways and for longer periods of time).

Within these parameters, there is a series of possible power relationships between dancer and customer; among dancers themselves; and among customers. The latter is subtle and difficult to spot but can be quite striking and revealing.

The performances in strip clubs consist of verbal and non-verbal exchanges between strippers and customers. There is a language of sex, money, and power that has developed in this setting. From my observations, the interaction between the dancer and his audience is not merely one of sexual display and gratification, nor is it concentrated solely in the purchase of intimate moments. Something more than sexual gratification takes place. Money changes hands seemingly in trade for minimal sexual intimacy or a moment's attention but, more than that, there is a power exchange–from dancer to customer and from customer to dancer. Both groups use sex and money to barter for the "resources" they want/need.

How do strip clubs operate? What goes on? As noted above, there are a variety of clubs and any number of ways for dancers to ply their trade in these venues. The clubs in which dancer-customer interaction takes place on a regular basis are the most typical and the ones in which power dynamics crackle.

These formats are present in heterosexual clubs as noted by Eaves (2002) and Frank (2002). In addition, these authors report that there is more variety, more sexual explicitness, and more leeway permitted by authorities in the "straight" setting. However, the gender trappings make everything seem different. The roles portrayed in heterosexual clubs, as noted by Chapkis (1997), Shteir (2004), and Wood (1998), tend to be traditional gender roles; thus, the power dynamics themselves are often traditional. The man is purportedly in charge and the woman is suppos- edly doing his bidding. However this gender role traditionalism raises several interesting points: (1) who is really in control? (Dancers would readily respond that they always exercise as much control as they wish.); and (2) does the male dancer take on the weakened power stance vis-à-vis the male customer? That is to say, is the male dancer, as an erotic laborer, seen as less powerful because he is working for another per- son's pleasure, doing someone else's bidding for money? Eaves (2002) claims that, as a female stripper, part of the thrill was her recognition that she had the power to give her customers the release they desired. Many of the male strippers interviewed echoed this sentiment.

Access to the stripper by the customer and attempts by strippers to influence/control customers allow the power game to be played out. Clubs in which dancers perform on the bar show the power game at its starkest. The major relationship is between the dancer and the customer. Customers, who desire to do so, beckon dancers to them for some "close-up" time. This close-up session consists of a number of elements. First, the dancer makes eye contact allowing the customer to know that he has been noticed. Next, the dancer will move toward the customer and perform for him, undulating in front of him, placing crotch and but- tocks in the customer's face and allowing the customer to touch or stroke his legs or more, depending on the locale. Following this, there is the slow descent to a squat so that the customer can place a tip on the dancer's person. This is a danger point for the performer because it pro- vides an opportunity for maximum access to his body. This also is the moment in which the dancer gives his full attention to the customer. This is what the customer has waited for since the dancer began his set. He now has the attention of the live sexual fantasy that everyone in the bar has been watching. He has the ability to hold on to that intimate moment by continuing to slide dollar bills into the dancer's g-string or in his socks, at least for a while.

For his part, the dancer is busy creating the fantasy that this customer is sexually desirable, and is a person with whom he wants to spend time. The stripper may intensify this fantasy by asking the customer's name, winking at him, stroking his cheek, placing a kiss on his mouth or forehead, or by whispering a few words in his ear. As one New York dancer put it, "You have to cruise the customers."

The delighted customer will usually continue to slip money to the dancer. Some patrons will give fives, tens, and even twenties. At a bar in Philadelphia, one customer was noted for giving several fifty dollar bills to his favored dancers during a single evening. Often the money is an attempt to keep the stripper dancing in front of the customer–to keep the performer's attention on him, which a customer may take as a sign of the dancer's interest in him. While most recognize this as being in the realm of pure fantasy, I have observed that some customers appear to give themselves over completely to the fantasy.

The dancer is interested in making as much money as possible in an evening. Unless the money from one particular customer is substantial, he needs to make the rest of the customers happy as well. Sticking to one customer for too long makes one an unpopular dancer. Customers begin to think of him as a mercenary creature and not the fantasy dream guy they hoped to find.

In these situations, customers can "flag down" a dancer. Dancers are alert to this signal. A customer will wait, dollar in hand, as a dancer performs for another patron. As the dancer rises to his feet, the next customer will make his "bid" for the dancer by subtly waving his dollar. This is a signal that the dancer's attention is desired. Some customers, new to the scene, do not give the correct signals. In one Washington, D.C. bar, a dancer told a patron, "I didn't think you wanted me to come over. It didn't look like you wanted me. I thought I wasn't your type." The signal had not been given clearly.

Customers will attempt to keep a dancer with them by means other than money; for example, they may attempt to engage the dancer in conversation–hoping to hear something about the dancer's private life. They also may physically hold onto a dancer's arm or hand or leg to keep him from withdrawing his attention. Many dancers have commented on this behavior. "They try to hold you so you can't go to anyone else," said one Philadelphia stripper.

WHO HAS THE POWER?

The dancer's power[2] to extract money from the customer lies not only in the erotic nature of the performance–though this is clearly a benefit of the show. His true power lies in attending to the customer, and making him feel attractive and desirable. Keeping this attention is what customers want.

In reality, this is the basis of a struggle between dancer and customer. The dancer wants the tips but does not want to be controlled or risk offending others by having his time monopolized. "A good dancer will maintain control," said Tyler, a dancer who works internationally. "There is no way that he will allow the customer to control the situation." The customer, conversely, desires the attention and intimacy the dancer can give, so that he looks more attractive and desirable and, thus, more powerful in the eyes of other customers.

Flowing from this craving for the attention of dancers, one sees competition arising between customers. By being able to monopolize a dancer's time and attention, a given customer may feel superior to others and may show this superiority by glancing around as he holds onto a dancer's arm. Casting side glances at other customers while one has the undivided attention of a stripper is one way to show that one is the most desirable customer, and that one has the most influence over the dancers. Some customers go to great lengths to become the center of attention in a strip club. "Mr. W came into the bar every night and once a week he would take his favorite dancers out to dinner. A whole group of us would go with him," said Mark, who dances in New York. What did this get Mr. W? Attention and the appearance that he was part of the strip club "in-crowd." Not only did he have a group of virile young men around him at dinner, he also commanded their attention whenever he entered the bar. He became an intimate of the dancers. His ability to treat them to dinner and to give good tips made him the envy of customers who could not do likewise. The heavy tipper is a type of customer who, by virtue of his ability to constantly shell out large bills, receives more attention from dancers than do other customers. Most often, dancers will pass the word that there is a big tipper in the house and that he should be the one on whom they concentrate.

Other customers, by virtue of being solid regulars at a club, also build up a cache of intimacy and receive kisses, hugs, and confidences from dancers which other less fortunate customers do not. One can observe the less fortunate looking on with envy.

As an observer and one known (to strippers and management) to be making a study of the world of the stripper, I was accorded the status of insider. I was treated to special attention by strippers both on and off duty, by bartenders, by managers and owners of stripper troupes. I often noticed other customers looking at me wonderingly.

Some customers, a decided minority, will try to show their power over dancers in less savory ways. It would appear that this abusive customer is trying to prove something not only to other patrons but also to the dancers themselves, something more than his ability to command attention. For example, Thom, a dancer at a bar in Philadelphia, tells the story of a customer who appeared each time he performed at this bar. On one occasion, the customer looked at Thom, indicating that he had a tip for him by waving his money in the air. Then, after Thom danced for him and was ready to accept the tip, the customer took his dollar bill, soaked it in liquor, and quickly shoved it into Thom's g-string pouch. "I asked him, 'Why are you doing this?' but he never said anything." Thom felt humiliated and angry as this represented a loss of control as well as a distinct feeling that the customer was declaring his superiority.

Often customers will insist on placing a tip on certain parts of the body or will withhold the tip until they are permitted access (i.e., permitted to touch the dancer's genitals or buttocks or, at the very least, see their penis in bars where genitals must be covered). Customers have been observed demanding that they be allowed to place a dollar bill in the crack of a dancer's ass or that a dancer should stoop and pick up the tip in some awkward way. In one Montréal bar, a patron would take Canadian two dollar coins and insist the dancers take them from his mouth with their lips. The dancers had to stoop and place their mouths against his in order to obtain the money.

Patrons try subtly and overtly to prove they can control the dancers or force others to see their power over strippers. However, as more than one stripper reports, their attitude is "So what if I have to stoop to get something, as long as it isn't demeaning? I've got the money and he's got nothing from me." They sometimes realize that the display of power is between the patrons, which certainly takes away some of the sting.

A few dancers have reported feeling demeaned by the ways in which customers have offered them money–crumpled bills tossed at the dancers as if to say, "You're trash and so is this money." Or, as was observed in several cases, patrons have given strippers coins which do not stay put easily in a g-string!

Another aspect of the power struggle is the propositioning of strippers by customers. Dancers often see this as a power play on the part of customers (i.e., the performers feel that customers act as if their money can make them do whatever the customers desire). Some dancers reported feeling offended at being offered money for sex. However, the dancer still holds the upper hand by refusing the offer. The refusal of money–the core of the customer's attraction–amounts to a show of power by the dancer. He has control of the situation, and not the customer, because he can accept or reject any offer.

Money also can be given in a paternal way, which sheds light on another aspect of power relationships in strip clubs: the paternal nature of masculine financial power. Wood (1998), who studied two heterosexual strip clubs in the Boston area, also saw this paternal pattern; men, she noted, have the idea that they are providers, breadwinners, and financial caretakers. This is particularly true of the dynamic between men and women, despite the image the female performer presents. Wood (1998) observed customers giving tips and gifts because, she says, they understand themselves "to be contributing to the dancer's financial security."

What happens to this dynamic when it operates between men? The power to provide for the welfare of another seems to be operative only if one of the parties is, or seems to be, in need. This can occur in the all-male strip club particularly if the stripper's image makes him seem dependent on the kindness of clients. Some of the images which may inspire paternal financial giving include: the little lost boy in need of guidance; the good-looking waifish ne'er-do-well in need of a strong hand; the intelligent boy with potential who is a student in need of a patron; and finally, the potential boy-toy or trophy boy who is too good-looking to have to provide for himself.

Despite the struggle to be on top, dancers usually have the edge. They are controlling the show, and the bouncers are there to handle anyone who gets out of control. Finally, the bar/club is a public venue which, in itself, provides a modicum of control for the performers.

Can anything tip the balance in favor of the patron? Perhaps one thing and not even this can throw a dancer who is really aware of what he is doing. Most, if not all, gay or bisexual dancers report sexier thoughts and feelings, and a much sexier performance when a client is attractive to them. When this happens, the pretense peels away, and the stripper is paying attention to someone he feels is deserving of such attention. If that person is a good tipper, the scene is set for changing the dynamic in favor of the customer. No dancer has reported fully losing control in such a situation. They have reported allowing such customers to "get away with" more than other clients (i.e., touching) and they often spend more time with attractive customers. Their evident arousal is a clear give-away of their feelings and puts them at a disadvantage if the customer chooses to reject or demean them. Their vulnerability at this point is maximized.

COMPETITION AMONG DANCERS

Occasionally, dancers speak about competition amongst themselves. This wasn't evidenced often and one dancer confided in me that he thought it was mostly straight dancers who tried to have a competitive edge over gay dancers. The competition takes many forms. Strippers may brag to each other about how much they have made in tips, or walk around counting their wad of bills and showing they have collected a bundle of money. As several dancers have noted, this is intimidating, especially if they have not earned as much. It psyches them out and throws them off in their performance, which may lead to even fewer tips.

The competition for tips is sometimes seen in the extent to which a dancer will allow a customer to touch him. A Midwest dancer said that he was unhappy in bars where touching was permitted because he personally didn't allow as much touching by customers as some other dancers, and they received more tips as a result.

Dancers have reported that they also subtly compete with each other on the dimensions of muscularity and penis size. They do this by preening and flexing as they get ready to go onstage. Dancers speak about feeling intimidated by watching the bigger, more muscled bodies or when they realize that another dancer has a larger penis (since, as more than one dancer pointed out, "It's all about a big dick.").

On the whole, however, dancers claim that such competition is rare. Mostly there appears to be a sense of camaraderie. As one man said, "We're all here for the same reason and we usually help each other out."

CONCLUSION

When all is said and done, who is really in control in the strip club: the dancer or customer? No one is forced to enter the strip club–both strippers and customers are there willingly. The dancer turns himself into a fantasy figure whose only desire is to please the customers while at the same time making money. Customers are there for a variety of reasons, all revolving around male beauty: Some wish only to see the dancer or, perhaps, touch him for a moment's pleasure whereas others want to suspend disbelief and give themselves over to the fantasy that these virile young men desire them body and soul. Both are willing participants in a theater that is more involving and interactive than Broadway. Each has a part to play but only one set of actors will come away with something tangible.

Though the casual observer might conclude that the customers seem to be luring dancers with dollars and succeeding at keeping their attention, this is not actually the case. Dancers gravitate toward waving dollars, but what is it that makes these dollars wave? It is the customers' craving for attention, the desire to touch and hold the erotic performers, and the need to feel desirable. In contrast, the dancers are *working*. Almost every stripper I interviewed said they are doing a job. Some enjoy it more than others, some put more into it than others, but all are working. One might call them, as Chapkis (1997) has, erotic laborers. If customers mistake the performance for reality, or if a dancer crosses the line and strikes up a relationship with a patron, the fact remains that this is and remains a performance. "A good dancer is always in control. No matter what happens, you're always in control," said Tyler.

Control is the operative word for workers in this arena. The male stripper who works for men may sway his hips and jiggle his flesh, but he also must understand and exercise the subtleties of control. Control, after all, is power and though a dancer does not want to lose control he also does not want to destroy the customers' illusion of possessing it. It is a delicate dance. He must maneuver this complex obstacle course without offending the customer or he risks losing tips and fans (who become regulars bearing gifts and bringing others to the club). Male strippers are engaged in the creation of fantasy, and they must juggle many factors: their own personal issues, their need to please, the needs of the customers, management pressures, local legal restrictions, limitations inherent in the physical setting, and any number of other elements all while engaging in a most intimate performance. For the male stripper, the creation of fantasy is work. The pleasure they give and the pleasure they seem to be getting from the work is the sum and substance of the job, but it is, for them, just a job.

NOTES

1. It should be noted that the terms stripper, male stripper, and dancer are used interchangeably as they are by the strippers themselves and other people involved in the business.

2. The stripper's body also may constitute a source of power. For example, according to Dutton (1995), the muscled body can be a power symbol or a pleasure symbol. However,

I believe that in the strip club, the body represents the power of brute force and the erotic simultaneously. Dutton's (1995) thesis about the muscular body being a power symbol resonates nicely with the current rise in popularity of the heavily muscled stripper. This popularity has created a power differential among strippers themselves. The less built (even if perfectly shapely and lightly muscled) dancer feels inferior. There is an evident envy of the muscle gods. Some strippers may harbor great resentment for their ripped and rippling brothers–resentment because the less developed dancers feel they are being pushed out of the field or left with fewer performance options. Bigger dancers get preferential treatment. In one New York bar that caters to a variety of tastes in body types, the smaller dancers complain that the bigger guys get to perform on better business nights. In Montréal, one dancer told me that "the bigger guys only dance at night, not during the afternoon hours" because they say more money is made during the evening (9PM to 3AM). This observation is borne out by the fact that crowds are naturally larger during those hours.

The idea of the muscled body as a power symbol–a representation of domination and strength–may or may not have a deeper significance in the world of the male stripper. I have observed that many of the more muscular dancers are heterosexual which makes for an interesting situation, especially if these musclemen are considered the epitome of what society considers "real men." Gay customers can exercise financial power over these representatives of "real" heterosexual masculinity and so money trumps muscle in this power game.

REFERENCES

Aldrich, R., & Wotherspoon, G. (2001). *Who's who in contemporary gay & lesbian history: From World War II to the present day.* New York, NY: Routledge.

Anonymous. (1997).*The full monty handbook.* New York, NY: St. Martin's Press.

Chapkis, W. (1997). *Live sex acts.* New York, NY: Routledge.

DeMarco, J. R. G. (2002, March/April). The world of gay strippers. *Gay and Lesbian Review Worldwide,* 12-14.

Dragu, M., & Harrison, A.S.A. (1988). *Revelations.* London, ON: Nightwood Editions.

Dutton, K. R. (1995). *The perfectible body: The western ideal of male physical development.* New York, NY: Continuum.

Eaves, E. (2002). *Bare: On women, dancing, sex, and power.* New York, NY: Knopf.

Frank, K. (2002). *G-strings and sympathy: Strip club regulars and male desire.* Durham, NC: Duke University Press.

Gibson, B. (1995). *Male order: Life stories from boys who sell sex.* London, UK: Cassell/Wellington House.

Goffman, E. (1959). *The presentation of self in everyday life.* New York, NY: Anchor Books/Doubleday.

Isherwood, C. (1996). *Wonder Bread and ecstasy: The life and death of Joey Stefano.* Los Angeles, CA: Alyson.

Jarrett L. (1997). *Stripping in time.* New York, NY: Pandora/HarperCollins.

Kline, T., & Bice, J. (1998). *Chippendales: The naked truth.* Mercer Island, WA: Pacifica Books.

McNamara, R. P. (1994). *The Times Square hustler: Male prostitution in New York City.* Westport, CT: Praeger.

O'Hara, S. (1997). *Autopornography: A memoir of life in the lust lane.* Binghamton, NY: Harrington Park Press.

Scott, D. (1996). *Behind the g-string.* Jefferson, NC: McFarland.

Shteir, R. (2004). *Striptease: The untold history of the girlie show.* New York, NY: Oxford University Press.

Tewksbury, R. (1993). Men objectifying men: The case of male strippers. In C. L. Williams (Ed.), *Doing women's work: Men in nontraditional occupations* (pp. 168-181). Newbury Park, CA: Sage.

Tewksbury, R. (1994). A dramaturgical analysis of male strippers. *Journal of Men's Studies, 2,* 325-342.

Weber M. (1993). *Basic concepts in sociology.* New York, NY: Citadel Press.

West, D. J., & de Villiers, B. (1992). *Male prostitution.* Binghamton, NY: Harrington Park Press.

Wood, E. A. (1998, March). 'Paper Doll Fantasies' and 'Inflatable Masculinities': Exchange and identity in strip club interactions. Paper presented at the Annual convention of the Eastern Sociological Association (Philadelphia, PA).

doi:10.1300/J082v53n01_05

Alienation of Sexuality in Male Erotic Dancing

David M. Boden, JD, PhD

Lake Forest College

SUMMARY. This ethnographic study investigates a male-for-male gender arrangement of erotic dancing. Analysis of the data suggests that the men in this occupation understand their labor as titillation, a pleasurable erotic flirtation, for the entertainment of the consumer. Central to the performance is a constructed sexuality that is not reflective of the desires of the dancer but, rather, those of the consumer. The alienation of the dancer from his sexuality may result in behaviors and encounters that violate his normative and moral expectations. doi:10.1300/J082v53n01_06 *[Article copies available for a fee from The Haworth Document Delivery Service: 1-800-HAWORTH. E-mail address: <docdelivery@haworthpress.com> Website: <http://www.HaworthPress.com> © 2007 by The Haworth Press, Inc. All rights reserved.]*

David Michael Boden, JD, PhD, is Assistant Professor of Sociology and Anthropology at Lake Forest College in Lake Forest, Illinois. He received his JD from the College of William and Mary in Virginia and his PhD from Northwestern University in Illinois. The author would like to thank the anonymous reviewers for their invaluable comments on an earlier version of this article. The author also wishes to acknowledge Kevin Novak for his assistance in reviewing and preparing the final manuscript. Correspondence may be addressed to Professor D. M. Boden, Department of Sociology and Anthropology, Box C-11, Lake Forest College, 555 North Sheridan Road, Lake Forest, IL 60045 (E-mail: boden@lfc.edu).

[Haworth co-indexing entry note]: "Alienation of Sexuality in Male Erotic Dancing." Boden, David M. Co-published simultaneously in *Journal of Homosexuality* (The Haworth Press, Inc.) Vol. 53, No. 1/2, 2007, pp. 129-152; and: *Male Sex Work: A Business Doing Pleasure* (ed: Todd G. Morrison and Bruce W. Whitehead) The Haworth Press, Inc., 2007, pp. 129-152. Single or multiple copies of this article are available for a fee from The Haworth Document Delivery Service [1-800-HAWORTH, 9:00 a.m. - 5:00 p.m. (EST). E-mail address: docdelivery@haworthpress.com].

Available online at http://jh.haworthpress.com
© 2007 by The Haworth Press, Inc. All rights reserved.
doi:10.1300/J082v53n01_06

KEYWORDS. Sexuality, males, strippers, eroticism, sex work, homosexuality

INTRODUCTION

I want to be everyman's fantasy, and I'm damn close.

(Dancer, 25 years old, White)

The occupation of the stripper, as with most occupations, is a combination of expressive and instrumental goals molded by organizational limitations and consumer expectations. The labor of the dancer is focused upon the production of an emotional state in the consumer. For the dancer, this entails more than the simple removal of clothing and display of the body. Dancers share a general belief that the consumer desires more than a visual inspection of their physique. (Even those consumers who "just want to watch" expect more from the dancer than a public physical examination.) The occupation of the dancer involves aesthetic choices. The dancer must demonstrate not only knowledge of the tropes of a performative self–those behaviors that are easily measured and reproduced–but also must manipulate and construct a deeper self, a self that adds a spark of life to the performance. The constructed self is the most subtle aesthetic element within the dancer's occupation.

Contrary to appearances, stripping is not a stage occupation such as acting, singing, or dancing. In stage performances, aesthetic judgment is leveled at the performer's interpretative skill. Aesthetic judgment in stripping is placed upon the ability to construct or manipulate a self that will generate an eroto-emotional response in the consumer.

[A] sign of approval is when they go from here [sitting upright in the chair] to when they go like this [slumped down in the chair with hand in crotch]. That's when you know that they like what they're seeing.

(Dancer, 33 years old, Black)

Another element that distinguishes stripping from other forms of entertainment is the immediacy and priority of consumer response; tipping is used to assess audience involvement and approval moment by moment.

> For that one dollar [...] they were really picky. [You've] got to
> know the tempo of the people. You got to feel them. You've got to
> be able to adjust if you have to. Even in one set.

(Dancer, 25 years old, White)

As with much of the service industry, the laborer is presenting a self
that is essentially under the control of the consumer. Unlike the labor of
stewardesses (Hochschild, 1983), bartenders (Cavan, 1966; Detman,
1990), taxi-drivers (Davis, 1959), and waitresses (Butler & .Skipper,
1980; Butler & Snizek, 1976), the dancer's emotional services are not
ancillary to another product or service. Stripping may be understood as
a sexualized extension of emotional work. The satisfaction of the patron
is based in his subjective satisfaction with the dancer as producer of a
consumable sexualized interaction.

For most of the dancers in the present study, the decision to strip was one
that made sense given their skills and opportunities. Identified benefits
of this occupation included fast "under the table" money, the apprecia-
tion of adoring audiences, and an introduction to, and immediate status
within, a new community. Dancers in this study often used their
stripping incomes to supplement or support other endeavors such as
gaining real estate licenses, "fun money," or paying for undergraduate
and graduate education. Instead of inquiring into the "function" of the
encounter between performer and audience, the present study focuses on
the occupational experiences of the dancers.

Performing as a male stripper entails involvement in what the dominant culture labels as disreputable identities–gay man[1] and sex-worker.
The dancer in the gay community may, however, be able to accomplish a
certain amount of subcultural prestige.

> I think sometimes when you're a dancer, like I'm a dancer, you
> have a certain place. Just like when you're a dancer who's a hot
> muscular guy, that's just a vision, something of beauty–and that is
> a coveted thing in the gay community.

(Dancer, 25 years old, White)

Elevation of strippers in the dominant culture generally is unheard of;
exceptions may be made for the burlesque stripper, such as Gypsy Rose
Lee and Lili St. Cyr. These women, however, were eventually defined as
part of a distinct entertainment genre within burlesque. The present-day

female stripper exists within a different, and far less legitimate, entertainment genre (Plachy & Ridgeway, 1996).

Explanations for entry into stripping as a profession tend to cluster around two explanatory frameworks: psychological and sociological. The psychological approaches typically delve into the personal histories of the strippers and explain their occupation decisions in terms of propensities toward exhibitionism for affectional and/or monetary gain (Boles & Garbin, 1974b; Salutin, 1971; Skipper & McCaghy, 1970), low self-esteem (Dressel & Petersen, 1982; Prewitt, 1988; Ronai, 1992; Salutin, 1971), laziness (Dressel & Petersen, 1982), self-perceived physical anomalies (Boles & Garbin, 1974a; Gonos, 1976; Skipper & McCaghy, 1970) and feelings of personal powerlessness (Prewitt, 1988; Prus, 1987; Ronai, 1992; Salutin, 1971).

The sociological approaches are similarly laden with pathologies. Patterns of social forces that are paraded as explanation include early sexual maturity and consequent early sexual experience (Ronai, 1992; Salutin, 1971; Skipper & McCaghy, 1970), familial abuse (Prewitt, 1988; Ronai, 1992; Salutin, 1971; Skipper & McCaghy, 1970), and economic crisis (Boles & Garbin, 1974a; Ronai, 1992). Larger social forces such as female underemployment, child dependency, poor education, and lack of marketable skills also are given as social causes of a drift into female stripping (Boles & Garbin, 1974a; Ronai, 1992; Salutin, 1971). For many of the heterosexual male strippers of Dressel and Petersen's (1982) study, the perception of the female audience as readily available sexual outlets was a powerful social motivator. Membership in a subculture that does not stigmatize stripping as an occupation is identified as conducive to entry into the occupation (Boles & Garbin, 1974a; Skipper & McCaghy, 1970). Entry was facilitated by the subculture described as "night people" (Boles & Garbin, 1974a). The urban gay and lesbian community may be understood as an analog to this accepting subculture. The lesbian community, for example, has embraced Annie Sprinkle and Carol "Scarlot Harlot" Leigh, sex workers who have defined themselves as pleasure and sexual activists/artists (Bussel, 2002; Leigh, 2004; Sprinkle, 2001).

The concept of deviance is common in the sociological literature regarding strippers and the venues in which they work. The work that occurs within these bars takes place as an exchange of economic resources for sexual titillation, ego gratification, and sexual interaction. The deviance of this occupation arises from its reliance upon, and invocation of, specific subjects including homosexuality, nudity, masturbation, and orgasm (Salutin, 1971). As well, the privacy of the sex act disappears and becomes impersonal; sexuality is packaged as a consumable product.

From a review of the literature, it appears that the decision to enter into stripping as an occupation is a complex intersection of various psychological, sociological, and social factors. The goal of the present study is to examine the occupation of the male stripper, once the decision to enter the career has been made.

METHOD

With the exception of two suburban sites, the venues are located within gay/lesbian neighborhoods of a large Mid-western American city. All of the bars are active centers of gay and lesbian socialization in their respective communities, frequently opening their doors for special fund-raising events, as well as supporting sports-teams and local gay community activities.

The data on the *Silver Bullet* and *Syncopation* and the other eight venues were collected during three years of observation and interviews. The dancer community was initially accessed via an affiliation network (i.e., a primary informant was located through which contacts were cultivated with local dancers). This snowball sample was supplemented by requests for research informants placed in several local gay newspapers. These advertisements resulted in both extended interviews outside the original sample, as well as the generation of discrete snowball samples. A final method entailed attendance at performances in eight venues, making direct approaches to dancers, patrons, and bar workers/managers/owners, notifying them of my role as researcher, and documenting on-site observations and interviews.

Three levels of data were generated: in-depth interviews, brief interviews on specific issues, and casual observations and field notes (see Table 1). The formal, open-ended interviews were tape-recorded with the consent of the respondent. In the case of informal interviews,

TABLE 1. Data Sources by Type

Source	Data Type	(*N*)
Dancer	1-3 hour interview	27
Dancer	Casual conversation	15+
Owner/manager	1-2 hour interview	3
Customer	Casual conversation	15+
Observation	Field Notes	120 hours+

which often occurred between sets at bars, notes were taken by hand. Passing observations and odd comments were recorded as elements of copious field notes.

Through interviews with the dancers, the representativeness of two venues was established. Most dancers identify the *Silver Bullet* and *Syncopation* as being typical of the dancing venues available in the city. Both bars exist within a "safe" zone of the city where a concentration of gay men may be expected to reside and frequent the businesses located therein. Both establishments also are "destination" bars–the patrons are a mixture of locals and visitors from the suburbs who come into the city for the purpose of attending the performances at these venues. The relationship between the two bars and the larger gay community is a positive one. Both venues participate in Gay Pride Parades by entering floats; hold special fund-raising events; are involved in neighborhood pride parties; and consistently promote awareness of topics of relevance to the gay community. The *Silver Bullet* and *Syncopation* serve alcohol and provide strippers as entertainment.

However, these sites differ with respect to the types of dancers they employ and the types of patrons they attract. The *Silver Bullet*, a gateway into erotic dancing within the city, is more likely to have the youngest dancers.

> Yeah. Everybody started at the [*Silver*] *Bullet*. You kinda learn what to do and what not to do.
>
> (Dancer, 27 years old, White)

These dancers may be typified using the subcultural term, *twink*. A twink is generally a male ranging in age from eighteen to twenty-four, having a slight and hairless build. Twink does not imply effeminacy–the emphasis is on the perception of youth and naïveté. *Silver Bullet* dancers often belong to a racial or ethnic minority. In addition, the dancers who work at the *Silver Bullet* are employed with an expectation of exclusivity. Violation of this rule is grounds for termination. Thus, the dancers may anticipate that, provided they adhere to the rules, they will have stable employment. The *Silver Bullet* has dancers seven days a week for upwards of fourteen hours per day; the dancers understand that they may be called in at a moment's notice. As a result, the dancers are much more limited in their ability to seek alternative employment.

The dancers who circulate through *Syncopation* are older than those at the *Silver Bullet* (ages ranging from mid-twenties to early forties).

These dancers may be typified as *jocks*. Jocks tend to have a wider acceptable age range, and the emphasis is on muscle, varying amounts of body hair (often shaved into "erotic" patterns), and a wholesome appearance. Latino performers are a specialty show on Sunday evenings; at most other times, the dancers tend to be white. Upon occasion, specialty dancers may appear as part of a troupe. The specialty dancers often wear fetishistic paraphernalia such as leather or uniforms. The dancers who work at *Syncopation* are free agents–the bar is one of several within a circuit that share a pool of independent dancers. This allows the dancers a higher degree of self-determination, but also reduces their ability to anticipate regular income. Thus, the dancers who are engaged in circuit-style stripping have a higher incidence of parallel employment; often the other career is dominant, and dancing work is supplementary.

Demographic characteristics of the participants in the current study, collapsed across type of venue, are provided in Table 2.

The patrons of the *Silver Bullet* are the antithesis of the dancers: they are older (usually fifty and upwards), generally of average or heavy build, and are primarily white. The patrons also are attired less fashionably than one would find at other gay bars/clubs in the vicinity. The patrons at *Syncopation*, on the other hand, are more uniformly upscale, younger (tending to be in their mid-thirties), and evidence greater attention to grooming and appearance. In general, the *Syncopation* dancers are less distinguishable from the audience than the *Silver Bullet* dancers and their patrons.

TABLE 2. Demographic Characteristics of Dancers in the Present Study

Race	(N)	(%)
African-American	6	22
Latino	4	15
White	17	63
total	27	100
Sexuality	(N)	(%)
Heterosexual	5	18
Homosexual	21	78
Bisexual	1	4
total	27	100

The present study posits an extension of Tewksbury's (1994) concepts of *actual* and *virtual social identities*. The *actual self* is the subjectively experienced self, whereas the *virtual* self is the objectified self. The *virtual self* (the Meadian "me") comprises two distinct components: the *performative self*, which includes those signs that are used to demonstrate some inner state of being, whether real or contrived; as well as a *constructed self* wherein the externally defined rules for internal experiences are played out. The latter is the realm of the externally mandated self. As an example, consider the situation in which an individual subjectively feels no anger or insult by a slanderous statement, but as friends insist that the statement should bring about anger or hurt, the individual "makes him or herself" feel the socially expected emotion. The emotion is truly felt, not simply performed; thus, distinguishing the present understanding from Goffman's (1959) deep acting concept. While the above example is based upon emotion, this experiential aspect of the virtual self includes a *constructed sexuality*. The ability to manipulate feeling and sexuality is both a resource that is exploited for financial gain and a source of alienation for the erotic laborer.

The performance of sexuality upon demand is illustrative of the ability of the social actor to manipulate elements of his behavior, as well as internal experiences, so as to bring them into alignment with an external agenda. The performance of these externally mandated constructions of self may be termed a virtual self–here intending to convey a self that is not simply a mask or managed impression, but a self that relies upon external expectations to define both execution and experience. The ability of the virtual self to extend beyond impression management (Goffman, 1959) may be attributed, in large part, to the constructed self, which buffers the individual from allegations of a cynical or disingenuous performance.

Most of us would nod in recognition to the statement, "I made myself feel grateful," or some other socially obligatory emotion. But would many of us recognize the experience of making oneself feel erotically excited or available by the touch or gaze of a person not of our selection? The alienation of the sexual self, as extension of the emotional self, probes even deeper into the essence of the worker's self that is open to external manipulation. This may tell us something of the ability of social actors to accommodate social sexual expectations if subjectively perceived benefits result. Some examples of this are: heterosexual marriage based upon familial expectations rather than felt erotic desire; reparative therapy to re-shape the erotic self of gay men and lesbian women based upon the spiritual belief of the immorality of homosexuality; and the ability to maintain a closeted sexuality while publicly working for its very eradication (for example, Roy Cohen and J. Edgar Hoover). We also may recognize these virtual erotic selves as occurring within the life stories of transgendered people. The mutability of sexuality is apparent in the erotic responses of men and women when placed within the confines of same-sex enclaves such as prisons, convents/monasteries, boarding schools and the military. The occupation of stripping exploits the human ability to redefine the erotic and to generate response sets that are simultaneously real and constructed.

The occupation of stripping does not require the production of any tangible object; rather, the dancer's sexual and corporeal selves are constructed as a product to be consumed in the course of the interaction (i.e., an aesthetic self). The dancer's performance is judged not upon criteria such as costume selection, music choice, or dance skill. Instead, the adequacy and appropriateness of the dancer's "product" is grounded in aesthetic judgment: judgment that is immediate and comparative.

The dancer's aesthetic self is based on a repertoire of gay subcultural conventions regarding perceived attractiveness, fetishism, and the meanings attached to certain forms of bodily contact. These conventions, through their enactment, construct particular types of social beings for both dancers and patrons. As Butler (1990) maintains, "acts, gestures, enactments, generally construed, are performative in the sense that the essence of identity that they otherwise purport to express are fabrications manufactured and sustained through corporeal signs and other discursive means" (p. 136). The fabricated self provokes an erotic sensory response in the audience. Over the course of his entire performance, the dancer negotiates the construction of this aesthetic self-as-product. As an airline attendant's performance often is assessed not in terms of efficiency, but "friendliness" or "warmth"–the product generally is not a reflection of the underlying "truly felt" experience of the performer. In the case of the dancer, the produced self is often described as "personality."

> There are some guys who have absolutely incredible bodies, but they have no *personalities*. And those guys are probably good for about five minutes. And then after that, nobody's interested, because once you've seen them, you realize, well, that's all there is.

> (Dancer, 30 years old, Black)

CONTEXTUAL DETERMINANTS OF THE PRODUCED SELF

The social setting within which the stripping performance occurs establishes the parameters within which the dancer's "personality" will be constructed, as well as the type and limitations of the emotions that will be manipulated. The space in which the dancer performs is a consciously created sexualized space. The showing of pornography on video monitors, the sexually explicit and titillating artwork, as well as the presence of the dancers themselves, are all calculated to create an arena in which sex is highly salient. The environment in which the performance takes place provides a root understanding of how the dancers should "feel" about the audience, and vice versa.

There also exists a well-known performance repertoire for stripping. Even so, dancers understand a "routine," "shallow" or "surface" performance—one overly reliant upon clichés—will be sensed as inauthentic by the audience. As a result, the audience will negatively sanction the dancer's failed performance: The tips may dry up, attentions may waiver or depart, and comments may be given directly to the dancer regarding his obvious disinterest. This may shock the dancer into correcting the faulty performance, or he may recoil into an even more shielded position.

By attempting to accommodate the consumer's tastes and desire, the dancer also is modifying his own expectations as to appropriate performance standards. The dancer is privy to immediate evaluation (tipping) and may make strategic adjustments as necessary. With little time for contemplation and assessment of the imposed standards, the dancer may construct a self-as-product that fails to embody his personal standards, but meets the exigencies of the moment. In this way, the immediacy of the encounter with the patron produces a context in which the dancer's actual self may become susceptible to the consumer's desire.

Other environmental factors must be accommodated by the dancer.[2] Behavioral limits may be established by law or the bar. Management will place boundaries upon the performance in terms of duration, music selection, lighting, spatial arrangements, and behavioral expectations.

SEXUALITY AND THE PRODUCED SELF

The production of an erotic and consumable self is the result of the effective dramatic staging of a persona. The production process encourages dancer self-consciousness and an awareness of himself as both a worker and an object of value. The dancer's self reflects his assessment of the desired sexuality of the consumer: "the performance serves mainly to express the characteristics of the task that is performed and not the characteristics of the performer" (Goffman, 1959, p. 77). The successful dancer manipulates the verisimilitude of the performance because he is manipulating aspects of a self that we generally do not recognize as open to manipulation: emotions and sexuality. This distinguishes the dancer from other types of stage performance. On the "legitimate" stage, the performance generally is recognized as illusion throughout. Magicians, for example, are praised for their ability to present the audience with illusions that are recognized as such but are experienced as reality; audiences understand the scripted identities of stage actors, and willingly suspend this in furtherance of their enjoyment of the actor's craft. The dancer, however, creates an illusion that is not often recognized as such; the performance is read as an aspect of the dancer's "true" self and "true" desires. Many dancers report problems with patrons who believe they have "made a connection" with the dancer–leading to occasional confrontations outside of the dance venue.

Unlike the performances of dancers described by Dressel and Petersen (1982), the dancers in a gay venue do not uniformly adopt a sexuality sympathetic to their audience. Among the patrons of these venues, heterosexuality is often fetishized and desired as a consumable sexuality. True knowledge of the dancer's sexuality might permit the audience to challenge the dancer's performance of sexuality as non-genuine. Therefore, he keeps his actual sexuality purposefully ambiguous. The concealment of actual sexual identity, rather than professional sexuality, is a pattern identified repeatedly in research on female strippers (Boles & Garbin, 1974b; Gonos, 1976; McCaghy & Skipper, 1969; Salutin, 1971) and male sex workers (Boyer, 1989; Kamel, 1983; Klein, 1989, 1994; Lowe, 1982; Tewksbury, 1992, 1993a, 1993b, 1994). Since the dancers in this study perform for a predominantly male crowd, dancer behaviors are homosexual in nature. The ascription of a gay sexual identity sits ill upon the dancers who identify as straight. Straight dancers explain their involvement as not a desire to make sexual contact with men; rather, it is a desire for money and admiration. Both of these resources are derived readily from working as a male erotic dancer in gay venues. Alternative venues are inefficient. Admiration of the male physique by other men is recognized as a type of homosocial bonding that occurs within different venues, most notably among the body building community (Klein, 1993)–but there is little opportunity to receive pay. Dancers, both straight and gay, recognize that larger tips generally come from a male audience. Further, female audiences are often perceived as demanding and intrusive.

> I'm not gay, but I'm not homophobic. I think there are a lot of very, very cool, successful gay people out there ... the majority of my work is gay work. [...] You can dance all year round when it comes to the gay scene, [...] to me, it's consistent money.
>
> (Dancer, approx. 30 years old, White)

Speculation as to the "real" sexuality of the dancers is a common occurrence among audience members, often leading to extended analyses of dancers' behavioral traits as clues to their "real" selves. Further, management, dancers, and patrons make the assertion that to engage in the types of behaviors expected by stripping establishes a framework in which to understand the dancer's "true" identity.

> If you can be in the milieu, and talk the talk, and smile the smile, and drape your arms around a guy's shoulder and give him a kiss on the lips because he gave you a twenty-dollar tip, or what have you, you cannot [...] say that you are one hundred percent straight and do not like men sexually if you can do all that. I don't care if it is professional survival–you learned it, and you do it, and you do it well; therefore, you must like doing it.
>
> (Dancer, 33 years old, Black)

Questions as to the sexual identity of the dancers are frequent, and proclamations of heterosexuality often are met with cynicism and disbelief. The self-identified gay dancers in this study, as well as the club managers, were skeptical of the presence of significant numbers of "straight" dancers.

> I would say that a lot of [dancers] are bisexual. And I would say about fifty/fifty. Half of them are gay and half of them are bisexual–none of them are straight–according to me.
>
> (Manager, approx. 55 years old, White)

> I don't think any of these guys are straight. [...] If you're walking around rubbing your organs against men and having them pinch your butt and caress your chest and [getting] an erection so [you]

look big [...] All of this [is] for men. That's not straight, even if you do like women.

(Manager, 50 years old, Latino)

Despite the protests of the "straight" dancers that they are manipulating their sexuality, it was widely believed that engaging in behaviors that are homosexual, even if only done professionally and within the context of a performance, is reflective of the sexuality of the actual self.

Hochschild (1983) refers to the conscious manipulation of emotion in the service of an external goal as the transmutation of feelings. This occurs within the constructed, virtual self. The present study expands the potential of transmutation beyond emotions to include behaviors and feelings associated with sexuality. Again, dancers consciously manipulate aspects of their sexuality in the service of the *perceived* erotic needs of their patrons. The transmutation involves not only the construction of a receptive interaction pattern, but also entails integrating elements of sexual play into the dancer's performance. Sexual transmutation is most apparent in the generation of specific paraphilias for the duration of one set, a show, or even a career; paraphilias that have little relation to the actual, subjectively lived, sexuality of the dancer.

I was hairy all over–chest, legs, back; you name it. But there were people who liked what I was. [...] The crowd liked me in leather. Nobody could do the leather the way I could. Put it on, pull it off, the way I did; and make it look right. So that was my big number.

(Dancer, 36 years old, White)

The potential for alienation in the dancer occurs as the occupation mandates a virtual self that becomes increasingly less representative of the dancer's aesthetic choices and desires and more a sexualized product shaped in anticipation of consumer evaluation and consumption. This potential may remain inchoate if the dancer's performative sexuality is consonant with his actual sexuality, and the dancer is able to maintain performance boundaries. However, as pressures and boundary trespasses increase, the possibility of this alienated sexuality emerging increases.

Dancers consciously manipulate their personal boundaries in the service of the erotic expectations of their audience. Boundary transmutation requires a level of surface acting to project the image of a valid intrusion. The dancer believes that the patron desires to gain entry into the private territory (behavioral, tactile, and visual) of the dancer in order to gain pleasure from this intrusion. The dancer's performance is then tied to presenting signals of invitation to intrusion, as well as signals that demonstrate that such an intrusion has occurred. For example, the dancer may have every intention of allowing the audience easy visual access to his genitals; yet, he makes a performance of granting "unanticipated" and "conspiratorial" access to a specific patron. The existence of a visual rule has been both reinforced and violated through this gesture of surreptitious display. The dancer must maintain this performance of boundary violation while convincing himself, at a deeper level, of the acceptability of such boundary trespass.

> I don't think anything is demeaning in itself; it is how you treat yourself, and how you let people treat you.
>
> (Dancer, 33 years old, White)

> There's a lot of crap; it just keeps chuggin' away at you. [...] But you know how easy the money is, so you still go. [...] You tease 'em. Yeah, somebody might grab my wee-wee right quick, or grab my butt, or pull on my nipple. But you know what? I overlook it. Let me get my money and take it home. Go home; take a shower and go to sleep.
>
> (Dancer, 27 years old, White)

As part of the work, the dancer encourages the consumer to press boundaries. Indeed, an integral element of the dancer's occupational skill set is his ability to anticipate those trespasses; in essence, he is always willing to give one inch more than his surface acting suggests. The continued existence of these boundaries provides much of the erotic titillation. Failure of the boundaries removes the titillation component of the performance. The dancer's performance then may be framed as simple advertisement and any boundaries are understood as arbitrary and trespass is justifiable/expected.

> Once you let your guard down, you let them do whatever, they're going to think, "Oh, he's a slut. He's a bar slut. He goes home with everybody. He lets anybody touch him." Once that is established, you can't be anybody's fantasy.
>
> (Dancer, 33 years old, White)

However, the trespassing of boundaries (and, in particular, the invasion of bodily privacy) is not without consequence (Vallelonga, 1986). First, the invasion of privacy may intensify the subjective experience of objectification. The individual may feel as though he is seen as a body, a body part, or a bodily process (e.g., an erection). In the case of a 25 year old white dancer, his performance of a virtual self re-defined his boundaries to such an extent that those boundaries became disconnected from his actual self. He expressed shame and some ambivalence about publicly masturbating, and described it as a violation of his privacy. He resigned himself to having to live with the knowledge that he is capable of creating these violations of "self."

> There was a private party. [...] When you strip, you strip completely nude. I ended up doing one of those parties and I made a lot of money. I walked out of there with a thousand dollars. I made my most money on my last set. That was because I jacked-off on stage. [...] In my last fifteen minutes that I was dancing, I was masturbating on stage and letting all these guys touch me and feel me ... I made close to four hundred dollars in fifteen minutes. [...] I don't regret doing it. But in a way, I do. Because all these men have seen me masturbate and would fantasize about it. Thinking, "He's probably masturbating right now at home ... I wonder if that's the way he looks every night."
>
> (Dancer, 25 years old, White)

A second consequence of invasion of bodily privacy is the erosion of distance between the dancer and the consumer. The consumer may "steal" some aspect of the dancer's intimate, actual self.

> [There] was this one guy. One time he tried to stick his finger up my ass! I was like, "Dude! Don't do that. I'm here to entertain you, not to spread my legs and enter at will." He just wouldn't stop. I got tired of that. I got him kicked out for a while. Other people would do that.
>
> (Dancer, 33 years old, White)

> If I say, "Stop," and they keep on going. If I say, "No, I'm done ..." Then they take off my G-string. You're not respecting me. Why should I respect you? So I walk off. I say thank you very much and get on my way. Business is business. You paid for my show, but

you didn't pay for my dignity. Let me act the way I want to act, and when I say "No" respect that.

(Dancer, 23 years old, White)

Despite such consequences, given the perception of strippers as essentially open targets for erotic observation, the invasion of bodily privacy may be trivialized. For example, aspects of actual sexuality may be co-opted for public consumption. One dancer states that he experienced this re-contextualizing violation of privacy when private nude photographs of him were placed on the Internet as advertising for a dance performance.

The concept of privacy invasion provides dancers with a repertoire of invasion types that may be manipulated to generate a desired effect.

There's some [strippers] who'll let [the audience] perform oral sex on them–right in the bar. As long as people are shelling out the money, it's okay with them. But then that really hurts the dancers like myself, who want to go in there [...] who look good, have a great personality, but I don't want everybody [touching me.] My body [...] if you're going to grab on it, is worth more than a dollar. You get other dancers that allow people to pull and tug, and poke and suck. It kills it for me and the other guys. Depending upon the parameters of the stripper–it's up to the stripper, you know.

(Dancer, 34 years old, White)

I'm fine with being on stage and masturbating and having people touching me that way. But I would never let somebody just put their mouth on my dick. That's disgusting. You're lowering your self-esteem. But a lot of the other strippers would. They're there kissing on all of these people [...] getting their dicks sucked. I found one in the bathroom getting fucked. I was like, "Wow, this is not me."

(Dancer, 28 years old, White)

On occasion, however, the manipulation of these boundaries may be surrendered to the control of the consumer via the constructed, virtual self.

[Stripping] does affect you [...] You can't forget. It's something that I'm sure I'll take to my grave. Something that I'll never totally forget. I'm sure after a while of being out of it for a couple of years, I'll be free and clear of a lot of it. But you've still done it.

(Dancer, 27 years old, White)

The dancer allows the constructed virtual self to guide the behavior, even to the point of violating the actual self's boundaries. After the encounter, the dancer looks back at his performance, and can appreciate it in terms of a satisfactory conclusion, but also may question the use or misuse of an ability to "make himself" feel a selected sexuality. The dancer may question the distinction between "real" and "generated" emotions.

> I think that's where my distance came in. I distanced myself from the fact that I was doing it. The same thing that other people were doing that I might not approve of. I had a certain distancing factor. Or a framing device–I framed it. Temporary necessity. It was something that I knew I was doing temporarily. Sometimes it wasn't awkward at all–it really wasn't.
>
> (Dancer, 33 years old, Black)

As an apparent response to their constant trespass, off-performance boundaries may be tenaciously patrolled. Dancers demonstrate a frequent pattern of reliance upon external authority to protect those boundaries most violated in the course of their work: groping, slapping, voyeurism, lewd language and gestures, and insistence upon sexual favors. When not performing, at least half of the dancers reported having used bouncers, managers, police officers, and other authority figures to aid in the protection of perceived trespasses upon personal boundaries.

Evidence of the failure of patrons to recognize the performance as a constructed sexuality is apparent in the frequent failure to limit the entertainment to the stripper encounter. The present study and previous research reveal that occurrences of prostitution among male-for-male dancers, while not unheard of, are rare (Tewksbury, 1992, 1993a, 1994).

> They [patrons] would leave their numbers on the dollar bills. They figured, "If he's dancing, then he must do his little tricks on the side." It [happened] all the time. No matter who you are. A new dancer would come in and they'd be "boom" right on top of him. What the hell are you thinking? That every dancer who walks through the door is going to go home with you?
>
> (Dancer, 34 year old, White)

When patrons are insistent that the dancer is essentially advertising his wares, the dancer must negate attempts to define his work as prostitution. The dancer may, for instance, resort to a tease. The tease will allow the dancer to link with a prior dancer's looser boundaries, while constructing and maintaining his own. The tease creates excitement through anticipation–thus the goal is shifted subtly to serve the interests of protecting the dancer's actual boundaries.

Straight dancers recognize that they *will* allow trespasses upon their own sexual boundaries in certain circumstances. These episodes are generally kept discreet and hidden from other dancers in order to maintain their straight "mystique." When preference patterns are discerned as to the straight dancer's choice of patrons, behavioral limits and permitted trespass, speculation arises among bar management and dancers as to the sustainability of his heterosexual identity.

> I know one guy, [...] He says, "I'm straight." I say, "No you're not. I can even tell you what kind of men you like." It's true; I know what kind of men he likes. I see him. He's got several girlfriends, and that's important to him. But there's a particular type of guy–he follows them around the bar. But he will still tell other people that he's straight.
>
> (Manager, 50 years old, Latino)

Gay dancers speculate as to the sexuality of the so-called straight dancers and often find amusement in making comments such as: "How straight could he be when he's naked and crawling on the ground while some guy strokes his ass?" or "Yeah, he's straight ... straight into the pants of the next sugar-daddy."

> I think maybe a lot more goes on here than they're willing to admit. The few guys that say they're straight–I can't find one that I consider that really is straight. [...] I think it's a struggle for a lot of them. If you do it long enough, it becomes second nature. [...] The more they're into it, the more normal it becomes and they keep having to remind themselves that they're really straight.
>
> (Manager, 40 years old, White)

Some dancers, when confronted by conspicuous evidence to the effect that another dancer is heterosexual (e.g., "conveniently" discarded straight pornography or messages from "girlfriends"), dismiss this evidence as window dressing. However, the presence of straight dancers is generally conceded.

Gay dancers will often demonstrate resentment of the straight dancers as possessing the mystique of being unattainable, yet curiously present and open to suggestion.

> I've had experiences with heterosexual dancers coming into a gay bar, and a lot of the gay dancers are like, "That really turns me off. Why does a straight person want to come into our rounds and make money off of them?" Because they can. It seems that the gay audience tends to know if they're straight. It's something new and different, and they become the star for that night. They make all the money.
>
> (Dancer, approx. 27 years old, White)

* * *

The men who attend the performances of male strippers demonstrate some minimal level of interest in being customers simply by walking through the door; they must, however, be "sold" on a particular dancer and drawn into the role of active consumer. The dancers select the patrons they will approach. The first exposure of the dancer to the patrons often occurs upon a stage, set above and separated from the audience; the second mode of exposure is the personal passage of the dancer through the audience. "Working the crowd" allows the dancer an increased ability to select the most receptive patrons–perhaps re-connecting with those who had approached the stage during the first phase of the performance, or moving quickly to patrons who indicate interest through signs such as prolonged eye-contact, hand gestures, winks, waves and flagging with dollar-bills.

The necessity for a receptive interaction partner is obvious. The dancer will not linger over patrons who are essentially "stealing" the erotic performance without providing payment. Bearing this in mind, the dancer will learn, both through personal experience and through knowledge passed on by other dancers, of the cues that allow identification of various types of patrons.

> You can pretty much tell what people want from where they sit. [...] The guys who want something more are against [the] wall. If they're at the bar, they wait for you to come to them–you can usually get

them to give you something. If they sit [at the tables] they want to watch–sometimes they're really good, but sometimes no. They are usually with people, so that changes things. If they are with a bunch of other guys, you can make some good money–usually you just have to work one of them–very hands-on. I'd rather work a crowd at the bar … you know what they want.

(Dancer, 30 years old, Latino)

Dancers also must be cognizant that the responses of patrons are driven by personal quirks of taste. They must develop the ability to "de-personalize" situations, to deflect the negative and accept the positive. For example, to not take it personally when patrons either do not tip or favor another performer. The odd corollary to this is that dancers *do* take compliments personally.

The patron typology aids in the generation of a performance. If the dancer engages non-interested parties in the encounter, motions become pro forma and self-conscious, thereby diminishing their likelihood of continued audience approval. The encounter, then, while superficially appearing to be a spontaneous connection between performer and audience, is often predetermined by the situational understanding and meaning of the use of space.

CONCLUSION

Researchers are fascinated with the ability of strippers to refuse full identification with their occupation. Dancers' statements are frequently interpreted as rationalization and deviance neutralizations (Perrucci, 1999; Reid, Epstein, & Benson, 1994; Thompson & Harred, 1992). Dancers often explain their involvement in the occupation as a form of sexual entertainment, a personal indulgence, an "ego stroke," sexual catharsis, or just a job until something else comes along. These subjective definitions of the situation are claimed by researchers to be rationalizations that deflect the affixing of stigma and its internalization by the dancer (Perrucci, 1999; Skipper & McCaghy, 1970, 1971, 1978; Thompson & Harred, 1992).

While most individuals may understand the rationale "I made myself feel happy," it is likely many find it difficult to comprehend how a person can make him or herself enjoy sexualized behaviors that are not a component of the actual self. The largest portion of the dancer's performance is the manipulation of those elements of the emotional self that are most directly associated with sexuality, which constitutes an element of the self that is generally understood to be of such "core" importance to the construction of the individual that it is not open to manipulation. As the dancer gains experience, he may generate an understanding that bridges the division between actual self and virtual self as aspects of his whole identity. Mature and experienced dancers appear more adept at managing constructed emotions and sexuality as being reflective of their complete identity. They identify a process of getting prepared for the performance; they "psyche" themselves up for the show. However, there remains an understanding of the artificiality of this performance as reflective of external, rather than internal, desire.

All dancers identified a satisfaction with successful construction of a consumable self–they made a desired product. As with many occupations that require the generation of emotions upon the demand of the consumer (e.g., nursing), instances of "burn-out" often occur amid claims that the laborer is emotionally exhausted from meeting the demands of the consumer. In the case of the male dancer, problems may arise, when the control of the emotional and sexual product shifts to an external locus. In this instance, the dancer may find himself subjected to participation in sexuality and behaviors that are alien to his own desires. As a result, the dancer may experience unease–he recognizes that the offending behavior was within his performative repertoire, but feels subjectively violated by having voluntarily engaged in such action. Dancer responses may include: (1) acceptance of the violation as part of his heretofore unknown limits, (2) refusal of responsibility, (3) shame, (4) numbing the experience with drugs and alcohol, and/or (5) removing himself from the occupation entirely. In all interviews within which this subject was discussed directly, dancers recognized having experienced this alienation of their sexuality. Some identified it as an occupational hazard and rationalized it away–something that will haunt them, but is irrefutable. Other dancers accept it and integrate it into a new pattern of interaction/performance. A final segment of the dancers claim to have learned from the pain of the experience, and have altered their performances to avoid those lapses of control.

In summary, stripping in particular, and erotic labor in general may pose a challenge to a person's sense of self. Mainstream society understands sexuality to be an expression of the deepest and most private aspects of the social actor as an individual. When those parts of the laborer's self are exploited for the entertainment of the consumer, the dancer may risk becoming alienated from his own sexuality, and bear the stigma of the consumers' desires. The memories and revelations of virtual sexuality are written upon the mind and soul of the dancer. He must come to terms with the knowledge that he is capable of these actions; actions that are read by society as reflective of his internal being, yet are reflections of desires and needs outside of him. The disconnection between a personally experienced actual self and the virtual self becomes a matter of consideration and requires accommodation in the dancer's identity. The moral conscience of the dancer is tested as an ongoing aspect of his engagement in erotic labor.

NOTES

1. Not all male strippers who perform in gay venues are homosexual. However, it is likely that many are perceived to be gay by virtue of what they do.
2. Environmental constraints are often manipulated by the dancer to serve his interests. For example, a legal proscription concerning the display of genitals provides the dancer with a structural boundary that may justify restricting audience access as well as provide a source of enticement and titillation through its violation.

REFERENCES

Boles, J. & Garbin, A. P. (1974a). The choice of stripping for a living. *Sociology of Work and Occupations, 1*, 110-123.

Boles, J. & Garbin, A. P. (1974b). The strip club and stripper-customer patterns of interaction. *Sociology and Social Research, 58*,136-144.

Boyer, D. (1989). Male prostitution and homosexual identity. *Journal of Homosexuality, 17*, 151-184.

Bussel, R. (2002, February). Annie Sprinkle up close. *Lambda Book Report, 10*(7), 20.

Butler, J. (1990). *Gender trouble: Feminism and the subversion of identity*. New York, NY: Routledge.

Butler, S., & Skipper, J. K. (1980). Waitressing, vulnerability, and job autonomy. *Sociology of Work and Occupations, 7*(4), 487-502.

Butler, S., & Snizek, W. E. (1976). The waitress-diner relationship. *Sociology of Work and Occupations, 3*, 209-222.

Cavan, S. (1966). *Liquor license: An ethnography of bar behavior*. Chicago, IL: Aldine.

Davis, F. (1959). The cab driver and his fare: Facets of a fleeting relationship. *American Journal of Sociology, 65*, 158-165.

Detman, L. A. (1990). Women behind bars: The feminization of bartending. In B. R. Reskin & P. A. Roos (Eds.), *Job queues, gender queues* (pp. 241-255). Philadelphia, PA: Temple University Press.

Dressel, P. L., & Petersen, D. M. (1982). Becoming a male stripper. *Work and Occupations, 9*, 387-406.

Goffman, E. (1959). *Presentation of self in everyday life.* Garden City, NY: Doubleday Anchor Books.

Gonos, G. (1976). Go-go dancing: Comparative frame analysis. *Urban Life, 5,* 189-220.

Hochschild, A. (1983). *The managed heart: Commercialization of human feeling.* Berkeley: University of California Press.

Kamel, G. W. L. (1983). *Downtown street hustlers: The role of dramaturgical imaging practices in the social construction of male prostitution.* Unpublished doctoral dissertation, University of California, San Diego, California.

Klein, A. M. (1989). Managing deviance: Hustling, homophobia and the bodybuilding subculture. *Deviant Behavior, 10,* 11-27.

Klein, A. M. (1993). *Little big men: Bodybuilding subculture and gender construction.* Albany: State University of New York Press.

Klein, A. M. (1994). Juggling deviance: Hustling and homophobia in bodybuilding. *Deviant Behavior, 10,* 11-27.

Leigh, C. (2004). *Unrepentant whore: The collected works of Scarlot Harlot.* San Francisco, CA: Last Gasp.

Lowe, A. (1982). *Socialization of role behavior in street corner prostitutes.* Unpublished doctoral dissertation, City University of New York.

McCaghy, C. H., & Skipper, J. K., Jr. (1969). Lesbian behavior as an adaptation to the occupation of stripping. *Social Problems, 17,* 262-270.

Perrucci, A. C. (1999). *Private parts in public places: A phenomenological study of the experience of privacy in erotic dancers.* Unpublished doctoral dissertation, Duquesne University, Pittsburgh, Pennsylvania.

Plachy, S., & Ridgeway, J. (1996). *Red light: Inside the sex industry.* New York: Powerhouse Books.

Prewitt, T. J. (1988). The exposed exotic dancer: A semiotic of deception in porno-active ritual. In T. J. Prewitt, J. Deely & K. Haworth (Eds.), *Semiotics* (pp. 241-247). Lanham, MD: University Press of America.

Prus, R. C. (1987). Developing loyalty: Fostering purchasing relationships in the marketplace. *Urban Life, 15,* 331-366.

Reid, S. A., Epstein, J. & Benson, D. E. (1994). Role identity in a devalued occupation: The case of female exotic dancers. *Sociological Focus, 27,* 1-16.

Ronai, C. R. (1992). A night in the life of an erotic dancer/researcher. In C. Ellis & M. Flaherty (Eds.) *Investigating subjectivity: research on lived experience* (pp. 102-124). Newbury Park, CA: Sage.

Salutin, M. (1971, June). Stripper morality. *Transaction, 8,* 12-22

Skipper, J. K., Jr. & McCaghy, C. H. (1970). Stripteasers: The anatomy and career contingencies of a deviant occupation. *Social Problems, 17,* 391-405.

Skipper, J. K., Jr. & McCaghy, C. H. (1971). Stripteasing: A sex oriented occupation. In J. M. Henslin & E. Sagarin (Eds.), *The sociology of sex* (pp. 275-296). New York, NY: Appleton Century Crofts.

Skipper, J. K., Jr. & McCaghy, C. H. (1978). Teasing, flashing and visual sex: Stripping for a living. In J. M. Henslin & E. Sagarin (Eds.), *The sociology of sex* (pp. 171-193). New York, NY: Schocken.

Sprinkle, A. (2001). *Hardcore from the heart: The pleasures, profits and politics of sex in performance (Critical Performance Series).* New York: Continuum International Publishing Group.

Tewksbury, R. (1992, August). Identity management and ceremonial performance: A dramaturgical analysis of male strippers. Paper presented at the annual convention of the American Sociological Association, Pittsburgh, PA.

Tewksbury, R. (1993a). Male strippers: Men objectifying men. In H. Brod & M. Kaufman (Eds.), *Theorizing masculinities* (pp. 168-181). Thousand Oaks, CA: Sage.

Tewksbury, R. (1993b). Men performing as women: Explorations in the world of female impersonators. *Sociological Spectrum, 13*, 465-486.

Tewksbury, R. (1994). Dramaturgical analysis of male strippers. *Journal of Men's Studies, 2*, 325-342.

Thompson, W. E., & Harred, J. L. (1992). Topless dancers: Managing stigma in a deviant occupation. *Deviant Behavior, 13*, 291-311.

Vallelonga, D. (1986). *The lived structures of being embarrassed and being ashamed-of-oneself: An empirical phenomenological study.* Unpublished doctoral dissertation, Duquesne University, Pittsburgh, Pennsylvania.

doi:10.1300/J082v53n01_06

The Closing of *Atlantis*

Jonathan David Jackson

SUMMARY. This article examines the author's experience of cultural bias as a spectator at a now-defunct, predominately white, working class American burlesque house called *Club Atlantis* in Baltimore, Maryland. The club was well known in the mid-Atlantic region for its all-nude male dancers. According to the author, *Club Atlantis* was less known for its sometimes subtle and sometimes overt unwelcome treatment of black American or dark-skinned patrons and its unwritten policy of banning black American or dark-skinned would-be strippers. Based on personal observations and informal interviews conducted between 2002 and 2004, and written in a manner common to the author's disciplines of creative nonfiction and the performing arts, the article argues for increased examination of erotic performance as a form of sex work. The article also argues for further study of the racial politics of commercial sex. doi: 10.1300/J082v53n01_07 *[Article copies available for a fee from The Haworth Document Delivery Service: 1-800-HAWORTH. E-mail address: <docdelivery@ haworthpress.com> Website: <http://www.HaworthPress.com> © 2007 by The Haworth Press, Inc. All rights reserved.]*

KEYWORDS. Cultural bias, erotic performance, stripping, racial politics, class, sex work

Jonathan David Jackson is a poet, storyteller, essayist, and former novelty burlesque performer. Correspondence may be addressed to Jonathan David Jackson at jonathan@jonathandavidjackson.net.

[Haworth co-indexing entry note]: "The Closing of *Atlantis*." Jackson, Jonathan David. Co-published simultaneously in *Journal of Homosexuality* (The Haworth Press, Inc.) Vol. 53, No. 1/2, 2007, pp. 153-172; and: *Male Sex Work: A Business Doing Pleasure* (ed: Todd G. Morrison and Bruce W. Whitehead) The Haworth Press, Inc., 2007, pp. 153-172. Single or multiple copies of this article are available for a fee from The Haworth Document Delivery Service [1-800-HAWORTH, 9:00 a.m. - 5:00 p.m. (EST). E-mail address: docdelivery@haworthpress.com].

Available online at http://jh.haworthpress.com
© 2007 by The Haworth Press, Inc. All rights reserved.
doi:10.1300/J082v53n01_07

> Being set on the idea
>   Of getting to Atlantis,
> You have discovered of course
>   Only the Ship of Fools is
> Making the voyage this year,
> As gales of abnormal force
>   Are predicted, and that you
>   Must therefore be ready to
> Behave absurdly enough
>   To pass for one of The Boys,
> At least appearing to love
>   Hard liquor, horseplay and noise.

—W.H. Auden, "Atlantis" (1976, pp. 315-317)

INTRODUCTION

In *Timaeus* and *Critias* (1971), two of Plato's late dialogues, two Athenian philosophers describe the treasures that were lost after an earthquake sank the mythic island of Atlantis into the Atlantic Ocean. Recalling a poem by the Greek poet Solon, the philosopher Critias describes a strong militarily advanced island that was rich with both economic and natural resources. It is from these ancient dialogues that Atlantis acquires its association with mysterious, fantastic, and ultimately lost wealth and power. Even in filmmaker George Lucas' *Star Wars Episode I: The Phantom Menace* (1999, 20th Century Fox), the lost riches of Atlantis are alluded to in the depiction of the vast glittering underwater world of a comic character named Jar Jar Binks.

But Atlantis has another meaning. The lost city also brings to mind illicit delights. For some, secret and even dangerous sexual enchantments are as synonymous with Atlantis as danger and tragedy are for the fabled Bermuda Triangle where waylaid vessels are rumored to disappear into the ghostly ocean. Surely it is to these associations that Auden's haunting poem "Atlantis" obliquely refers. In the poem, the journey to Atlantis simultaneously becomes a perilous and pleasurable fool's errand. One is likely to be caught–or pleasantly released, if you care for such men–into the company of rowdy sailors ("The Boys") with their "[h]ard liquor, horseplay and noise" on a storm-racked ship (Auden, 1976).

It is no doubt to these darker erotic meanings that the name of a now-defunct American nightclub called *Club Atlantis* in Baltimore, Maryland refers. At the top of the nightclub's building on 611 Fallsway, just south of Madison Street, were two green and white signs emblazoned with its name. One sign sits atop two nine feet tall poles. The other flanks the eastern side of the building's roof. Yet, because the space adjacent to the nightclub is shot through with the crisscrossing steel and concrete pillars that support the Jones Falls Expressway, it is difficult to see the building's signage from most angles. To identify the nightclub, one must stand just underneath the expressway on Fallsway. This is what I presume a photographer did when he documented the nightclub's signs for an article about *Club Atlantis*' closing in September 2004 (Chase, 2004). For a moment, as you drove around the bend from the South to the North on Fallsway, you might have seen the signs as you glanced sharply up to the right.

For over 24 years, *Club Atlantis* was partially hidden by a freeway and sandwiched between three landmarks without which it seems Baltimore city, given its high crime rate, would not function. The first landmark is the Central Booking building of the Baltimore City Police Department. Central Booking lies on the northeast side of Madison Street. In the pot-holed parking lot of the Central Booking station, a black Winnebago sold bail bonds 24 hours a day.

The second landmark is the dilapidated, but still well-used Maryland Penitentiary on 401 East Madison Street. The penitentiary, which is over 100 years old, runs for several blocks southeast behind the forty-car parking lot and the nightclub. The third landmark is the super-maximum state-of-the-art prison facility (or Super-Max) that houses Maryland's Death Row. On lock-down for 23 hours of each day, the mostly black American prisoners wait to be executed. (The actual executions occur in a chamber a block away within the old penitentiary.) Lethal injection is the preferred method since use of the expensive, dangerous (for witnesses and workers, to say nothing of inmates), and antiquated gas chamber was curtailed in the mid-1990s. The Death Row wing of the Super-Max is approximately seventy-five yards from the door to *Club Atlantis*. The high walls of the prisons loom so close to the club that sometimes, if you are standing in the other smaller ten-car parking lot reserved for the nightclub, you can hear the muffled voices of inmates.

Club Atlantis' partial concealment and baffling proximity to death and imprisonment seemed both to add to, and detract from, its appeal. The nightclub was an all-male burlesque house and one of the most legendary gay male hustler bars in the middle Northeastern states. Its main attraction was the semi-nude or nude white male dancers who performed on top of the oval bar in the center of the nightclub's front room six nights a week from Tuesday through Sunday.[1] During the time I studied the nightclub between January 2002 and August 2004, one of the dancers asked, "Where else could the *Atlantis* exist in the city but where the cops can monitor it and no one else in the city could be bothered?"

Club Atlantis' relative isolation and coveted zoning license for nude burlesque entertainment made it a hot property for its new owners. Negotiations for its sale were finalized in September 2004. Andrew Alley and Brian Shulman, the new proprietors, also own a small all-female burlesque club in Baltimore called *Chubbies*. However, their plans for the *Atlantis* may be far more ambitious (i.e., Chase [2004] reported that the nightclub likely will become part of the *Scores* franchise, which is a popular collection of upscale heterosexual burlesque houses in the Northeast).

I visited *Club Atlantis* on Tuesday or Wednesday nights twice a month from the beginning of 2002 until the nightclub closed in September 2004. The dancers and patrons that I mention here are not composite sketches and all names are pseudonyms. Some members' comments were said in passing, while others occurred during more personal interactions.

After beginning with a tape recorder and attempting sit-down interviews outside of the nightclub in February 2002, I took my cue from a dancer who suggested that I refocus my approach and "just be at the club, have fun, and still ask questions." This shift in information-gathering helped me establish rapport with a few of the performers and patrons.[2] I did not use a recording device for most of my interactions and, thus, do not include lengthy quotations. Instead, I use shorter quotes and paraphrases drawn from what I could reasonably write down inside the dimly lit and loud nightclub. I found that my particular information-gathering methods helped me to experience the moment-to-moment process of the nightclub and other sites.

Club Atlantis was not located in the gay commercial district of Baltimore city. Patrons often told me that the nightclub seemed to exist in a world of its own. One of the organizers of Baltimore's gay pride festivities, an activist named Jim Williams was quoted as saying, "For a lot of us regulars, the *Atlantis* was like a neighborhood bar, especially on Sundays. It has that same friendly atmosphere you expected from a neighborhood bar" (Chase, 2004). Two longtime patrons, Jack and Harry, told me that the club was like a "closed space." When I asked them to clarify what they meant, they replied that the club felt like a space reserved for regulars like themselves. While *Atlantis* was not a private club, patrons often told me that the club's distance from the gay commercial district, its close proximity to prisons, and its partial concealment under a freeway made it *seem* like a private establishment.

I originally set out to examine the kind of erotic performance that occurred at a place with *Club Atlantis'* peculiar geography. Little did I know that patrons' perception of the nightclub as a closed space had as much to do with its racial politics as with its location. *Club Atlantis* was not always hospitable to a black American writer who had resettled in Baltimore city. Akin to Plato's dialogue and Auden's poem, *Club Atlantis* was about the ways that myths and fantasies penetrate reality. It also was about the uncomfortable combination of geography, money, race, and sex.

I witnessed the frequently unwelcome posture of the nightclub's all-white older management and their anti-black and anti-Latino jokes; their refusal to hire black performers; the insularity of the predominately white patrons; and the tendency of many dancers to ignore me at the bar because they assumed I would not tip. These kinds of biases were taken for granted in a way that made me realize–all over again–how much racial politics are not just fringe issues in sex work but core concerns.

Yet, should I fault the men with whom I interacted for their perceptions and actions? After all, many of the white working class regulars had bonded for over 24 years at *Club Atlantis*. The bias that I felt was covert, hard-to-pin-down; subtle yet pervasive. Being ignored in a place where the performers are paid to interact with you is not the same as being physically or verbally attacked. Further, most patrons and dancers, told me that jibes and exclusions were "just jokes; all in good fun; not meant to harm." At *Club Atlantis* I found myself divided: reveling in its sexual expression, yet critical of its racial divisions. How did the environment of the club become so toxic that the pleasure of my spectatorship was diminished and it became impossible for me to "just get over it" as one bartender half-jokingly said?

Bringing up racial politics in a sex-charged environment where naked men were all-but masturbating on top of the bar was, for some dancers, a threat to their livelihood. I had several interactions with one performer who later told me that I was ruining his ability to "stay focused on business." When I asked him what he meant, he pointed to his genitals and his hands to indicate that he was referring to the work of appearing sexually aroused enough to get tips. Even though the nights that I visited were on Tuesdays and Wednesdays, when very few patrons sat at the bar and the nightclub was nearly empty, the manager would often berate dancers if they spent too much time dancing in front of me.

One performer named Rod said that he once asked the manager why dancers were scolded for talking with me. Rod told me that the manager felt he could not ban me from the club because it was illegal and because I paid to enter the establishment. But he *could* make it difficult for me to interact with the performers. When I tried to ask the manager about his own experience at the nightclub and about its hiring policies, he consistently ignored me. Some dancers claimed that the manager was always gruff and rarely expressive towards people he did not know, while others said that the manager was probably even more guarded around me because my questions unearthed the uncomfortable issue of race.

It seemed that in order for the patrons and dancers at *Club Atlantis* to accept me, I had to conform to their assumptions. More often than not, the chief (and false) assumptions were that I was either criminal or the kind of black person who has an unnatural fascination with white men. So entrenched were these assumptions that even when I interacted with the few blacks that passed through the nightclub, they sometimes shared these views. During my visits I saw four black patrons, one man whom I thought was Asian and no one that I thought was Latin American. The U.S. Census Bureau (2003) notes that Baltimore city is predominately African American and that neighborhoods in the city are divided along racial lines. How did the racial politics of *Club Atlantis* embody the city's own cultural divisions?

When I worked as a facilitator in a gay youth group during my teens, I was told that white gay men and lesbian women are less racially exclusionary than heterosexual men and women because of the pronounced discrimination they face. Yet, to date, everything in my life has shown that gay American worlds, regardless of race and class, are extremely divisive racially. What can be called *mainstream gay media*– magazines, newspapers, and even pornography–overwhelmingly favor the depiction of whites. When dark-skinned men or blacks are depicted in pornography they are marked as exceptions or even aberrations in a manner in which the very race of blacks is habitually over-sexualized (Westcott, 2004).

My visits to *Club Atlantis* left me with questions that I still find hard to answer. Is not all commercial erotica by definition a celebration of stereotypes, myths and fantasies? Wasn't *Club Atlantis* a place where the metaphysical property of synecdoche is a basic operation: where customers necessarily see *parts for the whole* and intentionally revel in erotic exclusion and inclusion? In this context, do I have a right not to be subjected to bias? Do I have a right to see erotic performance that does not objectify and hyper-sexualize individuals along racial lines?

Often dancers and patrons thought that my presence at the nightclub meant that I was exclusively sexually attracted to white men. Assumptions about interracial attractions seemed to overlap with white dancers and patrons' subtle racism. These assumptions raised other hard-to-answer questions: Are sexual attractions outside the realm of social justice? Is social justice outside the realm of the erotic?

In my first experiences at the nightclub in 1994 and 2002, two ideas—the stigma of cross-racial desire and the presence of racism—seemed to feed on each other. I do not remember what precisely brought me to the nightclub in 1994 while I was studying at a university in Baltimore city. I had worked as a novelty burlesque dancer off and on since I was seventeen years old. I also danced, sang and acted in floorshows, revues, and magic shows at hotels and on cruise ships to put myself through university. I was accustomed to commercial performance, be it erotic or not, and once I heard about *Club Atlantis* and decided to go out alone to socialize, I probably much preferred its brand of entertainment to that offered in a traditional bar. During my visit in 1994, I do remember noticing that the dancers performed in g-string underpants rather than in the nude. My sole interaction at the nightclub was with a bartender who said, as he passed me in the bathroom, "You know we don't let pool sharks in here." He did not seem to be joking. I remember immediately thinking to myself: What on earth about my appearance made him think that I was a pool shark? Isn't a pool shark a kind of thief? Did he make such an assumption because I was a solitary young black person who had entered a predominately white gay nightclub?

Reminiscent of DeMarco's (1983) description of what was once the widespread bigoted "carding" of blacks at many (though certainly not all) predominately white American gay bars and clubs before the 1980s, the doorman of *Atlantis* spent an inordinate amount of time perusing my ID. Things had not changed in the 21st century. Each time I visited in 2002 and 2003, various doormen consistently asked for, and painstakingly checked, my identification, turning over my card in their hands while glancing up at my face. Even when they clearly recognized me and acknowledged my presence as a repeat customer; even when I stood behind a group of white men of comparable age (who were invariably let inside without any presentation of identification), the doormen never, ever failed to check my credentials. While I would like to be flattered by the assumption that I was deemed too young to enter the nightclub, the covert exclusion and surveillance always carried the same hurt that being assumed to be a pool shark did in 1994. By the end of 2003, I learned to have my identification card out of my pocket and in my hand ready to be seen when I stepped up to the doorman.

The exclusionary door check at the *Atlantis* felt different than the sometimes ruthless door checks at the *Shampoo* nightclub in Philadelphia or the now-defunct *Limelight* in New York City where, regardless of race, if you were not on the guest list, or bizarrely attired or just plain "hot" to the doormen, you would not be let inside. *Club Atlantis*, a purported neighborhood club, seemed to have no illusions of nightlife grandeur like the large pansexual establishments in Philadelphia and New York City. Yet, there was something about its sensibility as a neighborhood club that seemed, in its own way, exclusionary.

When I returned after nine years to *Club Atlantis* on December 31st, 2001 in search for entertainment on New Year's Eve, it was not the carding ritual that I remember most. Instead, I recall that the only other black person in the nightclub–a short, heavy-set, quite funny, and effeminate man who some dancers claimed worked as a female impersonator and everyone seemed to call "Miss Oprah"–asked, cooing into my ear: "Here for the white boys, huh?"

What fascinated me most about Miss Oprah's question was that it seemed to provide insight into what I assumed was the nightclub's atmosphere as a whites-preferred space. Was Miss Oprah attempting to bond with me by commenting on the lack of blacks in attendance? This seemed to be the case and I wish that I had interviewed Miss Oprah further and inquired about his experience. His question seemed to function simultaneously as an invitation to bond; a recognition of *Club Atlantis* as a whites-preferred space; and a caustic half-put-down that made light of my apparent exclusive attraction to white men.

Miss Oprah's question exposed the extent to which assumptions about interracial attractions played themselves out in my visits to the nightclub. I often wondered if many blacks that frequent mostly white gay bars and nightclubs identify themselves as being exclusively attracted to white men. Or was this perception about class as much as race? Was I perceived in this way because I spoke with the diction I probably learned in a military boarding school: clipped and syntactically clear (as far as I can tell)? Sometimes, in my experience, when a black person does not use slang or speak with what is assumed to be a black urban or rural vernacular, they are thought to align themselves more with whites than blacks. When I was an adolescent, even some blacks called me "proper" and asked why I was "acting white" when I spoke.

Whatever the cause, it seemed that the assumption of exclusive attraction to whites was so enduring that black and white patrons and dancers alike marked me in this manner. When a dancer named Gene asked if I was "one of those blacks who are into whites," I told him that, on the contrary, my sexual experiences with white people were far fewer than my experiences with black people and I hadn't a clue why. Furthermore, things are not always what they seem: For not only am I a bisexual person whose only truly long term relationship has been with a bisexual woman, but I cannot imagine having limits and exclusions to my attractions. While I was drawn to erotic performance, my actual sexual contacts were few and far between. I told him that limiting myself by race excludes sizeable numbers of quite diverse people and those exclusions are fueled by assumptions and stereotypes that operate under the surface of declarations like "it's just my preference."

After I said these things, Gene asked me: "Then why are you here?" At the time, I had an answer: "Because I'm fascinated by nude dancers, and dancing in general, and I would be even more fascinated if there were a variety of races beyond only white dancers." But, after speaking with Gene, I was less sure: Did I have stereotypes and curiosities of white men that I wished to see played out in nude dancing? Today, tentatively, I would answer that I have sexual curiosities about a variety of different people regardless of gender and race. Further, I honestly feel that my sense of self-interrogation makes me question stereotypes even when they arise within me.

Most of the dancers were not as confrontational as Gene. One in particular–Max–was a study in shyness. Max was tall–well over six feet three inches by my estimate. His shyness and his height made go-go dancing at *Club Atlantis* a hazard. The low ceiling of the nightclub forced Max to stoop when he danced. Further, instead of dancing, Max would lumber slowly around, picking his way among shot glasses, beer mugs, elbows and hands until the rare time when he saw someone that excited him. When he was not fixated on a particular man that he found attractive, he was sullen and serious, only nodding his head in silent greetings to customers sitting at the bar. He seemed to have no aptitude for chatting up patrons to score better tips.

I once overheard a customer say that the long, straight, dark brown hair that flopped around Max's ears showed no respect for fashion. The customer was right. Max did not sport the "Caesar cut" that was so popular among the dancers, and among many white gay men in Baltimore. Max's long nose, pale skin, and lean build were all marvels of ordinariness. While there were a number of brown-haired performers at the nightclub, there seemed to be a preference for looks that underscored certain fantasies of whiteness: namely, blonde, thin, small-framed bodies (or the physicality of "twinks" as such looks are labeled in some gay male communities). Max's appearance–unstudied, dark, and "out of fashion"– made him stand out.

Invariably, the patrons that seemed to please Max were thin, dark-haired, young white men in their early twenties who occasionally wandered into the bar alone or with friends. When a man caught his fancy, Max lowered his great body into a squat and rocked slowly from side to side in a quiet effort to conceal his erection. He might not have bothered for, when it became erect, his thick penis curved so far downward that it nearly tucked between his legs. Max's private, shy world and physical remove from the looks valued at the nightclub fascinated me.

Since Max began working at *Club Atlantis*, I had noticed that regular customers would sometimes joke about his sullenness and move away from the bar when he came their way. Yet, while other customers ignored him and he interacted only fleetingly with white customers, I and a few other black patrons were the only ones that Max completely ignored. Dancers had to pass directly in front of every customer as they navigated around the bar, and when a dancer chose to ignore a customer, he did so conspicuously.

On the first Tuesday of November 2003, I decided to ask Max why he always passed by me without even nodding a greeting. When he came my way, I waved and smiled as demonstratively as I could. Even though the nightclub was nearly empty, he looked around to check that I was in fact waving to him. Then he came over and squatted down in front of me. I tipped him the entire quota of $1 bills that I had set aside for tips during his set. He said that he had not seen me at the *Atlantis* before. I sensed he knew that I could tell he was lying. I told him that I visited twice a month, mostly on Tuesdays because I was writing about the nightclub and could not afford the higher cover charge on weekends. He apologized for ignoring me and reached out to shake my hand.

Max was far more personable than I could have imagined, and after a few minutes, I asked him why he did not acknowledge me as he did other customers. He seemed disturbed by my question and tried to explain that the manager did not permit him to linger in front of any one customer for too long. "I'm sorry if the question offended you," I told him and, for good measure, I stuffed a few more dollar bills into his socks.

After exchanging our first names, he asked what I did for a living. "I'm a writer," I reminded him. He said, "Oh, you really *are* writing about the club." Then he added, "Well, I'm a closet freak." By "freak" he did not seem to mean "odd," but sexually adventurous, and the inflections in his voice registered that he was trying to speak in black slang. I asked him if he noticed that I did not use black American slang. Max laughed and said that I was "too polite." Then he tried to explain that he thought I would understand him better if he talked that way. I offered that, "I'm open to any way that you choose to speak to me."

When he came off the bar between sets, Max told me that he was studying at the University of Maryland at Baltimore County. I suspected that he was a college student but his age–twenty-five–confused me. As it turned out, after getting a woman pregnant, he dropped out of college because he could not focus on his studies. The child was stillborn. He became depressed and spent two years in a "haze," as he said, working on computers. He then reenrolled to complete his degree. For Max, go-go dancing was "college money," and he found out about the job through an advertisement in a gay newspaper that said "Always hiring male strippers." After talking about his history for a while, I asked him why he believed that I wouldn't tip. He answered honestly, saying, "That's what all the other dancers say: that blacks don't tip."

Here the reality of biased assumptions seemed to impinge on fantasy. It was impossible for me to participate in the environment without my race being an unstated liability. Even if I wanted to, I could not make fantasy precede the reality of my black identity. When Max finally spoke to me, he talked in what he thought was black slang, and he did this though I gave no indication that I spoke this idiom. It seemed that Max's interactions with me were guided by racial considerations.

Something about the history and geography of *Club Atlantis* seemed to make it amenable to social divisions. I asked Jack and Harry how the nightclub fit into the history of gay nightlife in the city. Our conversation quickly turned to the nightclub's close proximity to Baltimore's red light district and crowded, predominately black prisons.

Jack told me that the two friends were "bosom buddies, and not lovers," and "well past fifty years old." They both grew up in south Baltimore in all-white working class neighborhoods and had been regular patrons at the *Atlantis* for over 20 years. On a visit to the *Atlantis* on January 21, 2003, Harry and Jack patiently explained to me that Baltimore's downtown gay neighborhood proliferated in what they called "the usual way around the late 1970s." Gay men from other areas in the city or from all across the state of Maryland were searching for safer environments in which to live and play. Besides a greater sense of safety and a growing openness about their sexuality in the 1970s, no one knows why so many men turned to the area two blocks North of the Walters Art Gallery on North Charles Street to buy or rent houses and apartments, or open restaurants, art galleries, boutiques, bookstores, discos, and bars. Soon, the gay neighborhood became gentrified. The gay commercial district in Baltimore city is called Mount Vernon, and it is located between Madison and Chase along North Charles Street fifteen blocks North of the once thriving shipping docks that Baltimore residents call the Inner Harbor. Today, many artists and students–especially musicians who train at John Hopkins University's Peabody Music Conservatory–cannot afford the high cost of living in the gay neighborhood.

Jack said that the rise of a distinct gay neighborhood may have been assisted by Baltimore's first black American mayor, Kurt Schmoke, who during his unprecedented three terms in office from 1987 to 1999, laid the foundation for the revitalization of the entire downtown area from the docks to Mount Royal Avenue. Harry disagreed with his friend and said that it was really in 1978 when the Chase Brexton Clinic opened that the neighborhood began to feel like a "gay ghetto." Jack countered and said that the word "gay Mecca was more appropriate." Then he asked me to "please put the words 'gay Mecca' in your paper. Just because gay people get together doesn't mean they are in a ghetto."

Both men agreed that the rise of AIDS in the mid-1980s played the biggest role in the creation of Baltimore's gay neighborhood. Originally, Chase Brexton Clinic was set up to provide STI testing and treatment to gay men. I asked Harry what kind of gay men sought treatment at the clinic and lived in Mount Vernon. Were they mostly white gay men? "Yes," he answered and then without prompting said, "And it wasn't racist. That's just the way it was then." When I asked him to explain, he said that at the time, the idea of "a gay neighborhood" really meant "white gay men" and "not even lesbians." He added: "As far as I know, no one was treating lesbians for a disease at the Chase Brexton." Harry went on to say that today the Chase Brexton Clinic is separate from the gay community center, which is called The Gay, Lesbian, Bisexual and Transgendered Center because he joked, "Apparently drag queens don't want to take off their dresses after they perform at the *Hippo* on Saturday night." (The *Hippo* is one of the largest gay discos in town.)

I asked them if they knew anything about The Black Gay, Lesbian, Bisexual and Transgendered Community Center at 302 Park Ave. in West Baltimore. Neither of them had heard of Baltimore's black

American gay community center. Then Harry said, "That's part of the problem. Why do some gay black people want to separate themselves?" I asked them whether white gay men may be considered separatist if they choose, as often happens, to date, socialize, and live amongst other white gay men. Jack said, "But what if it's just the way it happens?" He explained that people grow up around the same kinds of people and you have to really go out of your way to live differently. But, I pressed him, why are the blacks who opened the black gay community center any more separatist than the predominately white men who proliferated in Mount Vernon? Jack broke off our conversation and said–and I smile every time I remember that moment–"Time for another round." I bought their drinks that night and, as the evening wore on and race inevitably arose in our conversation, our interaction became tense, but amicable.

I asked them how the *Atlantis* fits into the history of Baltimore's gay neighborhood. Jack tried to explain to me that, "The *Atlantis* fits and it doesn't fit. It really isn't in the gay part of town." But, I remind him, neither is the city's gay leather bar, the *Baltimore Eagle* at 2022 North Charles Street; nor are the two West Baltimore gay bars that cater primarily to black American male clientele: *Sportsman* at 410 Park Avenue one block from the main public library and *Club Bunns* at 608 W. Lexington Street. "But those places are different," said Jack. I asked them if these other establishments are "different" because the bars and clubs in Mount Vernon represent mainstream gay nightlife. "Of course," Jack told me. "There is always a mainstream for any lifestyle and the *Atlantis* is not mainstream." Harry said that they also patronize the *Eagle* with its backroom sex space and that "they must not be mainstream" if they go to the *Atlantis* and the *Eagle*.

As if to preempt my question, Jack said that they don't go to the black bars because he just didn't think he would fit in with anyone there and that it's uncomfortable to be the only one of certain kinds of people at a place. He added that there is nothing wrong with his opinion. I agreed. I also thought to myself that it was fascinating to hear a white man acknowledge the discomfort of being the only one of a certain race or one of a few in a particular environment. I wondered if he also knew that there were times when it seemed that I *had* to put myself into predominately white spaces to do the most basic of things, from banking to teaching. Is it not the majority's luxury to avoid potential discomforts?

Jack went on to tell me that one of the things that makes the *Atlantis* different is that it has always been a hustler bar and right on the edge of legality: "All these boys," he said, gesturing to the dancers, "are for sale and some are cheap." Harry chimed in that he could tell me which dancers had drug habits, which ones would "trick in the bathroom" and which ones ran escort ads in the back of the gay paper. He added, "I'm not even Alexander St. John." (Alexander St. John is the pseudonym for a local gay entertainer who writes a gossip column for one of the city's gay papers, and regularly visited the *Atlantis*.) "But," I whispered, "The dancers can't *all* be sex workers." Harry and Jack did not share my disbelief and they both laughed. "Look," Jack said, "most of these guys are 'gay for pay.' Taking off your clothes for money to a bunch of old gay men *is* what you call sex work."

Harry and Jack both agreed that the *Atlantis* is more akin to the go-go bars and peep show palaces that run along East Baltimore Street five minutes South of Fallsway. This once thriving, nearly ten-block long heterosexual red light district was the first stop for sailors on shore leave at the docks from the turn of the 20th century into the 1970s. Then, "The Block," as everyone in town calls it, began a gradual decline. Porn theaters and large burlesque houses closed down in rapid succession. The Block is now only two blocks long, and all activity literally dead-ends into a small division of the main police department building. The 2004 opening of the *Larry Flynt Hustler Club* with its huge, black and pink neon marquee may trigger a period of revitalization for The Block. The timing of the sale of the *Atlantis* and its eventual transformation into an upscale heterosexual go-go club may capitalize on this revitalization.

It is not only the comparison of the *Atlantis* to the establishments on The Block that fascinates me. It is Harry and Jack's contention that the *Atlantis* is situated in one of the worst locations in the city–between prison complexes and the main police booking center. Maybe, I tell them, the gay owner of the *Atlantis* thought that its location–literally on the fringes of the law–was its best protection in a mostly working class city where male stripping was rare. Jack said that, after over 20 years of relatively undisturbed business, my suspicion could well be true. But, surprisingly, Harry also interjected stinging words: "It's the animals on death row that just kill me." Then he added that, "Sometimes you can't get into bar [the *Atlantis*] without them yelling from their cells at you." I asked them what the prisoners were yelling. Harry said, "The usual nasty things" but that "like rap stars you can never understand fully what they're saying." While his comment about rap stars conveyed subtle bias, I was not offended. I, too, cannot tell what some rappers are saying in their songs, and I understood his fear of prisoners.

Harry and Jack's condemnation of the death row prisoners drew the attention of Ron, a small, dirty-blonde haired dancer who had finished his set. Ron laughed and said that most of the guys on death row are there because they raped or killed someone anyway. I wondered if Harry, Jack, or Ron knew anything about the politics of capital punishment in Baltimore city. But I was afraid to ask. A month before I spoke with these men, I had a conversation with Gene, one of the few overtly muscular, *Chippendales*-style weekend dancers at the nightclub who was working a rare shift during the week. Gene fascinated me because his girlfriend–who Gene said was a stripper herself in the county outside the city–waited for him inside their car in the parking lot while he worked at the nightclub.

Similar to Harry, Jack and Ron, Gene complained about death row. I began to tell Gene the story of Kenny Collins, a longtime black American death row inmate. The main witness against Collins, Andre Thorpe, later called Collin's attorney and admitted that he lied under oath in order to help convict Collins. Gene said that hearing what he called my "self-righteous" commentary was like "sniffing Clorox [bleach]," and he further noted that he was at the *Atlantis* to make money and have a good time. "Who cares," he said, "about death row when you [*sic*] up here [dancing on the bar at the *Atlantis*]?"

I have joined protests with white men against Maryland's capital punishment policies, and I realize that Harry, Jack, Ron, and Gene's harsh sentiments were not only a measure of their white identity. But Harry and Jack explained to me early in our conversation that they were born in a poor, white South Baltimore neighborhood. One of the reasons why they abhorred the newer bars in Mount Vernon was because they thought some of the other white gay men[3] were "uppity." As well, they complained about the over-emphasis on youth and appearance at the bars in Mount Vernon. They also noted that they did not identify with the black poor of Baltimore city or associate with any blacks. What was it that made Harry and Jack view themselves as transgressing mainstream middle-class white gay life in Baltimore at the same time that they did not usually associate with blacks?

Unlike Gene who said, "Who cares?" about the death row inmates, I found that I could hardly get the idea of death row and its striking closeness to the nightclub out of my mind. I *do* care about the way that many black Americans are treated when they encounter law enforcement. One experience, during the course of my visits to the *Club Atlantis*, may explain why. Three months before I talked with Gene for the first time, when I stepped outside at the end of an evening at the *Atlantis*, a police officer drove up silently behind me, flashed his lights and stopped me in the parking lot of the nightclub. He told me to sit on my hands on the tarmac while he ran a background check from his car. The officer chatted about women's bodies with two other police officers that came to his assistance. He took his time. The ordeal lasted forty-five minutes. What was my transgression that evening? It seemed to the officer that I was tampering with one of the cars of a patron of *Club Atlantis*, when all I had done was squat down to pick up a bag that I had dropped next to a vehicle. The officer did not think that I was a customer at *Club Atlantis* and, consequently, his treatment of me seemed racist and not homonegative.[4]

The customers and dancers passed by me, as they left the *Atlantis* at the end of the night. I tried to explain to the officers that I was a patron and I urged the customers and dancers with whom I had been speaking to vouch for me. None did. Were the customers afraid of possible homonegative treatment from police as they hurried out of the nightclub? Were they afraid that their identities would be revealed? Finally, one of the bartenders, a heterosexual man, came out and confirmed that I was a customer at the nightclub. Did the doorman fail to recognize me and call the police when he saw me stooping down beside one of the cars in the *Atlantis* parking lot? Was the incident racial profiling or over-zealous precaution? I have socialized with a few other black people at the *Atlantis*. Did anything similar happen to them? Before the nightclub's sudden closing, I never had the chance to pose these questions to other blacks that frequented the *Atlantis*. Indeed, my inability to find answers to many of my questions only exacerbates the sense of quiet helplessness that I feel in the face of these issues.

Gene thought I was being "self-righteous" about the politics of capital punishment but my aim was to draw attention to the credible research on the problem of black disenfranchisement in Maryland's implementation of the death penalty. Capital punishment was often in the news during the time period that I visited *Club Atlantis*. In the January 8, 2003 edition of a political newsletter called *CounterPunch*, Cassel reasoned that, "[w]hen [the] outgoing Maryland Governor Parris Glendening put a hold on all executions and commissioned a report on the administration of the death penalty in 2000, he was primarily concerned with finding out the answer to one question: [in Maryland] Is the death penalty more often imposed when the murder victim is white and the defendant black?"

After the State of Maryland released their report in January of 2003, the answer to this question turned out to be a resounding "yes." A January

7, 2003 press release from the National Coalition to Abolish the Death Penalty (NCADP) announced that:

> Of the 12 people currently on Maryland's death row, eight are black and four are white, and every person on death row was convicted in connection with the murder of a white victim. This is despite the fact that in recent years about 80 percent of homicides in the state of Maryland involve black victims. (American Civil Liberties Union, 2004)

The late 1990s were distinguished by an increased attention to what many gay and lesbian scholars called the "intersection" of race, class, and sexuality (Harper, Munoz, & Rosen, 1997). For me, nothing embodied the living reality of this intersection more than my overwhelming impression that, "I cared about death row" when I was at the *Atlantis*. When I sat on the tarmac in the parking lot some twenty-five yards from death row and just one minute from the police department's Central Booking Center, I viscerally understood the ways in which the racial politics of crime in the city inform both the *Atlantis*' geography and the ideology of its patrons. In one instant, I became emblematic of this pathology and, in effect, was uninvited from the premises.

After my 2003 chat with Harry and Jack, I stood outside of the nightclub at the end of the evening. The two men had said good night and already left in their cars. Standing there I realized that these two very personable gentlemen and I parted company in more ways than one. I remembered that a year earlier in February 2002, I had walked East beyond the *Atlantis*' parking lot. I was following what were probably the same muffled voices of the prisoners that Harry and Jack would refer to in my conversation with them the following year. As it turns out, the muffled cries came from the old correctional facility on the *other* side of the building where death row is housed. The muffled voices became more distinct as I walked closer to this other building. To my surprise, I found that the prisoners were talking at the top of their voices to two stout black women on the street. The women were calling out what seemed like the prisoners' names and making promises to visit. Over the next several months, as winter turned to spring, I found that these street-level visitations around the perimeter of the prison facility increased. I suspect that what Harry and Jack thought were muffled epithets being levied against them from the men on death row were, in reality, the greetings and endearments of an entirely different set of prisoners directed at visitors around the high walls of the old penitentiary.

If *Club Atlantis* exists in a world set apart from mainstream gay nightlife in Baltimore–and, for that matter, from all nightlife and sexual cultures in the city–then it truly may be a mythic "lost world." Yet, to be fair, *Club Atlantis* is not the only lost world divided along racial lines in the nightlife of the city. On Wednesday nights, I sometimes went to *Club Bunns*–one of the oldest continuously black (and black gay) owned nightclubs in the Northeast–for their all-black male stripper show.

Bunns is a neighborhood bar, with a mostly working class black American clientele and a few white and Asian men. The Wednesday night revue with the "Ghetto Boys" is a dynamic affair. In a small stage space, the nude dancers come out, strip, and, one by one, perform truly amazing acrobatic feats including sustained balances on both hands. A drag queen often acts as master of ceremonies offering outlandish off-color jokes between sets. Or a local male comedian will perform an *entr'acte*, cooling the sexual heat with jibes about bad fish at the Lexington Market two blocks away. The music is a fast, syncopated mix of 70s and 80s black soul music and hip-hop classics. Here, I always think, is a stripper show that emphasizes a variety of performance more akin to classic mid-20th century all-female vaudevillian burlesque entertainments. Yet even at *Bunns*, I am somehow separate. (I do not know any upscale, gay nightclubs in Baltimore that cater to wealthy men, regardless of race.) Though I was raised poor and my entry level teaching salary hardly makes me wealthy, when I order a drink, my speech (if I don't attempt slang) marks me as a visitor to an establishment bound as much by class as it is by race.

All of my experiences raise deeper questions about how we conceive sexuality and identity, fantasy and reason. I began by remarking that the myth of the island of Atlantis first appeared in Plato's dialogues, *Timaeus* and *Critias*. The fact is never lost on me that *Timaeus* begins with Socrates urging three scholars–Critias, Timaeus and Hermocrates–to describe an "ideal state and its citizens" (Plato, trans. 1971). (The characters in Plato's philosophical dialogues are imagined representations of actual thinkers who lived prior to or within Plato's time.) It is in his answer to Socrates that Critias describes the mythic island of Atlantis. Yet, as the title of the dialogue makes clear, the bulk of the text is set within the voice of Timaeus. Critias' brief account of Atlantis precedes Timaeus' far more extended discussion of the relationship between *being* and *becoming*–between rational understanding and knowledge drawn from the senses. Timaeus argues that a *form* or an *essence* exists behind real objects and experiences. In this late dialogue, Plato further develops the theory of "forms" that so distinguished his earlier political dialogue *The Republic*.

Aristotle took Plato to task for the imprecision of his teacher's definitions. While Plato believed that we are born with the capacity for rational exchange already formulated within us, Aristotle understood that we gain knowledge through our acts and experiences. These very old philosophical disagreements are still with us as we try to reconcile fundamental questions of nature versus nurture. Can social spaces like *Club Atlantis* achieve a reasoned sense of integration and still celebrate fantasy? Am I, are we, ruled by the seeming inexplicability of attractions and assumptions?

Without answers to these questions, I feel as unfinished as *Club Atlantis* was at the time of its premature closing. Remarkably, at the end of the poem by W.H Auden with which I began, the speaker never gets to the city of Atlantis. He gazes at the glittering city from outside its walls. Like the speaker in Auden's poem, I am left with the sense that I never actually made it to Atlantis, to a place of unfettered fantasy. Even before the nightclub was sold, what was it that made *Club Atlantis* closed to me?

NOTES

1. The nightclub was featured in John Waters' film *Pecker* (1998, New Line Studios).

2. Another reason why off-tape interactions proved to be the best approach was that the dancers and other staff *were working*. Some understandably wanted money that I did not have for off-site interviews. Instead I talked with dancers between sets, tipping an average of $3 to $5 a set when a dancer performed in front of me (but not paying for "private shows" or off-site interviews), and conducted informal interviews.

3. Harry and Jack's comments about this issue were restricted to white men.

4. Of course, one can not ignore the possibility that the police officer's homonegativity compounded his racism.

REFERENCES

American Civil Liberties Union (September, 2004). The death penalty in Maryland: University of Maryland study. Retrieved between January and February 2003, from http://www.aclu.org/DeathPenalty/DeathPenalty.cfm?ID=16518&c=62.

Auden, W. H. (1976). *Collected poems*. New York, NY: Vintage Books.

Cassel, E. (2003, January). Maryland's death penalty. Retrieved between January and February 2003, from http://www.counterpunch.org/cassel01082003.html.

Chase, M. (2004, August 2004). Club Atlantis sale pending. *Baltimore Outloud*, pp. 2-3.

DeMarco, J. R. G. (1983). Gay racism. In M. J. Smith (Ed.), *Black men, white men: Afro-American gay life and culture* (p. 110). San Francisco, CA: Gay Sunshine Press.

Harper, P. B., Munoz, J. E., & Rosen, T. (1997). *Queer transexions of race, nation, and gender*. Durham, NC: Duke University Press.

U.S. Census Bureau. (2003). *Maryland quick facts: Baltimore City*. Retrieved between January and February 2003, from http://quickfacts.census.gov/qfd/states/24/24510.html.

Westcott, C. N. (2004). Alterity and construction of national identity in three Kristen Bjorn films. *Journal of Homosexuality, 47*(3/4), 189-196.

doi:10.1300/J082v53n01_07

ON THE NET AND BEYOND

Porn Star/Stripper/Escort:
Economic and Sexual Dynamics
in a Sex Work Career

Jeffrey Escoffier

SUMMARY. This article explores the career dynamics of performers in the gay male pornography industry, by focusing on a common career path–from porn star to stripper to escort. Between 1995 and 2005, most men performing in gay porn films, unlike contract actresses in the straight porn industry, have been unable to earn enough income to work exclusively as performers in front of the camera. The industry's constant search for

Jeffrey Escoffier has written on sexuality, gay history, and dance. His most recent book is *Sexual Revolution* (Thunder's Mouth, 2003), an anthology of writings from the 1960s and '70s about sex. He is the author of *American homo: Community and perversity* (University of California Press, 1998), and *John Maynard Keynes* (Chelsea House, 1995). He edited, with Matthew Lore, *Mark Morris' l'allegro il penseroso ed il moderato: A celebration* (Marlow, 2001) on the choreography of Mark Morris. He is currently writing *Passport to fantasy*, an inside look at the gay porn industry, which will be published by Carroll and Graf in 2008. Correspondence may be addressed to Jeffrey Escoffier, 332 Bleecker Street, #K27, New York, NY 10014 (E-mail: jescoffier@msn.com).

[Haworth co-indexing entry note]: "Porn Star/Stripper/Escort: Economic and Sexual Dynamics in a Sex Work Career." Escoffier, Jeffrey. Co-published simultaneously in *Journal of Homosexuality* (The Haworth Press, Inc.) Vol. 53, No. 1/2, 2007, pp. 173-200; and: *Male Sex Work: A Business Doing Pleasure* (ed: Todd G. Morrison and Bruce W. Whitehead) The Haworth Press, Inc., 2007, pp. 173-200. Single or multiple copies of this article are available for a fee from The Haworth Document Delivery Service [1-800- HAWORTH, 9:00 a.m. - 5:00 p.m. (EST). E-mail address: docdelivery@haworthpress.com].

Available online at http://jh.haworthpress.com
© 2007 by The Haworth Press, Inc. All rights reserved.
doi:10.1300/J082v53n01_08

new faces and fresh performers creates what sociologist Paul Cressey has called "the retrogressive dynamic": The longer a person works in a sexual occupation, the less one is paid, and the lower the status of the work venue. In the porn industry, one aspect of this process is referred to as "overexposure," during which the performer experiences a diminishing "fantasy potential" as fans lose erotic interest in the porn star who has appeared too frequently in too many movies. Performers attempt to confront the retrogressive dynamic by limiting the number of adult films in which they appear in a year, diversifying their sexual repertoire, or shifting into other roles within the industry (behind the camera, marketing, production, etc.). One common option is to pursue work in economically complementary forms of sex work such as stripping and escorting. doi:10.1300/J082v53n01_08 *[Article copies available for a fee from The Haworth Document Delivery Service: 1-800-HAWORTH. E-mail address: <docdelivery@haworthpress.com> Website: <http://www.HaworthPress.com> © 2007 by The Haworth Press, Inc. All rights reserved.]*

KEYWORDS. Sex work, porn star, stripper, escort, pornography, gay porn industry, fantasy

INTRODUCTION

'Sex work' is a broad and rather vague term. Generally, it refers to work involving any kind of economic exchange for sexual services. While 'prostitution' is the classical term for such economic exchanges, 'sex work' has emerged as a more inclusive term for a wide range of occupations–everything from the street prostitute or escort to the phone sex 'actress,' stripper, or porn star. Thus, at times, journalists or even industry insiders identify the huge complex of businesses and individuals offering these services as 'the sex industry.' The services and products of the sex industry exist along a continuum: from pornographic videos which involve no direct interaction to phone sex, stripping, lap dancing, and prostitution, all of which involve some degree of interaction between customer and sex worker (Flowers, 1998; Frank, 2002; Liepe-Levinson, 2002; Plachy & Ridgeway, 1996; Weitzer, 2000).

There are a number of reasons why few aspects of the sex industry have been studied extensively. One reason is the stigma attached to sex work generally, and another is that access to sex workers is limited. The latter may reflect the fact that many people in the sex industry are self-employed and/or work for privately owned businesses (e.g., *Vivid Studios*, the largest producer of straight pornographic videos and *Falcon Studios*, long the most profitable producer of gay videos); hence, there are no publicly reported sales statistics, annual reports, or income data (Lane, 2001; Marvel, 2002). The third reason is that some of the industry's activities are, or have been, illegal or semi-legal. Indeed, certain activities–escorting is the best example–operate without explicitly alluding to their illegal status. This situation posed a dilemma in the composition of this article. I have referred to various performers who work as escorts indirectly, unless they have either publicly acknowledged working as escorts or advertised escorting services in local gay newspapers or on escorting Web sites. In this manner, I have observed the fine line between discretion and empirical verification.

Since so little research has been conducted on the gay porn industry, I have relied upon numerous sources that scholars may consider unconventional or, perhaps, even questionable. The most important of these is *Manshots* magazine, which between 1988 and 2002, when it ceased publication, operated as the 'magazine of record' for the U.S. gay porn industry. Over the course of its fourteen year history, it published almost 400 substantive interviews with performers and more than 130 interviews with directors and other assorted 'behind the scenes' personnel.[1] I have drawn on other magazines and Web sites, as well as more than fifty in-depth interviews that I have conducted since 2001 with individuals working in the gay porn business (including directors, film editors, producers, marketing directors, and performers). In addition, I have learned a great deal from both casual and formal conversations with people working in the industry. These interviews, conversations, and relationships have developed in the course of conducting research for a book on the gay porn industry. Much of the information and knowledge gleaned from these sources–such as personal conversations, Internet discussion boards, or popular magazines aimed at gay men–are not available in scholarly publications. I will cite such non-academic, though verifiable, sources whenever I can so that other researchers can critically examine them and test my arguments and conclusions.

Despite the huge revenues earned within the sex industry (revenues in the U.S. porn industry alone are estimated at $10 billion dollars a year), very little is known about the careers of people who work in it (Weitzer, 2000). The U.S. porn industry, according to one estimate, employs approximately 20,000 people–though it is unclear whether this figure includes occasional and part-time workers or just full-time equivalents (McNair, 2002). The gay porn business employs some fraction (arguing from standard estimates of the gay male population: 5-10%) of those working in the industry as a whole (Lauman, Gagnon, Michael, & Michaels, 1994). Although these figures are crude estimates, they are useful in suggesting that the overall number of people employed in all branches of the sex industry is much larger.

For many of the people employed in these jobs, sex work is a supplement to other forms of income. However, if it is a primary source of income, it usually lasts for a short period of time (months to several years). Thus, it may seem somewhat paradoxical to speak of careers in the sex industry. The concept of 'career' is usually applied to the sequence of jobs performed by individuals over the course of their work lives. However, Howard Becker (1963), Erving Goffman (1961), and others also have applied the term metaphorically to various stages in the development of social behavior that is not economic–such as the stages by which a person becomes a marijuana user, a patient in a mental hospital, a soldier, or a homosexual (Becker, 1963; Goffman, 1961). In this article, I will examine one set of interlocking sex-work roles that exists among performers in the gay porn industry and, in so doing, identify the key decision points and underlying sexual-economic dynamics of this career path. The set of interrelated jobs–'porn star-stripper-escort'–is one widely utilized by performers in the gay porn industry to create a more viable economic basis and, thus, constitutes a career, in both the occupational and sub-cultural senses of the term.[2]

PORN STAR: FANTASY AND HUMAN CAPITAL

Similar to movie stars or other celebrities, porn stars embody ideals and utopian fantasies and serve as cultural fetishes and commodified public figures. In the book, *Stars*, French philosopher Edgar Morin analyzes the psycho-cultural dynamics of stars and celebrities:

> The star becomes the food of dreams; the dream, unlike the ideal tragedy of Aristotle, does not purify us truly from our fantasies but betrays their obsessive presence; similarly the stars only partially provoke catharsis and encourage fantasies which would like to but cannot liberate themselves in action. Here the role of the star becomes 'psychotic'; it polarizes and fixes obsessions. (as cited in Dyer, 1998, p. 19)

Star personas crystallize both fantasies of identification (who we want to be) as well as fantasies of sexual desire (who we want)–a dynamic that is central to adult films (De Angelis, 2001; Rojek, 2001). In the complex dialectic between 'active subject' and passive 'object of desire,' most spectators of porn vacillate between the two positions, imagining themselves as both the active 'desiring' party and passive 'desired' object (Cowie, 1993).

The idea of the porn star owes a great deal to Hollywood and the star system that originated in the film industry in the 1920s and 30s. The star was and is both a featured performer and an iconic presence and, in the history of the movies, the making of 'stars' has exploited key aspects of film as a medium. Screen performers do not, like stage actors, create a role, but instead construct their personas and the roles they play as actors from their own psychological and physical characteristics (Braudy, 1977; Cavell, 1980, De Angelis, 2001; deCordova, 1990). As Braudy has pointed out:

> the film actor ... works on his self-image, carries it from part to part, constantly projecting the same thing–"himself." .... The stage actor .... project[s] a sense of holding back, of discipline and understanding, the influence of head over feelings, while the film actor projects effortlessness, nonchalance, immediacy, the seemingly unpremeditated response. (p. 197)

Thus, the emphasis on the 'role' in a theatrical production is replaced on the screen by the 'persona' with its sense of immediacy and its suggestion of 'authenticity'–a characteristic absolutely essential, I have argued, to the success of video porn. The porn star's persona is like a character, but it is his 'character'; one that he takes, at least partially, from his own sense of self (i.e., porn film as a medium requires certain 'reality effects' such as erections and orgasms) and from a certain projection of a marketable sustainable role (top, bottom, sex pig, etc.) across various movies (Escoffier, 2003a).

In the early days of the movie industry, stars were relied upon to distinguish between the films of various studios. Stars were an important means by which to promote and market the films of a studio. Each star offered a distinct personality and style which branded the studio that employed him or her. While stars exist in other performance media such as music, theater, or dance, movie stars in particular achieved wide recognition among the mass audience created by the film industry.

The *persona* of a star is constructed around the personality and performance of an individual, but 'star' also is a complex social role. The 'star' is an iconic *image* that signifies something about sexuality and gender and represents a distinctive personality or type. Also the star is a *worker*, a person who earns his or her income as a performer. Last, but certainly not least, the star is an economic asset, an investment or a form of *human capital* for the studio or company that has him or her under contract (Becker, 1964; Dyer, 1998). In addition, for the individual star, 'star quality' is something that can be consciously developed and is highly marketable. Stars are an essential component of the making and marketing of movies. Stars sell movies; they are marketing tools that help to stimulate and stabilize the demand for films.

The term 'star' is implicitly a term of value; not every movie actor is a star. However, in the porn industry–at least in the gay porn industry– 'porn star' is often used much more broadly and loosely. Almost every performer in a pornographic film is termed a porn *star*–at least to fans and viewers–though industry insiders generally use the term 'model' to refer to the performers in adult films.

Since its beginning years in the early 1970s, the gay porn business has created several generations of porn stars who became popular icons among gay men (Thomas, 2002). Casey Donovan, the star of Wakefield Poole's *Boys in the Sand* and Jerry Douglas' *The Back Row*, was the first gay porn superstar. He made 21 films between 1970 and 1986. Well-educated, culturally sophisticated, and sexually versatile, Donovan resembled and aptly represented the liberated gay man residing in New York City in the 1970s (Edmonson, 1998). Another iconic figure of early gay porn was Al Parker, who represented the bearded masculine man in a work shirt and jeans–an image that became the dominant gay male style ('the clone') of the late 70s and early 80s. Like Donovan, Parker was sexually versatile (Edmonson, 2000).

By the mid-1980s, a new type of gay porn superstar emerged in the person of Jeff Stryker. Identified as straight, Stryker was primarily known for his large penis. He performed exclusively as a top, was passive in oral sex, and did not engage in kissing (Spencer, 1998). Ryan Idol, a superstar of the late-1980s and early 1990s, was similarly identified as straight (Groff, 1998). Among the few 'gay' men who approached 'superstar' status in the mid-eighties were Leo Ford, Jon King, and Joey Stefano. Both King and Stefano were exclusively or primarily bottoms (Fairbanks, 1996; Isherwood, 1996). Ford's career was cut short by his death in a motorcycle accident (d. 1991), Stefano's from a drug overdose (d. 1994) and King's by his incarceration for auto theft, and death from AIDS shortly after resuming his career (d. 1995).

* * *

In the mid-1980s, the market for gay porn was booming. The new video technology and the extensive ownership of VCRs had lowered the cost of production and made pornography more accessible. It also became cheaper to purchase and easier to rent. Thus, pornography was more likely to be viewed in the privacy of one's home. The AIDS crisis reinforced this privatized experience, with some gay men turning to video porn in lieu of sex with another man (Fenwick, 1988). However, by the mid-1990s, the market for gay porn had experienced some set backs and the Internet was beginning to emerge as a competitor to scripted and produced porn films (Anatalek, 1998; Escoffier, 2007). In the 1990s, only Ken Ryker (6'4 with a 12' penis), who initially identified as a straight top, aspired to the status of a superstar.

Jeff Stryker, Ryan Idol, and Ken Ryker were 'made' by directors (Matt Sterling and John Travis for Stryker) or agents (David Forest with Idol and Dan Byers with Ryker) who consciously built a mystique around each of the prospective stars and heavily promoted their name-recognition. These efforts paid off in sales (as far as one can gauge without reported earnings) and industry awards. In each case, the mystique rested on a calculated strategy of aloofness, presumed heterosexuality, and a constricted sexual role that helped to sustain an air of mystery. Idol and Ryker found it is difficult to maintain that aloof Garbo-like presence over an extended period of time. In addition, both Idol and Ryker contended with personal problems and experienced ambivalence about their roles in gay porn (Douglas, 1998; Groff, 1998). Neither appeared able to achieve an economically secure career. Only Stryker attained economic security,[3] and was able to maintain a strategy of aloofness (possibly enhanced by working in the straight industry).

In the late 1990s, a new kind of gay porn star emerged: 'the professional.' These were performers (both gay and straight) who showed variety in their sexual performances, who could top or bottom, who kissed, who sucked cock, who rimmed, and who used sex toys. The well-known veteran porn star, Rod Barry, exemplifies the new professional. As the *Adam Gay Video 2003 Directory* (2002) noted, "Rod is one of those remarkable performers who was so good from the beginning, it was difficult to believe he was just a beginner" (p. 16). Although he has been married twice and is involved with women in his private life, Barry defines himself as 'sexual' rather than 'straight' or 'gay.'

Other performers who entered the industry in the mid-nineties were Kurt Young and Matt Easton, two lovers who migrated to Los Angeles in order to work in the porn industry. Both became major stars. Young, who performed frequently as a top, was the most recognized actor in the

history of gay porn, winning 14 industry awards in 4 years; Easton, created a persona as a butch bottom but, due to a lack of recognition, left
the industry. Other performers embodying the professional orientation
include Dino Phillips, a popular versatile performer, who left college to
pursue a career in porn; Jim Buck, a bookish young man from a small
town in Louisiana who went on to create a persona (in the movies of
Wash West and others) as a hot, masculine top; Dean Phoenix, a notable
top, who came out after leaving the Navy; Tanner Hayes, a cowboy
from rural Montana, who made his reputation as a power bottom; and
Harper Blake, a popular drag performer in the Bay Area, who trans-
formed himself into a well-built, sexually versatile, masculine body
builder. In addition, there was Logan Reed, who built a career around
the flip flop (when two performers alternate between top and bottom)
and Travis Wade, a Texas-born bisexual gym trainer who was one of the
most successful 'Exclusives' signed by *Falcon Studios*. These performers were among the most popular porn stars in the last five years of the
twentieth-century. Most of them were sexually versatile and performed
both top and bottom roles at some point in their careers.

Among the leading performers today, only Jason Adonis, a performer
who has evolved from gay-for-pay into a self-acknowledged bisexual,
and Matthew Rush, a "Lifetime *Falcon* Exclusive" and self-identified
gay man, approach superstar status. Both of these men occupy the aloof
role adopted by Stryker and Idol; however, unlike these superstars of
the 1980s, Adonis and Rush perform a wide variety of sexual activities.

The porn star is a major economic resource of the adult film industry.
Fans purchase movies specifically for the performers who appear in
them; thus, for the companies who produce the movies and for customers who purchase or rent them, the 'star,' is absolutely essential. As
O'Toole (1999) observed about *Vivid Studios*:

> [T]he most crucial strand of *Vivid's* capital investment has been in
> people.... It doesn't matter how good the script or the digitalia are,
> whether it is film or videotape in the camera, this kind of adult
> entertainment depends upon bodies and beauty. *Vivid* is famous
> for its beautiful contract players, also known as the 'Vivid Queens.'
> It was the first company to offer exclusive contracts to performers,
> with Ginger Lynn the original Vivid Queen in the mid-eighties.
> Though other companies have followed suit, *Vivid* still leads the
> field. *Wicked*, *VCA*, *Ultimate* and *Sin* are all doing it, but still only
> with a maximum of three contracted players at any given time.
> (p. 184)

The existence of contract players or exclusives would suggest that stars (i.e., performers with name recognition) would be able to command substantial salaries for their appearance. In the straight porn industry, contract female performers can earn $70,000 to $100,000 a year appearing in adult movies (Abbott, 2000; Jameson, 2004). In the gay porn industry, male performers, on average, earn more per scene than their straight counterparts; however, it remains difficult to earn an adequate annual income by performing exclusively in gay pornographic movies. While major stars can earn anywhere from $10,000 to $50,000 (as Jeff Stryker was reportedly paid several years ago), performers typically earn $500 to $2500 per scene (depending on their popularity, the sexual acts to be performed, and the prestige and wealth of the studio). Smaller companies pay closer to $500 per scene. Thus, if a performer is paid $2000 a scene and makes a movie every month, his annual income would be $24,000 (Adams, 2000; Adams, 2003; Escoffier, 2002).

Some individuals also feel that the use of 'exclusives' is much less common in the gay porn industry than in its straight counterpart. Veteran porn star Rod Barry, for example, contends that both the performer and the studio lose out if adult video companies fail to sign and nurture performers:

> I'm the biggest star that ever came out of *All Worlds*. And the biggest mistake that they ever made was not signing me to an exclusive contract.... They would have made much more money from my movies if they'd given me an exclusive contract.... They consider exclusives a lot of work, and lots of times they are, but you've got to create stars for your company. Straight porn companies are built on the followings of certain stars. In the gay business, only a few companies take advantage of that–*Falcon, Jet Set*, and *Studio 2000* to an extent. You have to create followings and I don't know why the people who ran *All Worlds* never wanted that. (Escoffier, 2004)[4]

Falcon Studios–the dominant and most economically successful of the gay porn companies–has long had a policy of having exclusive contracts with half a dozen or more performers. The studio strictly regulates the careers of exclusives by controlling their access to the gay press, their sexual repertoires, and the characters they play. Other studios may sign one or two performers as exclusives, but few devote resources to the development of exclusives or contract actors.

The star, however, is not only a performer, but also a form of human capital–an investment used to help guarantee the sales of movies. Like any other kind of human capital, the porn star is created through an investment–in porn, through the display of specific sexual skills and through construction of an image or persona that appeals to the individuals who purchase or rent porn videos. To be a successful porn star, the performer must maintain his or her *fantasy potential* (i.e., the ability to suggest that erotic possibilities will not be exhausted).

An exclusive contract acknowledges the performer as an essential asset of the studio's promotional and marketing effort. A successful investment strategy for stars and exclusives is one that does what is necessary to maintain the erotic appeal of the performer, protect him or her from overexposure, and carefully stage the expansion of the performer's sexual repertoire. However, without an exclusive contract–and in the gay porn industry, very few performers are signed to exclusive contracts–the performer must manage his 'career' on his own. Unless they are working with an agent, very few performers that I have interviewed employ a self-conscious 'investment strategy.' Instead, they must confront by themselves, and usually without much awareness, the risks of overexposure and the trap of unlimited sexual accessibility (i.e., the psychoeconomic dynamics of fantasy and retrogression).

PORNOGRAPHY AS A CAREER

It has often been said–more as an example of folk wisdom than as a demonstrable fact–that in the gay porn business a successful 'porn star' must have two of three characteristics: a beautiful face, a beautiful body, or a big penis. Performers are absolutely central to the gay porn industry; indeed, casting is considered one of the most significant aspects of making a successful porn film.

However, despite the fact that 'porn star' is a generic term, not all performers are stars. Becoming a porn star is rarely something that young men–especially young gay men who must address the issue of their homosexuality–anticipate as a career. The vast majority of the men interviewed by myself became performers in porn movies without much premeditation. They knew a friend who was doing it, were approached by a scout or photographer, or sent their photos on a lark to a porn company after they had become familiar with pornography.

The young gay men entering the gay porn business have frequently dropped out of college, often come from working class backgrounds, and from religious families or families uncomfortable with or hostile to their homosexuality. Performing in porn is, for many gay men, a path to glamour or sexual exploration.[5] In contrast, the young straight men entering the gay porn world do not appear to differ significantly from those identified by Susan Faludi in the straight porn business. "They had all bailed out," Faludi (1999) noted, "of sinking occupational worlds that used to confer upon working men a measure of dignity and a masculine mantle but now offer only uncertainty" (p. 538). For this group, the 'easy' money exercises a major appeal (Escoffier, 2003a).

* * *

In the early days of gay commercial pornography, it was difficult to recruit performers because homosexual behavior was stigmatized and production was illicit. Performers were often filmmakers' friends, casual sexual partners, and/or boyfriends (Douglas, 1996). There was no pre-existing network or agents. One early filmmaker, Barry Knight, described how:

> Central casting in those days was *The Gold Cup* restaurant on the corner of Hollywood Boulevard and Las Palmos [in L.A.]. Whenever they needed an actor, or an actor didn't show up, they'd go down to 'central casting.'... Kids who were hitchhiking with a backpack were offered a way to make extra money. That's how it happened. (Douglas, 1996, p. 11)

In contrast, the contemporary gay pornography industry has a highly developed infra-structure of production companies, distribution networks, technical services, agents, and scouts for performers.

Despite its greater sophistication, few individuals appear to enter the porn industry with any notion of what a 'career' in this business really means. However, one person who did was Jeff Stryker. He was fortunate to have John Travis and Matt Sterling, two of the most influential directors of gay pornographic films in the early 1980s, as his advisors. Travis initially responded to photos that Stryker submitted.

> He had no concept of what anything was about in the big city of Los Angeles, and he was at first very untrusting. And in the first three months I knew him, we planned his future, the strategy–what

could be done, how it could be done–and that strategy, that program still goes on today. (Douglas 1990, p. 10)

Stryker also was advised by Matt Sterling, a successful director for *Falcon Studios* in its early years and one of the most prominent directors of the 1980s. Sterling believed that Stryker closely resembled Elvis Presley and Marlon Brando in spirit, like "his passion for motorcycles … I felt it was the real thing, not a packaged thing. I just wanted to bring out as much as I could of the real, and it worked–he became a hero of sorts in the gay community" (Douglas, 1988, p. 50).

* * *

Performing in gay video pornography is a form of sex work and requires the performance of sex acts according to the direction of the paying party. While porn actors, like other sex workers, may exclude certain activities from their repertoire, their on-set sexual behavior is governed by the demands and constraints of adult video production. Thus, in gay pornography, even heterosexual actors must necessarily engage in homosexual activity. Further, the sexual acts that performers engage in are unlike those they might perform in their everyday lives; in pornographic sex constant interruptions occur. Therefore, to maintain their erections and stimulate their orgasms, they are allowed to use various forms of pornography–gay or straight, depending on their sexual orientation. "It's not what you would think," performer Dino Phillips told *Unzipped* magazine. "It's a lot of contrived, regulated, stop-and-start sex" (Phillips, 1999, p. 13). The final product shows scenes which, through editing and post-production manipulation, appear as credible sexual encounters.

How individuals are recruited, their sexual orientation, and the limits they place in terms of the sexual acts they perform determine the potential shape of their porn career. These factors help a performer shape the persona that he will adopt as his 'character' in the films he makes. The persona is based, in part, on his motivation for entering the gay pornography business–be it money, attention, and/or sex–but also on the image that he wishes to project as a sexual performer (an aggressive top, a submissive bottom, a sex pig, etc.). The persona is the porn performer's identity as a sexual performer. It is constructed from his beliefs about sex and sexual identity, from acceptable sexual scripts (romantic stories, leather, orgies, etc.) in which he may comfortably engage, and from his repertoire of acceptable sexual acts (active/passive oral, anal penetration, rimming, etc.).

The performer's porn persona is constructed for use within the confines of a porn career and the gay porn business. He must maintain it in his on-screen sexual activities, in his public appearances, and in his interactions with fans. It is a kind of identity or character; it helps him do his job, and it helps define the social expectations of his significant others in the business. However, a performer's persona also may have its limits. He may not be able to successfully perform his persona at all times, and others may be unaware of his persona or may choose to ignore it. His backstage behavior may vary greatly from his public persona. It also is little help in negotiating encounters with the people in the actor's life who may not know of his participation in the world of gay pornography (Escoffier, 2003a).

Whatever training new performers in gay porn receive often takes place relatively quickly. Usually the first few scenes expose the new performer to the knowledge and skills that are required. Learning to feel comfortable performing sexually in front of a camera and group of people is something a porn performer must develop with haste or he will be unable to continue working in the industry. Keeping an erection and regaining it quickly were essential skills in the days before erectile drugs. However, since their introduction, performers must discover the exact doses or brands which work for them. Several performers have told me of taking a whole pill, which gave them headaches and made it difficult to maintain their erections. However, not even an erectile drug can arouse a man if he feels no attraction to his partner or if there are no other aids (e.g., pornographic magazines or videos) on the set to stimulate his arousal.

Also important is the necessity of anal douching for the performer who will be bottoming or engaging in anal penetration by fingers, tongues, and sex toys. Occasionally, I have heard complaints from tops about inexperienced or careless bottoms that had not douched properly. As well, performers must be able to achieve an orgasm and ejaculate after many interruptions and delays in the sexual action of the scene. Again, one hears complaints about performers unable to hold off ejaculating or, even more problematic, unable to climax at the end of a sexual scene. Sometimes a director may choose to ignore a performer's inability to come, but others may call in a 'stunt dick' to fake the performer's final orgasm. One very successful gay-for-pay performer told me that in his first porn movie scene (a straight porn movie), he had been unable to get an erection and they had to fake his orgasm with a jet of hand cream on his partner's belly.

The most important decision a new performer must make is whether he wishes to pursue a career in porn as his primary source of income or to supplement money earned from a more conventional job. The performer who uses porn movies as a source of supplemental income has greater latitude in terms of how he relates to the industry. However, the performer who chooses, even temporarily, to pursue a career in porn videos as a primary source of income must face the dangerous currents of the retrogressive dynamic. As many performers have remarked, 'pornography is not a career.' It has a very short life-span, and it lasts only as long as performers can compete with new and younger entrants into the business. "You can't do porn as your main career," performer Rod Barry warned. "If you do, you'll end up starving and on the streets, back with your family, sleeping on the couch–it's a supplemental income" (Escoffier, 2003b).

THE RETROGRESSIVE DYNAMIC

In the gay porn industry (and in many other occupations in the sex industry), there is steady demand for new, young and attractive performers, and the search for such individuals is an integral dynamic of the porn industry.

In the 1930s, sociologist Paul Cressey formulated the theory of retrogressive life cycles to explain the careers of young women who worked as taxi dancers (dime-a-dance girls). The young women who sought work as taxi dancers usually had left their families and communities to work in an occupation that was closely associated with prostitution. At first, the young women found it exciting, but the longer they worked as taxi dancers the more difficult it was to compete with the newer and younger women who started after them. Usually, the longer each woman worked as a taxi dancer, the less money she made, and the shabbier the taxi halls in which she had to work (Cressey, 1932; Escoffier, 2006). The life cycle of performers in the porn industry is subject to the same dynamic.

Most porn actors are aware of the retrogressive dynamic and either attempt to postpone the impact of the dynamic or to develop a strategy that goes beyond their porn career. Though there are no numerical data, industry folklore suggests that the average porn career lasts between two to four years.

"One interesting thing about this business," porn director Kristen Bjorn observed, "is that the longer you are in it, the less money you are paid. Once you are an old face, and an old body, forget it. You're through as far as your popularity goes" (De Walt, 1998, p. 55). In the porn industry, the performer who is considered an 'old face' or an 'old body' is either over-exposed or sexually predictable. He has made too many movies in too short a period of time; he has been around too long; or his performances are too similar from movie to movie. Viewers are bored with him and do not expect him to provide anything new. This progression often leads to lower budget productions as well. The performers most victimized by the dynamic are those addicted to drugs, alcohol or otherwise locked in by class or economic limitations (Carson, 2001).

The retrogressive dynamic is rooted in the psychology of fantasy ('the laws of desire') that shapes viewers' sexual scripts. The successful sexual performance in a strip show, with an escort, or in a porn movie allows the person entertaining the fantasy, watching the movie, or engaging in sex to protect his sexual excitement from being undercut by anxiety, guilt, or boredom. It simulates a reality in which the subject controls the situation by virtue of its commercial or phantasmal nature, but without the emotional risks that attend everyday sexual encounters, which are often full of uncertainty and performance anxieties (Stoller, 1985). The fantasy scenario itself stimulates a subject's desire and, for many people, the erotic excitement is heightened when the fantasy's outcome is uncertain; when it includes an element of risk, danger, mystery, or transgression. Thus, the repetitive playing out of a porn movie, a fantasy encounter, or experience with the same cast will eventually reduce the uncertainty, mystery, or suspense necessary for an erotic fantasy to remain vivid (Escoffier, 2006).

When the *fantasy potential* of an erotic scenario (and the objects of desire it contains) is exhausted, the retrogressive dynamic emerges in full force as a challenge to the performer. Whether it is through over-exposure, repetition, or stasis, the diminishing rate of phantasmal investment produces boredom or irritability in the spectator. While the porn star's sexual heat is generated through a complex formula that includes personality, physical attributes, and sexual skills, his fantasy potential increases only when the erotic scenarios reveal new aspects of the performer. Every performance that shows new or hitherto unknown skills, that demonstrates new physical attributes, and that is energetically performed enriches the porn star's fantasy potential.

The star's durability and appeal are prolonged if he can continue to reveal new possibilities, make new fantasies possible, and re-invent and renew himself without closing off the original fantasies that inspired his fans. His failure to do so makes him vulnerable to the retrogressive dynamic. Performers who refuse to broaden their sexual repertoire must rely exclusively upon their screen partners and the scenarios in which they appear. The muscle bound performer who only bottoms and never gets an erection will seldom generate much fantasy potential. The trade top who doesn't suck dick, doesn't kiss, and doesn't rim soon becomes boring; his fantasy potential quickly exhausted after only a few movies. Similarly, the ambitious performer who starts out as an aggressive top, performs increasingly as a bottom (but without having an erection), and then appears in a series of gang bang movies as a sex pig (a persona characterized by an aggressive and insatiable enjoyment of all forms of sex) will soon deplete his fantasy potential if he doesn't maintain himself as an aggressive top. Most of these performers will have short careers unless they limit their over-exposure, diversify their sexual services or related career activities, modify their physical attributes, or engage in new promotional efforts.

Performers react to the retrogressive dynamic in different ways. On a practical level, most performers worry, quite reasonably, about "over-exposure"–that is, they are concerned that viewers will lose interest in them if they appear in too many movies too quickly or play roles that are too similar. The most common way to limit overexposure is to appear in a limited number of productions, perhaps a handful a year, though most successful performers usually pursue a number of different activities. Veteran performer, Jon Galt (who is widely considered an exciting and dependable performer, but not a major star) summarized his strategy:

> If you want to have any kind of longevity in adult entertainment, it is probably better to do a couple of very good things a year and stretch your career out over a number of years, instead of doing 50 really bad films at once, shooting your wad and overexposing yourself.... Do a few things a year and keep it interesting. I have a full-time job outside of porn that I love that pays me very well, so I'm not doing movies or involved in an escorting career for my livelihood. (Hitman, 2005, p. 42)

Such an approach is most feasible if one has chosen not to make a career in the sex industry one's primary source of income.

Superstar Jeff Stryker is the most famous example of a prominent performer who prolonged his career by rationing his film appearances–approximately one a year. His sexual range was extremely limited–he only fucked, never kissed, never sucked a penis, and never rimmed or bottomed; yet, he was able to maintain his popularity for more than a decade. Stryker explained his rationale to *Manshots* magazine:

> See, I never hustled or tricked on the side, and that way, I was un-obtainable. The only way they could get it was on video. So with that in mind, my objective was to make as few movies as possible, but make sure they were the best. That's what I tried to do and to do that, you've got to start out from a position of power. I negotiated deals in which I was covered–my rent and everything, so that I wasn't having to take jobs to get by or to get food, rent or whatever. (Spencer, 1998, p. 33)

Falcon exclusive Travis Wade is another example of a porn star who built his strategy around limiting the number of movies in which he appeared. Wade was discovered by *Falcon Studios* and signed with them to make 5 movies in his first year. When he completed his contract, he decided to re-sign after a short break because he decided that the "money is way too easy to make [at *Falcon*] for me to be ... doing 20 films with all these different companies" and being forced to leave the business because "nobody cares who you are" (Holden, 2000). Over the course of his career, he gradually expanded his sexual repertoire from his original stance as a trade top, and eventually bottomed in *The Crush*, his last movie for *Falcon*. According to Wade, bottoming

> increased my overall worth in the business. It appeals to a different audience. Some people just want to see me as a top. And then there are those people out there that have been saying how beautiful my butt is . . . I wanted *The Crush* to take me to that next level, so that when I'm ready to stop making movies, I'll still have the option of another year or two of performing in clubs, doing video signings and doing appearances. (Holden, 2000)

Throughout the period he performed in porn movies, Wade also danced and escorted. He eventually left the business to work as a gym trainer–a common post-porn career for many of the more gym-conscious performers.

Periods of 'retirement' and subsequent 'comebacks' offer another strategy for avoiding overexposure. Any performer who has worked in the industry for more than five years has taken extended leaves from film production. They may continue to perform live on stage, to escort, or work behind the scenes, but their absence from the screen can help rejuvenate their fantasy potential. As the turnover of performers is fairly rapid (2-3 years), older high-profile performers can re-enter the business and perform in new combinations with new partners. Comebacks are often associated with additions to the performer's sexual repertoire as well.

Expanding what one does sexually is a common strategy adopted by performers to postpone the retrogressive dynamic, enhance their fantasy potential, prolong their careers, and maintain their fan base. For example, Rod Barry increased his fantasy potential and extended his fan appeal by adding new elements to his sexual repertoire. During his first year in the business, Barry developed a persona as an aggressive, verbally abusive, dirty-talking top. After about a year or two, he began to bottom and gave a new spin to his persona by performing as a similarly aggressive bottom, trash-talking and shouting such things as "Fuck me! Fuck me harder, you motherfucker!" Then, after taking a four-year break, he staged a comeback in 2003-2004, winning a GAYVN Award for his performance as an aggressive, trash-talking, hillbilly top in *White Trash*. In performances on various Web sites, he expanded the range of his anal eroticism and bottoming, using a variety of dildos (including a baseball bat), and ultimately achieving orgasms while being fucked, without ever relinquishing his persona as an aggressive top.

Others will choose to stay in the porn industry and work behind the scenes while some will rely increasingly upon escorting or some other form of sex work–which often stretches out the retrogressive dynamic over a longer time period. Many, of course, will leave the industry and go into other occupations or businesses.

STRIPPER: FANTASY AND TIPS

The retrogressive dynamic affects most seriously those performers who wish to rely on work in the adult film industry as their primary source of income. Performers begin to experience the dynamic when they are offered less money to perform in a scene than they received earlier in their career or when they are hired and paid less for smaller roles, asked to perform sexual acts they had rejected previously or to be an extra in an orgy scene (i.e., neither topping nor bottoming). Some performers may decide to leave the business at that point, while others may accept the lower paying jobs until they can diversify their sex work activities or find some other way to increase their fantasy potential.

Once the retrogressive dynamic kicks in, it affects the income that performers earn from appearing in porn movies. At that point, some performers may choose to combat the decline in the economic potential of their career by engaging in other forms of sex work that are complementary to their employment in pornography. The most frequently exercised options are stripping and escorting, but other pursuits are not uncommon; many go on to work 'behind the scenes' as videographer (Colby Taylor) or director (e.g., Gino Colbert, Michael Lucas, Dino Phillips, Doug Jeffries, Chad Donovan, and Chris Steele). A number of performers have worked as personal gym trainers (e.g., Chad Conners, Travis Wade, and Matthew Rush) which, though not strictly a form of sex work, may draw on the fantasy potential of their porn careers.

Performing live, dancing, stripping, or whatever is the appropriate term (the word that is used depends often on local laws, whether the venue serves liquor or not, whether it is a club or theater, etc.) is probably the most common remunerative activity engaged in by porn stars to supplement their income. Whereas performers in porn videos are usually paid by the scene, the primary form of income for live performances comes from tips–bills stuffed into briefs or thrown on stage. Female strippers can make thousands of dollars a night, but male strippers usually earn considerably less (Burana, 2001; DeMarco, 2002).

As noted by Travis Wade, the porn star comes with an advantage; his name recognition, or merely his status as a performer in porn, serves as an attraction for the club putting him on stage. The porn star, by virtue of the national distribution of porn videos or through adult sites on the Internet, has a reputation that reaches beyond the local gay community. In the clubs, he is a 'featured entertainer' in contrast to the local talent or relatively anonymous dancers that routinely perform. Travis Wade asserted that:

> The money is not in the movies really. The money is good for movies, but if you're a dancer at the same time–which is what I was before I was a film star–it quadruples your money when you're performing in a club. (Holden, 2000)

Thus, the porn star not only may be paid a fee (though more often, only travel and hotel are paid for), he also earns more in tips than local strippers and promotes his career as a porn performer. The downside is that giving live performances usually requires traveling extensively outside the area where the performer lives.

Stripping and dancing on stage also enable the porn performer to recreate, in the flesh, his porn persona. This allows him to elaborate on it, and give his fans a chance to interact with him while he enacts it. Stripping, like porn, projects a fantasy–but with a difference: It is physically present to the spectator and permits a degree of interaction. The manager of a straight strip club explained the relationship between stripping and prostitution like this: "We sell the *idea* of sex. We do not sell the act of sex. We sell a sexual fantasy without actually copulating" (Frank, 2002, p. xix). Live performances allow performers to take the fantasy persona of their pornographic movies into close proximity to their audience. Thus, it can help to increase the performer's fantasy potential–although, of course, a lackluster performance can have a damaging effect.

I recently witnessed a performance by Rod Barry that both reenacted and elaborated on the aggressive 'sex pig' persona he portrayed in his videos. He came on to the stage and stripped relatively quickly, then presented his ass to the audience, spreading his anus and allowing spectators near the stage to finger it. Then he inserted a beer bottle in his ass and penetrated himself (and then afterwards, drank the beer that had remained in the bottle). After that he moved along the perimeter of the stage reaching out and pulling in the older or less attractive men to him, rubbing himself up against them. He spit on the bald head of one man dressed in leather, spreading the spittle out affectionately over the man's naked scalp, and kissed the man's head. Then, swinging from the pipes along the ceiling of the bar, Barry moved over the heads of the audience, landing and planting his naked ass on the faces of patrons who sought his attention. It was an extremely provocative and even shocking performance; the audience, however, was delirious with excitement and surprise.

For the most part, stripping is a way, like performing in porn, of earning 'extra cash.' As a supplement to a career in pornographic movies, it can be, as Travis Wade suggested, quite lucrative. By itself, however, even when combined with performing in gay sex videos, it probably cannot produce a sustainable income. "Movies and dance gigs," observed Rod Barry, "they're just a little extra cash. I can go out and do a film–and get a motorcycle" (Escoffier, 2003b). Only escorting can provide an adequate full-time income. In this regard, stripping is a somewhat ambiguous enterprise. While many strippers may not work as escorts, stripping can serve as a point of contact for escorting. Traveling around the country dancing in gay clubs and burlesque theaters allows the porn star to demonstrate his appeal and meet clients in the smaller markets away from the gay triumvirate of Los Angeles, San Francisco, and New York.

FROM PORN STAR TO ESCORT:
PORN MOVIES AS ADVERTISING

When a performer pursues work as an escort, his relationship to porn and to stripping change; the economic weight of escorting transforms the work in porn and as a stripper into adjuncts of escorting. The appearances in porn movies become akin to infomercials, and the dancing and stripping in the gay club circuit become a modern triple-x version of the traveling salesman. "I don't think that porn stars really make a living doing porn; they have to have some kinds of other income," notes director Kristen Bjorn. "They just cannot make that much money. So those who are totally into just doing porn movies are basically prostitutes who use the porn movies as publicity for what they really do" (De Walt 1998, p. 55).

The term 'escort' has a broad significance, but it is only one kind of male prostitute (Adams, 1999; Luckenbill, 1986). Compared to hustlers, who often work on the streets or out of bars, escorts more generally work by phone, through advertisements in the local gay papers, escort agencies, or increasingly through Web sites. When successful porn stars (those with name recognition) become escorts, they have a degree of national recognition and a scope of operation that local escorts cannot match. A quick glance at a local gay publication reveals many ads for 'models/escorts' that list non-porn escorts by their first name only (Adam, Luis) or by some descriptive phrase ('Str8 Italian,' 'Hot Black, Hard Body,' 'Donkey Dick'). Conversely, ads for porn star escorts usually supply the performer's entire name ('Talvin Demachio,' 'Ken Ryker,' 'Billy Brandt'). Ryker was one of the superstars of the gay porn industry. Brandt also is well known, though not very active. Similarly, Demachio has not been a particularly active xxx performer in the last four or five years (i.e., the annual installments of the *Adam Gay Video Directory* show him active from 1997-2000), but his ad suggests that he clearly assumes there is an audience out there who knows who he is. The ads range from merely listing the porn star's name, cell phone number, or Web site to detailed information about availability. In a recent issue of *Frontiers* magazine, one porn star escort announces in his advertisement: "I will be escorting in the following cities: Toronto, Canada Oct. 4-6 (In/Out), Los Angeles, CA Oct. 7-10 (In/Out), Vancouver, Canada Oct. 11-12 (In/Out) ... Berlin, Germany, Oct. 21-23. Return to the USA Oct. 24" (Frontiers, 2004). This national or even international visibility puts the porn star (or even the former porn star) at the top of the hierarchy in the male prostitution market. This porn star escort is able to travel for his escort work without needing to reach potential customers through the retail marketing that stripping and dancing represent.

Fantasy is a significant component of any sexual encounter between the porn star escort and customer. As long as the porn star appears only in movies, he remains to some degree unattainable (e.g., Jeff Stryker) and exists only in a fantasy mode. However, the spectator's ability to imagine access to the star, whether by gossip, strip show, Web site, or escort ad, helps to sustain the fan's desire and fosters a fantasy scenario of connection between performer and audience member. Thus, the possibility of hiring the porn star as an escort is integral to the spectator's fantasy (even if he never hires one) and to the economic link between working as a porn star and working as an escort.

Many of the spectator's fantasies are generated through interviews (sometimes completely fabricated) with their favorite porn stars in soft-core porn magazines. However, interviews in local gay magazines and newspapers (when the porn star is in town dancing at a local club or promoting his latest film) also feed the fantasy of connection. The proliferation of chat rooms, Web-cams, voyeur sites, and interactive Web sites allow fans to engage in conversations and have contact with porn stars. On some sites, fans can purchase 'exclusive' time with the performer/star, interact with him and together they enact a fantasy scenario. Voyeurs, who pay a lower fee, can watch the interaction but not interact with the performer. For example, in one interaction that I witnessed, a fan (using the name Topman) bought exclusive time with one of his favorite porn stars and engaged in a fantasy scenario: Topman wanted to 'top' the performer, so the porn star penetrated himself with a dildo and verbally played out the fantasy scenario, shouting "Fuck me harder, Topman," masturbating until he reached orgasm. This is the cyber-fantasy equivalent of an escorting encounter.

In-person sexual encounters between porn star escort and their clients also involve a degree of fantasy, which is sometimes one of intimacy (Bernstein, 2001). This sort of encounter can be disappointing if the porn star fails to live up to his persona, performs badly, is drunk, high on drugs, or uninterested in pleasing his customer. However, porn escorts are often as professional in their escort work as in their video work. One prominent porn star told me that he experienced a comparable problem; he often found that his clients expected him to live up to his film persona and that he had difficulty sustaining that without the presence of the camera or an audience.

Some escort sites (e.g., male4malescorts.com) have review sections for clients to review the men they hire. In the case of well-known porn stars, the reviews often seem to navigate between the fantasies that clients may have entertained before they hired the performer and the quality of the sexual encounter itself. Two themes that recur in many reviews are how 'authentic' the escort seems as a person ('not a stuck up porn star!') or how genuine the escort's enjoyment of the sex is—which may go some way to compensate for the fact that the escort has been paid to have sex with the client. One reviewer commented on that very dynamic:

> Let's be real. They are doing it for money. Some are better at hiding that then others. Some just have a great time getting paid for something they find fun. (Topdawg, 2003)

While working as an escort has a great deal more economic potential than working as a performer in porn, escorting can affect a model's porn career by enhancing his fantasy potential. In other words, the availability or accessibility of the performer as an escort may itself contribute to his erotic appeal. While information about a porn star's escorting circulates in a realm of innuendo and euphemism because of the illegality of prostitution, it also enhances the performer's transgressive appeal. The fan's knowledge of the escorting may never result in an actual purchase of the porn star's services, but it contributes to the fantasy of accessibility (de Angelis, 2001). Thus, as it helps to make the porn career economically unnecessary, it also ironically may help to prolong that career.

CONCLUSION:
CAREERS, NETWORKS, AND MARKETS IN SEX WORK

I have explored the economic and sexual interrelations of a career path—porn star/stripper/escort—frequently adopted by performers in gay pornographic movies. The focus of this article has been on the individual; in particular, on the impact of the diminishing erotic appeal of the performer over time—called the retrogressive dynamic by sociologist Paul Cressey—and the measures that performers adopt in order to counteract its economic effects. These measures include (1) performers enhancing their fantasy potential through activities such as elaborating their persona, working out at a gym, dyeing their hair, or expanding their sexual repertoire; and (2) performers engaging in complementary forms of sex work such stripping (live performances) and escorting.

The career path–porn star/stripper/escort–consists of a sequence of jobs that are allocated in overlapping, but quite distinct labor markets. These markets are heavily mediated by networks and brokers (e.g., recruiters, scouts, agents, and escorting services), and each of them is very loosely organized (Ellingson, Lauman, Paik, & Mahay, 2004). There are no systematic means by which performers for adult videos are hired. There are no want ads or 'adult' employment agencies, no labor laws governing their employment, and no minimum wage requirements.

These markets function primarily through networks: Individuals may be linked through informal or casual connections, often involving a certain degree of reciprocal relations, and embedded in social contexts that are not necessarily explicitly oriented to sex work–though they may be sexual (Ellingson et al., 2004). For example, two men may meet at a club. One, let's call him Jake, who is porn star, is a friend of a friend and is introduced to another man at the club, let's call him Ed. Merely curious, Ed may inquire about working in porn or Jake may be attracted to Ed, but if Ed expresses some interest in performing in a porn movie, Jake then may contact a recruiter, a scout, or even a director of one of the companies for whom he performed. It is through these network traits that the labor market for performers emerges (Powell & Smith-Doerr, 1994).

While the labor market for adult video performers continues to be loosely organized, the porn star as stripper and escort implicitly helps to arrange these disparate and overlapping labor markets into a single hierarchical structure. Performing in porn movies is the most visible form of sex work on a national level as well as the most prestigious. However, the three overlapping markets–for escorts, strippers, and porn stars–interact on a number of levels both nationally and locally. Porn performers operate in a quasi-national market, while both strippers and escorts who haven't worked in porn, are hired in local markets. In the case of adult video performers who are engaging in other forms of sex work, the markets for strippers and escorts tend to be more national because of the distribution pattern of pornographic movies. The latter serves as a form of publicity, provides relevant information about sexual performance and capabilities, and may enhance the performer's fantasy potential.

ACKNOWLEDGMENTS

This article is based on research, currently underway, for a book on the gay porn industry. The author would like to thank all those performers in the industry who have talked to him, on the record and off, about their experiences as sexual entertainers and the complicated relations between performing in porn movies, dancing on the live stage, and other forms of sex work. Also, the author would like to thank Andrew Spieldenner, Aaron Tanner, the anonymous readers who read earlier drafts of this article, for their many useful comments, and Todd G. Morrison for his invitation to contribute an article to this volume.

NOTES

1. It should be noted that, as *Manshots* was not associated with any porn production company, these interviews were not puff pieces.
2. Porn star-stripper-escort is not the only possible career path. There are several others, one of the most common being the path that leads from stripper to porn star (and then, perhaps, to escort) in which working as a stripper serves as the means through which performers are recruited by scouts or porn company representatives. Another is a career path that opens up for veteran performers within the industry itself (e.g., as production assistants, videographers, producers, or directors). Each of these paths requires different kinds of skills, degrees of training and, especially important in the porn industry, psychological investment on the part of the individual performer (e.g., the loss of glamour and public recognition, the different kind of engagement with sexual performance, etc.).
3. I doubt even Jeff Stryker supported himself by making gay porn.
4. In 1997, at the beginning of Barry's career, *All Worlds* had not yet signed performers as exclusives. Partly, as a consequence of Barry's meteoric success, the studio began to sign potential popular performers as exclusives (e.g., Dean Phoenix and Tanner Hayes). In recent years, smaller studios also have begun signing performers as exclusives.
5. Many of the interviews in *Manshots* illustrate these points.

REFERENCES

Abbott, S. (2000). Motivations for pursuing an acting career in pornography. In R. Weitzer (Ed.), *Sex for sale: Prostitution, pornography and the sex industry* (pp. 17-34). New York, NY: Routledge.
Adam gay video 2003 directory. (2002). Los Angeles, CA: Knight Publishing Group.
Adams, J. C. (2000, March 31). Less bang for the buck. *HX, 447,* 29-30.
Adams, J. C. (2003, April). Pay 4 porn. *Badpuppy, 5,* 56-57.
Adams, M. (1999). *Hustlers, escorts, porn stars: The insider's guide to male prostitution in America.* Las Vegas, NV: The Insider's Guide.
Anatalek, J. (1998, November). Porn in the USA. Retrieved May 25, 2001, from http://qsfmagazine/qsf9711/porn.html (Link no longer active. Article available from author upon request.)
Becker, G. S. (1964). *Human capital.* New York, NY: National Bureau of Economic Research.
Becker, H. (1963). *The outsiders: Studies in the sociology of deviance.* New York, NY: The Free Press.
Bernstein, E. (2001). The meaning of the purchase: Desire, demand and the commerce of sex. *Ethnography, 2,* 389-420.

Braudy, L. (1977). *The world in a frame: What we see in films.* Garden City, NY: Anchor Books.

Burana, L. (2001). *Strip city: A stripper's farewell journey across America.* New York, NY: Hyperion.

Carson, H.A. (2001). *A thousand and one night stands: The life of Jon Vincent.* Bloomington, IN: Authorhouse.

Cavell, S. (1980). *The world viewed: Reflections on the ontology of film.* Cambridge, MA: Harvard University Press.

Cowie, E. (1993). Pornography and fantasy: Psychoanalytic perspectives. In L. Segal & M. McIntosh (Eds.), *Sex exposed: Sexuality and the pornography debate* (pp.132-152). New Brunswick, NJ: Rutgers University Press.

Cressey, P. (1932). *The taxi hall dance.* New York, NY: Greenwood Press.

De Angelis, M. (2001). *Gay fandom and crossover stardom: James Dean, Mel Gibson and Keanu Reeves.* Durham, NC: Duke University Press.

deCordova, R. (1990). *Picture personalities: The emergence of the star system in America.* Urbana, IL: University of Illinois Press.

DeMarco, J. R. G. (2002, March/April). The world of gay strippers. *The Gay and Lesbian Review Worldwide,* 12-14.

De Walt, M., (1998, January). The eye of Kristen Bjorn. *Blueboy,* 52-55.

Douglas, J. (1988, September). Behind the camera: Matt Sterling. *Manshots,* 4-8, 50.

Douglas, J. (1990, March). Behind the camera: John Travis. *Manshots, 2,* 6-10, 72-73.

Douglas, J. (1996, June). Jaguar Productions: Interview with Barry Knight and Russell Moore. *Manshots, 8,* 10-15.

Douglas, J. (1998, November). Comeback: Interview with Ken Ryker. *Manshots, 10,* 30-33, 80-81.

Dyer, R. (1998). *Stars.* London, UK: British Film Institute.

Edmonson, R. (1998). *Boy in the sand: All-American sex star.* Los Angeles, CA: Alyson Books.

Edmonson, R. (2000). *Clone: The life and legacy of Al Parker, gay superstar.* Los Angeles, CA: Alyson.

Ellingson, S., Lauman, E. O., Paik, A., & Mahay, J. (2004). The theory of sexual markets. In E. O. Lauman, S. Ellingson, J. Mahay, P. Paik, & Y. Youm (Eds.), *The sexual organization of the city* (pp. 3-38). Chicago, IL: University of Chicago Press.

Escoffier, J. (2002, April). Unpublished interview with Aaron Tanner, New York City.

Escoffier, J. (2003a). Gay-for-pay: Straight men and the making of gay pornography. *Qualitative Sociology, 26,* 531-555.

Escoffier, J. (2003b, September). Unpublished interview with Rod Barry, Cherry Grove, Fire Island.

Escoffier, J. (2004, October). Unpublished interview with Rod Barry, Los Angeles.

Escoffier, J. (2007). Scripting the sex: Fantasy, narrative, and scripts in pornographic films. In M. Kimmel (Ed.), *The sexual self: The construction of sexual scripts* (pp. 61-79). Nashville, TN: Vanderbilt University Press.

Escoffier, J. (2006). The retrogressive dynamic. In M. H. Ditmore (Ed.), *Encyclopedia of prostitution and sex work* (pp. 400-402). Westport, CT: Greenwood Publishing Group.

Fairbanks, H. (1996, September). Fade out: Jon King (1963-1995). *Manshots,* 82.

Faludi, S. (1999). *Stiffed: The betrayal of the American man.* New York, NY: William Morrow.

Fenwick, H. (1988, February 2). Changing times for gay erotic videomakers. *The Advocate,* 36-37, 63-65.

Flowers, A. (1998). *The fantasy factory: An insider's view of the phone sex industry.* Philadelphia, PA: University of Pennsylvania Press.

Frank, K. (2002). *G-strings and sympathy: Strip club regulars and male desire.* Durham, NC: Duke University Press.

Frontiers (2004, October). Los Angeles, CA: Frontiers Publishing.

Goffman, E. (1961). *Asylums: Essays on the social situation of mental patients and other inmates.* New York, NY: Anchor Books.

Groff, D. (1998, June). Letter from New York: Fallen Idol. *Out,* 43-50.

Hitman, T. (2005, April). Atlas Shagged: Interview with Jon Galt. *Unzipped,* 40-48.

Holden, B. (2000, September 1). An interview with Travis Wade. Retrieved on July 21, 2005, from http://www.radvideo.com/news/article.php?ID=130 (Link no longer active. Article available from author upon request.)

Isherwood, C. (1996). *Wonder Bread and Ecstasy: The life and death of Joey Stefano.* Los Angeles, CA: Alyson.

Jameson, J. (2004). *How to make love like a porn star: A cautionary tale.* New York, NY: Regan Books.

Lane, F. S., III (2001). *Obscene profits: The entrepreneurs of pornography in the cyber age.* New York, NY: Routledge.

Lauman, E. O., Gagnon, J. H., Michael, R. T., & Michaels, S. (1994). *The social organization of sexuality: Sexual practices in the United States.* Chicago, IL: University of Chicago Press.

Liepe-Levinson, K. (2002). *Strip show: Performances of gender and desire.* New York, NY: Routledge.

Luckenbill, D. (1986). Deviant career mobility: The case of male prostitution. *Social Problems, 33,* 283-296.

Marvel, B. (2002). Porn: As profits explode, stigma persists. Retrieved on April 15, 2002, from http://www.dallasnews.com/041402dnlivporn.1c4od.html (Link no longer active. Article available from author upon request.)

McNair, B. (2002). *Striptease culture: Sex, media and the democratisation of desire.* London, UK: Routledge.

O'Toole, L. (1999). *Pornocopia: Porn, sex, technology and desire.* London, UK: Serpent's Tail.

Phillips, D. (1999, December 7). 12 questions. *Unzipped,* 12-13.

Plachy S., & Ridgeway, J. (1996). *Red light: Inside the sex industry.* New York, NY: Powerhouse Books.

Powell, W. W., & Smith-Doerr, L. (1994). Networks and economic life. In N. J. Smelser & R. Swedburg (Eds.), *The handbook of economic sociology* (pp. 368-402). Princeton, NJ: Princeton University Press.

Rojek, C. (2001). *Celebrity.* London, UK: Reaktion Books.

Spencer, W. (1998, September). Interview with Jeff Stryker. *Manshots,* 30-33, 72-73.

Stoller, R. J. (1985). *Observing the erotic imagination,* New Haven, CT: Yale University Press.

Thomas, J. A. (2002). Porn stars. *GLBTQ: An encyclopedia of gay, lesbian, bisexual, transgender and queer culture*. Retrieved July 21, 2005, from http://www.glbtq.com/arts/pornstars.html

Topdawg. (2003, February 10). Male escort Rod Barry–San Diego. *HooBoys M4M Escort Reviews*. Retrieved on February 1, 2004 from http://wwwmale4malescorts.com/reviews/rodbarrysd.html

Weitzer, R. (2000). Why we need more research on sex work. In R. Weitzer (Ed.), *Sex for sale: Prostitution, pornography and the sex industry* (pp. 1-13). New York, NY: Routledge.

doi:10.1300/J082v53n01_08

"Nobody's Ever Going to Make a Fag *Pretty Woman*": Stigma Awareness and the Putative Effects of Stigma Among a Sample of Canadian Male Sex Workers

Todd G. Morrison, PhD

National University of Ireland

Bruce W. Whitehead

SUMMARY. The purpose of this study was to examine male sex workers' awareness of the social stigma surrounding involvement in the sex industry and the possible effects of that stigma. Personal interviews were conducted with 21 men (9 independent escorts who advertised via the Internet and 12 escorts/erotic masseurs who were on contract with an agency). Results indicated that a majority of interviewees believed sex

Both authors contributed equally to this work; thus, authorship is in alphabetical order. Todd G. Morrison is a lecturer at the National University of Ireland, Galway, Ireland. Bruce W. Whitehead is an independent scholar. The authors would like to thank the men who graciously agreed to be interviewed for this study. Correspondence may be addressed to Dr. Todd G. Morrison, Department of Psychology, National University of Ireland, Galway, Ireland (E-mail: Todd.Morrison@nuigalway.ie).

[Haworth co-indexing entry note]: ""Nobody's Ever Going to Make a Fag *Pretty Woman*": Stigma Awareness and the Putative Effects of Stigma Among a Sample of Canadian Male Sex Workers." Morrison, Todd G. and Bruce W. Whitehead. Co-published simultaneously in *Journal of Homosexuality* (The Haworth Press, Inc.) Vol. 53, No. 1/2, 2007, pp. 201-217; and: *Male Sex Work: A Business Doing Pleasure* (ed: Todd G. Morrison and Bruce W. Whitehead) The Haworth Press, Inc., 2007, pp. 201-217. Single or multiple copies of this article are available for a fee from The Haworth Document Delivery Service [1-800- HAWORTH, 9:00 a.m. - 5:00 p.m. (EST). E-mail address: docdelivery@haworthpress.com].

Available online at http://jh.haworthpress.com
© 2007 by The Haworth Press, Inc. All rights reserved.
doi:10.1300/J082v53n01_09

work was stigmatized but attributed this stigma to society's tendency to conflate escort/erotic masseur with street-based prostitute and society's negative view of human sexuality in general and homosexuality in particular. It should be noted that interviewees did not necessarily perceive the gay community as more tolerant than the heterosexual community of persons involved in the male sex industry. In terms of how participants saw the sex trade, both prior to and during their involvement, multifarious viewpoints emerged (i.e., some engaged in "whore mythologizing" while others reported having no clearly defined perception of male sex workers). Finally, results suggested that some participants believed their involvement in a stigmatized industry was deleterious to them personally whereas others maintained that the consequences of being an escort/erotic masseur were largely positive. doi:10.1300/J082v53n01_09 *[Article copies available for a fee from The Haworth Document Delivery Service: 1-800-HAWORTH. E-mail address: <docdelivery@haworthpress.com> Website: <http://www.HaworthPress.com> © 2007 by The Haworth Press, Inc. All rights reserved.]*

KEYWORDS. Male prostitution, sex work, Canada, gay men, escorts

INTRODUCTION

Sex work may be defined as any occupation in which an individual provides sexual services in exchange for money and/or other items of value (Minichiello & associates, 2001). Two points should be noted. First, our interpretation of the phrase "provision of sexual services" is broad and, thus, includes all aspects of the sex industry (e.g., pornography performer, phone sex operator, escort, and stripper). Second, we eschew a value-laden perspective of this industry and, consequently, avoid the irresolvable debate of whether sex work is inherently good or inherently bad. As a corollary to the latter point, our emphasis is on the *subjective* experience of the sex worker and his client.

The importance of understanding the individual's perception of what he does is underscored by research identifying experiential variability among male sex workers. For example, Joffe and Dockrell (1995) reported that some of the prostitutes in their sample evidenced little agency. They felt that clients were in control of the sexual encounter and, due to their "[d]esperation for money, drugs, and … a place to stay"

(p. 339), capitulated to clients' demands for unsafe sex. Similarly, Calhoun and Weaver (1996) observed that the decision to enter and/or leave street-based prostitution may not be directly under the prostitute's control. Contextual variables such as poverty, history of abuse, and a lack of education strongly influence entry into this form of sex work, while factors such as "increased age and physical maturity" (p. 213) may hasten exit from the industry. Conversely, in a qualitative study of male sex workers, Browne and Minichiello (1995) provided comments from various interviewees that problematize the discourse of prostitute-as-powerless-victim. Two illustrative quotations are: "The worker is providing a service for the client to use and enjoy, but he's not providing himself for the client to use" (p. 603) and "I won't negotiate safe sex. It's safe sex and that's it" (p. 614). Morrison and Whitehead's (2005) study of independent Internet escorts similarly revealed that participants saw themselves as possessing agency vis-à-vis their career (e.g., "I'm in control of the situation. I don't do anything that I'm uncomfortable with ... that I think might be dangerous for me" [p. 174).

One issue that researchers have ignored, due, in part, to their singular focus on HIV/AIDS (e.g., Allman & Myers, 1999; Boles & Elifson, 1994; Weinberg, Worth, & Williams, 2001) and safer sex (e.g., Marino, Browne, & Minichiello, 2000; Minichiello et al., 2000) is the stigma[1] associated with sex work. Although prostitution is stigmatized by society (Pheterson, 1990), few researchers have attempted to understand how sex workers perceive this stigma. Instead, they operate from the presumption that male sex workers *must* (or should) perceive their employment as "stigmatized" and "deviant" because what they do contravenes the dictates of hegemonic masculinity–in particular, notions of male erotic subjectivity. For example, Joffe and Dockrell (1995) reported that several participants in their study appeared to "distance themselves from the stigma of their working life by talking of a private life of intimacy, unfettered by the tools and connotations of their trade" (p. 343). Unfortunately, these researchers do not present any evidence to suggest that participants felt degraded by their involvement with sex work or saw it as a stigmatized form of employment. Further, the "distancing technique" of relegating love and romance to the private, rather than public (or work), sphere may be seen as the hallmark of a talented employee and not necessarily a response to social disapproval.

Suggesting that male sex workers do not necessarily perceive this form of employment in deviant or stigmatized terms does not mean they are impervious to the (hetero)sexual standards embodied by hegemonic masculinity. What it does suggest is that being cognizant of stigma is not tantamount to internalizing and accepting it. Indeed, sex workers may engage in strategies of resistance (Morrison & Whitehead, 2005); they may reject "society's ubiquitous cultural norms [surrounding prostitution]" (Scambler, 1997, p. 109) and, in so doing, formulate their own ideas of good, bad, honor, and dishonor. Awareness, but not internalization, of stigma seems particularly likely to occur among gay-identified sex workers, given that they fall within a subculture that has a problematic relationship with hegemonic masculinity and, consequently, is subject to social opprobrium itself.[2]

In addition to focusing on a narrow range of topics, researchers have only recently extended their scope beyond street-based prostitution. The reliance on one category of sex work has resulted in "a body of literature that has been inappropriately generalized to all men who are paid for sex ..." (Uy, Parsons, Bimbi, Koken, & Halkitis, 2004, p. 14).

The current study will expand understanding of male sex workers in the following ways. First, participants will consist of two infrequently studied groups: gay-identified independent escorts who promote their services via the Internet and contractual escorts/erotic masseurs (i.e., those who pay a fee to work at an agency). Second, HIV/safer sex will not comprise the analytic focus of this investigation; instead, the objectives will be to explore participants' awareness of stigma and the possible effects of working in a stigmatized industry.

METHOD

Participants

Twenty-one male sex workers (9 independent and 12 contractual) served as interviewees. Although their ages ranged from 20 to 57 ($M = 29.4$, $SD = 9.0$), in many cases, their stated "working ages" were substantially lower (i.e., the individual who was 57 listed his age as 44). The ethnic composition of participants was as follows: sixteen identified as Caucasian (or being of European heritage), two as Black, one as Spanish, one as Asian, and one as being of mixed ethnicity. With respect to location, a majority of participants resided in Vancouver, British Columbia. Finally, six of the participants had obtained university degrees (4 undergraduate; 2 graduate); five were post-secondary students at the time the interviews were conducted, two had partial university educations, six had no post-secondary experience (with one not graduating high school), and two had received job certification prior to becoming sex workers.

The majority of participants were employed primarily in the sex industry; however, a small number also held "straight" jobs (e.g., financier, researcher, and hairdresser). In addition to escort/erotic massage work, participants also reported involvement with adult films (production and performance), modeling (Internet and print), brothel work, erotic dancing, and domination/slave training.

Procedure

Participant recruitment. Different methods of recruitment were used for the independent escorts who advertised via the Internet and those who worked on contract as escorts/erotic masseurs. Each method will be outlined briefly.

For the independent escorts, an Internet search engine was used to locate sex worker review boards.[3] These boards were regarded as favorable initial contact sites because they provide workers with an opportunity to engage in public dialogue with past clients about service-related issues. As well, bulletin board posts from clients offer information about a sex worker's employment status—specifically, is the individual still involved in sex work and, if so, is he self-employed or affiliated with an escort agency?

Internet links from the review boards and the sex workers' personal sites were used to locate additional prospective interviewees. Other review boards (i.e., similar sites that participate in advertisement/banner exchanges) were located by following all appropriate "links" from one site to another. Sites whose sole purpose was to advertise escorts also were investigated. Upon identifying potential participants, their e-mail addresses and primary work locations were recorded.

Five main sites (2 review boards and 3 escort lists) were used to locate 118 potential participants. The men who were initially considered had personal e-mail addresses listed in their postings or advertisements. This criterion sought to eliminate agencies that advertised on these sites and listed a number of sex workers (i.e., 'worker's_name@name_of_agency. com'). Recorded contact information then was cross-referenced by city, name, identifying information (i.e., photos), and e-mail address to ensure that men advertising under different names (or professional identities) would not be contacted multiple times. This process resulted in 70 men serving as potential interviewees.

These individuals received an introductory letter via e-mail which outlined the purpose of the study as well as standard requirements for social scientific research with human participants (e.g., data were confidential and anonymous, participation was voluntary, etc.). Ten e-mails were undeliverable and 42 went unacknowledged. Of the 18 individuals who provided a response, two refused to participate and five would agree only to an e-mail interview. The latter's refusal to be interviewed in person or by telephone did not abate even after the researchers informed them that this means of communication was undesirable because it permitted the interviewee to scrutinize the contents of disclosure. Such scrutiny was of concern because it may diminish the spontaneous exchanges that accompany the personal interview and its potential for harnessing individuals' "propensity for self-reflection and narrative construction" (Flowers & Buston, 2001, p. 54).

Eleven men agreed to participate; however, only 8 were able to commit to an interview during the data collection period. One of the eight men recommended another person for participation in the study, resulting in a final sample of 9 independent escorts. Each interviewee received a copy of the consent form via e-mail, the details of which were reviewed with the second author. Three interviews were conducted in person and six by telephone.

To identify contractual escorts/erotic masseurs, the owner of an escort agency was contacted via e-mail to determine his willingness to participate. This individual granted his permission for on-site interviews, and a data collection period was agreed upon (approximately four days). Interviews were conducted in person by the second author, with the interview schedule being determined by participant availability (i.e., some were interviewed before or after their shift and others between clients). Of 15 potential participants, 12 were interviewed. Among the three who did not participate, one refused, one was not on-site during the data collection period, and one was too busy. Details regarding informed consent and the purpose of the research were given to all interviewees.

Data collection. Personal interviews were conducted in this study. According to Asher and Asher (1999), this method of data collection is appropriate when: (a) the topic under investigation is one about which there is a dearth of information; (b) the objective is to examine how a particular group of individuals view an aspect of themselves that is "notoriously difficult to quantify" (p. 137) such as their beliefs, attitudes, and/or values; and (c) the researchers are committed to the "authenticity of the participants' point[s] of view" (p. 137). Research by Calhoun and Weaver (1996) and Lasser and Tharinger (2003) underscore the utility of a qualitative approach when examining research questions that are not grounded in the motivation to test specific theories; questions that are exploratory in nature and, thus, may be addressed most satisfactorily by "examining the words of the subjects themselves" (Calhoun & Weaver, 1996, p. 214).

All interviews were semi-structured (i.e., participants were asked a series of general questions, which were followed by supplemental "trigger" items if required). For example, each participant was asked, "How do you think the gay community perceives male sex workers?" In some cases, this item was sufficient. However, in other cases, follow-up questions were necessary such as "Do you think gay men are jealous of you, admire you, etc.?" "How does gay popular culture portray male sex workers?" "In what ways is this portrayal accurate/inaccurate?" Key topics concerning awareness and possible effects of stigma were explored with all interviewees; however, since participants largely dictated the direction, depth, and length of disclosure, variations in the interview schedule occurred.

Interviews ranged in length from approximately 20 minutes to three hours. They were tape-recorded and transcribed verbatim (i.e., paralinguistic cues such as "um" and "M-hmm" were included). Three hundred and ninety-one pages of single-spaced text were produced and analyzed to identify themes concerning participants' views about stigma and sex work. Although individual differences in interpretation were acknowledged, the goal was to pinpoint commonalities among interviewees–assuming, of course, that such similarities existed.

The two authors reviewed the text separately and then compared themes. Given the exploratory nature of this study, discrepancies in the authors' analyses were not resolved (i.e., no attempt was made to "prove" that one author's interpretation was more "correct" than the other's); rather, the authors' assessments were combined resulting in a more expansive view of the data.

RESULTS

The first objective of this study was to identify whether interviewees perceived sex work as stigmatized (or, at least, provided textual information which connoted stigma). This information then would be used to inform the second objective, which focused on the possible effects of stigma. Although the two objectives are inter-related, for ease of presentation, they will be discussed separately.

Stigma Awareness

Most participants agreed that sex work was stigmatized, but attributed the stigma largely to public representations that focused on street prostitution and ignored other aspects of the industry–in particular, gay male escorts.

> ...it really bugs me when [people] just think of you as a whore. I mean, we are more than that: we're therapists, we keep marriages together. (Interviewee 19)

> I mean you see [the words] sex industry... you don't think of escorts, you think of hookers on the street. [People think] you live this dismal life and maybe your mom was a prostitute and she made you a prostitute.... They're glorifying five percent of the industry ... [There's] a difference between your street hookers, and your escorts and, like, your high paid escorts. [Those] are the three categories [I use] ... [So] even though I'm working [in] the same sex industry, I look down on street prostitution. I can't stand it. (Interviewee 9)

> Well, the only kind of representation I've come across is, you know, the street worker ... I think people need to realize that it's not just, you know, some drug addict runaway or whatever that's out there selling a blowjob for 20 bucks. (Interviewee 1)

> I do not live a ... marginal existence. It's not like I'm on the street, barely surviving ... doing people for drugs. (Interviewee 12)

Some interviewees believed that another contributor to the stigma surrounding the male sex industry is Western society's negative views of sexuality in general and homosexuality in particular.

> We're taught that [sex is] bad or we're taught that it's kinda gross and that, you know, you have to wait until you're married and all this other stuff. (Interviewee 17)

> People are very narrow-minded. Anything to do with sexuality or nudity ... we live in a very Puritan-type society. (Interviewee 7)

> We live in a generic Christian world so that's the morality of the majority. (Interviewee 14)

> I think we [male sex workers] are in an even worse position because ... we're men. Men aren't supposed to be prostitutes. I'm sure you could go to the library and look up a book on prostitution and find it only discusses women. (Interviewee 12)

I think we as gay people are seen as promiscuous PERIOD, from a heterosexual [viewpoint] ... (Interviewee 20)

Nobody's ever gonna make a fag *Pretty Woman*. (Interviewee 1)

Perceptions of whether the gay community stigmatizes male sex work were diverse. Some participants believed that the views of gay men were comparable to or, in some cases, more disparaging than those evidenced by their heterosexual counterparts.[4]

[Sex workers] are completely eroticized but also derided ... and really the rudest motherfuckers I deal with all day are the gay men.... The gay men are evil cunts. And I say this as a gay man, but like it's just pathetic the way, you know, they're totally happy to worship you, and then as soon as it's over ... you can feel the scorn. (Interviewee 14)

There's a sort of ... admiration-revulsion ... part of it is, um, a revulsion of, you know, "You're in the sex trade. You're a whore or prostitute or hustler or whatever you want to call it." But the other side of it is "Wow, this guy must be really hot and sexy." (Interviewee 13)

Negatively. Surprisingly. (Interviewee 17)

There are a lot of gay men [who] ... will judge people in the trade using the rest of society's moral standards. (Interviewee 11)

I think gay culture is just as intolerant as the straight culture ... I don't think as much as they [the gay community] demand equality that they are as willing to give equality ... [So], I don't think there's much difference between gay perception or straight perception when it comes to [the sex industry]. (Interviewee 7)

Just as in the heterosexual community, within the gay community ... you can have your left and your right ... your extremes. I'm sure there [are] some people out there within the gay community that feel that ... working in the sex industry only demeans or ... kind of brings down the image of homosexuals within the rest of society. (Interviewee 1)

However, other participants saw members of the gay community as less inclined to stigmatize those in the male sex industry, particularly those perceived as "higher end."

I don't think there's a big stigma on it [escorting] because if you're in the gay community, I mean, there's sex everywhere. (Interviewee 9)

I think a lot of people actually have a fantasy of doing it [escorting and/or pornography], and we're just the ones that took it a little further ... Some people look in awe of it because it does give you ... a bit of a celebrity status. So people tend to actually revere you a little bit more than look down on you. (Interviewee 5)

In the gay community it's a lot more acceptable ... I have a lot of friends that have bought hookers . . . when I worked in [city omitted] ... very young attractive men would be my clients. They were just very wealthy and they didn't want to go play the bar game. (Interviewee 10)

...the gay community is a very diverse community ... being a rent-boy is just one of the common quintessential positions that a gay man could do ... it's not outrageous ... so much of our identity is sexual anyways. (Interviewee 12)

When asked to particularize how they perceived sex workers prior to their involvement in the industry, a majority of interviewees evidenced positive perceptions.

I thought they were cool. (Interviewee 21)

...as soon as I saw one or read anything [about sex work], my instant impression was ... that they were heroes ... [It's] embarrassing to ... say this, but it was like ... I want to be the male Annie Sprinkle. (Interviewee 4)

I just lay in bed at like 15 reading ... *Our Lady of the Flowers* and *City of Night* ... and wanting to be that young man out there on the street. (Interviewee 14)

I was excited by it ... I thought a lot of it was very glamorous. (Interviewee 10)

Other participants did not report having a clearly defined perception of sex workers or saw them as qualitatively similar to themselves.

I never thought of it as really negative ... I generally thought of women ... like, male sex workers are generally ignored [in mass media]. (Interviewee 11)

I neither had a negative impression nor did I ever glamorize it ... It just is. (Interviewee 13)

I actually didn't see myself as being that much different. (Interviewee 5)

I figured that people doing escort work were pretty much kind of like me. (Interviewee 1)

Despite awareness of the stigma surrounding the male sex industry, only a minority of participants reported possessing negative views prior to their involvement.

I thought they were all crack whores. (Interviewee 19)

[My opinion of sex workers] used to be very low because that was how I was brought up...[I] didn't know anyone who was a sex worker ... so ... I was very prejudiced against them. (Interviewee 12)

Putative Effects of Working in a Stigmatized Industry

Inspection of the transcripts revealed that, for some participants, working in the male sex industry appeared to have a deleterious effect on them or on sex workers they knew.

[During a session] you could just cancel out on your body ... you could leave your soul, and then afterwards you'd come back and you're, um, like "Oh my God." You're back in your body and you need some sort of substance or something to sort of allevi-ate that experience. (Interviewee 10)

You know I wish I had reported it (being raped).... Part of the reason why I was so incapable of doing anything about it for a while was just because ... there's a tendency in this job to get used to ... a client-attendant relationship that is manipulative, that is exploitive. (Interviewee 20)

I've been assaulted emotionally. One [instance] that stands out in my mind was a regular client of mine was invited to a dinner party. We got there and the host said [to the client], "Ok ... come in and have drinks. We're sending the tricks upstairs in the bedroom, we'll see them later." (Interviewee 13)

Others believed that, despite society's negative views of male sex work, their involvement in the industry was largely positive.

I think you have to care about yourself a lot to give yourself away like that. (Interviewee 21)

...working here made me realize that I'm not damaged. That I'm pretty smart.... I had body issues too. This job has given me a lot more [confidence] ... I take my shirt off at the beach now. ... I'm starting to like my body image now when I look at it in the mirror. (Interviewee 19)

I don't feel I'm damaged in any way ... I can hold normal friendships and relationships and stuff like that. (Interviewee 7)

Working in a stigmatized industry also may have ramifications in terms of individuals' willingness to disclose their employment to family, friends, and significant others.[5] Again, variability was noted in the transcripts, with some individuals reporting maximal disclosure or claiming that disclosure was irrelevant.

Q: Who knows you're employed in the industry?

Everybody.... There's no one I've particularly excluded.... If they ask, I tell them. (Interviewee 13)

My family ... My mom was like, "Whatever makes you happy." My mom supports me. If you ask me, you've got to be happy with who you are. (Interviewee 16)

All of them. (Interviewee 15)

My family don't live in Canada anymore so ... it's sort of a non-issue ... (Interviewee 18)

Others, however, reported downplaying their involvement to certain individuals such as key parental figures.

I told my father, but I told [him] that I'm here as a manager only. (Interviewee 19)

I told my mother ... last year, but [I] focused more on the s/m master work because it is less about 'sex' and my mother is 65 and doesn't need to know everything. (Interviewee 4)

I do have one my closest friends who ... thinks I'm doing it [modeling] over the Internet [rather than working with an escort agency]. I just didn't tell her because I think she'd get worried. (Interviewee 10)

Most interviewees, however, evidenced partial disclosure (i.e., they told some individuals they were involved in the male sex industry, but not others).

> I haven't told my sister and my dad just because they're very religious. (Interviewee 12)

> The only people who don't know are my immediate family. ... My mother is a very conservative Christian and would be [pause] absolutely devastated. And it's like, why cause her grief? It just [pause] ... serves no purpose. (Interviewee 3)

> [Q: Does your family know?] No. I haven't even come out to my family. It's pathetic. (Interviewee 21)

> I mean I keep it select. I keep it to a small group ... basically, [people] I feel I can trust. People I hope can keep a secret. (Interviewee 20)

DISCUSSION

These findings suggest that most interviewees evidenced awareness of the pervasive negative cultural norms that surround the sex industry in dominant (heterosexual) culture and, according to some participants, in gay subculture as well. They attributed the negativity surrounding the male sex industry to society's erotophobia, homonegativity, and myopic focus on street-based prostitution. Some interviewees believed that gay men were just as punitive as their straight counterparts which, due to the community's emphasis on sexuality, many regarded as a hypocritical stance. However, others felt that the gay community regarded involvement in sex work as a legitimate and, in some cases, high-status form of employment.

In terms of their involvement in a stigmatized profession such as sex work, some participants believed that it was deleterious to them psychologically. The primary concerns raised were the emotional distancing techniques required to cope with specific aspects of the job and the normalization of exploitation/abuse. Conversely, other interviewees felt that their involvement in the sex industry assisted in their personal development.

These findings suggest that the stigma associated with participation in sex work is a multifaceted construct. With one exception, none of the participants saw their employment as escorts/erotic masseurs in uniformly negative terms. Yet, even those who presented the most positive view of their involvement in the industry acknowledged that sex work could be damaging to some escorts (e.g., those who were not "emotionally stable"–Interviewee 4). As well, most interviewees reported there were key parental figures/significant others from whom they had withheld details concerning their choice of employment. Even among the minority who reported "full disclosure," most presented their employment in a more socially acceptable manner (e.g., they reported being managers rather than escorts or engaging in sex work via the Internet rather than in person). It should be noted that the motivation to limit disclosure was not presented as self-serving but, rather, appeared grounded in the desire to protect others from vicariously experiencing the stigma of sex work.

A number of issues warrant consideration in future research. For example, many of the independent escorts clearly differentiated themselves from other categories of sex worker:

> The difference for me [is] you're a hooker ... you work for drugs. [With] escorts ... it's a little, maybe a little class ... you don't have to stand on the corner of the street. I think if I [were] a street prostitute, I would have no respect. Zero. Absolutely none. (Interviewee 9)

Those who were employed contractually as escorts/erotic masseurs were less apt to establish such demarcations:

> I don't like throwing fancy words around like escorting and masseur. To me, it's just prostitution basically ... I think what I'm doing in here and what the guy on the corner is doing is no different whatsoever. The only difference is the environment I'm doing it in and the price point ... (Interviewee 10)

Researchers should investigate the possible reasons underlying these differences.

Issues of stigma awareness and the "effects" of involvement in a stigmatized profession also should be explored from the vantage of clients, a group that has gone largely unstudied by researchers (Allman, 1999). Do clients perceive the act of hiring a sex worker as transgressive or as a legitimate transaction? Do such perceptions vary as a function of clients' sexual identity and immersion in the gay community? Do they perceive sex work as a multifaceted construct or do they embrace interviewees' perception that people tend to conflate street-based prostitution with other categories of sex work? The possible influence of venue vis-à-vis clients' perceptions also warrants assessment. For example, one contractual employee noted that [the escort agency] provided "... a façade of respectability ..." (Interviewee 11). Do clients perceive such environments as "respectable" and, if so, why?

Given that personal interviews were conducted, an important limitation of the current study is the veracity of participants' responses. It is possible, for example, that individuals may have tailored their disclosure to map onto what they believed the interviewer wanted to hear. As one participant remarked, "... bringing your book forward [can] hopefully broaden people's horizons in terms of how they see this industry" (Interviewee 20). The determination to broaden horizons and, in so doing, engender a more "sex positive" view of male sex work may have motivated interviewees. As well, the possibility that some participants adopted a specific persona during the interview process cannot be discounted.[6]

In summary, the results of this study underscore the need to abandon narrow emphases that mythologize sex work or present involvement in the industry as horrific. As one interviewee pointed out:

> [O]n a good day, I have two or three clients that are clean and well-to-do men; that are nice and respectful, and give me a great blowjob, and I walk away with 900 dollars that day... I have days like that and I'm like "Hmmm. Jeez. Life ain't so bad." (Interviewee 10)

NOTES

1. Social stigma may be defined as a "social construction that involves at least two fundamental components: (1) the recognition of difference based on some distinguishing characteristic or 'mark'; and 2) a consequent devaluation of the person" (Dovidio, Major, & Crocker 2000 as cited in Hebl & Dovidio, 2005). Hebl and Dovidio (2005) suggest that the constructed nature of social stigmas underscores the fact that they are contextually based (i.e., an identity that is stigmatized in one environment may not be stigmatized in another).

2. There is ample social scientific evidence to suggest that "... stigmatization of GLB [i.e., gay males, lesbian females, and bisexual males and females] is a serious and prevalent social problem in North America" (Banks, 2003, p. 12). Research by Banks (2003), Flowers and Buston (2001), and Herek, Gillis, and Cogan (1999) detail the prevalence, acceptability, and pernicious effects of homonegativity (i.e., negative attitudes and behaviours directed toward GLB persons).

3. Escort review boards are Internet bulletin boards that allow escorts both free and paid advertising and allow clients to access and post "reviews" of the men and women

in the sex industry. Some of the boards are mere checklists with less than ten items, while others allow unlimited space for clients to detail their experiences. Additionally, a few sites allow the worker being reviewed to post rebuttals.

4. Some interviewees suggested that it was hypocritical for gay men to stigmatize the male sex industry:

I've had several conversations with guys that I know just through friends or hanging out with people and they're always like "Well, how can you have sex for money?"... And I'm like "Well, you go to the club and pick up a guy and bring him home and have sex for free." How is that any different? (Interviewee 18).

I mean half the people that are judging me are the ones that walk around the parks or around the bathhouses every week, fucking everyone left and right...I'm a whore, they're a slut. What's the difference? (Interviewee 19).

5. For some participants, disclosure to prospective partners was deemed irrelevant because they could not envision having a relationship while involved in the male sex industry.

If I was to meet a man ... who I would like to share a relationship with, I couldn't do this sort of work....Sometimes I think maybe I keep myself in this industry, too, so that I don't have to venture down that road ... (Interviewee 10).

6. One interviewee remarked that prostitute as victim may be "part of the [sex worker's] shtick"; a role that he "plays" because it maps onto what clients expect (Interviewee 13).

REFERENCES

Allman, D. (1999). *M is for mutual, A is for acts: Male sex work and AIDS in Canada.* Toronto, ON: Health Canada.

Allman, D., & Myers, T. (1999). Male sex work and HIV/AIDS in Canada. In P. Aggleton (Ed.), *Men who sell sex: International perspectives on male prostitution and HIV/AIDS* (pp. 61-81). Philadelphia, PA: Temple University Press.

Asher, N. S., & Asher, K. C. (1999). Qualitative methods for an outsider looking in: Lesbian women and body image. In M. Kopala & L. A. Suzuki (Eds.), *Using qualitative methods in psychology* (pp. 135-144). Thousand Oaks, CA: Sage.

Banks, C. (2003). *The cost of homophobia: Literature review on the human impact of homophobia in Canada.* Saskatoon, SK: Rochon Associated Human Resource Management Consulting.

Boles, J., & Elifson, K. W. (1994). Sexual identity and HIV: The male prostitute. *Journal of Sex Research, 31,* 39-46.

Browne, J., & Minichiello, V. (1995). The social meanings behind male sex work: Implications for sexual interactions. *British Journal of Sociology, 46,* 598-622.

Calhoun, T. C., & Weaver, G. (1996). Rational decision-making among male street prostitutes. *Deviant Behavior, 17,* 209-227.

Flowers, P., & Buston, K. (2001). "I was terrified of being different": Exploring gay men's accounts of growing up in a heterosexist society. *Journal of Adolescence, 24,* 51-65.

Hebl, M. R., & Dovidio, J. F. (2005). Promoting the "social" in the examination of social stigma. *Personality and Social Psychology Review, 9,* 156-182.

Herek, G. M., Gillis, R. J., & Cogan, J. C. (1999). Psychological sequelae of hate-crime victimization among lesbian, gay, and bisexual adults. *Journal of Consulting and Clinical Psychology, 67*, 945-951.

Joffe, H., & Dockrell, J. E. (1995). Safer sex: Lessons from the male sex industry. *Journal of Community & Applied Social Psychology, 5*, 333-346.

Lasser, J., & Tharinger, D. (2003). Visibility management in school and beyond: A qualitative study of gay, lesbian, bisexual youth. *Journal of Adolescence, 26*, 233-244.

Marino, R., Browne, J., & Minichiello, V. (2000). An instrument to measure safer sex strategies used by male sex workers. *Archives of Sexual Behavior, 29*, 217-228.

Minichiello, V., Marino, R., Browne, J., Jamieson, M., Peterson, K., Reuter, B., & Robinson, K. (2000). Commercial sex between men: A prospective diary-based study. *Journal of Sex Research, 37*, 151-160.

Minichiello, V., Marino, R., Browne, J., Jamieson, M., Peterson, K., Reuter, B., & Robinson, K. (2001). Male sex workers in three Australian cities: Socio-demographic and sex work characteristics. *Journal of Homosexuality, 42*(1), 29-51.

Morrison, T. G., & Whitehead, B. W. (2005). Strategies of stigma resistance among Canadian gay-identified sex workers. *Journal of Psychology and Human Sexuality, 17*(1/2), 169-179.

Pheterson, G. (1990). The category "prostitute" in scientific inquiry. *Journal of Sex Research, 27*, 397-407.

Scambler, G. (1997). Conspicuous and inconspicuous sex work: The neglect of the ordinary and mundane. In G. Scambler & A. Scambler (Eds.), *Rethinking prostitution: Purchasing sex in the 1990s* (pp. 105-120). New York, NY: Routledge.

Uy, J. M., Parsons, J. T., Bimbi, D. S., Koken, J. A., & Halkitis, P. N. (2004). Gay and bisexual male escorts who advertise on the Internet: Understanding reasons for and effects of involvement in commercial sex. *International Journal of Men's Health, 3*, 11-26.

Weinberg, M. S., Worth, H., & Williams, C. J. (2001). Men sex workers and other men who have sex with men: How do their HIV risks compare in New Zealand? *Archives of Sexual Behavior, 30*, 273-286.

doi:10.1300/J082v53n01_09

Looking Beyond HIV:
Eliciting Individual
and Community Needs
of Male Internet Escorts

Jeffrey T. Parsons, PhD
Juline A. Koken, PhD (candidate)
David S. Bimbi, PhD (candidate)

City University of New York

Jeffrey T. Parsons, PhD, is Associate Professor of Psychology at Hunter College and the Graduate Center of the City University of New York, and also is Director of the Center for HIV/AIDS Educational Studies and Training. His research focuses on the intersections between sexuality, HIV/AIDS, and substance use, and he also has conducted research in the areas of sex work, HIV medication adherence, and sexual compulsivity. He is actively involved in the Society for the Scientific Study of Sexuality and the Society for the Advancement of Sexual Health.

Juline A. Koken is a doctoral student at the Graduate Center of the City University of New York and Center for HIV/AIDS Educational Studies and Training (CHEST). Her research interests focus on issues facing female and male sex workers, and how sex workers experience positive marginality.

David S. Bimbi is a doctoral student at the Graduate Center of the City University of New York and Center for HIV/AIDS Educational Studies and Training (CHEST). His research interests focus on male sex workers, barebacking, and sexual behaviors of gay and bisexual men. Correspondence may be addressed to: Jeffrey T. Parsons, PhD, Hunter College-CUNY, Department of Psychology, 695 Park Avenue, New York, NY 10021 (E-mail: jeffrey.parsons@hunter.cuny.edu).

The Classified Project was funded by a Faculty Development Grant to the first author. The authors acknowledge the assistance of James Kelleher and the willingness of participants to share their stories and experiences.

[Haworth co-indexing entry note]: "Looking Beyond HIV: Eliciting Individual and Community Needs of Male Internet Escorts." Parsons, Jeffrey T., Juline A. Koken, and David S. Bimbi. Co-published simultaneously in *Journal of Homosexuality* (The Haworth Press, Inc.) Vol. 53, No. 1/2, 2007, pp. 219-240; and: *Male Sex Work: A Business Doing Pleasure* (ed: Todd G. Morrison and Bruce W. Whitehead) The Haworth Press, Inc., 2007, pp. 219-240. Single or multiple copies of this article are available for a fee from The Haworth Document Delivery Service [1-800-HAWORTH, 9:00 a.m. - 5:00 p.m. (EST). E-mail address: docdelivery@haworthpress.com].

Available online at http://jh.haworthpress.com
© 2007 by The Haworth Press, Inc. All rights reserved.
doi:10.1300/J082v53n01_10

SUMMARY. In evaluating the needs of male sex workers (MSWs), past research and community-based outreach efforts have assumed they should receive counseling and be educated regarding drug abuse and HIV/STI prevention. These assumptions have been based upon studies that predominantly sampled heterosexually identified men who work on the street as 'hustlers.' The purpose of this study was to set aside previous assumptions, and elicit directly from MSWs their perceived needs. Semi-structured interviews were conducted with 46 gay and bisexual male escorts who advertise on the Internet, an understudied group that is expected to differ greatly from street-based MSWs. The men identified several areas where attention should be directed beyond safer sex, such as business advice (e.g., taxes, income investment) and assistance with navigating legal issues. These findings have direct implications for community-based organizations, advocates for MSWs, and men in the commercial sex industry. doi:10.1300/J082v53n01_10 *[Article copies available for a fee from The Haworth Document Delivery Service: 1-800-HAWORTH. E-mail address: <docdelivery@haworthpress.com> Website: <http://www. HaworthPress.com> © 2007 by The Haworth Press, Inc. All rights reserved.]*

KEYWORDS. Male escorts, gay men, sex work, advice, education

INTRODUCTION

Most research concerning the psychosocial and physical health of male sex workers (MSWs) has focused on non-gay identified hustlers and those who work the streets (Hickson, Weatherburn, Hows, & Davies, 1994). However, male escort agencies providing sexual services for men have been in operation for nearly 20 years (Salamon, 1989), and individuals have been advertising their services as models, masseurs, body workers, or escorts in magazines and newspapers targeting the gay community for approximately the same amount of time (Lumby, 1978). Further, recent research has found that MSWs are increasingly likely to be gay-identified, regardless of whether they are hustlers or escorts (Browne & Minichiello, 1995; Cates & Markley, 1992). With the advent of the Internet, a new sex work venue has emerged. The ease, availability, and relatively low cost of advertising for commercial male-to-male sex work have led to the increased use of this venue by MSWs. Many Internet-based escorts have their own Web sites, including photos and descriptions of their services, and potential clients are able to e-mail these escorts or find them in popular Internet chat rooms.

It is likely that escorts who advertise via the Internet using their own Web sites, rather than that of an agency, differ substantially from other types of male sex workers. As independent contractors, they can be more selective about their clients and the sexual activities they engage in, charge more for their services, and exercise greater control over their work schedule. Whereas hustlers and street-based sex workers risk arrest, exposure to violence, and not being paid for services rendered (Calhoun & Weaver, 1996), these problems are less likely to occur among independent male escorts who advertise over the Internet (Joffe & Dockrell, 1995).

Most of the research on MSWs has emphasized their potential role in HIV transmission and infection (Vanwesenbeeck, 2001). In the past, such men have been referred to as "vectors of transmission" of HIV infection into the heterosexual society, even in the absence of reported unsafe sex (Morse, Simon, Osofsky, Balson, & Gaumer, 1991). Implicit in this derogatory label is the assumption that MSWs pose greater risk to others than they do to themselves, and that they are more dangerous to heterosexual than to homosexual populations in terms of the potential to spread HIV (Coutinho, van Andel, & Rijsdijk, 1988). A problem with this perspective, however, is the growing body of research showing that the majority of MSWs consistently use condoms during sexual encounters with their clients (Estcourt et al., 2000; Estep, Waldorf, & Marotta, 1992; Minichiello et al., 2000; Overs, 1991; Perkins, Prestage, Sharp, & Lovejoy, 1994; Pleak & Meyer-Bahlburg, 1990; Ziersch, Gaffney, & Tomlinson, 2000).

In trying to evaluate the needs of MSWs, the tendency is to assume they need (and thus want) information on HIV and sexually transmitted infection (STI) prevention, drug abuse, sexual addiction or compulsivity, and counseling for other psychological or physical problems. Additionally, outreach efforts aimed at non-gay identified MSWs have frequently focused on coping with the cognitive dissonance that may result from the threat homosexual activity poses to their heterosexual identity (Gaffney, 2003). Failure to enable MSWs to particularize their own needs may explain, in part, why previous efforts by community-based organizations to provide services to MSWs have been unsuccessful (Boles & Elifson, 1998).

It is likely that gay-identified male escorts who advertise on the Internet have different needs and desires in terms of information, advice, and programs than street-based MSWs and those with less independence in their work practices. As evidenced by their method of advertising, these men have greater access to the vast wealth of health-related facts available via the information superhighway. However, whether Internet-based MSWs know where to find this information, and if they are in fact accessing it, has not been addressed in the available literature.

In order to understand the needs of Internet escorts, we asked a sample of these men about their desires and interests for programs and education. Further, we asked these men what advice or recommendations they would provide to other male escorts or gay and bisexual men considering this profession. The underlying premise behind this investigation, called The Classified Project, was to set aside our a priori assumptions about what these unique MSWs want or need, and instead let them tell us.

METHOD

Participants

The mean age of participants ($N = 46$) was 31.8 ($SD = 6.5$; range = 22 to 47). The majority identified as White, gay, and indicated having at least some college education (see Table 1).

TABLE 1. Participant Demographics and Health Characteristics ($N = 46$)

	n	%
Sexual Orientation		
Homosexual/Gay	38	82.6%
Bisexual	8	17.4%
Ethnicity		
African American	5	10.9%
Asian/Pacific Islander	3	6.5%
Caucasian	31	67.4%
Latino	7	15.2%
Education		
High School or Less	2	4.3%
Some College	14	30.4%
Bachelor's Degree	21	45.7%
Graduate Coursework/Degree	9	19.6%

Thirty-eight participants (82.6%) reported being HIV seronegative; six (13.0%) reported being HIV seropositive, and two (4.3%) said they had never been tested for HIV due to their belief that it was unnecessary because they did not engage in receptive anal intercourse. Twenty-one (45.6%) of the men reported a history of STIs other than HIV.

More than a third of the sample (37%, $n = 17$) reported currently having a male primary partner. None of the men indicated having female primary partners. All but three of these primary partners knew about the participant's sex work. In the past three months, the men reported engaging in sexual activity with an average of 44.8 ($SD = 40.7$; Median = 32) work-related and 25.0 ($SD = 51.8$; Median = 15) non-work-related sexual partners.

The average length of time participants reported working as escorts was 2.7 years ($SD = 5.0$; range = 3 weeks to 25 years). Half ($n = 23$) reported spending at least 12 hours a week escorting or performing related activities, such as answering phone calls, talking with potential clients online, and maintaining their appearance (e.g., going to the gym and tanning); 26% ($n = 12$) reported spending more than 20 hours a week escorting and could be considered full-time or nearly full-time sex workers. The median range of income reported from sex work was $20,000 to $29,999 U.S. per annum. The median range reported from sources other than sex work was $10,000 to $19,999 U.S. per annum. Most men (70%, $n = 32$) charged $200 an hour, with a range from $75 for "body work" to $250 for "full service." Those escorts who reported engaging in "body work" provided massage with full release, meaning that the escort would massage the client and then masturbate the client to orgasm. Those escorts who reported "full service" work engaged in various forms of sexual activity with clients, including masturbation, oral and anal intercourse, and specific fetish-oriented behaviors.

Procedure

The e-mail addresses of potential participants were identified through the user profiles from Internet Service Providers and from male escort Web sites. An e-mail describing "The Classified Project" was sent to each valid e-mail address (370 addresses in total), and men were invited to call to be screened for the study. The e-mail assured potential participants of the confidential nature of the study, which was approved by an Institutional Review Board, and also disavowed any link to law enforcement. A total of 60 phone calls were received. These men were screened by telephone to determine eligibility (i.e., they self-identified as a gay or bisexual male, reported engaging in sex work during the past 90 days; were over 18 years of age; and served as an independent escort with an online presence). Fifty-seven men were scheduled for in-person appointments. Of these, seven men failed to keep their appointments.

Participants provided informed consent and then completed a qualitative interview, followed by a self-administered quantitative survey of demographic characteristics and other psychosocial factors, such as sexual compulsivity (Parsons, Bimbi, & Halkitis, 2001), and attitudes about barebacking (Bimbi & Parsons, 2005). Each participant received a total of $75 for participating in the qualitative interview and the quantitative survey. Due to equipment failure, four interviews were neither transcribed nor analyzed, thus resulting in a final sample of 46 interviews.

Materials

The data reported here are based on the qualitative interviews of The Classified Project. The interviews took from 45 to 75 minutes to complete and covered a variety of areas, including participants' initiation into sex work, their perspectives on what skills and resources are needed by men to work successfully as an escort, as well as what advice they would offer to a friend who expressed an interest in working as an escort.

The open-ended questions in the interview encouraged participants to elaborate on their thoughts, feelings, and experiences. This allowed participants to express themselves freely, and highly salient experiences arose naturally in the course of the interview without substantial probing on the part of the interviewer. All interviews were conducted in a private, one-on-one setting by trained male interviewers. Interviews were audio recorded, sent to an independent firm for transcription, and subsequently verified for accuracy by having a member of the research team listen to the tape and compare what he or she heard to the produced transcript, making changes when necessary. All identifying details were removed from transcripts to protect participants' privacy.

Analytic Strategy

Transcripts were analyzed utilizing qualitative software (NUDIST, 1997), which allowed participants' statements concerning their feelings about sex work, strategies for staying physically and emotionally healthy while maximizing profit, and narratives on what advice they would give to a potential escort to be identified and captured. After reading and reviewing each interview several times, broad codes for *advice* and *what escorts want* were created and applied to passages where these themes arose. Using a grounded theory approach (Strauss & Corbin, 1990), emerging themes and patterns were noted as they arose from the transcripts. After reviewing these, new codes were created and applied, or simply noted with a flag code to connote areas for future exploration and research.

RESULTS

Getting Started as an Escort

Several of the participants (24%, *n* = 11) emphasized the importance of doing their own research on the realities of sex work prior to beginning work as an escort. Other men in the sex work industry were described as valued sources of specialized knowledge, and reviewing the experiences of a variety of escorts was suggested as an excellent way to get an idea of what the work "is really like." In explaining how he would describe his work to those interested in escorting, one participant said: "I think [I would] describe the experience, or a few experiences. So it would be less emotionally draining sometimes because they [potential escorts] would be able to prepare" (41, White).[1]

Four of the eleven men suggested specific techniques for preparing to get started as a sex worker, such as contacting one or more escorts in person or online or through reading books written by male escorts.

> I have a friend, he didn't start doing it [escorting] until after we knew each other. And when he met me, [I was] a great resource. He asked me lots of questions. He considered it, talked about it, and it was about six months before he started doing it. (29, Latino)

One technique mentioned by four of these participants was to hire an escort so they could experience a session from the client's perspective, and also have the opportunity to discuss ways of getting started in the business. As one participant describes:

> I went through a period of hiring body workers and saw different ranges of the people who gave massages and things. I was just happy experimenting. I didn't think I was attractive enough or whatever enough to be able to do it myself. And so I called a guy

up, and he came over, and he was a body worker, and we had a session. And we actually really clicked. So I had enough connection with him to be able to really grill him and say, "How do you do it?" "What's it like?" "How do you handle yourself when you walk through the door?" "What do you take with you?" So he told me everything, and he said, "If you're that interested, you should try it." So I thought about it for six months, and in the end, I decided, well, let me try advertising as a body worker. I'll do a client. If I don't like it, I will never do it again. So I did. (35, Asian/Pacific Islander)

This man hints at one function hiring an escort may serve for those considering entering the business–the opportunity to "get their feet wet" in the business by adopting the role of a client. Through hiring escorts, these interviewees were able to access insider knowledge about working in the business, as well as receive what could be termed "hands-on training."

The Basics of the Business

When asked what information participants thought would be helpful to MSWs, many of the men requested information about basic business practices for escorts. Participants reported that appropriate marketing of one's self and learning how to interact with clients in a positive way were essential to building and maintaining a client base.

I would like to see some information that describes dealing very, very nicely with clients, because it's a job. A lot of escorts, they are really nasty. "What do you want to do? That's two hundred dollars." And they don't even say, "Hi, how are you?" They just care about the money, and they forget that the money comes from a customer. (27, Latino)

You have to basically market yourself, find a way to market yourself, and deliver what you say you'll deliver. I send thank you notes to my clients. I'm literally a customer service business. (33, White)

In making customer service a priority, these men indicate a clear awareness that they are in the *business* of pleasure. Previous studies (e.g., Browne & Minichiello, 1996) have noted that maintaining an "occupational perspective" towards escorting makes good business sense and also may contribute to a positive feeling of professionalism and self-efficacy on the part of the worker. This occupational framing was observed among the men in the current study.

Some participants ($n = 10$, 22%) mentioned that they would like more information about the financial aspects of working as an escort. Uncertainty over how to set rates and negotiate financial matters with clients were common themes: "Well, for me, I'm always confused about money, so I would love to see information about that. I never know how much I'm supposed to be charging or getting" (30, White). Another frequently mentioned topic concerned how to pay taxes and manage income from escorting. Several participants stated that such information would be useful to the majority of MSWs, given the amount of income a typical escort may earn, and the young age of many of the men entering the business.

> Here's one thing I would like. For the last year or so, I've been very focused on personal finances. I finally decided to start declaring all my income, which is a big decision. And I think a workshop for people in the sex industry regarding financial matters [would be attractive]. It would involve a lot of emotional and psychological issues as well. Because I think a lot of people may hide in a lot of different ways, including hiding their money in a way which is not beneficial to them. Money that you don't declare, you can't invest. (29, Latino)

As this participant points out, decisions regarding how to handle money made in the commercial sex industry are complicated by the extralegal status of sex work.

Staying Healthy, Staying Safe, and Staying Out of Jail

Due to the physical and sexual nature of escorting, the fact that it frequently involves private sessions in the client's home or in a hotel room, and its marginal legal status, many of the men reported health and safety as high priorities. Nine (20%) of the men commented that while safety information is vital to the welfare of MSWs, many escorts may not know where to access such information. This indicates a gap in services available to men in the commercial sex industry. Further, even when such services are available, MSWs may not know of their existence.

Nearly half of the participants ($n = 22$, 48%) called for the creation of a reliable, frequently updated, accessible source of safer sex information. Previous studies (Halkitis & Parsons, 2000; Wolitski & Branson, 2002) have found that, in spite of years of safer sex campaigns, many gay and bisexual men still feel uncertain about the level of risk involved with certain sexual practices, such as oral sex. As well, information on available vaccinations (e.g., Hepatitis A and B) does not seem to have reached many in the MSW community. In explaining the information he felt he lacked as an escort, one participant said: "Detailed listings of safe sex practices. That would be the most important for me. Like, I go next month for my final Hepatitis vaccine. I didn't even know a vaccine existed. I had no idea" (33, White).

While many MSWs may benefit from clear explanations of the degree of HIV/STI risk involved with various sexual acts, some researchers view the safer sex negotiation strategies developed by escorts as a rich source of knowledge that could benefit sexually active individuals (Browne & Minichiello, 1995). Many MSWs, through their interactions with diverse clients and requests for varied sexual experiences, have developed a repertoire of strategies that ensure safer sex is practiced with clients and also provide clients with education regarding the potential risk of behaviors requested (Parsons, Koken, & Bimbi, 2004). The notion of the "sex worker as sex educator" is clearly exemplified in the following narrative:

> There was one time, actually quite recently, where a guy that I had seen once before–and, we had been safe before–and then he actually, he tried–he tried to fuck me without one [a condom]. He just tried to stick it in before, you know. But, obviously, that wasn't going to happen. So I said, "Here, take this and put it on." Because he really just wanted to, you know, ram me. I said, "Do you want me to leave?" … But, I said, "No, no, no. You have to put it on." And he said "I don't like condoms." And I said, "Well, I do." And he said, "Well, I'm negative." I said, "So am I, and I plan to stay that way. Slip it on." Those were my exact words. And he said, "Okay," [and] then he did. (27, White)

The following participant, one of the older men in the sample, describes a more proactive and "fatherly" approach to educating his clients and initiating safer sex practices:

I have two older brothers and a really great father, and it's just in my nature to always be protective, whatever. So I mean, I'm protective of these guys–I feel very strongly about safe sex. I usually take the first step to bring up the issue. If you, the sex worker, make the first thing about safe sex, then they know you're serious and responsible, and it's not just about money. It's about your will. For a sex worker to make the first comment about "it has to be safe," you risk losing business, and they know that. So that impresses them, and that makes them know you really are going to be safe. I mean, by the late '80s, I met so many men and didn't remember who the hell they were, calling me up and saying, "Gee, my God, you know, when you pulled out those gloves and started using condoms or dildos, I thought you were a lunatic. But I realized when, after I left you that, you know, that you had woken me up to safe sex, and I just want to say thank you, you saved my life." (42, White)

As seen above, MSWs may utilize both reactive and proactive strategies as sex educators in their interactions with clients. These two narratives illustrate the importance of looking at both sides of the equation when investigating motivations and practices of unsafe sex in commercial sex interactions. Clients who are resistant to safer sex practices or who seek out unsafe sex with MSWs are potentially the "vectors of disease transmission" that escorts are so often assumed to be.

Some participants ($n = 9$, 20%) stated that escorts would benefit from information on resources for drug and alcohol counseling. The theme of sex work as a risk factor for drug and/or alcohol abuse arose in the interviews of these men:

There's just so many things about the nature of sex work that encourage you, you're around it [drugs and alcohol] all the time and the money's quick and easy. And it's so much easier to do sex work. You can take a pop of Viagra, do some coke, do some crystal. (42, White)

Clearly these men view substance abuse as a problem facing many MSWs in the industry. As one man stated: "Sex work, being so marginal, it can be so psychically taxing that people self-medicate and then they have to recover from their medication" (35, Asian/Pacific-Islander). Community-based organizations would do well to note this issue and reach out to these men to raise awareness about their services.

Safer sex and substance use were not the only concerns faced by the participants interviewed for this study. As stated previously, physical safety is critical for MSWs, due to the "behind closed doors" nature of their work. Many of the participants ($n = 19$, 41%) described strategies for ensuring their physical safety when screening and visiting clients. These strategies included ways of discerning potentially dangerous clients over the phone and by e-mail, verifying the client's identity, and telling a friend or family member where they were going.

> Don't go by yourself. And if you do go by yourself, make sure you let somebody know where you're going, get an address. I use *54 [a mechanism in the United States by which you can obtain the phone number of the person calling you] and I'll check the address to the telephone number, that it's not going on a wild goose chase—always leave a trail because you never know where you're going. And, if you have a bad feeling, don't go. (31, White)
>
> I actually leave it on my computer. The name, address, and picture of the person is actually left on a computer, so that when I leave the house ... if somebody [opens] the computer, and hits any key, it all flashes up on the screen. (37, White)

One specific safety issue brought up by participants, in terms of their needs as escorts, was how to deal with clients who are inebriated or high. Many participants warned that this could be a potentially unstable situation, such as one man who said: "They [potential escorts] should know how to tell people are wasting your time or leading you into dangerous situations. There are all kinds of little things that are a red flag. The whole drug thing, to me, is a problem. Dealing with clients [who are] on drugs or high" (31, White).

Aside from screening out potentially dangerous clients, some escorts ($n = 16$, 35%) stated that the ability to be able to discern whether or not a potential client was a police officer was a critical unmet need. One participant explained that he would like to see programs for MSWs that train men "how to screen someone over the phone. How to discern if someone's on drugs or masturbating or could possibly be a cop. How to word your ad in a non-incriminating way" (28, White).

These men expressed a need for clear, concise legal information on what they could put in their advertisements, what could be spoken about over the phone, and how to negotiate payment and services in person. Several expressed that this information would be extremely helpful if posted on an Internet Web site. Another theme arising from the interviews was the desire to network with other escorts or have peer support systems in order to exchange information about police crackdowns:

> I think more of a community thing where we help each other that way, also for legal advice as well. If you're in the middle of these busts and things in New York, how do you handle it? What do you do? How do you word your ads to get around the legal issue? (36, White)

> Legal information is something that's really important. There's so much confusion out there about what's allowed, and what's not allowed. And if you are going to have a police sting–what do you do, where do you go, who do you call? I wouldn't know… If you end up with someone who is scary or who harms you in some way, where do you turn? Is there someplace…a number you can call for someone to meet you at the hospital? These kinds of informational things are really, really useful. (44, White)

Much like the confusion surrounding how to manage money and pay taxes on income made from sex work, the illegal nature of exchanging sex for money in the United States complicates negotiation with potential clients and limits the ability of MSWs to be completely honest and forthcoming. For example, going to the police to complain about an abusive client is not an option for someone engaged in illegal activities. Many sex worker advocates (Almodovar, 1999; Bimbi & Parsons, 2005; Vanwesenbeeck, 2001) argue that this illegality makes sex work more difficult and more dangerous.

Got Personality?

Nineteen (41%) interviewees asserted that successful escorts have special traits or characteristics. Qualities specified as valuable included being outgoing, patient, caring, having an open-minded approach to a wide variety of clients, treating clients with empathy and respect, and having the ability to set and maintain personal boundaries.

> It [escorting] is really hard work, and it takes a certain type of well-rounded personality and some savvy to be successful in it, and not just burn out in a year as some sort of little hustler. (33, White)

> It really takes a specific type of personality [to escort]. It's not something that everybody can just go into. It takes somebody who's extremely outgoing. I think it takes more intelligence than we're given credit for . . . I think one of the reasons I've been so successful with my clientele is because I can read people. I know what they're looking for. I can change mid-stream. (47, White)

Within the general theme of MSWs as possessors of certain skills and characteristics, some men singled out the issue of comfort with one's own sexuality and sexual identity.

> I would tell them [potential escorts] they have to know what their sexuality is. I think it's probably bad if you consider yourself straight. Those guys seem not to like it. They seem to have a lot of trouble with it emotionally. I would say that if the guy is gay and really comfortable being gay-identified, I would tell them it's something that is reasonable to consider if they have clear-cut thoughts about what they want out of it financially. If they're doing it because they just want to party and do drugs, it's a bad idea. If they're doing it because they want to pay off their student loans, or just improve their life, I think it's a great way to make a lot of money in a short period of time. The important thing is to be okay with it emotionally. (31, White)

In addition to being comfortable with one's own sexuality, the ability to be sexual with a wide variety of clients was stressed. Participants emphasized that sexual performance with clients was part of the *work* of escorting and not only for the escort's sexual pleasure:

> Don't think this is some porno fantasy of, you know, if someone hires you and they look like Tom Selleck or whatever, it just doesn't happen. That's a fantasy, and the people who hire you are going to be fat and old and married and ugly and whatever. So if that's an issue for you, you can't do this. (44, White)

Therefore, part of being a "professional" is having the ability to bring the client's fantasy to life, without expecting reciprocity from the client. MSWs with a well-developed sense of their own sexuality may be more comfortable working with the sexual needs of their clients and, consequently, less likely to suffer job-related stress.

While many of the respondents stated that men considering sex work should be comfortable with their own sexual identity, the issue of being prepared to deal with clients who may not be comfortable with their identity was raised: "He [the client] may have gay tendencies, but basically a straight mentality. He could become a jerk or something, and how are you going to react to that?" (28, African American). The possibility of dealing with clients who are uncomfortable with same sex desire is a challenge somewhat unique to male escorts. A few participants welcomed this part of the work, as they enjoyed subverting heterosexual norms.

> But more importantly, I like the married men, you know. I'm releasing this tension that society has created. We're pushed [in]to marrying, we're still pushed to be straight in this country . . . but there are still many gays and bisexuals, and they're married, and I'm the release, and it's great to be a part of that. And so that's what I say about undermining the American system. (28, Latino)

In this way, MSWs may be a source of comfort and support to men struggling with feelings of internalized homophobia, or who have yet to come to terms with their sexual identity.

Taking Care of Yourself

Much like workers in other sectors of the service industry and "helping professions," MSWs also must manage their emotions effectively in order to maintain their well-being and have longevity in the business (Chapkis, 1997; Hochschild, 1983). For example, one participant, in discussing advice he would offer to potential escorts, pointed out how easily MSWs can lose their sense of self through their work:

> The money's great, but there's a price you pay for it. It can be yourself. It can be losing yourself to it. If you don't have a really strong sense of who you are, and know yourself, you can get just kind of wrapped up in it, and you don't even realize it until you get to a point where you feel really empty doing it. And when you start to feel like that, that's when you should stop. (28, African American)

The men interviewed for this study reported that getting emotional support from other MSWs or nonjudgmental loved ones outside the industry was an essential component to staying healthy in sex work and maintaining a strong sense of self. However, many participants ($n = 17, 37\%$) expressed a need for a forum (either in person or online) where escorts could make contact with each other to access this type of support: "People who are in the business actually really want to talk with others who are in the business because they feel isolated. So possibly there could be some sort of networking thing" (27, White). Another participant highlighted the need for emotional support from other MSWs when coping with the more difficult sessions: "It's amazing how many times I have finished a job and thought, 'Oh, that was awful.' But I've needed someone to talk about it and say, 'Oh, that was horrible what I just did'" (31, White).

These participants underscore one of the pitfalls that may be associated with escorting for some men: a sense of isolation or loneliness. Coming together for support in a safe space could help ameliorate these negative feelings. Counseling also was an advised option for MSWs having emotional difficulties with their work or other parts of their life: "I guess information on low-cost counseling. I find that these things are not existent. A list of counseling support and services–that would be good" (37, White). Were a list of counselors available to MSWs, as this man suggests, it would be advisable to first screen practitioners to assess their attitudes about and knowledge of issues faced by male escorts. This would be no different than the ethical concerns that guide a therapist when attending to gay-identified clients. The common goal is compassion in a non-judgmental setting.

Some of the interviewees ($n = 11, 24\%$) remarked that one way of maintaining emotional health while working as an escort was drawing and maintaining personal boundaries. These boundaries may enable the individual MSW to differentiate between work and personal sex, between clients and lovers, between one's "work personality" and one's "real identity":

> You know, I think maturity gives you . . . you know when to say no. You can really stand your ground. I think you really have to be able to establish boundaries with clients . . . saying, this is not my personal life. You don't get my home number. You don't get my name. (39, White)

As stated previously, independent male escorts can be more selective about their clients and their sexual services, compared to other MSWs. One man talked about setting up boundaries regarding the types of clients he will see and the behaviors he will engage in: "Be picky. Be picky, yeah. Know what you want. Know what you won't do; know what you will do. Know how much you'll charge and stand by it" (22, White).

Proceed with Caution

A small number of men (*n* = 3, 6.5%) warned of the possibility of becoming "addicted" to escorting. They mentioned that the sex, money, and attention they received from escorting could make it difficult to leave the business.

> You get hooked on it. It's like any other addiction. The money is good. You get lazy. You don't want to do anything else and it doesn't lead to anything. I mean, you're not paying taxes on the money. It [the negative aspects of escorting] will catch up with you at some point. (37, White)

One escort, who had recently stopped escorting only to go back into the business, described his experience as follows:

> It's [escorting] a very big ego trip. And you can get addicted to it very easily. You're getting paid by somebody who's giving you a lot of attention for an hour, and that becomes extremely addictive. Last year when I stopped [escorting], I had to go through withdrawal because I had been doing it for a whole year. And it was–all of a sudden, I wasn't getting all this attention like I was used to getting. And I wasn't having the sex that I was used to either. And it was serious withdrawal. (46, White)

While some of the men interviewed expressed what appeared to be symptoms of sexual compulsivity, the quantitative data from this study revealed that these men were not more sexually compulsive than other gay and bisexual men (Parsons et al., 2001).

In response to the query 'If a friend of yours came to you and said he was considering becoming an escort, what advice would you give him?' a small portion of the participants (*n* = 5, 11%) flatly stated: "Don't." For example, one man said, "I would say 'Don't,' because if a person is stable and they have a mommy or daddy or have anything just to get by–stick with that. I do this because I have to" (22, Latino).

These few men described the stress and emotional difficulty that came with escorting and warned others to stay out of the business if they had the choice. These warnings were often accompanied by the recommendation that if such a friend truly felt he had to escort, he should remember to have safer sex: "I wish I could give them [potential escorts] advice, don't do the escorting stuff. But then I'm doing it. If they're going to do it anyway, the only thing I can tell them, be safe, wear condoms" (26, Latino). The type of advice offered by other participants, such as maintaining one's boundaries, doing research prior to entering the business, or getting support from friends, was not provided by these men.

DISCUSSION

I think there should be a place you could call if you're an escort [and] you need to ask a question to someone. Where you can call for information, free information. Or if they get in trouble, or they're in jail. We could help get them out. I think in a way it shouldn't be illegal and I think there should be people out there that can help. Maybe an organization that can sort of [provide] aid. (29, White)

The men interviewed for this study identified several areas where they would benefit from services that are currently lacking or, when services are available, may not be known about or accessed. Confirming prior assumptions about MSWs, the men did report that male escorts serving a male clientele would benefit from clear, specific information on safer sex practices, in addition to instruction on how to negotiate such practices with clients. While much of this health information is available on the Internet, MSWs may need a map to navigate the overwhelming number of sites available, which sometimes offer conflicting, confusing, or out of date information. This "map" would conceivably consist of a widely publicized Web resource specifically developed for MSWs, featuring regularly updated information about HIV/STIs and safer sex. This resource also could include other needs identified by participants, such as where and how to locate drug and alcohol treatment or low cost counseling. Further, opportunities for networking, possibly through well publicized escort-only listservs and chat rooms, could be made available to help decrease the potential for isolation and improve social support. Although some such resources currently exist, many are poorly maintained and somewhat transient. A Web site targeted specifically to MSWs, and developed and maintained by current and former

MSWs, HookOnline (www.hookonline.com), is one such resource that has emerged in the community.

Due to their status as self-employed independent escorts, those without other full-time jobs which provide health benefits may have limited access to health care, an issue that needs to be addressed in this community. In recent years, sex work advocates in the United States have taken steps to meet this need, forming organizations such as the Adult Industry Medical (AIM) Health Care Foundation (www.aim-med.org). The services offered by AIM, founded by former adult film actress Sharon Mitchell, help to fill a gap in the services available to both male and female sex workers and those involved in the adult film industry by offering access to medical insurance and general health care, in addition to HIV and STI testing. Similar programs providing medical services to MSWs exist in places where sex work is less criminalized, such as the United Kingdom where The Working Men Project (www.wmplondon.org.uk) has been in operation for over ten years.

Often overlooked in past assumptions about the types of information and services MSWs need and want, but identified in the current study, was information more in line with what is required by self-employed people running their own small business. The men who participated in this study clearly stated that there is a need among Internet-based MSWs for information on how to effectively manage their business. Specifically, the men raised topics such as negotiating sales, marketing their services/product, filing taxes, and investing their profits. Also frequently mentioned were strategies for how to successfully screen clients (e.g., determining the client's intention for calling; gauging whether he might be dangerous or a member of a law enforcement agency, etc.). The men in this study have explicitly stated needs and wants; thus, it is hoped that individuals or agencies who endeavor to provide services to MSWs keep these needs at the forefront of future programmatic efforts. Hopefully, this will avoid the pitfalls encountered by organizations that were unable to remain operational, such as the Coalition Advocating Safer Hustling (CASH), in which the needs identified by MSWs were secondary to the needs identified *for* them *by* others (Boles & Elifson, 1998).

The extralegal status of sex work further complicates the efforts of male escorts when dealing with potential and actual clients. Many participants expressed confusion and frustration with the limitations on what they could and could not say over the phone, in e-mails, and in person due to their fear of arrest. Many sex worker advocates/activists have been hampered in their efforts to make specific guidelines for avoiding arrest available to sex workers, due to existing laws that prohibit pandering or instructing individuals in how to go about engaging in acts of prostitution. Additionally, these laws vary from state to state, and even from year to year, making the task of keeping abreast of them difficult even for experienced attorneys.

It should be noted that the findings of the current study are constrained by several factors. First, although The Classified Project is novel in its sampling of MSWs that utilize the Internet for advertising and soliciting clients, the number of participants is small. Additionally, it is difficult to know how the men who participated differed from those who did not. It also is not possible to know if the participants were honest with the interviewers about their behaviors, feelings, and needs. Also, while the sample included men of diverse ethnicities and backgrounds, it mostly comprised European-Americans. This may reflect an inequality of minority involvement in Internet technology (*New York Times*, 2000). Finally, this study sampled only Web-based escorts in New York, and the findings may not generalize to other locales, especially less urban settings.

In closing, the MSWs who participated in this study do not appear to be the vectors of disease transmission so often portrayed by past authors (Morse et al., 1991). In fact, many of our participants are successfully negotiating safer sex with their clients, even when faced with resistance or specific requests for barebacking (Bimbi & Parsons, 2005; Parsons et al., 2004). The marginalized status of commercial sex work too often has resulted in the conflation of the work with the worker and subsequent disregard for the needs of the individual within the occupation. Our findings indicate that their needs beyond HIV and STI prevention are not unlike those of self-employed individuals or other small business owners.

NOTE

1. Excerpts from the interviews for this paper are accompanied by the participant's self-reported age and ethnicity.

REFERENCES

Almodovar, N. J. (1999). For their own good: The results of the prostitution laws as enforced by cops, politicians, and judges. *Hastings Women's Law Journal, 10*, 119-133.
Bimbi, D. S., & Parsons, J. T. (2005). Barebacking among gay and bisexual male escorts. *Journal of Gay and Lesbian Psychotherapy, 9*, 89-110.

Boles, J., & Elifson, K. (1998). Out of CASH: The rise and demise of a male prostitutes' rights organization. In J. E. Elias, V. L. Bullough, V. Elias, & G. Brewer (Eds.), *Prostitution: On whores, hustlers and johns* (pp. 267-278). New York, NY: Prometheus Books.

Browne, J., & Minichiello, V. (1995). The social meanings behind male sex work: Implications for sexual interactions. *British Journal of Sociology, 46*, 598-622.

Browne, J., & Minichiello, V. (1996). The social and work context of commercial sex between men: A research note. *The Australian and New England Journal of Sociology, 32*, 86-92.

Calhoun, T. C., & Weaver, G. (1996). Rational decision-making among male street prostitutes. *Deviant Behavior, 17*, 209-227.

Cates, J. A., & Markley, J. (1992). Demographic, clinical, and personality variables associated with male prostitution by choice. *Adolescence, 27*, 695-707.

Chapkis, W. (1997). *Live sex acts: Women performing erotic labor.* New York, NY: Routledge.

Coutinho, R. A., van Andel, R. L. M., & Rijsdijk, T. J. (1988). Role of male prostitutes in the spread of sexually transmitted diseases and human immuno-deficiency virus *Genitourinary Medicine, 64*, 207-208.

Estcourt, C. S., Marks, C., Rohrsheim, R., Johnson, A. M., Donovan, B., & Mindel, A. (2000). HIV, sexually transmitted infections, and risk behaviors in male commercial sex workers in Sydney. *Sexually Transmitted Infections, 76*, 294-298.

Estep, R., Waldorf, D., & Marotta, T. (1992). Sexual behavior of male prostitutes. In J. Huber & B. E. Schneider (Eds.), *The social context of AIDS* (pp. 95-109). Newbury Park, CA: Sage.

Gaffney, J. (2003, March). *Cost of living: Men who sell sex.* Oral presentation at the 6th National CHAPS Conference, Leicester, UK.

Halkitis, P. N., & Parsons, J. T. (2000). Oral sex and HIV risk reduction: Perceived risk, behaviors, and strategies among young HIV negative gay men. *Journal of Psychology & Human Sexuality, 11*, 1-24.

Hickson, F., Weatherburn, P., Hows, J., & Davies, P. (1994). Selling safer sex: Male masseurs and escorts in the UK. In P. Aggleton, P. Davies, & G. Hart (Eds.), *AIDS: Foundations for the future* (pp. 197-209). Bristol, PA: Taylor & Francis.

Hochschild, A. (1983). *The managed heart: Commercialization of human feeling.* Berkeley and Los Angeles, CA: University of California Press.

Joffe, H., & Dockrell, J. E. (1995). Safer sex: Lessons from the male sex industry. *Journal of Community & Applied Social Psychology, 5*, 333-346.

Lumby, M. E. (1978). Men who advertise for sex. *Journal of Homosexuality, 4*, 63-73.

Minichiello, V., Marino, R., Browne, J., Jamieson, M., Peterson, K., Reuter, B., & Robinson, K. (2000). Commercial sex between men: A prospective diary-based study. *Journal of Sex Research, 37*, 151-160.

Morse, E. V., Simon, P. M., Osofsky, H. J., Balson, P. M., & Gaumer, H. R. (1991). The male street prostitute: A vector for transmission of HIV infection into the heterosexual world. *Social Science and Medicine, 32*, 535-539.

New York Times. (2000). *The New York Times 2000 almanac.* New York, NY: New York Times.

NUDIST. (1997). *Non-numerical unstructured data indexing, searching, and theorizing, Version 4.0.* Thousand Oaks, CA: Sage Publications Software.

Overs, C. (1991). *To work or not to work? Questions facing HIV-positive sex workers.* National AIDS Bulletin (Australia).

Parsons, J. T., Bimbi, D. S., & Halkitis, P. N. (2001). Sexual compulsivity among gay/bisexual male escorts who advertise on the Internet. *Sexual Addiction & Compulsivity, 8,* 101-112.

Parsons, J. T., Koken, J. A., & Bimbi, D. S. (2004). The use of the Internet by gay and bisexual male escorts: Sex workers as sex educators. *AIDS Care, 16,* 1021-1035.

Perkins, R., Prestage, G., Sharp, R., & Lovejoy, F. (1994). *Sex work and sex workers in Australia.* Sydney, Australia: University of New South Wales Press.

Pleak, R. R., & Meyer-Bahlburg, H. F. L. (1990). Sexual behavior and AIDS knowledge of young male prostitutes in Manhattan. *Journal of Sex Research, 27,* 557-588.

Salamon, E. (1989). The homosexual escort agency: Deviance disavowal. *British Journal of Sociology, 40,* 1-21.

Strauss, A. L., & Corbin, J. (1990). *Basics of qualitative research: Grounded theory, procedure and techniques.* Newbury Park, CA: Sage.

Vanwesenbeeck, I. (2001). Another decade of social scientific work on sex work: A review of research 1990-2000. *Annual Review of Sex Research, 12,* 242-289.

Wolitski, R. J., & Branson, B. M. (2002). "Grey area behaviors" and partner selection strategies: Working toward a comprehensive approach to reducing the sexual transmission of HIV. In A. O'Leary (Ed.), *Beyond condoms: Alternative approaches to HIV prevention* (pp. 173-198). New York, NY: Kluwer Academic/Plenum.

Ziersch, A., Gaffney, J., & Tomlinson, D. R. (2000). STI prevention and the male sex industry in London: Evaluating a pilot peer education program. *Sexually Transmitted Infections, 76,* 447-453.

doi:10.1300/J082v53n01_10

'Western Union Daddies' and Their Quest for Authenticity: An Ethnographic Study of the Dominican Gay Sex Tourism Industry

Mark B. Padilla, PhD, MPH

University of Michigan

SUMMARY. This article draws on ethnographic research among two categories of male sex workers in the Dominican Republic in order to describe the relationships between gay male tourists and the Dominican men they hire on their trips to the Caribbean. Drawing on both qualitative interview data and quantitative surveys, the discussion examines the usefulness of theories of 'authenticity,' as they have been applied in the analysis of tourist practices more generally, in accounting for the

Mark Padilla is Assistant Professor in the Department of Health Behavior and Health Education, University of Michigan. His work focuses on the ethnographic analysis of gender, sexuality, HIV/AIDS, and commercial sex work in the Hispanic Caribbean. In addition to his ongoing work among Dominican male sex workers discussed in this article, he is conducting anthropological research among Dominican and Puerto Rican men who have sex with men in New York City, and is initiating a new research project on HIV/AIDS and the informal tourism economy in Cartagena, Colombia. Correspondence may be addressed to Mark B. Padilla, PhD, MPH, Department of Health Behavior and Health Education, University of Michigan, M5515 SPH11, 109 South Observatory Ann Arbor, MI 45109-2029 (E-mail: padillam@umich.edu).

[Haworth co-indexing entry note]: "'Western Union Daddies' and Their Quest for Authenticity: An Ethnographic Study of the Dominican Gay Sex Tourism Industry." Padilla, Mark B. Co-published simultaneously in *Journal of Homosexuality* (The Haworth Press, Inc.) Vol. 53, No. 1/2, 2007, pp. 241-275; and: *Male Sex Work: A Business Doing Pleasure* (ed: Todd G. Morrison and Bruce W. Whitehead) The Haworth Press, Inc., 2007, pp. 241-275. Single or multiple copies of this article are available for a fee from The Haworth Document Delivery Service [1-800- HAWORTH, 9:00 a.m. - 5:00 p.m. (EST). E-mail address: docdelivery@haworthpress.com].

Available online at http://jh.haworthpress.com
© 2007 by The Haworth Press, Inc. All rights reserved.
doi:10.1300/J082v53n01_11

behaviors and practices of male sex workers and their foreign gay clients. While the flow of international remittances from 'Western Union daddies' to their Dominican 'boys' creates a continuous reminder of the utilitarian nature of the exchange, both sex workers and clients are motivated to camouflage this instrumentality in their construction of a more 'authentic,' fulfilling relationship. The article examines the consequences of this ambivalent negotiation for the emotional and economic organization of gay male sex tourism in the Caribbean. doi:10.1300/J082v53n01_11 *[Article copies available for a fee from The Haworth Document Delivery Service: 1-800-HAWORTH. E-mail address: <docdelivery@haworthpress.com> Website: <http:// www.HaworthPress.com> © 2007 by The Haworth Press, Inc. All rights reserved.]*

KEYWORDS. Male sex work, prostitution, tourism, authenticity, gay men, bisexuality, Dominican Republic

INTRODUCTION

A few blocks from the bustling pedestrian mall at the heart of the Colonial Zone in Santo Domingo, Dominican Republic is a small, inconspicuous corner bar called *Charlie's*.[1] Every night of the week, as the sun goes down and Santo Domingo's colonial architecture begins to take on its distinct amber-gold hue, the forty-something, slightly overweight bartender, Héctor, opens the wooden front door facing a narrow side street. The iron security gate remains noticeably closed, allowing passersby a hazy view of the darkened interior through the black metal bars. At this early hour, children are still playing along the adjacent sidewalks of this mostly residential barrio, and the men who gather at the *colmado* (small corner store) across the street prepare for a lazy evening of dominoes, rum, and animated political commentary. After nearly 20 years of operation, *Charlie's* seems to blend imperceptibly into the local rhythm of life and, in many ways, is situated within a social space that is reminiscent of traditional anthropological descriptions of masculinity and street life throughout the Caribbean.[2] Nevertheless, few of the activities that occur there are explicable within the conceptual frameworks offered by Caribbean ethnographers for understanding masculine behavior and sexuality. Neighbors in the area have grown accustomed to the taxis that pass by to drop off or pick up their passengers–tourists staying at one of the gay-friendly hotels or, perhaps, arriving directly from the airport–and often stop by to chat with the *bugarrones* (a local term for male sex workers)[3] who prop themselves for hours against the weathered concrete wall outside the establishment.

Leonardo, the husky *portero* (door man) and well-known *maipiolo* (pimp), arrives around 7:30 p.m. and takes his usual seat on the stool just inside the iron-gate. From here, he maintains a steady watch over the activities on the street, prepared to come to the assistance of clients whose incautious display of dollars or jewelry occasionally attracts the attention of muggers, or to warn his fellow *bugarrones* at the first signs of a police patrol. It was Leonardo who came to my rescue one night when a side window of my car was smashed and a backpack full of research materials stolen by a young *tíguere* (tiger)[4] known to torment tourists in the neighborhood. But on a busy night at *Charlie's*, most of the patrons and sex workers that gather inside the bar do not appear concerned with these potential dangers. They are too occupied with *la búsqueda* (the search). Gay tourists, often bleary-eyed from ingesting obscene amounts of rum, and red-faced from a weekend at the beach, size up the young, muscled men who strategically display themselves at the tables along the perimeter. During the high tourist season, or when gay tour groups are in town, the small bar can become so crowded that *bugarrones* who can no longer squeeze through the doorway gather along the street outside and solicit clients as they stumble into their taxis. Translators and *guías*–such as the famous *El Loco* (the crazy one), an ex-*bugarrón* whose age and diminishing physical condition now preclude direct sexual exchanges–function as middle-men between clients and sex workers, hoping to broker contacts that will bring commissions roughly equivalent to five dollars each. Héctor, in his relatively powerful position as bartender, manages to make a living by strategically over-charging the drunken tourists, extracting commissions from sex workers or flirtatiously soliciting generous tips.[5] Police officers pass by on their motorcycles and attempt to extort payments from *bugarrones* as they leave the bar with a client or walk home after an unsuccessful evening.

All of this is presided over by *Charlie's* somewhat unlikely owner, Simon, a gay British ex-patriot whose air of sophistication–symbolized by a large picture of the Queen of England that graces one wall–seems somewhat out-of-synch with the bar's otherwise humble surroundings. Simon, enticed years ago by the erotic allure of the Dominican Republic, sold his businesses in Spain and England and began *Charlie's* as an extension of his private home, which is located adjacent to the bar and easily accessible through a door that simply reads *Privado* (Private). A slight old man and self-defined alcoholic who continues to sip his imported gin despite advanced cirrhosis of the liver, Simon appears to take a certain pleasure in quietly watching over his 'boys' and joking with the tourists who make their way in and out of his otherwise insular world. Despite the fact that he speaks little Spanish and rarely leaves his home, he continues to advise his tourist clientele–who treat him as a sort of grandfatherly expert on the local men-for-hire–on the best ways to enjoy the *bugarrones*. "One of the most common questions they ask me is 'How big is he?'" Simon commented in an interview. "That's foremost on their mind. It's just the interest in their dick. But, of course, you would expect those kinds of questions in a bar of this type." Perched on his personal barstool with a cigarette balanced precariously in one hand and a drink in the other, Simon seemed to enjoy discussing his past with me amidst the cacophony of *merengue* [a type of lively music] mixed with inebriated laughter. "It's not a bad life they're leading," he reflected when I asked him about the *bugarrones'* choice of profession. "I don't know what the average Dominican wage is right now–maybe 2000 pesos a month [approximately US $117 in the year 2001]–and they can make that with a tourist, you know, in four or five days, maybe less. Maybe all at one go." As we watched a middle-aged, overweight New Yorker select three sex workers and the entire entourage squeeze into a taxi outside, I commented to Simon (who was giving them a delicate wave goodbye) about the variety of tourists that come into his bar/home. "Oh, dear, here we get the kinky ones and the first-timers. We've had several porno directors who film the boys in one of the hotels around here. And, of course, we get the weird fantasies." With an unexpectedly loud shriek of laughter, Simon proceeded to tell me about the infamous repeat visitor, "Mr. Poo-Poo," so-named because of his notorious fecal fetish. "But he always manages to pay enough to get what he wants," he reflected, in a suddenly hushed tone–as if out of fear that one of his 'boys' might overhear him.

It is useful to begin with this description of *Charlie's* bar because in many ways it is emblematic of a kind of sex tourism in the Dominican Republic that has been given relatively little attention in the existing literature on 'beach boys' and male sex workers in the Caribbean. As described below, through an analysis of ethnographic evidence based on three years of anthropological fieldwork with male sex workers in Santo Domingo and Boca Chica, Dominican Republic, a significant and growing number of Dominican men are involved in sexual-economic exchanges with gay male tourists, a phenomenon that is related to the rapid growth of the tourism industry in the country. This phenomenon has been described more extensively for female sex workers, as demonstrated by Brennan's (2004) recent book on Dominican women involved in the sex industry in the tourist town of Sosúa. The clandestine nature of same-sex relationships in the tourism economy has, perhaps, contributed to the general lack of analysis concerning the influence of the gay sex industry on the local terrain of sexuality and masculinity in the region. Further, it has marginalized discussion of the ways that gay identity in the industrialized West has produced–through its consumption of 'foreign' bodies and identities–a market for particular performances of gender and sexuality. Indeed, a closer look at the Dominican gay sex tourism industry reveals why an understanding of the contemporary meanings of Dominican homoeroticism requires an analysis of how local sexualities are being commodified by foreign gay tourists.

Through a multi-method approach incorporating ethnographic observations, in-depth interviews with sex workers and clients, and a behavioral, demographic, and social survey of sex workers, this paper offers a theoretical framework for understanding the process of sexual commoditization in the sex tourism industry and its intersection with the subjective experiences of sex workers and clients. Focusing primarily on the longer-term relationships between sex workers and gay tourists that lead to ongoing economic support through regular cash remittances from abroad, the analysis developed in this paper draws on the theoretical literature from tourism studies to examine the usefulness of the notion of 'authenticity' as an explanatory framework for understanding these sexual-economic exchanges. MacCannell's (1973, 1976) discussion of 'staged authenticity' in tourist settings argues that the quest for authentic experiences through tourism is linked to the contemporary desire to experience genuine, rather than 'staged,' expressions of intimacy. However, the performative dimensions of tourist spaces, which offer somewhat artificial and constructed forms of intimacy, can lead to a highly ambivalent experience on the part of the tourist. The concluding section draws on the ethnographic material presented to examine the specific expressions of this ambivalence for the gay sex tourists and Dominican sex workers with whom this research was conducted.

METHODOLOGY AND DEFINITIONS
OF THE RESEARCH POPULATION

This research involved three years of multi-sited ethnographic fieldwork between January, 1999 and December, 2001. Access to the study population and data collection were facilitated by my research association with the staff at the non-governmental organization *Amigos Siempre*

Amigos (ASA), a non-governmental organization whose primary donor support comes from the US Agency for International Development (USAID) and which has nearly twenty years of experience conducting HIV prevention work among gay-identified men. The methodology used was both qualitative and quantitative, and involved three basic phases. First, the primary areas and social spaces in which male sex work occurs in the two study sites of Santo Domingo and Boca Chica were identified, described, and mapped. This exploratory phase also included three focus groups with male sex workers in Santo Domingo to examine issues related to self-identification practices, catalogue local terms and definitions for types of male sex workers, and check the maps of sex work sites against sex workers' lived experience. Second, a face-to-face quantitative survey was conducted with a total of 200 sex workers in both research sites, following a brief validation phase with 20 sex workers. (The number of usable surveys was 199.) Surveys included measures of sociodemographics (e.g., socioeconomic status, household composition, marital and extra-marital history, patterns of spousal support, education, occupation, and income); self-identifications [e.g., as *bugarrón, sanky panky, trabajador sexual* (sex worker), see below]; social norms about sex work (e.g., preferred types of clients, perceived behavior of social peers); sexual behaviors and condom use with clients (both male and female) as well as with girlfriends, wives, or intimate partners; affective and emotional bonds with clients; substance use history; frequency of internal and transnational migration experiences; and numerous relatively standardized measures of co-factors of HIV and STD risk (e.g., access to condoms, perception of risk, knowledge of HIV, and social support). In the third stage of the research, audio-taped semi-structured interviews were conducted with 98 sex workers, exploring issues such as childhood experiences and traumas; current and past relations with parents and siblings; stigma-management techniques; initiation into sex work; relationships with girlfriends, spouses, and children; stories of worst and best clients; beliefs and fears about HIV/AIDS; and future aspirations.

Finally, ethnographic techniques–most importantly, participant observation, informal interviewing, and ethnographic note-taking–were used throughout the research. This involved many hours of socializing with male sex workers and clients in various contexts, at first largely in sex work areas–such as bars, discos, parks, restaurants, and streets–and later in more private settings, including sex workers' homes. The ethnographic data continually informed the emerging results from the more formal methodologies, allowing for triangulation and verification of data as well as the cultural contextualization of particular findings. This was especially important in the case of the surveys, since straight frequencies of responses can often be misleading when interpreted without reference to sociocultural or political-economic context. This qualitative and quantitative approach is reflected in the dialogue between the different methods developed in this paper.

The local terms *bugarrón* and *sanky panky* generally correspond to the categories of self-identity used by the male sex workers described here, although not all of the men who participated in this study used these terms as forms of self-reference (see Table 1). As described in prior studies (De Moya & Garcia, 1996; De Moya & Garcia, 1998; De Moya, Garcia, Fadul, & Herold, 1992), the *sanky panky* identity, which is based on a linguistic Dominicanization of the English phrase 'hanky panky,' emerged in the seventies and eighties in response to the growing presence of young, well-built Dominican men who made a modest living by hustling foreign men and women in beach areas popular with tourists. The term, therefore, connotes both a particular masculine style–including, for example, the small dreadlocks often mentioned by sex workers as a signature feature of the classic *sanky*–and a specific location, that is, the beach. The spatial specificity of the *sanky panky* identity explains its more common self-attribution among sex workers in Boca Chica, a beach town and a primary tourist destination on the country's southern coast, as shown in Table 1. The word *bugarrón*, which De Moya and Garcia (1998) argue takes its root from the French *bougre*, has a deeper history in the Dominican Republic and, consequently, does not have the same connection to the development of the tourism industry as *sanky panky*. Rather, *bugarrón* was a preexisting identity that was

TABLE 1. Residence of Survey Participants by Self-Identified Sexual Identity (*N* = 199)

	Homo-sexual	Gay	Bisexual	Hetero-sexual	*Bugarrón*	*Sanky Panky*	Other	Totals
Santo Dom.	3	1	29	17	63	7	5	125
Boca Chica	1	0	8	18	7	25	7	66
Other residence	0	1	4	0	2	1	0	8
Totals	4	2	41	35	72	33	12	199

subsequently incorporated into, and commodified by, gay sex tourism in the Caribbean. As an ideal type, *bugarrón* refers to a man who engages in insertive anal sex with other men, often for money or other instrumental benefits, but who in other domains of life may not be noticeably different from 'normal' men.[6] Neither the *bugarrón* nor the *sanky panky* identity is socially ascribed in a way that is analogous to the public self-ascription practices typical of many gay-identified men in the contemporary Euro-American sexual system. Therefore, these terms are best understood as situational identities that are generally veiled in public, and especially in familial and social contexts.

RESULTS

Miguel's Story

During an interview, Miguel–a 32 year-old *bugarrón* who has 20 years of experience in the Dominican sex trade–recalled events in his childhood that were anything but idyllic. Born in the eastern pueblo of La Romana, an area that would later be developed into one of the Dominican Republic's most lavish tourist zones, he remembered:

> My father was, as they say, an alcoholic. Everything he earned he drank, and he never gave a dime to my mother, because everything was–everything he earned he drank. There were problems between them, so I decided to leave the house, and that way they avoided [another] problem. . . . The problem with me when I was little was that I was really mischievous and my mother was always beating me, and I always had little problems. And between the beatings that she gave me, and the tormenting, what they did to me is tear me apart, and I got so that I didn't even want to *see* my house. When I looked at my family, it was like looking at the Devil, so when I left, it was like fleeing. . . . At the end of it all, you have to leave the house and get by alone.

At age nine, Miguel left his family home and became, in his words, "*niño de la calle* (street kid): "I was raised in the street. Mainly I was raised with the tourists. I worked with them. Some were gays and I stayed with them, and that's how my life went. I raised myself alone." Two years after leaving home, he relocated from La Romana to Santo Domingo to try his luck in the city:

Well, when I came to Santo Domingo the first time, I began working with a *triciculo* [tricycle][7] in the street … looking for bottles,
looking for cardboard in the street. And I always stopped there in
El Conde around a hotel that was called the Hotel Anastasia, and
they [the tourists] always waved to me, and they started to give me
things, and they said "Come," and from there I continued. I went
every day, I passed by every day, since then I knew that they gave
me–that they gave me a sandwich; they gave me ten dollars; they
gave me five pesos … And I got a person, a guy, an American
friend, and from the age of twelve I stayed almost–almost four or
five years working with him in the hotel. I was the one who–who
did it to him. And there I stayed.

Today, Miguel is a well-known *bugarrón* in Santo Domingo with relatively lucrative connections to the international sex trade, a success
which he attributes to his sociable personality and his English language
proficiency. "I learned [English] easily," he commented, "because aside
from the fact that I don't know how to read or write, I'm very intelligent."
These language skills have served him well, since they have allowed
him to continue making a living in the sex industry despite competition
with younger *bugarrones* who are often in higher demand. Now, as a
well-connected *maipiolo*, he has even been able to reduce his direct
involvement in sexual exchanges without seriously compromising his
income, since his networking services earn him regular commissions:

> Basically, I don't have to be wandering around having sex with lots
> of people, because I always get something translating, or taking him
> [a tourist] to Boca Chica, or taking him to such and such a place to
> buy this or that. And they send for me if they need a person: "Hey!
> Get me that one." And I go and I look for him. In general, I don't
> have to have sex, since now I almost don't use sex to, to get money.

Miguel's success with the tourists has allowed him to provide a relatively stable income for his common-law wife, Sonia, and their three
children, the eldest of whom is now twelve. The family has a small
house in *Los Mameyes*, a lower-class barrio just across the Rio Ozama
from the city's colonial zone. Miguel believes that the higher income
one can attain through sex work has allowed him to provide a better life
for his children. "I was a kid who suffered a lot on the street," he reflected, "and I know what that is like, and I don't want to throw kids out
to suffer on the street because I can't take care of them." Sex work also

has provided other benefits for his family, including a more flexible schedule, since "In my free time, I can be at home with my kids, sometimes playing Nintendo, sometimes we go to San Cristóbal to the river, to the beach, lots of things."

Nevertheless, he admits that when he is busy with tourists, he sometimes has "problems" with Sonia, who, though she is aware of his work and has even entertained tourist-clients in her home, is not wholeheartedly supportive of Miguel's occupation:

> You know how women are. They always want to have their husband beside them, so the problems always come because of that, because I have to go out to the street and sometimes I'm out until two, three o'clock in the morning, and those are, most of the time, the problems that we have. We've argued to the point of hitting each other.

Despite these arguments, Miguel feels that his wife has no grounds to criticize him for what he considers legitimate work that provides for his family's needs:

> The man always has to be in the street looking for money for the woman's food, and from that she eats ... You can't go on what everyone tells you in the street, because you know that I'm in this environment and, if you're my partner and we're living together, you're eating from what I bring here, you have to accept what–what I'm involved in.

Many of these tensions come to the fore when one of Miguel's regular clients, Larry–a North American executive in his early sixties–comes to Santo Domingo on his annual vacations. For the past eleven years, Larry has been traveling to the Dominican Republic to visit Miguel at least once a year, usually staying for two months at a time. Miguel recalls being introduced to Larry through another *bugarrón* who had established him as a regular client. When he was invited to accompany the couple to dinner, Miguel took the opportunity to impress the tourist:

> I took him a basket of fruit, and I got him with that, because when I went [to the hotel] I took him that present and he said to my friend, "Of the two or three years we've been seeing each other, you've never given me anything. I'm always giving you things. And look, yesterday I invited this boy to have dinner here and look what he

came here with!" . . . And then we went on a trip to La Romana, with my friend driving and us in back, and he started falling in love with me. And that was when he told my friend that he didn't want to have anything to do with him anymore. . . . And later [from New York] he called me at my house and he told me that he was coming at such and such time and that I should wait for him. And that's when he started sending me money.

Larry now sends Miguel "a monthly payment of 150 dollars and mainly with that I can get by."

During Larry's trips to Santo Domingo, Miguel has to spend signifi- cant amounts of time away from home in order to accompany him and serve as his tour guide and translator: "The problem when he's here is that I have to spend one night there [in the hotel] and one night in my house, one night there and one night in my house–because I have to divide myself." While Sonia complains of these absences, Larry under- stands when Miguel needs to spend time at home with his family. In fact, Larry "is the one who buys me what I need, if I need a fan, if I need a television, if I need a radio–it's always him that buys everything." Miguel emphasized that "he's bought almost everything I have in the house," either indirectly through his remittances or directly in the form of gifts. Nevertheless, Larry is not accepting of Miguel's involvement with other male tourists, warning that "if [anybody] tells me that you're working I'm not going to Santo Domingo anymore." This is a tangible threat, since Miguel has come to depend on the regular remittances he receives from New York. When asked how he convinces Larry that he is not working with other tourists, Miguel shrugged and remarked, "No, it's not about convincing, because he's in the United States and I'm here; he doesn't know what I'm doing."

Despite his feeling that his career in sex work has provided him *"dinero fácil"* (easy money), Miguel does not conclude that it is harmless:

The foreigners come here and do a lot of damage. . . . How can I explain it? It's never really known because it stays with them, but the foreigners sometimes do a lot of damage to the boys. . . . They're the ones who get them used to it [*los acostumbran*] because if I'm a person who's making two hundred or three hundred pesos a day [ten to fifteen dollars] and you come to me and say, "Look, come with me and I'm going to give you four thousand or five thousand pesos" that boy will get used to it. That boy gets used to a life. And what life? Drinking every day, and drugs. And he gets used to it. And that's where the problem comes from: when the boy doesn't have a dime, he has to rob the tourist.

However, he feels that this world of *"vicios"* (vices) in which he has spent most of his life has helped him to provide for his family, including his parents, whom he has continued to visit on occasion. Until his fa- ther's recent death, he had regularly supported both of his parents–who subsequently had been divorced and remarried–with whatever he could manage; despite the fact that he feels they neglected him as a child. He continued these contributions even though his father's new wife treated him very poorly, and often objected openly to his occasional visits. Miguel feels that his father, though certainly a neglectful parent, suf- fered from a weakness and inability to control his drinking and his women. Indeed, Miguel seemed to find a certain poetic justice in the manner of his father's passing, which–at least in Miguel's own imagi- nation–was partially related to the father's agonizing sense of guilt about his life-long neglect of his child:

> That was something that tormented him a lot, and he started drink- ing, because he was saying, 'Damn, I wasn't with my son when he was a boy'... And he started drinking, and drinking, and drinking, and then he fell off the bed and had a stroke.

The 'Western Union Daddy' and the Performance of 'Love'

I remember the first time I encountered one of my 'informants' in a Western Union office in Santo Domingo. His name was Rogelio, and he worked as a stripper at one of the gay discos near the *Parque Olímpico*. Rogelio, known for his impressive physique, was one of the *bugarrón* success stories–at least for the moment–and was enjoying the peak of his popularity among the tourists. As I was filling out my paperwork for a balance transfer from the U.S., I overheard Rogelio chatting in ex- tremely broken English over one of the international phone lines along the wall. A few moments later, he strolled over and stretched out his hand to me and, by way of greeting, we exchanged the obligatory *"¿Como tu 'ta?"* (How are you?). Before I could stop myself, I blurted, *"¿Qué tu haces aquí?"* (What are you doing here?). Perhaps the abrupt- ness of my question, which I later regretted, was motivated by the cog- nitive dissonance that I, like many sex workers themselves, felt upon encountering a 'knowing other' in the context of a public space. In any case, Rogelio seemed not to notice. "I'm here picking up a little present from a friend," he winked, as he flashed me the wad of bills he held in his hand.

I had several such encounters with *bugarrones* in Western Union offices, and even assisted some of them in receiving payments from their "friends" abroad.[8] As described above for Miguel, these remittances can make the difference between meeting basic expenses and living on the street, particularly for those who have no support from family. Thus, while exchanges with tourists often are transient encounters, they can be highly lucrative if they develop into longer-term relationships that transcend direct sex-for-money exchanges. Indeed, a prior study of 76 male sex workers in Santo Domingo found that half of them had foreign clients who sent remittances from abroad or brought them gifts during their regular visits to the Dominican Republic (Ruiz & Vásquez, 1993).[9] Tourists such as Larry, who send regular payments to their Dominican 'boys' while abroad, do not appear to be seeking the impersonal, de-humanized sexual object associated with a certain modality of sex tourism. In many ways, these relationships resemble what Pruitt and LaFont (1995) have described as "romance tourism," a phenomenon which is given considerable attention by the contributors to the recent volume on Caribbean sex tourism, *Sun, sex, and gold* (Kempadoo, 1999).[10] Nevertheless, these analyses have focused exclusively on 'romantic,' long-term exchange relationships between male sex workers and female clients. Are these dynamics the same or different in same-sex interactions?

The men referred to here as "Western Union daddies"–because of the nature of their remittances and their generally older age–resemble the male clients of female sex workers in the coastal town of Sosúa, Dominican Republic, as described by anthropologists such as Cabezas (1998, 1999) and Brennan (1998, 2004). Cabezas (1999), for example, observes that many of the female sex workers with whom she spoke preferred entering into longer relationships with foreign clients who sent them monthly remittances for "buying gifts such as electrical appliances and clothing for [their] children" (p. 99), and who often returned to visit. She notes that sometimes these clients provide the women "plane tickets and visas for travel," the latter being the goal of many female sex workers who fantasize about reaching "*La Gloria*" (The Glory) (p. 99). Cabezas (1999) reports that many of these women express a clear preference for foreign tourists over locals:

> The majority of the women interviewed in this category had not worked with a local clientele. Those that had, indicated that they

much preferred to work with foreigners because Dominican men are considered rough with the women, mistreating them and calling them names; they are verbally and sexually abusive, and they are always reluctant to wear condoms. Foremost, women make a lot less money in these establishments [those oriented toward local clients], they cannot control their hours, and the business owners dominate and abuse them. In comparison, foreigners pay them a lot more money, and they have the possibility of migrating or traveling to other countries. (p. 98)

This preference for foreign clients also is reflected in prior studies among male sex workers in the Dominican Republic. In a survey study by Ruiz and Vásquez (1993) of 76 lower-class *bugarrones* in Santo Domingo, the average number of male clients per year was 36, of which nearly half (17) were foreign tourists. They were described as "better" clients because of the higher price they were generally willing to pay for sex, a finding which is consistent with De Moya et al.'s (1992) study among *sanky pankies* in the tourist town of Sosúa. Similarly, in a 'KABP' (Knowledge Attitudes Beliefs and Practices) study of 188 Dominican bisexual men, Ramah, Pareja, and Hasbún (1992) found a high rate of participation in sex work among lower-class men, for whom foreign tourists or higher-class men were their preferred clients.

In their exchanges with male clients, the *bugarrones* and *sankies* in the present study similarly show a strong preference for foreigners, often alluding to the fact that such clients represent "*dinero fácil*" in the context of an otherwise difficult economic environment. Martín, for example, explained to me as follows the reasons he prefers tourists as clients:

I've gone for about 10 or 12 years without work. So, you know, here in the Dominican Republic things are really hard, so since there are some opportunities with some guys who come from abroad, and they offer you money or something to be with them, you grab it, you understand? It's the easiest way to get money. That's what's going on.

The preference for foreign clients is evident in the survey data summarized in Table 2, which shows an overwhelming bias toward foreigners.[11]

A preference for foreign clients also is reflected in the nationalities of sex workers' last male clients, of whom 64% (107/168) were foreigners. For these 107 sex workers, the breakdown of last client nationality is

TABLE 2. Who Would Be Your Favorite Client (*N* = 166)[*]

	Frequency	Percent (%)
Foreign tourist	96	57.8
Local tourist (Dominican)	4	2.4
Foreign executive	18	10.8
Local executive (Dominican)	18	10.8
Married man	3	1.8
Transvestite (*travesti*) / '*Loca*'	2	1.2
Gay man	16	9.6
Don't know	1	.6
No Answer	8	4.8
Total	166	100.0

[*] Only those respondents with experience with male clients are included (*N* = 166).

shown on the left side of Table 3. Of interest here is the fact that the greatest proportion of tourist-clients originated from the United States (36%), followed by Italy (14%). These percentages are roughly similar to the distributions for sex workers' last *regular* male tourist-clients. For the purpose of this survey, regular male clients were defined as those with whom participants had at least three encounters, generally considered a marker for a more involved, steady relationship. These regular clients also are those with whom it was more likely for sex workers to develop long-term economic relationships involving remittances from abroad, a pattern typical of the Western Union daddies described in this analysis. There were 118 participants who indicated they had had regular male clients, of whom 72 (61%) indicated that their last regular client was a foreigner. The breakdown of client nationality for the last regular tourist-client is shown on the right side of Table 3.

Survey participants also were asked to estimate the age range of their last regular tourist-client, and the modal age range was between 35 and 39 years old (19%). Interestingly, last tourist-clients were significantly older when they were classified as regular clients as opposed to new clients ($p < .05$). That is, the modal age distribution is significantly higher for regular tourist-clients than for first-time tourist-clients, a finding that is consistent with ethnographic observations. Tourists who I observed on repeat trips to the Dominican Republic for the purpose of visiting one or two specific sex workers were generally older than those who divided their time between numerous men or expressed interest in a

TABLE 3. Nationality of Most Recent Tourist-Client, by Regularity of Encounters

	Last male tourist-client (N = 107)		Last *regular* male tourist-client (N = 72)	
	Frequency	Percent (%)	Frequency	Percent (%)
U.S.A.	38	35.5	27	37.5
Canada	9	8.4	6	8.3
Spain	5	4.7	1	1.4
Italy	15	14.0	12	16.7
Germany	8	7.5	5	6.9
France	1	0.9	1	1.4
Other*	29	27.1	20	27.8
Don't know	2	1.9	0	0
Total	107	100	72	100

* Those countries of origin falling within the "other" category include: Colombia, Cuba, Curaçao, Denmark, England, France, Greece, Holland, Mexico, Norway, Surinam, Switzerland, and Yugoslavia.

greater variety of erotic experiences. This suggests a life-course pattern in which younger clients use sex tourism as a means of erotic exploration with multiple partners, while older clients seek more stable and intimate relationships with specific sex workers. Further, to the degree that older clients are more oriented toward regular, intimate relationships, it is likely that they provide a steadier source of income than younger clients. It also is quite possible that older clients, by virtue of their occupational stratum, have more disposable income, enabling them to provide more extensive economic support through remittances and gifts. These findings are consistent with those of Ruiz and Vásquez (1993), who report that 62% of the male sex workers they surveyed preferred older clients, often because these "*viejos*" (old men) were believed to have more money.

Regular clients, whether foreign or local, often provide a safety net for men who have no steady wage or whose income does not meet their basic needs. Sex workers often explained to me that these longer-term relationships are more reliable than simple one-night stands. For example, when I asked Martín why he had chosen to focus more attention on his regular clients, he replied:

Listen, what happens with the gays and the money is that most of
the time it's momentary. You grab a guy, he gives you something,
and that's what you made that night, like I told you. But if you have
two regular ones, they're more definite than those that you grab for
the night, you understand? Because when you need them, they're
going to be there to help you.

The types of economic support received from steady foreign clients further demonstrate the importance of regular clients to sex workers' economic situation. Of the 72 sex workers who reported having regular
male tourist-clients, 66 (92%) said these clients had provided economic
support that went beyond direct payments for sex. When asked an
open-ended follow-up question about types of support from steady clients, responses demonstrated a more diverse range of types of support
received than was characteristic of exchanges with new clients. While
frequently including cash or regular monthly remittances, support from
Western Union daddies is often oriented toward assisting sex workers
with regular household and living expenses including items such as
construction materials, automobiles or motorcycles, clothes and sup-
plies for children, household furniture, university tuition and fees, cellu-
lar phones, and food. It also is noteworthy that sex workers often
emphasize support for children in their descriptions of regular clients'
forms of assistance, a pattern that parallels statements by Dominican female sex workers (Cabezas, 1998).[12]

Importantly, regular remittances from foreign clients must be understood within the larger context of dependence on remittances from abroad
that characterizes the Dominican economy more generally. Grasmuck
and Pessar (1991) estimated that in 1981, the single city of Santiago,
Dominican Republic, received approximately US $13 million dollars in
the form of regular remittances from migrant family members abroad.
As their work aptly demonstrates, the influx of remittances from abroad
functions for many Dominican families as a means to cope with falling
wages and the restriction of local employment options, while enabling
them to acquire foreign consumer goods that are increasingly symbolic
of the 'middle class.' Indeed, in Latin America and the Caribbean, the
volume of remittances to the Dominican Republic is surpassed only by
Mexico and Brazil and, in 2001, the value of Dominican remittances
was three times the value of all its agricultural exports (MIF, 2001).
Georges (1990) reports that by the mid-1980s, remittances received by
Dominicans from migrant family members, primarily from the U.S.,
were already nearly equal to the annual profits from the country's sugar

exports and equivalent to the total budget of the Dominican government. In addition, "the contribution of remittances to the Dominican balance of payments was considerably greater than in some other major Caribbean [migrant] sending nations, such as Jamaica and Barbados" (p. 236). Viewed in this light, the cash gifts sex workers receive from their regular clients abroad is a microcosm of a global economic flow from the 'core' to the 'periphery' upon which the local Dominican economy has come to depend. It is not surprising, then, that sex workers value their regular foreign clients, since the commonality of support from migrant family members has undoubtedly taught many of them about the importance of regular remittances from abroad. It is worth noting that standard estimates of the value of foreign remittances entirely neglect the payments received from sex work clients abroad, which may be quite significant in countries with a large sex tourism industry.

Given the level of economic support from regular male clients and the relatively greater intimacy that characterizes these relationships, how do sex workers feel toward the men with whom they develop such long-term relationships? This is a complex question, since such exchanges are infused with contradictory interests, motivations, and emotions. As discussed in Padilla (2003), many sex workers mitigate the shame they feel about their same-sex encounters by employing information management techniques which decrease the possibility of discovery by family, friends, and neighbors. This, however, does not necessarily eliminate the anxiety and emotional turmoil many of them feel regarding their sexual behavior and identity. These anxieties can intensify when relationships with male clients develop into longer-term arrangements involving a certain degree of intimacy because clients may expect more 'authentic' expressions of affection from their partners, and because sex workers may begin to develop feelings for their long-term clients that conflict with their own self-perceptions and definitions.

The ambivalence sex workers feel toward regular clients manifests itself in a number of ways. In my study, sex workers frequently avoided using terms of emotional attachment when describing their relationships with regular clients. This is related to the common belief that it is gay men, not "*hombres normales*" (normal men), who develop strong emotional feelings for other men. Thus, the denial of an emotional bond with regular clients–and especially a bond that would imply an inappropriate level of attachment to another man–served to preserve their *macho* self-image and allay any fears about becoming a *maricón* (gay man or effeminate man). Nevertheless, their efforts to maintain a safe emotional distance from their regular clients were often complicated by their growing affection for them, and many emphasized how well their "*amigos*" treated them. The result is that their descriptions of relationships with regular clients often revealed a tension between expressions of genuine affection and the desire to maintain an appropriate level of emotional distance.

Sex workers' tendency to distance themselves emotionally from regular clients is demonstrated by survey responses about affective relations with last regular clients. Several Yes/No questions were designed to explore participants' reactions to a series of phrases describing progressively deeper emotional attachments to regular male clients. These questions followed an extensive inquiry into the history of participants' relationships with their last regular tourist-clients that included questions about sexual activities and safer sex practices. The relevant questions are:

- Do you feel your last regular client treats you well?
- Do you trust your last regular client?
- Do you feel affection for your last regular client?
- Do you love your last regular client?

As expected, sex workers tended to answer affirmatively in lower proportions to questions that implied a greater degree of emotional involvement. While 100% of the participants agreed that their most recent regular male client treated them well, only 67% felt that this relationship involved "trust," 60% characterized it as "affection," and 22% as "love." From one perspective, this seems to be a logical result, since it is reasonable that fewer relationships would develop to a level that would represent mutual love. Nevertheless, there is more to these patterns than is immediately apparent. For example, the comparison of answers to two additional survey questions is telling. When participants were asked a general question about whether a *bugarrón*–that is, *any bugarrón*–could fall in love with another man, responses were overwhelmingly positive, with 79% (158/199) agreeing that this was possible. On the other hand, when they were asked a direct personal question about whether they themselves could fall in love with another man, only 35% (70/199) acknowledged this possibility. This difference represents the degree to which sex workers are motivated to deny their own emotional attachments to other men, as these are considered 'abnormal' expressions of eroticism and signs of homosexuality that are threatening to their sense of self. De Moya's (1989) study of Dominican adolescents reported similar uses of same-sex behavior.

In our conversations, the ambivalence that sex workers felt regarding their emotional attachments to regular clients often manifested itself in a rhetorical emphasis on the performative aspects of their 'love.' That is, they sought to depict their outward affection for their regular clients as an exigency of their occupation, and often joked about the 'ridiculous' things they have to do to convince their partners of the authenticity of their feelings. "I feel like an idiot sometimes," one *bugarrón* explained about his romantic performances for clients, "but I do it super well." These performances are often necessary because the credibility of their 'love' and affection can have a direct bearing on clients' willingness to continue visiting Santo Domingo or to send remittances from abroad. It is useful in this context to recall the explicit threat by Larry, Miguel's regular client, that "if [anybody] tells me that you're working I'm not going to Santo Domingo anymore." This sets up a financial scenario in which Miguel is forced, if he is to continue receiving the lucrative remittances from New York, to give a convincing show of love, affection, and–in this case–fidelity.

Precisely because of the need to perform romance, a certain proportion of sex workers refuse to enter into longer term relationships with clients, preferring the more mechanistic, instrumental, and impersonal encounters typical of exchanges with new clients. Rafael, for example, explained to me that he avoided steady clients because they required him to do things that made him feel uncomfortable as a "*macho*," and therefore were not worth the potential economic benefits:

Rafael: Actually, the ones that come from *allá* [over there, meaning 'abroad'], some of them want to have, like, a relationship. But you see, you have to do lots of things for that, and that doesn't happen with me.

Author: Why doesn't it happen?

Rafael: Because I'm not going to make you feel–I don't do whatever you want. You have to satisfy a *maricón* with things that you don't–if you're a *machista*–you wouldn't do, you understand? So, they tell me, like, that I'm cold, but I tell them, "No, man!" because I don't do that ... I'm telling you, honestly, sometimes you try to make them fall in love with you and they don't give you anything. It's not worth it, you see? Keep that away from me! Look, shit, I treat

> you with affection [*cariño*] and nothing … You know, you
> go with them and you give them a little caress [*acaricia*],
> and later you tell him, "Sweetie, I'm in love" [*estoy
> enamorado*]. And me, lying down with him hugging me–
> It looks bad. I don't like that shit.

Thus, individual sex workers must weigh their own willingness to perform romance–which occasionally requires behavior that is decidedly
un-*macho*–against the potential economic benefits of these performances.[13]

It is important to emphasize that a significant proportion of sex workers acknowledge feeling affection for, or even being "in love" with, one
or more of their regular clients. How are we to understand the affective
dimensions of these relationships, particularly when they are fraught
with differences of race, class, and nationality? In fact, even in those
cases in which affection or love was expressed openly, emotional attachment was often framed within the context of the material benefits
that resulted from these relationships. In sex workers' discourses about
favorite clients, for example, one of the primary rationales for feeling
genuine "*cariño*" for a client was the provision of extensive economic
benefits and gifts. "Best clients" are almost always described as those
who are financially generous, as opposed to the contemptible "*tacaños*"
(stingy ones) who are constantly devising ways to cheat the 'boys.' Often, these stereotypes are couched in nationalistic terms. That is, there
are those countries from which clients tend to be more generous or more
tacaño, although there appears to be no clear consensus among sex
workers on this point. What is clear is that a positive emotional valence
toward a client is more consistently associated with generous material
benefits than with nearly any other personality trait. And, as described
in the following section, this is precisely the source of anxiety for many
Western Union daddies, since the fact of their economic contributions
never allows them to feel entirely secure about the authenticity of their
partners' affection.

"No Romance Without Finance":
Gay Tourist Narratives of Authenticity

I met Jeffrey, an early-forties paralegal from New York, through an
Internet chat group oriented toward gay tourism to the Dominican Republic, where I had posted a message about conducting interviews with
sex work clients during their trips to Santo Domingo. After corresponding
with Jeffrey, we agreed to meet during his next trip to Santo Domingo,

and we conducted our first interview at a gay hotel near the *Zona Colonial* (Colonial Zone) in May, 2000. This interview was the beginning of a regular correspondence that lasted two years in which Jeffrey kept me informed of his 'adventures' in the Dominican Republic and his developing relationship with Fernando, a regular *bugarrón* at *Charlie's* bar. I also interacted regularly with Fernando, both in the presence of Jeffrey and during his long absences in New York, and Fernando participated in various formal stages of this research. In addition, Fernando and Jeffrey solicited my translation services for their phone calls between Santo Domingo and New York, since the occasionally complex negotiations of their transnational relationship often required a linguistic precision that exceeded their language abilities. The longitudinal quality of the ethnographic material with Jeffrey and Fernando is useful in illustrating many of the dimensions of authenticity that are central to sexual-economic exchanges. It also permits a glimpse into the complex emotional attachments and economic arrangements that develop as relationships based on sex tourism are gradually reconfigured into those based on romance—a transformation that is fraught with questions of authenticity.

During our initial interview, Jeffrey described his relationship to the *bugarrones* as one based primarily on anonymous sexual exploration, although he had already established a regular relationship with two sex workers, one of whom was Fernando. Nevertheless, as he later wrote to me from New York, his initial infatuation was not with Fernando, but with Leonardo, the husky doorman from *Charlie's*:

> I remember telling you something along the lines of I have no problem separating my emotions from the whole scene and not emotionally falling for these boys. Well, I've been having a little bit of a problem with that since returning to NYC this time. I certainly wouldn't call it Love (if it is–I will REMAIN in denial). But I have a strong infatuation with Leonardo. Now I've been through enough in life to know that infatuations don't last. But still, all in all, I'm feeling these things for him. And I don't particularly like it. All of his kindness and sincerity put aside, the bottom line is that he is a PROSTITUTE. But feeling this infatuation with him leaves me open and vulnerable. For instance, I told him that I would wire him $50 on my payday. Now, Mark, honestly, I live paycheck to paycheck and really can't afford to be sending these boys money. Unlike a lot of these queens who go there all the time, I have to save money for my little jaunts to Santo Domingo. And then I think that if I send Leonardo $50, then I should send Fernando the

same–to keep from hurting Fernando's feelings. It's crazy. But I know I'll do it anyway.

This initial correspondence represents the beginning of Jeffrey's ongoing internal debate about the fundamental nature of his relationship with Dominican *bugarrones*, a debate that centered principally on the meanings of his financial contributions and the underlying motivations for his "boys" to continue their relationships with him. These questions intensified as his trips to Santo Domingo became more frequent, trips which he described to me in an interview as a kind of "obsession." The latter is epitomized by the compulsive nature of his remittances, which is a theme of his letters, and is represented in the above correspondence by the final line, "But I know I'll do it anyway." Such linguistic constructions demonstrate the degree to which Jeffrey perceives his remittances as something beyond his voluntary control, and much of his correspondence focuses on his attempts to understand the psychological roots of his own obsessive financial relationships with Dominican men. Indeed, he confided in one letter that he often found his correspondence with me somewhat cathartic, in contrast to his conversations with fellow sex tourists who display similar compulsive tendencies:

> You know this corresponding with you has really helped me to sort out my feelings. I tried to get into a similar dialogue on the phone with one of my fellow traveling sisters in Atlanta, but Miss Thing is already carrying around so much emotional baggage of her own, that she really couldn't offer me any constructive feedback. She's been to Santo Domingo 15 times in the last 10 months! But Miss Thing is loaded and can afford it like that. God only knows if I had that kind of money, I'd be doing the same! She said she has 3 of these boys constantly calling her for Western Union gifts.[14]

In later correspondence, Jeffrey began to reflect more directly on the psychological motives behind his own financial contributions, as well as on the authenticity of the affection that Fernando and Leonardo expressed to him. He narrated, as follows, the final day of one of his trips to Santo Domingo:

> You see, I was running out of money on my last day (as I always do), and I knew I wasn't going to have anymore to give them, and I certainly wanted some more *Pinga*[15] before I left! They have both told me that, unlike their other clients, I can give them what I want.

Matter of fact, Fernando never asks for anything. And the only thing Leonardo will say is 'I have to go to see my family now and I need to take them 500 pesos,' or something similar. They tell me that I am their friend not just a tourist. It is very touching. Whether it is an orchestrated and rehearsed scene or not (but I don't think it is), it is very touching to me. But after I had said to them at the beach that I would wire them money next week, somehow I felt in control and in charge of the whole situation again. Nothing changed about them after I mentioned money. They were their same festive selves as before. Would they have continued to stay with me the last night if there had been no money offered? I would like to think so, and I think that may have been the case–but I don't know for sure. At any rate, they never allow me to go from point A to point B in Santo Domingo without one of them escorting me. And that's very touching.

Here, Jeffrey displays more introspection in his understanding of his own financial contributions, making reference to feeling "in control" after paying Fernando and Leonardo. Nevertheless, he is unable to entirely dispel the suspicion that their affection is actually "an orchestrated and rehearsed scene," despite the fact that he ultimately finds their 'act' convincing and "touching." In this narrative, Jeffrey makes one of his first references to what he later calls the "what-if question"–referring to the hypothetical consequences if he were to discontinue his financial support; a question that seems to cause him considerable emotional turmoil. In one message, for example, he writes, "If I REALLY wanted to know the answer, I'd stop with the $$." As far as I am aware, however, Jeffrey has never carried out this test, preferring to continue sending remittances and coping with the constant questions about the authenticity of his partners' affection. This is preferable to the pain of verifying what he has suspected all along, as illustrated by his closing remark in one message: "Is it really 'No Romance without Finance?'"

In several of Jeffrey's letters, there are scattered references to the distinctions between Dominican *bugarrones* and hustlers in New York, which is a pattern in gay sex tourists' narratives and a primary motive for their attraction to the country. Jeffrey, for example, described to me the "jaded" attitude of the "strung-out," drug-addicted hustlers in New York, and the fact that Dominican *bugarrones* are "clean" and "predictable" (not displaying aggressive or erratic behavior) in comparison. Such tourist narratives often incorporate references to cultural differences that are eroticized, including, for example, the ways Dominican men move their bodies when dancing the *merengue* or the *machismo* expressed in their gestures. Many gay sex tourists with whom I spoke during fieldwork eroticized the fact that Dominican sex workers do not generally consider themselves to be gay, allowing the tourist to realize a fantasy that is not 'thinkable' within the sex-gender logic of the United States and Europe: to have sex with a truly 'straight' man. The erotic charge of this fantasy seems to be reflected in the fact that many gay sex tourists do not object to their 'boys' being sexually involved with women or married, and may even prefer this arrangement. Finally, the poor economic condition of the Dominican Republic–and of sex workers in particular–is a common feature of these tourist narratives, and often functions as a justification for continued remittances as well as a way to mitigate ambivalence about the combination of 'romance' and 'finance.'

Many of these narrative features are evident in a notable passage in one of Jeffrey's messages from June, 2000:

> In March, Leonardo took me to meet his family and have dinner with them (his sister, nieces, nephews and mother–I saw no girl-friend or wife). And I saw the conditions they live in. Granted, it was very clean considering the circumstances but they had no running water, electricity was haphazardly strung up everywhere, and cement floors. Which is something I love about the Dominican people who have never been here [in the U.S.A]. They haven't been exposed to the blatant materialism we have here, and they appear to have a tranquility about them. They seem to love their culture, their language, the food, their music, etc. But when I saw the way they lived I knew that even a few dollars would go a long way to help them. And it seems that almost all the money that Leonardo gets goes back to them. And I'm sure Fernando's family is the same way. And Leonardo and Fernando are not alcoholics or drug addicts who are going to blow every dime you give them on getting fucked up. They put the money to good use–whether it's for their family or for something for them to wear or eat.

Here, Jeffrey is explicit about the fundamental differences between North Americans and Dominicans, particularly those who have not been "exposed" to the negative (modern) influences of the developed world–an ironic contrast given the commonality of transnational migration and exchange that characterizes Dominicans of all social classes. The idea that his remittances are "put ... to good use" seems to be one of the primary ways that he was able to reach a tentative resolution to the "what-if" dilemma of his financial contributions. This is because his focus on the conditions of poverty and deprivation allowed him to psychologically reconfigure his payments as a kind of humanitarian assistance, rather than (or, perhaps, in addition to) compensation for sex, affection, or companionship. Thus, while providing a way to configure himself as an empathic benefactor rather than a sex tourist, his focus on the conditions of poverty in which Fernando and Leonardo lived permitted him to alleviate the ambivalence he felt about sending regular remittances to them. In this context, it is important to note that sex workers are well aware of the potential economic benefits of 'performing' poverty for their regular clients, and often expressed this as a strategy for gaining empathy that could lead to more generous payments from tourists. Gregorio, a 21 year-old *bugarrón* in Santo Domingo, for example, explained in one interview how the passing of Hurricane Georges in September, 1998, was his "best period," since he was able to convince all of his regular clients to send him sympathy payments totaling 46,000 pesos (nearly $3000 U.S.) to help him rebuild his house. "But my house was fine," he joked heartily, "since it's made of brick!"

By March, 2001, more than a year after his first remittances to Fernando and Leonardo, Jeffrey reported that he had begun to suspect Leonardo's motives, particularly because he seemed to be trying to cheat Fernando out of his portion of the payments. "I'm wondering if Leonardo wasn't going to one Western Union to pick up his money with his I.D.," he wrote in one letter, "and then going to another Western Union and getting Fernando's money." The conflict that ensued between Leonardo and Fernando typifies the tension that often develops between competing sex workers when a regular client proves to be particularly generous. Subsequent correspondence with Jeffrey revealed that Leonardo and Fernando were no longer in communication, and each had a different–and conflicting–story about the other's motives in relation to Jeffrey. At the same time, Jeffrey began to express greater affection for Fernando, and his subsequent trips to Santo Domingo focused almost exclusively on this relationship.

Some of the correspondence from this period is noteworthy in that it demonstrates the ways that sex tourism can become a fundamental feature of one's psychological coping style–a kind of "drug," as Jeffrey once described it to me–leaving one feeling empty and depressed between vacations. Jeffrey often spoke to me about his desire to live in the Dominican Republic, but his linguistic limitations and "paycheck-to-paycheck" existence in New York made this untenable. In one message, he clearly expresses his emotional state upon his return to New York following a trip to Santo Domingo:

> I am still in a FUNK. I feel like as if I'm walking around like a pro-grammed robot. Get up, get dressed, take the fucking 7 train to the City, work all day and half the night, go home, go to sleep and do it all over again. And all this just so I can go back to the DR again. I have absolutely no interest in anything going on in this City. My dearest friend is not speaking to me now because he says all I have is the DR on my mind. He's right, you know. I am so fucking DEPRESSED! I feel so NEEDY!!!

Passages such as this, echoed in various messages from Jeffrey, illus-trate a dimension of sex tourism that is rarely addressed in scholarly dis-cussions: the ways that it can be used, perhaps largely unconsciously, as a means to deal with emotional problems 'back home.' For obvious reasons, I cannot (nor do I wish to) assess Jeffrey's emotional health. However, his behavior—including a highly obsessive relationship with Dominican *bugarrones*; a compulsive overtime work schedule in order to pay for the next trip to Santo Domingo; and a generally depressed attitude toward life in New York—suggests that his participation in sex tourism can only be understood within the larger framework of his emo-tional life. As a forty-something, somewhat overweight gay man living a marginally middle-class life in New York, the Dominican Republic has provided him with the opportunity to see himself as desirable by men whom he views as fundamentally different from the hustlers (and, perhaps, all gay men) in New York. *Bugarrones* are *real* men; they are true *machos* who are not "jaded" by the "materialism" of the modern world; they are happy in spite of their circumstances; and they are pleased to accept whatever he is willing to send them to "help out." In-deed, in Jeffrey's conceptualization, Santo Domingo is everything that New York is not, suggesting a kind of splitting or bifurcation of his emotional / geographical universe into the modern turmoil of New York and the idyllic fantasyland of the *bugarrones*. Being able to control the affection of others through economic resources—something that would be impossible for him among the more expensive hustlers in New York—allows him to gain a degree of control over what might otherwise be a difficult erotic terrain at home. Thus, Santo Domingo allows him a temporary escape not only from the unsatisfying grind of work, but also from a sense of himself that he finds, in some way, unfulfilling. As a Western Union daddy, he is able to see himself in a different light, as someone worthy of the attention of men, as an empathic benefactor–as anything but ordinary.

At the time of this writing, Jeffrey and Fernando continue their visiting relationship, which has developed into one they both characterize as "love." Jeffrey has continued to send regular remittances, and provides Fernando with relatively expensive gifts, most recently a car. They have spoken of the possibility of Fernando moving to New York, although this is a step they are still negotiating, partly because of Jeffrey's insistence that Fernando become literate before moving abroad. Despite the progression of their relationship, Jeffrey continues to express doubt about the authenticity of Fernando's affection. His last update on the status of their relationship ends with his typical combination of hopeful romanticism, nagging suspicion, and gay camp:

> It has been confirmed and verified that Fernando no longer goes to the *bugarrón* spots anymore. I know this is most likely because I give him a monthly allowance, but it's still a lifestyle change for him ... Maybe I'm a fool, but right now I'm just a fool in love.

DISCUSSION

Homoeroticism and the Quest for Authenticity

The performances used by sex workers to market themselves and gay tourists' desire for authentic erotic experiences demonstrate an intriguing expression of MacCannell's (1973, 1976) classic analysis of the techniques that people in host countries use to 'stage' particular features of 'authentic' local culture for consumption by the tourism market. The motivation for tourist experiences, according to MacCannell, is partly the product of the search for authenticity that increasingly characterizes the contemporary world. "Under modern conditions, the place of the individual in society is preserved, in part, by newly institutionalized concerns for the authenticity of his social experiences" (1973, p. 590). Tourism provides an outlet for these desires through the consumption of 'authentic' cultural experiences, but achieving this goal requires access to what MacCannell, following Goffman (1959), describes as "back regions"–the domain of private life that transcends the barriers to 'truth' and intimacy that nearly always characterize public social spaces.[16] Nevertheless, this quest for authenticity is a partial one: "Sightseers are motivated by a desire to see life as it is really lived, even to get in with the natives, and, at the same time, they are deprecated for always failing to achieve these goals" (1973, p. 592). MacCannell (1973) summarizes the ambivalent position of the tourist in relation to his or her quest for authenticity:

> Touristic consciousness is motivated by its desire for authentic experiences, and the tourist may believe that he is moving in this direction, but often it is very difficult to tell for sure if the experience is authentic in fact. It is always possible that what is taken to be entry into a back region is really entry into a front region that has been totally set up in advance for touristic visitation. In tourist settings, especially in modern society, it may be necessary to discount the importance, and even the existence, of front and back regions except as ideal poles of touristic experience. (p. 597)

MacCannell's framework is useful in relation to the construction of sexuality more generally, and homoeroticism in particular, in sex tourism encounters. This is for two primary reasons. First, same-sex desire is a domain of experience in which gay-identified tourists have invested their sexual identity, and gay identity itself is a means by which men in the industrialized West have asserted their authenticity and legitimacy as sexual subjects. Thus, one might say that gay identity is already 'about' authenticity, in that it operates to articulate and validate a certain kind of non-normative sexuality. Second, if MacCannell is correct, then gay men's sexuality in most tourist-sending countries is already embedded in the structure of late modern capitalism; a system which tends to facilitate the personal alienation that motivates touristic experience. While MacCannell himself did not seek to apply his theoretical framework to the sphere of homosexuality, it would seem that it helps to explain certain broad features of the contemporary economy which frame same-sex practices in the global, 'postmodern' era. Indeed, if–as some social scientists have argued (D'Emilio, 1983)–the historical development of gay identity itself was tied to the emergence of urban industrial capitalism in the West, a 'postmodern' gay identity might be said to be increasingly tied to a new expression of global capitalism. This expression requires the consumption of certain kinds of homoerotic experiences, and sex tourism might be said to be the vehicle through which some contemporary gay men gain access to certain 'authentic' sexual experiences. In the case of the *bugarrones* and *sanky pankies* described here, it is quite clear that these consumptive practices are linked to the global marketability of *non-gay-identified* Dominican men, who are seen to be more 'macho,' more 'real,' and more available in the Caribbean than they are in the industrialized West. Therefore, gay sex tourism sets up a global division of sexual labor in which the market demand for certain authentic homoerotic experiences–particularly those with 'straight,' masculine men–is fulfilled by the Dominican men who provide sexual services to visiting gay tourists.

MacCannell's (1973, 1976) theory is useful in another way, since it also articulates an ambivalence that is at the heart of the tourist's quest for authenticity. This ambivalence recalls the discussion of Jeffrey, who is tormented by the 'what if' question of his financial contributions, never entirely confident about the authenticity of Fernando's shows of affection. As in MacCannell's description of the quandary of the tourist, travel to the Dominican Republic allows Jeffrey to purchase exotic experiences that, at least in his view, are not possible in New York. Yet, the instrumental nature of these experiences undermines his sense of their authenticity. Importantly, ethnographic evidence described above and elaborated further in the ethnography upon which this discussion is based (Padilla, 2003), demonstrates that *bugarrones* and *sanky pankies* are highly aware of the suite of meanings associated with a certain notion of Dominican masculinity, and they use this knowledge strategically in marketing themselves to clients. In MacCannell's terms, they perform–with their bodies, their masculinity, and their sexual services–a 'back region' for consumption by gay sex tourists. However, this 'strategic' deployment of sexuality should not be considered a purely rational or conscious phenomenon since, in many cases, it is impossible to distinguish between 'performances' that are instrumental in nature from those that are more deeply integrated into one's sense of self or personhood. Consequently, sex workers' performances are fundamentally 'over-determined,' that is, they are informed by multiple meanings and interests simultaneously.

What is clear from Jeffrey's narrative is that sexual experiences with Dominican men fill certain psycho-emotional needs. As Western Union daddies, men like Jeffrey–vis-à-vis their experiences of travel, cultural and racial difference, and the consumption of sexual services–are able to envision themselves and their erotic lives in a new light. Thus, as suggested by Kempadoo (1999, p. 26), "Caribbean masculinity and femininity alike ... become the tableaux upon which a reshaping and retooling of Western identity occurs." Nevertheless, for at least two reasons, this "Western identity" is never entirely stable. First, the erotic power of the Other depends on a particular construction of essentialized difference that, in turn, necessitates a certain degree of *distance*. A consequence of this is evident in a comment that Jeffrey made repeatedly when we discussed the possibility of him moving permanently to the Dominican Republic: "But if I *lived* there, it just wouldn't be the same." According to Mullings (1999), the inverse relationship between familiarity and eroticism that characterizes sex tourism is one of the reasons that 'traditional' destinations for international prostitution, such as Southeast Asia, are now showing signs of market saturation, as tourists are seeking unspoiled, 'virgin' areas for sexual exploration. For clients seeking 'romantic' encounters abroad, sex tourism requires a compromise between distance and intimacy, permitting a degree of emotional involvement while keeping the erotic charge of otherness intact. As illustrated by Jeffrey's story, however, the drawback of this division of one's erotic universe is that it sometimes leads to a fragmenting of identity, an aching nostalgia, and a sense of personal alienation upon return 'home.' As one's identity and fantasy world become rooted in an exotic faraway place, it becomes increasingly difficult to deal with the mundane grind of 'modern' urban life.

A second reason this so-called Western identity, as constructed through the Other, is unstable is that it depends on socioeconomic differences whose very existence undermine the authenticity of a partner's fantasized 'love.' As more intimate relationships develop, the dramatic economic inequalities that frame global sex work never permit the sex tourist absolute security about the degree to which his affection is genuinely reciprocated, despite the various strategies that both parties employ to obfuscate the instrumental aspects of the relationship. As O'Connell Davidson and Sanchez Taylor (1999) argue, in global sex tourism, the commercial nature of the sex worker-client exchange essentially strips all mutuality from sexual relations and "provides a conveniently ready-dehumanized sexual object for the client" (p. 40). Yet, in the context of 'romance tourism'—or the longer-term, more intimate relationships typical of Western Union daddies—this tendency toward dehumanization must be resolved, insofar as it is understood to be antithetical to true intimacy and emotional mutuality. Thus, while sex tourism in places such as the Dominican Republic opens certain avenues by which Westerners can rework their identities vis-à-vis the 'Other,' it also can create dilemmas for them as they struggle to imagine themselves as worthy beings amidst the inequalities that can never be entirely erased from consciousness.

NOTES

1. Due to the sensitive nature of the subject matter, all place names and proper names for sex workers and clients have been changed to maintain confidentiality. Certain biographical or event details may be modified slightly to further protect the identities of study participants.

2. See, for example, ethnographic accounts of Caribbean masculinity in Chevannes (2001), Dann (1987), and Wilson (1969, 1973).

3. This ethnographic study was conducted with two local identity categories of male sex workers, *bugarrones* and *sanky pankies*. These are glossed here as 'male sex workers,' but also have other local meanings that are not addressed in this article. For a more thorough description, see Padilla (2003).

4. *Tíguere* is a specifically Dominican term used to describe a masculine gender figure that is stereotypical of lower class men (particularly those engaged in delinquent or non-normative behavior), but is so pervasive culturally that it has become a key metaphor for Dominican masculinity more generally (Krohn-Hansen, 1996). In this specific example, Leonardo chased the *tíguere* for several blocks and managed to retrieve my belongings, confirming his status as a skilled *portero* as well as solidifying my relationship with him. This was one of three occasions in which he came to my rescue in the course of my fieldwork.

5. In the informal and fluid economy of Dominican male sex work, commissions do not follow a rigid structure or hierarchy, and the boundary between 'sex worker' and 'pimp' is permeable and changeable. Individuals with specific services to offer (such as language translation or tour guide services) or who hold particular positions of power (such as Leonardo in his role as doorman at *Charlie's*), take advantage of these circumstances to sell their services or extract commissions from both sex workers and clients.

6. Indeed, as discussed in Padilla (2003), traditional constructions of Dominican homoeroticism blur the boundaries between *bugarrone*s and 'normal' men, since gender normativity is defined in relation to one's position in sexual intercourse rather than sexual object choice. Similar arguments have been made in other Latin American and Caribbean contexts (Carrier, 1995; Kulick, 1998; Lancaster, 1992; Lumsden, 1996; Parker, 1999).

7. Hirschman (1984) estimates there are 5,000 *tricicleros* (tricycle riders) in Santo Domingo who make a meager living by distributing fruits, vegetables, coal, and a variety of other items. Driving *triciculos* is a common source of employment among poor urban males.

8. Some sex workers lack the identification sometimes required to make Western Union pickups, which was the motive for my assistance on two occasions.

9. Ruiz and Vásquez (1993, p. 58) report as follows: "Around 9 of every ten [sex workers] preferred foreign tourist-clients, mainly because they say that they pay better (74%), even though one of every ten thinks that these clients can transmit diseases. Virtually all of them (92%) had had sexual relations with foreign tourist-clients. The average number of lifetime foreign clients was 21, mainly from the United States, Italy, Spain, and Canada" (translation by author).

10. Mullings (1999, p. 66) summarizes Pruitt and LaFont's argument as follows: "Pruitt and LaFont (1995) have argued that male sex workers are involved in romance rather than sex tourism, because there is often a level of emotional involvement that is not often present in sex tourism. These holiday relationships tend to be longer term,

involving a much higher level of social and economic commitment on the part of both parties in the exchange."

11. Survey participants were read a list of client types from which they were requested to choose the one that represented the 'best' client according to their own preferences or personal criteria. It was thus a forced-choice question for which only one response was permissible. The client types included in this question were established in prior focus group discussions with sex workers. Separate categories were created for 'executives' (both local and foreign) since these presumably wealthy businessmen were understood by sex workers as a distinct type of male client that should not be conflated with 'tourists.' These executives were the preferred clients of a sub-group of *bugarrones* and *sanky pankies*, totaling approximately 22% of the sample.

12. Support for children as a primary motive for involvement in sex work is much less common among male sex workers than female sex workers. This is consistent with Espinal and Grasmuck's (1997) finding that male informal entrepreneurs contributed 60% of their income on average to their households, whereas their female counterparts contributed 80%.

13. In his study of male sex workers in a Costa Rican brothel, Schifter (1998) similarly argues that *cacheros* (an identity of male sex workers roughly analogous to Dominican *bugarrones*) "cannot conceive of how two men can love each other" (p. 60). He quotes one informant who commented that clients often "want you to tell them they're attractive and interesting and I just don't give a shit" (p. 60).

14. The feminine pronouns frequently used in Jeffrey's correspondence are a gay discourse style, and invariably refer to gay men.

15. *Pinga* is colloquial Spanish for dick, and is frequently used by gay sex tourists and the pornography industry as a racialized reference to the Latin phallus.

16. The use of 'front' and 'back' in MacCannell's terminology derives from Goffman's (1959) use of the dichotomy of "front stage" / "back stage" in his theoretical model, which employs theatrical performance as a metaphor for the contextual nature of public and private social relations.

REFERENCES

Brennan, D. E. (1998). *Everything is for sale here: Sex tourism in Sosúa, the Dominican Republic.* Unpublished doctoral dissertation, Yale University, New Haven, CT.

Brennan, D. (2004). *What's love got to do with it? Transnational desires and sex tourism in the Dominican Republic.* Durham, NC: Duke University Press.

Cabezas, A. L. (1998). *Pleasure and its pain: Sex tourism in Sosúa, the Dominican Republic.* Unpublished doctoral dissertation, University of California, Berkeley, CA.

Cabezas, A. L. (1999). Women's work is never done: Sex tourism in Sosúa, the Dominican Republic. In K. Kempadoo (Ed.), *Sun, sex, and gold: Tourism and sex work in the Caribbean* (pp. 93-123). Lanham, MD: Rowman & Littlefield.

Carrier, J. (1995). *De los otros: Intimacy and homosexuality among Mexican men.* New York, NY: Columbia University Press.

Chevannes, B. (2001). *Learning to be a man: Culture, socialization, and gender identity in five Caribbean communities.* Kingston, JM: University of the West Indies Press.

Dann, G. (1987). *The Barbadian male: Sexual attitudes and practice.* Kingston, JM: Macmillan Caribbean.

D'Emilio, J. (1983). Capitalism and gay identity. In A. Snitow (Ed.), *Powers of desire: The politics of sexuality* (pp. 100-113). New York, NY: Monthly Review Press.

De Moya, E. A. (1989). *La alfombra de guazábara o el reino de los desterrados.* Paper presented at El Primer Congreso Dominicano sobre Menores en Circunstancias Especialmente Dificiles, Santo Domingo, Dominican Republic.

De Moya, E. A., & Garcia, R. (1996). AIDS and the enigma of bisexuality in the Dominican Republic. In P. Aggleton (Ed.), *Bisexualities and AIDS: International perspectives* (pp. 121-135). Bristol, PA: Taylor & Francis.

De Moya, A., & Garcia, R. (1998). Three decades of male sex work in Santo Domingo. In P. Aggleton (Ed.), *Men who sell sex: International perspectives on male prostitution and AIDS* (pp. 127-140). London, UK: Taylor & Francis.

De Moya, E. A., Garcia, R., Fadul, R., & Herold, E. (1992). *Sosua sanky-pankies and female sex workers: An exploratory study.* Santo Domingo, Dominican Republic: La Universidad Autónoma.

Espinal, R., & Grasmuck, S. (1997). Gender, households and informal entrepreneurship in the Dominican Republic. *Journal of Comparative Family Studies, 28,* 103-128.

Georges, E. (1990). *The making of a transnational community: Migration, development, and cultural change in the Dominican Republic.* New York, NY: Columbia University Press.

Goffman, E. (1959). *The presentation of self in everyday life.* Garden City, NY: Doubleday.

Grasmuck, S., & Pessar, P. (1991). *Between two islands: Dominican international migration (1st edition).* Berkeley, CA: University of California Press.

Hirschman, A. O. (1984). *Getting ahead collectively.* New York, NY: Pergamon Press.

Kempadoo, K. (1999). Continuities and change: Five centuries of prostitution in the Caribbean. In K. Kempadoo (Ed.), *Sun, sex, and gold: Tourism and sex work in the Caribbean* (pp. 3-33). Lanham, MD: Rowman & Littlefield.

Krohn-Hansen, C. (1996). Masculinity and the political among Dominicans: 'The Dominican tiger'. In M. Melhuus & K. A. Stølen (Eds.), *Machos, mistresses, madonnas: Contesting the power of Latin American gender imagery* (pp. 108-133). New York, NY: Verso.

Kulick, D. (1998). *Travestí: Sex, gender and culture among Brazilian transgendered prostitutes.* Chicago, IL: University of Chicago Press.

Lancaster, R. N. (1992). *Life is hard: Machismo, danger, and the intimacy of power in Latin America.* Berkeley, CA: University of California Press.

Lumsden, I. (1996). *Machos, maricones, and gays: Cuba and homosexuality.* Philadelphia, PA: Temple University Press.

MacCannell, D. (1973). Staged authenticity: Arrangements of social space in tourist settings. *American Journal of Sociology, 79,* 589-603.

MacCannell, D. (1976). *The tourist: A new theory of the leisure class.* New York, NY: Shocken Books.

MIF. (2001). *Conference document: Remittances to Latin America and the Caribbean: Comparative statistics.* Washington, D.C.: Multilateral Investment Fund.

Mullings, B. (1999). Globalization, tourism, and the international sex trade. In K. Kempadoo (Ed.), *Sun, sex, and gold: Tourism and sex work in the Caribbean* (pp. 55-80). Lanham, MD: Rowman & Littlefield.

O'Connell Davidson, J., & Sanchez Taylor, J. (1999). Fantasy islands: Exploring the demand for sex tourism. In K. Kempadoo (Ed.), *Sun, sex, and gold: Tourism and sex work in the Caribbean* (pp. 37-54). Lanham, MD: Rowman & Littlefield.

Padilla, M. (2003). *Looking for life: Male sex work, HIV/AIDS, and the political economy of gay tourism in the Dominican Republic.* Unpublished doctoral dissertation, Emory University, Atlanta, GA.

Parker, R. (1999). *Beneath the equator: Cultures of desire, male homosexuality, and emerging gay communities in Brazil.* New York, NY: Routledge.

Pruitt, D., & LaFont, S. (1995). For love and money: Romance tourism in Jamaica. *Annals of Tourism Research, 22,* 422-444.

Ramah, M., Pareja, R., & Hasbún, J. (1992). *Lifestyles and sexual practices. Results of KABP conducted among homosexual and bisexual men.* Santo Domingo, Dominican Republic: AIDSCOM.

Ruiz, C., & Vásquez, R. E. (1993). *Características psicosociales y motivación para la prevención del sida en trabajadores sexuales homotrópicos.* Santo Domingo, Dominican Republic: La Universidad Autónoma.

Schifter, J. (1998). *Lila's house: Male prostitution in Latin America.* Binghamton, NY: Harrington Park Press.

Wilson, P. J. (1969). Reputation and respectability: A suggestion for Caribbean ethnology. *Man, 4,* 70-84.

Wilson, P. J. (1973). *Crab antics: The social anthropology of English-speaking Negro societies of the Caribbean.* New Haven, CT: Yale University Press.

doi:10.1300/J082v53n01_11

CONCLUSION

Musings on Male Sex Work:
A "Virtual" Discussion

Rebecca L. Harriman, PhD (candidate)

University of Saskatchewan

Barry Johnston, MA (candidate)

Birkbeck, University of London

Paula M. Kenny, MA

SUMMARY. Contributors and editors were asked to respond to a series of questions concerning male sex work in order to stimulate an informal

Rebecca L. Harriman is a graduate student in Clinical Psychology at the University of Saskatchewan. Her research interests include attitudes towards minority group members, and issues related to gender and sexuality.

Barry Johnston is currently a postgraduate student in the School of Psychology at Birkbeck, University of London. His research interests include factors influencing the development of masculinities in young men.

Paula M. Kenny, MA, completed postgraduate training in International Security and Conflict Studies in Dublin City University, Ireland. Her research interests include all areas of political psychology, particularly political terrorism and international relations.

Correspondence may be addressed to Rebecca L. Harriman, Department of Psychology, 9 Campus Drive, University of Saskatchewan, S7N 5A5 (E-mail: rebecca.harriman@usask.ca).

[Haworth co-indexing entry note]: "Musings on Male Sex Work: A "Virtual" Discussion." Harriman, Rebecca L., Barry Johnston, and Paula M. Kenny. Co-published simultaneously in *Journal of Homosexuality* (The Haworth Press, Inc.) Vol. 53, No. 1/2, 2007, pp. 277-318; and: *Male Sex Work: A Business Doing Pleasure* (ed: Todd G. Morrison and Bruce W. Whitehead) The Haworth Press, Inc., 2007, pp. 277-318. Single or multiple copies of this article are available for a fee from The Haworth Document Delivery Service [1-800- HAWORTH, 9:00 a.m. - 5:00 p.m. (EST). E-mail address: docdelivery@haworthpress.com].

Available online at http://jh.haworthpress.com
© 2007 by The Haworth Press, Inc. All rights reserved.
doi:10.1300/J082v53n01_12

"conversation." Some of the topics explored include: why people seek the services of prostitutes; is the term "sex work" favorable to "prostitution"; is it right to pay for sex; and is exploitation a necessary part of the sex worker/client interchange? Contributors' responses were compiled and listed in the order they were received. Common elements of their responses are summarized and the advantages of this informal approach are articulated. doi:10.1300/J082v53n01_12 *[Article copies available for a fee from The Haworth Document Delivery Service: 1-800-HAWORTH. E-mail address: <docdelivery@haworthpress.com> Website: <http://www.HaworthPress.com> © 2007 by The Haworth Press, Inc. All rights reserved.]*

KEYWORDS. Male sex work, sex work, prostitution, sex industry

INTRODUCTION

Each of the contributors has taken a unique approach to the topic of male sex work, emphasizing different aspects of this topic and drawing on samples from diverse regions such as the Dominican Republic, Australia, Canada, and cities across the United States. This broad approach is important in advancing our understanding of this topic; however, an equally important task is to combine the contributors' insights and engage in a meaningful discussion of different issues. In an attempt to accomplish this task, the current chapter involves a "conversation" among the different contributors allowing them to offer their views on various questions pertaining to male sex work.

This chapter is admittedly not a replacement for a rigorous interactive discussion on male sex work, but it does provide an important opportunity to discuss themes rarely focused on by media and society in general. It is hoped that these questions will encourage not just the contributors, but also the readers, to explore the moral, social, and psychological controversies that surround male sex work. Further, exposing readers to different arguments and viewpoints simultaneously may enable them to reach their own conclusions and, in so doing, achieve a deeper understanding of this provocative topic. Finally, it is hoped that contributors' responses may stimulate more academic inquiry into this under-researched area.

Although the researchers will no doubt draw on their academic experience, this chapter was designed to reflect personal viewpoints and opinions; thus, contributors were advised that it was not necessary to provide references or to remain strictly objective. Furthermore, to facilitate the "dialogue," a conversational, rather than formal, tone was encouraged. Contributors, along with the editors of this chapter, were free to respond to as many questions as they wished. The questions are presented in the order in which they were received, with no changes apart from correction of typographic errors.

QUESTION 1

Why do you think people seek the services of prostitutes? Do the reasons differ if it's a male client with a male prostitute, male client with a female prostitute, female client with a male prostitute, etc.?

Mark Padilla:

> I don't believe an answer to this question is generalizable to all times and places, since there are clearly cultural and historical dimensions to the ways that sex work is understood and practiced, as well as a diversity of personal and developmental reasons for seeking sexual-economic exchanges. As an anthropologist working on sex tourism in the Caribbean, my work seeks to understand the linkages between the cultural and historical context of sex work and the ways that exchanges between sex workers and clients unfold in practice. This includes particular notions of race and class, as well as the meanings associated with Caribbean masculinity, which are not necessarily applicable to other cultural contexts. For example, there is reason to believe that male tourists seeking men in the Caribbean are eroticizing quite different aspects of race and sexuality than are the clients of male sex workers in places such as Thailand. Such differences, which are still in the preliminary stages of ethnographic description, demonstrate that the motives for sex work are not interpretable outside of the meanings of sex and prostitution in specific historical and cultural contexts. It is a challenge for future work on male sex work to begin to understand the cross-cultural similarities and differences in the practices and meanings of sex work in specific locations and historical moments.

Todd G. Morrison:

> The reasons are as multifarious as the individuals seeking the "services" of prostitutes. Some want a hassle-free encounter in which

specific sexual activities are performed for a specific price. They
don't want the uncertainty of the bar scene, where you may or may
not receive physical attention commensurate with the price you
have paid in watered-down drinks and tedious conversation. I
imagine that, for some, the ability to focus on one's own sexual
needs (to the exclusion of the other person) is quite appealing.
Within the sexual realm, most of us are given few opportunities to
be unapologetically self-absorbed. (And I don't mean "self-absorbed" in a pejorative sense.) In socially approved sexual encounters, mutuality is stressed: We can't (or, at least, believe we
shouldn't) focus on our own orgasm, and ignore our partner's.
"I'm done. Good-bye." Such a utilitarian emphasis on the pleasure
of one's own body connotes a lack of sensitivity or–even more cat-
astrophic–suggests that one is a bad fuck. Certainly, this sort of
emphasis on the self is permissible within the client/prostitute interchange. Another obvious answer to this question is the "illicit
thrill" that some individuals derive from having sex with a prostitute. These individuals can escape the confines of their traditional,
ordered existence and, for a brief time, enter into a perceived
demimonde of sex and sin. Finally, one shouldn't ignore those
who rely on prostitutes to gratify erotic tastes that are more eso-
teric in nature; those who may have difficulty interacting sexually
outside the protective realm of a consumer transaction; and those
who seek the services of prostitutes for the express purpose of de-
basing and abusing them.

Jonathan David Jackson:

So rich and dynamic are persons' reasons for seeking the services
of sex workers, and so prevalent might sex work be in many social
worlds, that there is some danger in generalizing about the motivations of customers or audiences. With this caveat in mind, let me
offer one reason that people, regardless of sexuality, may seek interactions with sex workers. The transactions and exchanges involved in sex work (whether they involve paying out, tipping, or
long-term set-ups) foster a psychic remove between sex worker
and client. This remove is a performance: The transactional structure advances a "fourth wall" (to use a theater-person's lingo). The
fourth wall is the invisible barrier through which audiences consider performers and performers project to audiences. The three walls
of a traditional proscenium arch stage open out to an invisible

*performance
metaphor*

fourth wall in a manner that allows us to gaze upon or overhear world making. The fourth wall in sex work allows both sex worker and client to "suspend belief" regarding depth of intimacy and bio-graphical truth. Yes, the performer-audience separation in sex work–be it on the street, in hotel rooms, at nightclubs, bordellos or at any locale–is porous and dynamic. Yes, the performer-audience separation does break down in all kinds of ways. But it exists in sex work. I believe that the performer-audience divide, *defines* sex work and motivates both clients and sex workers to participate in the exchange.

[margin note: "suspend belief" in interaction]

Obviously, I am conceptualizing sex work as performance. Let me explain my reasoning here further. The fourth wall of sex work inscribes it as inherently performative. Here I *am NOT* refer-ring to the Butlerian or queer-theoretical definition of perfor-mative. "Performative" *is NOT* for me a wholly theoretical problem of identity politics, or a high academic speculative fetish as it often seems to be in some queer and performance theory. For me the term "performative" signifies events of structured action involving considered choreographic or theatrical practice whether seemingly quotidian (like being a house-boy or street-walking) or apparently stage-bound (like stripping and having sex for video, DVD and film on a studio set).

[margin note: performance not in a Butlerian sense]

If we accept that all social action reflects diverse cultural val-ues, then the sexuality and gender of the client and the sex worker matter. While the exploitation of sex workers is a problem regard-less of gender and sexuality, in my experience such exploitation is talked about more for woman-born sex workers. A lot of boys or male-identified persons begin sex work at a young age. I started novelty and burlesque dancing when I was under-age (and I con-sider stripping, novelty dancing and other erotic performance to be types of sex work). When you're a teenager trying to survive a low-income existence, be it on the streets or otherwise, you don't always make the best decisions. Yet, some sex workers choose the work for its variable time commitments, and because they identify with and even value the skills involved in the work (and yes, strip-ping requires theatrical and social skills, and even street walking requires social skills). I've met a great deal of male and female strippers and sex workers who choose to do it and who do not feel exploited. Many of these people feel as I do that sex work is a performance that merits as much pay and labor equity as any other profession.

[margin note: reasons for choosing sex work]

I will say that often street walking–selling sex on the stroll–
for female, male or transgendered persons overlaps with drug
abuse and other problems. Personal problems of self-worth and
addiction are as much a problem in sex work as they are in any
profession. Yet, because sex work does not, for the most part,
involve labor equity, and because it is generally illegal, the social problems of a sex worker are magnified. The labor conditions of street walking or hustling in nightclubs are deplorable
and the social problems for the sex worker are magnified on the
street.

So, for me, the issue is one of accepting sex work as a profession and a performance; analyzing the performance as well as
the cultural politics of labor; gathering more views of sex workers and clients (or audiences); and improving the labor conditions towards equitable pay scales and improved quality-of-life
concerns.

David M. Boden:

I think there are as many explanations for seeking the services of
prostitutes as there are clients. I think, however, that they might be
summarized as convenience: The convenience of receiving a service that satisfies a primary human drive. Time spent in bars,
phone lines, print and computer personals, dates, etc. as well as the
monetary investment with no assurance of sexual satisfaction may
be a motivator to seek the services of a professional. Convenience
may also encompass the ability to direct the sexual activity–it
diminishes the need to negotiate with the partner, to compromise,
to consider their subjective pleasure. It is sometimes convenient to
focus simply upon one's own pleasure. With a prostitute, the actions
are pre-negotiated, established in their type, duration, and sequence.
The scenario has a greater likelihood of completion and subjective
satisfaction. Finally, prostitution may allow the individual access
to experiences that would otherwise remain hidden for shame or
fear of stigma.

Bruce W. Whitehead:

Sometimes you want a double latte with foam, and sometimes you
want a skinny decaf. (I know I have read that analogy recently,
regretfully I cannot recall where, so I thank the "unknown" writer

for that comparison and apologize for not crediting you.) I have been involved in various facets of the sex trade as a worker, customer, and researcher so the answers to that question are endless. I will not delve too deeply into the possible reasons for why a person may choose to engage the services of a sex worker, except to say that sometimes you want a particular person to do particular things to/for you at a particular time. At its height, sex work is the sale of orgasms, and at its least the sale of attention and time, with or without sexual arousal being present. Some may seek the attention, closeness, and intimacy they lack in other areas of their lives. Yet, while I fully acknowledge that visits to a sex trade worker may give rise to (or feed) various pathologies, I will refrain from commenting on whether these visits encourage or diminish the likelihood that these pathologies will occur outside the relationship, as then we degenerate into the prostitution is good, prostitution is bad debate, which is cyclical and pointless. So I'll end with the not-so-clever note that I personally prefer a double shot, short, with extra foam, and if my usual server won't give it to me, then I can go elsewhere and am willing to pay extra, which I don't mind doing if I'm getting what I want and the server is smiling.

Jeffrey Escoffier:

There must be many reasons why men—and women sometimes—seek the services of prostitutes. Of course, sex is probably the most important, but " intimacy," conversation, and companionship are also factors. I think that it is commonly thought that someone who pays for sex is somewhat pathetic. But, again, the range of motivations must be quite large: Playing out a fantasy, people who are single and work long hours, people with disabilities who might be limited in their access to casual sexual contacts. I don't think it makes any difference if it's a man hiring a male prostitute or female prostitute.

Joseph R. G. DeMarco:

I think people seek out prostitutes for a lot of different reasons, some of which we'll never know. There are those who buy sex because it's easier and less time consuming than playing games in bars or online. There are people who just want sex with no involvement—a prostitute does his job, takes his money, and goes home–which is exactly what some clients want. Some feel they are not good-looking enough to attract another man (whether this is objectively true or not, it is how they feel). Some may feel they are too old to have any success in the sexual arena. There are also those people who think they may never get the type of man–in terms of physical qualities–that is available as a prostitute and hiring one is the way to solve that problem. It may be trite, but there are probably as many reasons as there are clients.

David Leary:

My observations and intuitions are around male-to-male sex work or prostitution at a street-based level. There appear to be a variety of reasons that people have at any given time for seeking the services of a male prostitute or sex worker and while the reasons may not sit comfortably or even coherently together in the rational world, I suspect they invariably hold together in some coherent fashion for the "seeker" of the "service." Among the reasons for seeking the service of a prostitute: sexual satisfaction, excitement, clandestine encounters, anonymity, intimacy that can be controlled and ended quickly, company to fend off isolation, sexual experimentation, the possibility of exploring fantasy, having power over another, and/or the thrill of danger in darkness. Perhaps one of the more sinister expressions of prostitution arises where a loose network of men share their interest in children and adolescents, and this moves further to a sharing of young males engaged in prostitution; a swapping of young males between older males, this happening after the older male has had enough of the prostitute. Although I haven't talked with these men, I have experienced the "seeker" through my research and where young males provide evidence in criminal proceedings. From the young males' narrative and their evidence, the motivation of the "seekers" is incredibly complex; the desire for sexual satisfaction is coupled (often in incongruent ways) with a desire to control, even punish, the young male who himself has very little control in his life and who, inevitably and unreflectively, rides the wave of whatever experience passes by that may have the potential for "goodies" to be gained. The motivations of both the older men and the young males could not be more complex.

Jeffrey T. Parsons:

> I think people seek the services of sex workers because they can!!!! I don't really think the reasons would differ by gender of sex worker or client. The bottom line is that sex is a basic human need, and important for healthy living. Sometimes other partners are unavailable or unwilling to engage in certain activities, so sex workers can fill this important need. There's a level of excitement and thrill to it that I think is enhanced by the novelty, the stigma, and the potential illegality of paying for sex.

David S. Bimbi:

> I can't recall the source, but the saying goes "Clients don't pay you to 'cum,' they pay you to go." Men (and some women) pay for the services of prostitutes to meet unfulfilled sexual and intimate needs. Any attractive gay or bisexual guy who does not need "discretion" can get laid easily; if it were not for the closet and the culture of male beauty, male prostitution would have a smaller market. Female prostitution is mostly based on the unavailability of women for casual sex.

QUESTION 2

Some researchers recommend using the term "sex work" because it avoids the moralistic baggage associated with the word "prostitute" and focuses, instead, on labor issues such as wages, working conditions, etc. What do you think about the term "sex work?"

Mark Padilla:

> I think sex work is useful analytically as both a general term to refer to all expressions of sexual-economic exchange that are at least partially based on a desire to satisfy economic or material needs. It is also useful politically in some circumstances where positioning sexual-economic exchange as "labor" may permit access to certain kinds of human rights, social legitimacy, or basic human dignity—all of which are frequently denied to persons engaged in sex work. On the other hand, the term is potentially problematic when it is used as an identity term or assumed to be meaningful to individuals who

[margin note: term "sex work" maybe problematic]

are engaged in various forms of sexual-economic exchange. In my own research in the Dominican Republic, "sex worker" was not a term of self-reference that was very meaningful to most of the men I interviewed, and when it was used it was more a reflection of international discourses of public health than something that was meaningful to the men themselves. The terms "sex work" and "sex worker" therefore need to be used cautiously and those of us studying sex work should always be mindful that in many settings the terms have emerged more from academic, advocacy, and public health contexts that may not reflect the local meanings of sexual-economic exchange to the individuals we "study."

Kerwin Kaye:

I generally agree that the term "prostitution" carries some negative connotations. This is clearly seen in the ongoing use of phrases such as "to prostitute oneself" in referring to situations in which one's "inner self" is compromised in job situations. Nevertheless, the term "sex work" refers to a much broader range of commercial sex activity than sex for cash exchanges (e.g., phone sex), and I therefore find a need to use the more specific–if politically compromised–term "prostitution" on many occasions.

Todd G. Morrison:

I don't mind the term because it makes it clear that getting people aroused sexually and getting them off (be it through dancing, performing in an adult film, giving a hand-job, etc.) is work! The effortful nature of this work is compounded when the target of one's ministrations is unattractive, smelly, rude, etc. But let's be honest: "sex work" is a neologism that attempts to counter pejorative words like prostitute, whore, and hustler. As such, I believe the primary goal of this term isn't to heighten awareness of labor issues but, rather, to engender social acceptability through language. Unfortunately, in our desire to find the "right word" (read: less threatening, more palatable term), a key issue is elided: namely, regardless of whether one self-identifies as a prostitute, hooker, whore, ho, skank, sex worker, or pleasure provider, why should one be prohibited from selling sexual services to another person?

Jonathan David Jackson:

I would like to argue for a broad definition of sex work. I define sex work as a transaction involving sex or sex-related acts for money or goods. This includes any activity where money or goods are passed in exchange for any kind of sexual experience, and it also includes any *relationship*, long-term or otherwise, where it is understood that the psychological or physical rapport is *quid pro quo*. This means that I define a lot of cross-generational relationships in gay worlds to be forms of sex work. For me, sex work also includes *erotic performance*. This means I believe live sex shows (be they burlesque or for video, film, DVD or any other kind of technology) are sex work because sex in all its diversity centers the entertainment.

I witnessed or became acquainted with many forms of live erotic performance in my performing life, including stripping, go-go dancing, and even "jerk-off shows" where the performer's dance involves masturbation culminating in ejaculation. Jerk-off shows were once, and may still be, famous at San Francisco's *Nob Hill* and Washington D.C.'s *Follies Theatre*. When I worked as a novelty burlesque dancer at New York City's *Show Palace* in mid-town I knew full well that the "live sex show room" and the burlesque room were both sites for sex work. In fact, everything about the *Show Palace* on 8th Avenue between 42nd and 43rd streets in New York City was about selling sex. (The *Show Palace* is not to be confused with the *Show World*.) Inside the *Show Palace* there was a screening room where one could watch a porno flick and masturbate; a burlesque room where all-nude go-go dancers (mostly black and Latino dancers from the late 1980s until it closed in the early 1990s) danced 24 hours and 7 days a week; a canteen; and a live sex room. Sometimes headliner strippers (who were usually white porn-performers–a form of racist programming given that the other, lesser paid strippers were non-white) worked in the live sex room. We were all being paid to demonstrate a talent for sexual suggestion or sexual action.

In my definition of sex work, I also include shows that involve auto-fellatio like those made famous by a simply marvelous and quite well known (in erotic art circles) gay performer named Aldo Ray whose manhood-self-swallowing counts as one of my fondest memories of theatrical creativity. Anal-play (non-bondage) shows like those that were once famous at Chicago's *Bijou*

Theater on North Wells Street when they had male strippers are also forms of gay male sex work. Further still, bondage shows are sex work, and truly, many gay worlds have and continue to abound with structured entertainment involving sexualized discipline, punishment, humiliation, and psychological or physical pain. Pornography for film, video, DVD and still images–all of which thrive upon live sexual performance at some point in the media's development– is sex work.

You see, broadening the definition of sex work in this manner sheds light on the extent to which many American and European classifications of sex work as illegal activity are quite arbitrary and confusing. Frankly, when someone sucks, fucks, or wanks on screen, strips for a tipping customer, escorts in a hotel room, or pumps the stroll and stops cars at 5 a.m., they are selling sex. Why is one form of sex work illegal and another not? Limited answer: complex cultural bias.

David M. Boden:

I don't have a problem with the term–except that it is extraordinarily vague. While it may remove some of the moralistic baggage of the term "prostitute," it presents some definitional and functional problems. For example, does any work that entails the performance of some sexuality fit into this definition? Would, for example, pornographic performers be included? What of actors in so-called, soft-core porn? What of swimsuit models in men's magazines? Are telephone fantasy operators included? Authors of erotica? What of sex therapists? Erotic dancers? Belly dancers? What of the people who document and distribute sexually-associated products? Are they sex workers? Or does the label only attach to the performer? Is a brothel-owner a sex worker? A pornographic film producer? Photographers? Videographers? Distributors?

While I might agree that the term prostitute is laden with moralistic baggage, I think the answer is not to replace a specific term with a vague term. Rather, I think the answer is to reform the use of the original term. To a certain extent, this is what has happened to the use of the terms *faerie, queer*, and *faggot* among the gay community. By insisting upon a definition and use that empowers the identified group, the negativity of the term is deflected and eventually fades. If, however, there is resort to use of an alternate term (such as "sex worker"), the original term, "prostitute," retains its stigmatizing bite.

Bruce W. Whitehead:

> What I appreciate about the term sex work/er is that it is inclusive, and does not identify the person working in the industry as a prostitute, which is a term that I personally don't mind. (I'm all for the "whore" positive reclamation movement with its grit, playfulness, and provocation.) I think it is up to the individual to find the "label" he or she identifies with most, whether that is "whore," "prostitute," or "sex trade worker." But, as a researcher, I think sex worker is a term that addresses what for me is critical: that the individual is involved in an exchange of sexual activity for money or monetary gain. Politically it helps to define an occupational field (and yes, I know there are people who object to the use of the word occupation when addressing sex trade workers–I am not one of those people) and, in so doing, narrows the focus and gives a definitive boundary around those whose work is included. An actor in a "legit" film or a server in a bar may be engaged in "sexualized work," but they are not sex workers. By invoking the term sex worker, we include all the individuals who are engaged in the sale of sex for money (in its myriad forms), from the fluffer to the phone sex operator, and beyond. I think it is a useful term that addresses the diversity of occupations within the industry, and therefore acknowledges those who may have been overlooked; yet the need for specificity still exists (i.e., Does a sex trade worker organization lobby on behalf of phone sex operators?). Again, I am speaking on behalf of someone whose interest is in Sexology, but I am sure a similar justification *may* be echoed by those whose interests lie in a social service capacity, and for those who are involved at a grassroots political level.

Jeffrey Escoffier:

> "Prostitute" seems very respectable (as it should be, I believe) to me, but it does have other meanings which are quite negative. Sex worker is a good term because it equates the work of a prostitute to other forms of labor. I interpret "sex work" as a broader term that includes many different kinds of work: phone sex operators, performers in porn, strippers, lap dancers, etc.

Joseph R. G. DeMarco:

> Personally I don't like the term "sex work." Aside from it being
> too clinical, it is also not descriptive enough. It covers too many
> people and you can never know if you're talking about a prostitute,
> a stripper, or any of the others who are lumped into that term.
> There's no poetry or history in the term and that offends me. There
> may be moralistic baggage associated to the other terms, but seri-
> ously, do you think people bubble over with respect when they
> hear the term, "sex worker?"

David Leary:

> In my research, I have avoided taking a hard line on terminology,
> preferring to use the term that the particular participant chooses.
> Not surprisingly, that changes from person to person, with some
> (usually the older participants) regarding the scene as sex work,
> while others (some older but mostly younger) regard their involve-
> ment as prostitution. For me as a clinician and a researcher, when a
> person begins their involvement in street-based prostitution at 10
> or 11 years of age, it can hardly be regarded as "work"; other more
> precise and negative descriptors come to mind. Where the person
> begins at an older age (say 16 or 17 years), they are more likely to
> have a greater capacity for insightful decision-making and control,
> and these are two of the capacities that affect the development of a
> perspective around both the experience and the terminology that is
> used by the young male. This is a particularly relevant feature in
> respect of street-based sex work or prostitution, where it is gener-
> ally more chaotic and the experience is more likely to be laced
> with an urgency resulting from homelessness, poverty, and sub-
> stance use. In such situations, thoughtfulness is less likely to be
> present, free choice is limited or skewed by necessity or urgency,
> and the tone in their description of these street-based events is more
> likely to be pejorative; it is referred to as prostitution. I have been
> affected by the stories of neglect, abandonment and pain, and
> violence; these move me to doubt the validity or usefulness of using
> the term "sex work." This is particularly the case where the experi-
> ence appears to be dominated by necessity, abuse, and the pres-
> ence of a calculated manipulation of the young male without regard
> for or recognition of his inherent dignity, rights, vulnerability, or the

potential for negative outcomes for the young person. This appears to be almost definitional to the experience of street-based prostitution. In street-based prostitution, the term "sex work" appears to me to be an unreflective and misleading gloss on a largely negative and destructive experience for the person who, because of his age and a level of background disadvantage that dominates his thinking, is largely incapable of avoiding the inherent negatives within the experience. For me, the pivotal point is not the morality of the issue but the experience of the person and this is what helps clarify the language. It is not about making judgments on the basis of a moral code; rather it is about reflecting on the experience and language of the person involved. This gives us some idea of how accurate and useful the terminology is around this phenomenon. Sex work is too simplistic a notion; it fails to capture the fullness of the experience. Then again, what term could?

Jeffrey T. Parsons:

> I like the term sex worker and prefer it to prostitute. I think sex worker is a broader, more inclusive term, and puts the focus on the work rather than on the person. The word prostitute, at least in the US, still has too much stigma attached to it.

David S. Bimbi:

> This definition of a prostitute, "one who sells one's abilities, talent, or name for an unworthy purpose," could be applied to many jobs because of what they involve or how they make the worker feel–like waiting tables always made me feel like I was prostituting myself, having to bend over backwards to please someone in the hopes that they will leave you a tip. I think it's unworthy to prostitute to support one's own or another's drug habit. Most other reasons for hooking are about having an income that no other job can offer.

QUESTION 3

Assume that two adults voluntarily consent to an economic arrangement concerning sexual activity and this activity takes place in private. Do you think there is anything wrong with this sort of arrangement?

Mark Padilla:

The exchange of sex for money or other instrumental benefits happens all the time–whether or not it is understood or defined as "sex work"–even in the morally sanctified context of heterosexual marriage. In most Western societies, individuals are taught to downplay the instrumental aspects of their affective relationships because "true love" is believed to be free of all material interests. As such, we rarely recognize the parallels between marriages that are based on economic arrangements and the more explicit exchange of sex for money typical of prostitution. In many ways, however, there are clear parallels between such exchanges and certain kinds of marital arrangements, particularly when we consider the case of long-term relationships between sex workers and clients that begin to resemble stable partner relationships. Clearly, then, the moral outrage so commonly expressed against sex workers is more the product of the scapegoating of particular classes of persons–what social scientists might refer to as "moral panic"–than the result of clear or categorical distinctions between sex workers and those presumably "normal" people who do not engage in such sexual deviance.

With this said, I should add this does *not* mean that sex work is always free of exploitation, or that it never reflects certain dimensions of inequality and differences in social power. Just as marital relationships can be exploitative, so can relationships based on sexual-economic exchange. Indeed, the fact that sex workers are much more often of a lower class status than the clients they service requires us to be critical of the social inequalities and political-economic circumstances that may drive some persons to engage in sexual-economic exchanges as a way of coping with extremely difficult life circumstances. But this critical stance should always avoid making facile generalizations about sex work as *inherently* exploitative, since such assumptions tend to contribute to, rather than alleviate, the suffering of persons engaged in sex work.

Thus, while we cannot claim that prostitution is inherently wrong any more than we can claim any other consensual sexual relationship is inherently wrong, we can take a moral position against the social inequalities–principally inequalities of gender, race, class, and sexuality–that contribute to the *potential* exploitation of persons engaged in sex work.

Kerwin Kaye:

In and of itself, of course not. I do not think, however, that consent should stand as the "only" criterion for sexual ethics. People often speak of prostitution as a form of "exploitation," and while this is a term without much of a defined meaning, I think there are cases in which the notion of one person taking advantage of another's desperation and vulnerability has relevance. There are also issues in terms of racism, sexism, etc. which might not rise to the level of making an individual act "unethically," but which nevertheless render it "problematic." On the other hand, I think it is important to note that ethically suspect behavior takes place regularly within socially valued sex as well (such as sex within marriage), and I do not automatically presume that the sex happening within prostitution is *ipso facto* more "exploitative" or "problematic" than what regularly happens within marriage, within one-night-stands, etc. Even if we were to somehow decide that sex within prostitution is *generally* more ethically suspect than sex in non-commercial contexts, I would ask how we might ameliorate these specific difficulties rather than take the position that prostitution in-and-of-itself should be eliminated. Many of the sex workers that I have come to know through my research and my activism on this issue have found that in their circumstance not only is there "nothing wrong" with sex work, but there are numerous positive benefits associated with the work (not the least of which is the money). In my own brief experience as a sex worker, I also found many positives, though I personally felt there was insufficient remuneration overall to justify the times when particular clients posed emotional challenges.

I think it is unfortunate that we get so caught up in the "good versus bad" argument, because it presumes that if prostitution is "bad" then it should be criminalized, and I generally think criminalization is one of the least effective ways to address situations that are actually problematic within prostitution. As has been argued by many others, criminalization usually makes things worse by turning the police into persecutors rather than protectors. At the same time, there are very few people (and I am not one of them) who take an absolutist libertarian position that all forms of sex work (including that done by young minors) should be allowed without any sort of regulation whatsoever. The question then is: What sorts of regulations make sense? Are there any sorts of criminalization that are actually useful? More generally, how could one best foster workers' rights within sex work? How best to address safety concerns? How best to address the ways in which sex work is *not* like other forms of work; the ways in which it has very specific occupational requirements to make it ok (including a basic willingness to do the job in the first place)? Questions of "good versus bad" tend to shut down discussions on these specific concerns. We need to look at *what* is the "bad" within prostitution and figure out ways to address those specific concerns rather than demonize the entire enterprise.

Todd G. Morrison:

Framed in this way, it is difficult to imagine *why* anyone would object to such an arrangement. However, it is important to acknowledge that this scenario represents an idealized account in which "adults voluntarily consent."

David M. Boden:

How is this any different from much of what happens in the domestic sphere? Negotiations regarding what we will and won't do for each other occur all the time–arguments terminate the likelihood of some actions, apologies increase others. I do not see any real difference between economic valuation/negotiation and the more subtle exchanges wherein sexual activity is given as reward for subjectively beneficial action or withheld as punishment for offensive behavior. I believe that the imposition of a statement of "wrong" to this arrangement reflects a cultural understanding of sex as associated with certain emotions (e.g., "love"). The commercialization of affection is almost incomprehensible to our culture; the fact that a specific value is placed upon a behavior that is idealistically and romantically understood as an expression of love and desire may sully the interaction. "Lust" may be understandable, but seems to be understood as a reflection of the baser animal component. It would seem as we shift toward a culture that celebrates the experience of "love," it also necessarily demeans the expression of "lust." We create a dichotomous understanding of sexuality. One is good and one is bad. To submit to lust, as evidenced by purchase of sexual activity, is to demonstrate a weakness of morals and absence of an emotional compass.

Jeffrey Escoffier:

> Not at all. It's not so different from some kinds of marriage–as the feminist Charlotte Perkins Gilman once pointed out.

David Leary:

> I think the key issues are contained in the words "adult," "voluntarily," "consent," and "private." While various sectors in any community will find reason to disparage such an arrangement, whenever these four concepts and experiences are present, the arrangement appears to me to be "wrong" only if other more negative factors are present (such as abuse).

Jeffrey T. Parsons:

> Absolutely not. Voluntary, mutually agreed upon, private sexual encounters are NEVER wrong, in my opinion. If money or other goods change hands, so be it.

David S. Bimbi:

> Private consensual sex is just that: private and consensual. It is when prostitution is public that it makes people uncomfortable. It just strikes too many raw nerves. We don't want to think about any of our boyfriends paying for it on the side. We don't want to think about what led some of these young men onto the streets when we know we can't help them. It's a case of: out of sight, out of mind.

Rebecca L. Harriman:

> I think it depends on the position of the person who is being paid. If they are fully and freely consenting to engage in the sexual activity, then I think it is fine. If the person is under the influence of any substance, or if they are being coerced (maybe by a third party) in any way, then I don't think that it is okay. But that's a hard question to answer, because what about all those people who buy each other drinks, and then are drunk and hook up when the bar closes? Same thing? Who knows? The lines are so blurry, there are no clear answers.

QUESTION 4

Why do those who provide sexual services appear to experience greater levels of stigma in our culture than those who buy such services? Is this disparity evident to a greater or lesser extent in gay "subculture?"

Mark Padilla:

> I think this generalization needs to be put into context, since there is cross-cultural variation in the degree to which sex workers versus clients experience social stigma, and these arrangements are not stable historically. In certain settings, it is the purchase of sexual favors that is now subject to greater state surveillance and control, for example. However, if we make the assumption–generally a fair one–that sex workers are at greater risk of stigmatization than their clients, there are several potential explanations. Sex workers are generally more visible, and they must make themselves so in order to be marketable to clients. As such, they are more frequently in the public view and therefore come to represent the "impurity" and moral depravity that are often associated with prostitution. In the contemporary era, the epidemic of HIV/AIDS further contributed to this stigmatization, as described by a number of social scientists, since the high prevalence of HIV among sex workers appeared to confirm their moral and sexual impurity. There is a psychoanalytic explanation for the stigmatization of sex workers in that clients purchase sex workers in order to enact or experience their dark or repressed sexual fantasies, and sex workers therefore come to embody or represent the ambivalence individuals feel in relation to their own sexual impulses.
>
> Regarding gay versus straight stigmatization, my own research in the Dominican Republic found that male sex workers often preferred gay men over women as clients because gay men were believed to be less ambivalent about the direct exchange of sex for money, and required less investment of time and energy in order to consummate a deal. This may suggest, as my research does, that gay men are generally less reluctant to participate in sex work as clients, although certainly not all gay men are nonchalant about this.

Todd G. Morrison:

> Despite the apparent success of the feminist movement, Western culture remains profoundly misogynistic, especially in the sexual realm. Men's unease with the internality of women's genitalia; their fear that women can rely on technology as a substitute for the almighty penis (and a superior substitute at that); and the phenomenon of "hate fucking" are a few examples that underscore men's ambivalence toward women and their sexuality. Traditionally, women were the providers of sexual services and men were the consumers. Thus, it is hardly surprising that the former have been demonized to a far greater extent than the latter.

David M. Boden:

> This is a crucial element of the occupation. Perhaps this arises from the perception that such occupations are predatory. While we may empathize with the consumer for experiencing desire/lust, the sex worker encourages this indulgence and benefits from the moral distraction of the consumer. Essentially, the stigma is attached to moral predation. I would question whether there is a coherent morality present in the gay subculture. Since the gay "subculture" is held together by a shared stigmatized sexuality, it would seem more difficult to maintain a moral high ground. It appears that hustlers are treated with a certain amount of disdain and distaste, but it appears that the consumers of their services are also stigmatized– this would appear to be a different type of stigma than that attached to heterosexual consumers. It may be that, within this community, resort to prostitutes amounts to an admission of failure; failure to effectively package oneself as sexually desirable. Given the liberation from many of the heterosexual constraints on sex, members of the gay community *should* be able to accomplish satisfaction without having to pay for it. In the instance of a "closeted" homosexual consumer, where access to the gay community is limited to prostitute/sex worker contact, there may be a conscious avoidance of any obvious engagement with the gay community. By minimizing the contact to individualized economic interactions, stigma of identity is avoided. For the larger community, the concealment of the transaction allows the stigma to attach not to the consumer, but to the worker.

Bruce W. Whitehead:

> Accessibility and discrimination? The sex worker is perceived as being an indiscriminate sexual being accessible to all, while the client's actions are temporary and transgressive. When a client engages the services of a sex worker she/he is engaging in behavior, whereas the sex worker is perceived as having an identity. Therefore, one "does" and the other "is." Clients of sex workers are stigmatized when their transgressions are discordant with, and threaten, their identity (i.e., family man, Christian, moralist, etc.)–and only if their actions are uncovered. This manner of stigmatization tends to rely heavily on entrenched mores of purity and contamination (the virgin/whore dichotomy), and those that the client has put "at risk" are held up as innocent victims (spouse, children, etc.). Therefore the cause of the contamination or transgression is the existence of the prostitute and not the actions of the individual. I think there are variations between gay and straight communities' perceptions and resultant stigmatization of sex workers, with the straight community demanding the person providing the service (a woman) own more of the stigma, and although male sex workers may achieve some status within the gay community, I feel this status has the potential to be transitory and hierarchical.

Jeffrey Escoffier:

> I think that most forms of prostitution and sex work are stigmatized because sex and love are often closely connected (or thought that they should be–WHY?) in people's lives. People feel that a commercial sexual transaction "betrays" the emotional intimacy that sex facilitates. But also because sex has a sacred aspect, the ecstasy of the orgasm can be a transcendent experience.

David Leary:

> Regardless of the institutional, ethical, cultural, or religious point of origin, the provision of sexual services appears largely to have been demonized within the mainstream of society. Procuring sex, and especially male-to-male sex, is demonized (in part) because it is seen as a threat to social stability and order; a threat to the morals of a community with the young particularly at risk from "perverted" individuals and groups. While there may be some validity to this belief (e.g., the presence of street-based sex work does change

the character of an area attracting criminal activity including intensified drug selling and substance use), sex workers (especially
those engaged in street-based work) are a very misunderstood and
targeted group. They experience greater levels of alienation within
the community and are often the target of violence, sometimes
from young people of a similar age. So, the threat is not simply to
social order at a macro (societal) level but also at a micro (individual) level. Having said that, sex work or prostitution is evident in
most gay bars within my city and perhaps this is one indicator of its
relative acceptance or tolerance within the gay subculture.

Jeffrey T. Parsons:

> I think the clients maintain a level of anonymity more so than the
> sex worker so they tend to escape more of the stigma. It's certainly
> less of an issue in the gay community, where being a sex worker
> has, in some situations, achieved a certain level of positive status.
> The sheer number of gay escorts, bodyworkers, models, and mas-
> seurs advertised on the Internet and in the gay press has had a nor-
> malizing effect on sex work so people are less likely to look down
> upon it or view it negatively.

David S. Bimbi:

> In the gay world it is a double-edged stigma. We exalt male beauty
> and can understand wanting to capitalize on one's own good looks,
> but then we resent them because they can do it and we can't because
> we are not as "marketable" or we can't get over our own sexual
> shame that prevents us from cashing in!

QUESTION 5

*When examining a commercial sex transaction, is either party being
exploited? Do traditional ideas of exploiter and exploited vary when
the prostitute is male versus female? And if so, why?*

Mark Padilla:

> I believe my answer to question 3, above, addresses this issue to a
> certain degree, so I will focus on the second part of the question. My

feeling is that gender relations are essential in understanding the relations of power that influence how sexual-economic transactions unfold. In this sense, being male or female necessarily influences how these relationships unfold, since gender relations permeate all of these interactions. An example is that the male sex workers I studied frequently threatened their male clients with physical harm if they did not pay what was deemed appropriate. It is much less likely that female sex workers would engage in such behavior (although certainly not impossible), and women are much more often the victims of sexual violence than the perpetrators. Clearly, in the case of the men I interviewed, the line between "exploiter" and "exploited"–which are themselves somewhat problematic terms– is blurred. As described above, I don't believe we can make a claim that any individual in a given sexual-economic exchange is *inherently* exploited, although the potential certainly exists. So, there are no generalities that can be made here, except to say that in my experience the perception among clients that they had been exploited (duped?) by sex workers was fairly common, and this is likely to be quite different in the context of female sex work.

Todd G. Morrison:

It would be disingenuous to provide a simplistic "sex positive" view of prostitution. All hookers have hearts of gold, and love, love, love what they do. They are agentic professionals, who share their positive sexual energy with persons in need, and, in so doing, make the world more erotophilic. No offense to Annie Sprinkle, but exploitation *does* occur. What I find interesting, however, is individuals' tendency to *focus* on exploitation when discussing prostitution and others categories of sex work. Why do we assume that the common variety prostitute is more likely to be exploited than the common variety *Wal-Mart* employee? If the potential for exploitation is an inherent characteristic of any relationship marked by a power differential, then couldn't most sexual interactions be viewed as (potentially) exploitative? For example, I believe that when gay men interact sexually, they seldom do so from a point of equivalence (i.e., one person will have a better body, a bigger dick, be more attractive, more sexually experienced/talented, and/or have less invested in the encounter than the other person). The individual who has more "assets," so to speak, is certainly in a position to exploit his partner. Finally, for those interested in the topic of exploitation and sex work, I think it is important to devote at least *some* attention to the consumers and the ways in which their (potential) vulnerabilities may be manipulated by the sex worker. Again, simplistic dichotomies, in which prostitute = exploited and client = exploiter, are inimical to achieving a fuller understanding of the prostitute/client interchange.

David M. Boden:

Is either party in *any* economic transaction necessarily being exploited? I think that the transaction itself is probably not exploitive. However, the context in which the transaction occurs may be another matter. First, institutionalized oppression and exploitation may create a systemic filter that disproportionately presses some persons into the occupation (youth, women, minorities, the disenfranchised, etc.). Second, the context in which the exchange occurs may facilitate an exploitive unbalance in power. The immersion of prostitution in the criminal subcultures would allow the consumer to wield the threat of exposure and formal sanctions to bolster their power in the bargaining relationship. Third, the continued criminalization of the occupation would facilitate the interests of the consumer by minimizing the ability of sex workers to unionize, to insist upon police protection, and ultimately to be forced out of the business. In this forced exit, new laborers would enter the market to replace the retiring workers. The consumer benefits from a constantly renewed labor force–all kept at a minimum of occupational benefits. As I stated earlier, however, this exploitation is the result of the institutional discrimination against portions of the population and continued criminalization of the occupation. The dynamics of the exchange itself do not seem to me to be qualitatively different from most relationships wherein the laborer and the consumer negotiate for some specialized service.

Bruce W. Whitehead:

I don't feel there is an inherent exploitation occurring beyond any other financial or commercial transaction. If I buy lights for my house, I have to pick the company, find the fixture, navigate the salesperson, hope for the best deal and not piss off anyone along the way. With sex work transactions, ideally, I am only dealing with one person, so the chances of being exploited decrease, on my part at least. If I am an unpleasant customer, I may receive less service, time, or intensity of service but I'm not being exploited. I'm just receiving less than adequate service. I'm sure I have engaged the services of many paid staff throughout my life who would rather be anywhere in the world than serving my cranky self, so how is that individual any less exploited than the person selling sexual services? A shitty job is a shitty job regardless of what you're doing and I tend to view exploitation as being more dependent on levels of management, which inevitably means less profit (and autonomy) for the person providing service. Conversely, and I thank JoEllen A. Morrison for pointing this out, some jobs are inherently more risky than others so the potential for exploitation is higher in some shitty jobs than in other shitty jobs. Therefore, as an aside, I assume (and I think it is a fair assumption) that most people consider the pimp, agency, or significant other that benefits from the prostitute's earnings as being an exploitive party; yet, in a society that criminalizes and marginalizes sex workers we create a need for such a service (i.e., in some cases significant others may aid in physical protection, provide social support, and help the individual circumvent legal constraints). Does one level of exploitation negate, neutralize, or balance another? Does having a pimp, who *exploits* you, or an agency that takes a fixed percentage of your wage, yet acts as an intermediary party, prevent the consumer from exploiting you? Or does it give you an edge in which you have control so that ultimately you are in a greater position to exploit the consumer? The question could be rephrased in reference to an individual who is working independently. I think this is an area of research lacking in the social sciences, as we (researchers) tend to want to know the experiences of those in the sex trade, yet we often do not truly listen to *their* definitions of exploitation. In the course of my research this is something I have had to deal with on several levels, and something that at times I have had difficulty resolving. Overall, I do not think the exploitation of either party (worker/consumer) is inherent in the act, but rather is dependent upon the context, the subjective experience(s) of each party, and the individual power dynamics occurring at the time of the sex for money transaction. The best way to find out if someone is being exploited, or more precisely, *feels* they are being exploited is to ask them.

Jeffrey Escoffier:

> It certainly can be exploitative, particularly if the prostitute or sex worker is in a weaker bargaining position such as when the prostitute is exchanging sex for money out of desperation, poverty, or the need for drugs.

Joseph R. G. DeMarco:

> The issue of exploitation is deep and complicated. Most people think that prostitutes are being exploited either because they are "owned" by a pimp or forced into that type of work because they have no abilities to do otherwise. And there's some truth in that. Women who work for pimps are most likely being exploited as are those people (male and female) who are driven to prostitution out of desperate circumstances. But there are people who do it because they enjoy the sex and the economic independence this work affords them or so I've been told by those I've interviewed. Some prostitutes argue that we are all whores; some of us sell our minds, some of us sell our ability to design or create things. We are all on the market with some skill or ability so what makes sex different? Why is selling sex stigmatized while being paid for the ability to entertain with humor, or lectures, or anything else is not?

David Leary:

> Exploited? When the individuals involved are older, there seems less likelihood of exploitation, but then age is not the only variable in any effort to understand the experience of exploitation. There are some situations that lend themselves to a simple conclusion that exploitation exists, but in the main, it is rarely that simple. Sex between an adult and a 10- or 12-year-old who is involved in prostitution appears almost by definition to be a clear case of exploitation. How could it be otherwise? No doubt there are situations where each party experiences exploitation even where both are consenting adults. The more complex scenario is where exploitation exists and is fluid, ever-changing, rebalancing itself with every encounter, even shifting ground during a single encounter; as such, this experience defies easy or simplistic explanations where dichotomies of right or wrong, good or bad, exploited or exploiting are put forward.

Jeffrey T. Parsons:

> I think it depends on the context and the parties involved. Certainly exploitation can happen. That might actually be part of the allure and the thrill of the experience. As long as both parties are comfortable with this, then it's fine. It's in situations where exploitation is not consensual that problems arise.

David S. Bimbi:

> The whole concept of exploitation in prostitution is based on the assumption that the prostitute is only doing this because they have to (e.g., "Those poor kids"). Yeah, it is very exploitive when gay kids have to turn tricks to survive because their parents threw them out, but is it exploitive when gay kids who are out and comfortable at home turn tricks so they can buy themselves the things they want? I just saw a posting on a Web site from an 18-year-old the other day that said, "Seeking generou$ guy–I really want an iPod."

Paula M. Kenny:

> I think it's more likely that the prostitute will be exploited than the client, but obviously as client/prostitute interactions are so varied, it is certainly possible for the reverse to occur. For one thing, the client generally is more financially secure than the sex worker and, thus, can wield more power. Also, I think the psychological effects of the "sex transaction" can be more problematic for the sex worker. Sex (usually!) involves mutual pleasure, but instead, the focus is exclusively on the pleasure of the client. Obviously, the sex worker can still enjoy the encounter, but their enjoyment is not considered important (unless, of course, their pleasure adds to the pleasure of the client). Prostitutes must accept that their needs are always secondary to the client's desires, particularly if they are already financially desperate. I know most prostitutes accept this as part of a job–it is work and not many people work purely for their own pleasure. However, I wonder if *all* prostitutes find it that easy to separate conventional ideas of sex from the sex engaged in during prostitution? Having said that, if an individual chooses to engage in sex work, why should they be prevented from doing so because someone else decides they are being exploited? It is obviously incredibly condescending to inform the sex worker "Yes, I

know you might not *realize* you're a victim, but we've had a think about it, and it turns out you are." I believe the difficulty in deciding whether or not prostitution is a form of exploitation is the fact that most sex work is a mixture of exploitation and benefit. Yes, a lot of the work is unpleasant, there may be negative psychological consequences, and the sex worker has less freedom in what he or she can choose to do sexually, but they also earn a lot more than they would otherwise, have flexible working hours and, for some, gain a sense of belonging. The extent of exploitation versus benefit will vary in each interaction: A homosexual male engaging in sex work to explore his sexuality seems to benefit more and be exploited less than a young heterosexual male who engages in sex work for basic survival. Also, the level of exploitation sometimes depends on the perceptions and beliefs of the prostitute himself.

Regarding the second question, I think differences in the level of exploitation between male and female sex workers are probably not any greater than differences within each group.

QUESTION 6

Is it the formality of payment that differentiates "prostitution" from a "one-night stand?"

Mark Padilla:

> Making formal payment definitional of prostitution may be less useful than a broader definition that includes payments in kind, since in my research it is clear that payments in kind are often more important to sex workers' economic situation than formal payments for sex. This blurs the boundaries even more with the "one night stand," particularly if the latter is accompanied by dinner and a movie.

Todd G. Morrison:

> I'm going to restrict my answer to a comparison of "one-night stands" among gay men and male-to-male sex work. Although payment marks a key difference, I think that another area of divergence lay in the expectations of those involved. With "one-night stands" there is always the possibility that the encounter will lead

to something more "substantial" (i.e., a relationship) or, at least, another night. I doubt that many clients share this expectation. As well, what the man may legitimately expect from the other person is quite different. A client has paid money to a prostitute for specific services; the provision of those services is expected. With a "one-night stand," one may *hope* that the other person will be amenable to engaging in certain activities, but one certainly does not have the right to expect them.

David M. Boden:

No. The economics are not the only differentiating factor. The transfer of funds is reflective of a negotiation and agreement as to the transaction that will occur. In a one-night stand the scenario or agenda of action is essentially a negotiation–both parties are expecting some sort of satisfaction. When the prostitute negotiates, their subjective enjoyment of the experience is essentially irrelevant. The prostitution exchange is innately a power relationship: the power in the relationship is manifest most in terms of convenience. The exchange is not an exchange of pleasure; it is an exchange of cash for the ability to shape and define the interaction.

Bruce W. Whitehead:

That is certainly one component, but I think time and level of "potential" intimacy may figure quite prominently. I know there is a chance that my one-night stand may still be hovering while I get dressed for work the next day (or it could be me hovering), but my time with my sex worker is up when the clock/wallet combination comes to fruition. Further to this, my one-night stand may come back the next night, or may pursue me further (good or bad depending on how you look at it). My sex worker will (likely) rely on me to initiate contact and will only come when I call, that is if we have managed to maintain a functional working relationship. What is the most important distinction though is the expectation. If I am a self-absorbed and self-indulgent lover, fully focused on my own pleasure, then my one-night stand may remain just that: a one-night experience (depending on the level of subjugation/submission being sought–but we'll assume mutuality is an expectation). Alternately, my sex worker (ideally) would not only tolerate this but also encourage my sexual satisfaction, as that is a critical component in whether or not our relationship is maintained. I have talked to enough people in the sex trade to say with some certainty, that although, at times, the sex may be fun and the client may be engaging, and there exists the potential for a mutually gratifying experience (and even long-term relationship), if there were no money exchanging hands the relationship would cease to exist. For those in the sex industry, this is a critical distinction that the client must not only know, but also honor wholly.

Jeffrey Escoffier:

Exchange for money or survival needs changes the transaction significantly. A one-night stand can be as enjoyable or alienating as a commercial sexual transaction. There is nothing inherently the same or different about them.

David Leary:

Payment certainly dominates the encounter and creates a climate for the encounter that is unmistakable but there other boundaries that are established that equally affect the encounter, differentiating it from other sexual experiences. Even the person engaged in street-based sex work develops, for a variety of reasons, boundaries that set limits and differentiate it from the "one night stand."

Jeffrey T. Parsons:

There are a lot of similarities. The thrill and excitement one gets from either paying for sex or having sex from hooking-up with a one-night stand are probably very similar. The payment though, for some people, becomes a critical element to the process, and is one of the things that make it more exciting and thrilling.

David S. Bimbi:

"One-night stands" are usually based on some sort of mutual attraction and the payoff is getting off, boosting your ego if the one night stand is hotter than you think you are, or part of the search for "Mr. Right." But it is the cash that differentiates some one-night stands from prostitution. We all know the feeling of being "used" sexually: "Oh yeah, you came and you're just waiting for me to finish off so you can ask me to leave." You might as well be paid for sex like that.

QUESTION 7

What factor (or factors) differentiates those men who seek the paid sexual services of other men from those who do not?

Mark Padilla:

> There is nothing absolute that distinguishes men who exchange sex for money from those who do not. Indeed, a certain percentage of gay men who have purchased sex with men have done so without being fully aware of their participation in prostitution, or–as demonstrated by my own work–may even seek to deny the instrumental nature of the exchange by thinking of it simply as a form of economic "help." Further, some men who do not normally pursue sex workers may do so while on vacation and justify doing so because it is simply "what people do here" or because "it's part of their culture." Whether these men think of their activities as prostitution is an open question, at the very least, and I have no reason to believe that there is some fundamental difference between these men and all other gay men. In fact, in the Dominican Republic, sex workers will occasionally try to convince gay tourists that they are not sex workers, and later seek to charge them for their services or otherwise rob them or threaten them physically to extract payment. This may lead to some gay tourists participating, somewhat unwittingly, in sexual-economic exchanges. Did they know this was the basis of the exchange when they agreed to it? Perhaps. Perhaps not. Is there some basic difference between them and other gay clients? I don't think so.

Todd G. Morrison

> The characteristic that comes to my mind is a willingness to disregard social convention. (I'll refrain from using the word "courage.") Even within gay subculture, which is sexually liberal (though far more proscriptive than one might imagine), I think it is difficult to deviate from what is socially permissible. At present, paying for sex

is considered unacceptable by many. As a result, many gay men will be reluctant to do so (or, at least, reluctant to admit doing so). Finally, to be realistic, attractiveness and age are two additional characteristics that distinguish those who seek paid sexual services from those who do not. While one wants to avoid the cliché that "only ugly people pay for it," common sense dictates that younger and more attractive men will be less likely to procure the services of a sex worker than their older and less attractive counterparts.

Bruce W. Whitehead:

This is a question that I tend to grapple with a bit, as I have not talked to many clients of sex workers regarding this matter. But having spoken to workers, the reasons are limitless. So rather than answer this directly, I shall take the easy way out and give a few reasons that I have heard from others keeping in mind these examples are more representative of patterns of engagement, rather then differentiations between those *who do* and those *who do not*. There appears to be a difference in regards to age, with younger men seeking out sex workers as a means of acting out fantasies, engaging in sexual exploration, and marking special occasions (i.e., holidays, birthdays, promotions, etc.). For others I believe that it is a means of maintaining sexual balance/satisfaction when one doesn't have an intimate partner. Finding sex (and intimacy) can be a huge investment of time and money, and there are times when you want to meet those needs with minimal investment (and I personally think that is a valid way to approach the issue). Perhaps as one becomes more established these elements become more pertinent. When your companion is a professional, you can meet sexual needs and experience minimal change in the structure of your life, and perhaps "avoid" the expectations placed on gay men in regards to aging and maintaining a masculine ideal. On a completely personal level, and in support of the above, no matter how much I plead with my partner he won't dance for me, but he knows that I know guys that will (and do).

Jeffrey Escoffier:

Desire, financial capacity!!

Joseph R. G. DeMarco:

I suspect there are a few factors that differentiate men who pay from men who do not. If a guy is at the peak of attractiveness and has men turning up around every corner–that's a factor. Although, I've had some interviewees say they often have clients who are gorgeous men. And these clients tell them it's because they have problems with people they meet which the casual observer may not notice such as bad treatment because of their looks. Some of the very handsome have trouble meeting people because others are intimidated by their looks. Another factor is money. I'm guessing that there'd be a few more buyers if more men had money to burn. Pride is probably the biggest thing preventing a man from buying sex or, at least, from admitting that he buys sex. It's an ego thing–no one wants to be thought of as having to purchase something that everyone else seems to be getting for free.

Jeffrey T. Parsons:

I don't think any factors do!! Our research certainly shows that clients (and sex workers) cross all sociodemographic and psychosocial characteristics. I don't think there is a certain "type" of person who seeks sex workers.

David S. Bimbi:

I don't think there is one way to separate this out. Men pay other men for sex for so many reasons: convenience, discretion, fantasy, affection, attention, etc. Maybe you could say that people who pay for sex are more concerned with their own pleasure, especially the submissives that get their pleasure by doing what they think is giving pleasure.

QUESTION 8

We pay for food. We pay for clothing. We pay for shelter. Why should we not also pay for sex?

Mark Padilla:

This is a leading question! It seems there is a particular answer you are seeking.

Todd G. Morrison:

My motto: if you have the discretionary income and the motivation, then by all means go shopping!

David M. Boden:

We should be allowed to pay for it. Sex is a natural human drive. The manner of its satisfaction, as with food, clothing and shelter, will vary from community to community. I think this question goes to a much deeper issue than simply the commercialization of sexuality, but to the meaning of sex to our society. In our community we associate sex with affectional ties to a partner. In other communities, economic interests may take precedence in which case prostitution is not placed on the periphery but is integrated into the social and cultural structure of the community. The sexuality standards that dominate the U.S. are suspicious of behaviors that reflect a sybaritic and self-expressionist aspect of the individual. While there may be some truth in the assertion that the U.S. has "loosened up" since the sexual revolution of the 1960s, most of this liberation appears, to me, to be in two areas: acceptance of female sexuality and a limited expansion of sexual repertoires.

Our culture may demonstrate titillation and fascination in the sexual exploits of "freaks" but safely returns to traditional heterosexual morality. Sexuality has become not a means of expanded self-expression, but a means of increasingly intrusive labeling. The tyranny of heterosexual, monogamous, affective and procreative sex has not been removed. It has simply shifted to less obvious modes of enforcement and control. The privilege associated with satisfaction of sexual desire is culturally allocated to those persons who adhere to the cultural agenda–others may achieve some satisfaction, but it is at the sufferance of the ruling class. The continued criminalization of the sex worker limits the legitimacy of alternate sexualities by constricting sexual expression to models that most easily are assimilated into the dominant sexual paradigm.

Bruce W. Whitehead:

You're preaching to the converted. I say ditto. In my life I have "paid" for sex in myriad ways. So I can thoroughly appreciate the forthrightness of a sex for money transfer. Looking back, I can think of many times I would have been better off giving a few 100s and leaving it at that.

Jeffrey Escoffier:

> It's the stigma that is the problem. Sex is somehow "special." In the eyes of some people, its sacredness or intimacy seems violated by the commercial aspect.

David Leary:

> It is hard for me to think about this question outside the context of sex work as I know it: street-based, regarded largely as a negative experience by those who engage in its practice, imbued with substance use and abuse, a dangerous preoccupation, involved as they are because they inevitably feel they have little choice in the matter. When males purchase these young men, they do so within this context. Yes, we pay for clothes, but those of us who like to think and act ethically pay for clothes but reject sweat shops and try to find clothes that are not made within a context where the rights and sensibilities of others are neglected and often denied. If I think about the phenomenon of sex work beyond a single plane (say, the physicality of a sexual encounter), considering other equally significant layers within the human experience, such an experience must be considered more than simply a negotiated sexual experience; you don't just purchase a sexual experience when you seek out a prostitute or sex worker.

Jeffrey T. Parsons:

> I agree. Why not? My feeling is that it's perfectly fine and acceptable to pay for sex. Of course, anything can be taken to excess and become problematic. Just like someone can overeat, or compulsively shop for clothes and get themselves into debt, or spend more than they should on their apartment, people can take paying for sex too far. At the point at which it becomes compulsive, or lands the person in debt, or other negative consequences emerge, then it's a problem, but no more (or less) of a problem than anything else.

David S. Bimbi:

> We already "pay for sex" in so many ways not involving money. It's all been said. What's the difference between a high society housewife and a streetwalker? The housewife had to suck the same dick over and over to get her fur coat.

Paula M. Kenny:

> Because it is not necessary to consider the needs of the food, cloth-ing, or shelter. (My apologies to the animal rights activists and environmentalists.) It is not buying "sexual pleasure" that is prob-lematic but the (perceived?) subjugation of another person to ser-vice this need.

Rebecca L. Harriman:

> I think we do pay for sex in more ways than one. Is the formal ex-change any different? Yes, it's more blatant, but essentially I feel that an individual being paid cash is the same as an individual be-ing wined and dined.

QUESTION 9

Why do you feel some individuals feel the need to use terms such as "high class" callboy/girl? Does this distinction serve to benefit the sex worker or the consumer (or both)?

Mark Padilla:

> Everybody likes status. For many sex workers, perhaps particu-larly in the developing world, access to social status may be highly constrained, and sex work can offer additional benefits beyond the purely material by permitting access to certain icons of pres-tige–from designer clothing, to exclusive hotels and restaurants, to travel and tourism. Clearly, this status can benefit the sex worker if it makes him more marketable, but the effect on his marketability cannot be determined out of context. It depends on what sells in a particular setting. If it sells to be "high class," it could have clear benefits to the sex worker. If "working class" men are what the buyers are seeking, on the other hand, it may not have material benefits to project oneself as "high class." But, in general, my feeling is that everyone likes status, and will seek to project a higher status if the cost of doing so is not excessive, or may do so in relation to their peers, but not necessarily in rela-tion to their clients.

Todd G. Morrison:

> As with any consumer enterprise, there is a need to differentiate one product from another. An obvious way to achieve this difference is to frame product A as being somehow "better" than product B. (Although the precise nature of these differences may be ambiguous.) When we travel, we can fly economy class or first class (or gradations between these end points). We can purchase sparkling wine or champagne; Vaseline intensive care or Crème de la Mer; a Toyota or a Porsche. So, too, individuals can seek the services of a "high class" callboy/girl versus a regular class (?) sex worker. The distinction creates an illusion of exclusivity which, in turn, may serve to enhance the client's experience. Further, use of the term "high class" may serve a justificatory function for some sex workers i.e., "At least, I'm a high class sex worker and not a street prostitute." (I will refrain from delving into why the need to make such distinctions is problematic.) For clients who are concerned about the moral implications of their actions, seeking the services of someone labelled "high class" may result in them perceiving the interaction as less taboo, less "dirty."

David M. Boden:

> It seems that the use of the term "high class" removes the possible taint of association with criminal elements. Prostitution, as it exists on the streets and in bars, is tainted by ancillary issues such as theft and drugs, for example. Also, in the case of the "high class" callboy, the parties have defined their exchange as one of greater power parity. The consumer need not experience the guilt or social responsibility of possibly exploiting the "poor" hustler. The prostitute attains an aura of exclusivity and social similarity with the consumer. In this situation, the motivations of the prostitute are reframed as purely economic and distinctly a matter of professional choice–not desperation. Investments made in advertisements, cellular phones, paging systems, switchboards, offices, etc. provide a luster of legitimacy to an otherwise "illegitimate" transaction. For many I would suggest this also continues the theme of convenience–limiting their concerns about disease, danger, arrest, and searching for " just the right guy."

Bruce W. Whitehead:

> I think it serves many functions. It justifies to consumers that they are buying a professional product and engaging the services of a professional (if that is important to the consumer–some consumers respond to "designer labels" and some do not). Additionally, for the customer, qualifiers such as professional and high-end imply discretion, something that I am sure is important to many clients, possibly more so for higher profile individuals. It may help some sex workers to justify what they are doing by drawing demarcations between themselves and those perceived to be experiencing less agency (e.g., street workers). Not to mention that workers can tap into consumers' investment in such qualifiers and as a result charge more, work less, and receive (perhaps) a higher end clientele. Lastly, I feel that, at times, it has proven to be a useful way of introducing the concept of sex work into mainstream culture. Not to say that this has ultimately benefited the sex trade, or those working in it, but I think it did have some impact in regards to normalizing the existence of prostitution and humanizing the prostitute.

Jeffrey Escoffier:

> It's the stigma again. I think the distinction is, in part, due to the fact that the callgirl and/or escort operates via phone, Internet or escorting agency, while the street prostitute, hustler, etc. operates in public spaces. "Private" provision of services is often assumed to be better, more high class, more expensive, while "public" sales of services is seen as more retail-like, lower quality, less "professional" and, thus, "lower-class."

Joseph R. G. DeMarco:

> It's my guess that the term "high class callboy/girl" may benefit both buyer and seller. It allows the buyer to see himself as doing something classy as opposed to wallowing in the sexual ghetto. It might benefit the seller in terms of what he can charge, who his clients will be, and where the "work" is done.

David Leary:

> It's about "spin": an attempt at advertising in a way that adds a gloss to the service and attracts a particular type of client. As with any spin, there is probably some reality to the advertising.

Jeffrey T. Parsons:

> I think people want to differentiate themselves from "street" based sex workers. There is a sense that a "high class" sex worker will be more "healthy" (e.g., not have HIV or STIs) and more attractive to clients and can command a better rate of pay.

David S. Bimbi:

> These words just make the consumer and the operator feel less "icky" about prostitution. These phrases distance themselves from the exploitation of prostitution, particularly street prostitution which tends to attract those in more dire circumstances. It is also a way of saying "I'm a pro. I'm safe. I won't rip you off."

Barry Johnston:

> Similar to the issue raised in question 2, the use of such classifications reflects a growing trend of labeling-up whereby bin-men become "waste disposal technicians" and window-cleaners become "professional daylight enhancers." But talk is cheap. Let's call a spade a spade and not a manual implement for the transferal of material. The psychological detachment fostered by such language games may serve a purpose but in attempting to come to a clearer understanding of these, and other social interactions, we must peel away the layers of spin; a process which, like removing make-up, may reveal something a lot less pretty beneath.

Rebecca L. Harriman

> There is a totem pole in every domain of life/work, sex work is no different.

CONCLUSION

The above responses are framed by personally held beliefs and experience and, though inevitably shaped by each contributor's prior research and study, it is hoped that the chapter will act as a counterpart to more academic and abstruse inquiry on the topic. The reader may think of this "discussion" as the literary parallel of conversations that take place at the reception following a symposium. Contributors' responses are, at times, honest, forthright, humorous, shocking, sad, brief, extensive, or a combination of the aforementioned. However, despite their variability, basic points of agreement emerge.

One commonality appears to be that all questions are best answered within the specific cultural and historical context of a given sexual transaction. Each contributor expresses caution against making any overarching generalizations that can be problematic if not downright futile. Even in this informal "conversation," respondents are reluctant to simplify their opinions or to disregard the complexities and nuances of the male sex industry. It is against this backdrop of social mores, power relationships, and personal histories that all discourse on sex work must be played out.

This explanatory balancing act is evident in the discussions on exploitation that surface throughout contributors' responses. There is broad agreement that sex work is neither inherently degrading nor exploitative. There are some who choose such a *career* and who take pride in the skills and services they provide but beyond this "idealized scenario" the opportunity for exploitation exists. Commentators point to inequalities of gender, race, and class but contend that exploitation is due to institutionalized discrimination against minorities and continued criminalization of sex work and is not intrinsically linked with the sale of sex per se. While some contributors argue that there is an ever-increasing and positive normalization of sex work in certain societies, others take a more pessimistic view arguing that this industry is continually and systematically "demonized."

Much of the insight given above can no doubt be found in numerous scholarly works already published. However, for myriad reasons, in academic writing some things are left unsaid. The burden of proof, the ideal of objectivity, and the need to appease funding agencies and editors can all conspire to muzzle even the most provocative of voices. Here contributors were encouraged to share thoughts that may not have been suitable in another milieu. There is also the danger that increasingly cerebral rhetoric and theorizing can become detached from the real world thus losing its relevance. Theory and practice can sometimes drift far apart and the meaning and utility of research can suffer. This forum, wherein contributors were asked to respond freely, allows the expression of opinions, some of which are informed by first-hand experiences in sex work. The value of articulating such opinions publicly and in a way that is accessible to the layperson is that it allows them to be criticized and revised to something that more accurately reflects the "truth." We hope that the content of this chapter has, in some small part, captured the complexity of male sex work and fostered thought and discussion in you, the reader.

Index

Actual self, 136
Addictions, 282
Adonis, Jason, 180
Adult Industry Medical (AIM) Health
    Care Foundation, 237
Adversity, adaptation to, 104
Aesthetic judgment, stripping and,
    130,137
African Americans, Club Atlantis and,
    158-161
Agency, presence of, 41-42,202-203
Alienation, 141
Alley, Andrew, 156
American Psychiatric Association
    (APA), 19
Amigos Siempre Amigos (ASA),
    245-246
Amsterdam, callboys in, 23-24
Anal douching, importance of, 185
Aristotle, 171
"Atlantis" (Auden), 154
Auden, W. H., 154,157,171
Authenticity
    gay tourist narratives of, 261-268
    search for, tourism and, 268-271
Avocational male sex workers, 21

Baltimore Eagle (bar), 165
Bar dancing, 114-115
Bar hustlers, 18,20
Barry, Rod, 179,181,190,192
Bars. *See* Gay strip clubs
Bathrooms, male street sex workers
    and, 52-53
Bijou Theater, Chicago, 287-288
Bimbi, David S., 3,4

on economic arrangements for
    sexual activity, 295
on exploitation in sex transactions,
    304
on paying for sex, 312
on payment for "prostitution" *vs.*
    "one-night stands," 307-308
on reasons people seek services of
    sex workers, 285
on status of sex workers, 316
on stigma of sex workers *vs.* clients,
    299
on use of term "sex work," 291
Bisexual male sex workers, 24
Bjorn, Kristen, 186-187,193
Black Gay, Lesbian, Bisexual and
    Transgendered Community
    Center, Baltimore, 160-161
Blake, Harper, 180
Boden, David M., 4
on economic arrangements for
    sexual activity, 294
on exploitation in sex transactions,
    301
on paying for sex, 311
on payment for "prostitution" *vs.*
    "one-night stands," 306
on reasons people seek services of
    sex workers, 282
on status of sex workers, 314
on stigma of sex workers *vs.* clients,
    297
on use of term "sex work," 288-289
Boundary transmutation, 141-143
Brandt, Billy, 193
Buck, Jim, 180
bugarrón, 242-243,246,269

© 2007 by The Haworth Press, Inc. All rights reserved.

defined, 247-248
Bulletin boards, 29
Business basics, male escorts and, 226-227
Byers, Dan, 179

Call book men, 22
  vs. hustlers, 23
Callboys, 18,20
  in Amsterdam, 24
  types of, 22-23
Canadian male sex workers, study of
  discussion of results for, 213-215
  methodology for, 204-207
  results for, 207-213
CASH. See Coalition Advocating Safe Hustling (CASH)
Charlie's (bar), Santo Domingo, Dominican Republic, 242-243
  Simon presiding over, 243-244
Chase Brexton Clinic, Baltimore, Maryland, 160
Chat rooms, 29
Class, male street sex workers and, 68
Classified Project, The, 222,223,238
Club Atlantis, Baltimore, 155-171
  African Americans and, 158-161
  Baltimore's gay neighborhood and, 165
  dancers at, 161-163
  doorchecks at, 159-160
  history and geography of, 155-156,163-165
  as hustler bar, 165-166
  Miss Oprah at, 160
  police harassment and, 167-168
  proximity to death row inmates and, 155,166-169
  racial politics and, 4,157-158
Club Bunns, Baltimore, 165,170
Coalition Advocating Safe Hustling (CASH), 27-28,237
Colbert, Gino, 19

Community norms, enforcement of, 63
Competition, among male dancers, 124
Conners, Chad, 191
Constructed self, 136
Control, male strippers and, 124
Conversation, capacity for, sex work and, 104
Coquettes, 18
Cressey, Paul, 186,195
Critias (Plato), 154,170
Cross-racial desire, stigma of, 169
Cyber fantasies, 194

Daddies, Western Union, 252-261
Dancers, male. See Male strippers
Delinquency paradigm, of male sex work, 9-10
Delinquents, male sex workers and, 19,20
Demachio, Talvin, 193
DeMarco, Joseph R. G., 4
  on exploitation in sex transactions, 303
  on payments to men for sexual services vs. men who are not, 309-310
  on reasons people seek services of sex workers, 283-284
  on status of sex workers, 315
  on use of term "sex work," 290
Deviance, strippers and, 132
Disease paradigm, of male sex work, 10
Dominican male sex workers. See also Male sex workers (MSWs)
  study of
    discussion of results for, 268-271
    methodology for, 245-248
    results of, 248-268
Dominican Republic
  gay sex tourism industry in, 4,244-245
  remittances to, 257-258

Donovan, Casey, 178
Donovan, Chad, 191
Douching, importance of, 185
Drag male sex workers, 20

Easton, Matt, 179-180
Emotional health, male escorts and, 233-235
Erotic masseurs, 22
Escoffier, Jeffrey, 4
  on economic arrangements for sexual activity, 295
  on exploitation in sex transactions, 303
  on paying for sex, 312
  on payment for "prostitution" *vs.* "one-night stands," 307
  on payments to men for sexual services *vs.* men who are not, 309
  on reasons people seek services of sex workers, 283
  on status of sex workers, 315
  on stigma of sex workers *vs.* clients, 298
  on use of term "sex work," 289
Escort agencies, 11
Escorting, 192. *See also* Internet escorts
  addiction of, 235-236
  fantasy and, 194
  porn stars and, 193-195
Escorts, 22. *See also* Internet escorts; Male escorts
Escort Web sites, 194-195
Exclusive contracts, 182
Exploitation, in sex transactions, 299-305

Falcon Studios, 175,181,184,189
Fantasy
  as component of escorting, 194

psychology of, 187
Fantasy potential
  effect of escorting on, 195
  of porn stars, 182,187-188
Flirters, 20
Follies Theatre, Washington, D.C., 287
Ford, Leo, 178
Forest, David, 179
Fourth wall, in sex work, 280-281

Galt, Jon, 188
Gay male sex workers, 24
  retrogressive dynamics and, 4
Gay male strippers, 146-147
Gay porn industry
  achieving orgasm and, 185
  research on, 175
Gay pornography
  as career, 182-186
  contemporary, 183-184
  early days of commercial, 183-184
  market for, 179
  performing in, 184
Gay porn stars, 22,182. *See also* Porn stars
  backgrounds of, 182-183
  developing persona of, 184-185
  as economic resource, 180
  escorting and, 192,193-195
  expanding sexual repertoire and, 190
  fantasy potential and, 182
  as human capital, 182
  importance of anal douching, 185
  labor markets for, 195-196
  overexposure and, 188-190
  persona of, 177-178
  popular icons, 178
  post-porn careers of, 189
  professional, 179
  retrogressive dynamic and, 186-190,190,195
  salaries of, 181
  as strippers, 191-192

training of, 185
Gay sex tourism industry, 4,269-270
Gay strip clubs, 4,112. *See also* Male
        strippers
    formats of, 119
    methodology for study of, 133-137
    performances in, 117
    power dynamics in, 113-116
    power of customers in, 122-124
    power struggles in, 116-117
    racial politics of, 4
    resources of male strippers in,
        117-118
    study of
        methodology for, 113
    types of dancing in, 114-115
Gay tourists, 242-243
Gilman, Charlotte Perkins, 295

Habitual male sex workers, 21
Harriman, Rebecca L., 5
    on economic arrangements for
        sexual activity, 295
    on paying for sex, 313
    on status of sex workers, 316
Hayes, Tanner, 180
Health care, male escorts and, 237
Health concerns, male escorts and,
        227-231
Heterosexuality, appearance of,
        147-148
Heterosexual male sex workers, 24.
        See also Straight male
        strippers
Heterosexual sex work, 15
Hippo (gay disco), Baltimore, 164
HIV
    emergence of, and shift to disease
        paradigm of male sex work,
        10,25-26
    research on male sex workers and
        transmission of, 221
Homosexuality, as mental illness
        paradigm, 11-12

HookOnline, 237
Humiliation, need to conceal, 66-67
Hustlers, 23
    bar, 18,20
    vs. call book men, 23
    periodic, 20-21
    permanent street, 20
    solitary, 21
    street, 18,20
    use of term, 9

Identities
    actual, 136
    virtual, 136
Idol, Ryan, 178,179,180
Internet
    advertising escort services on, 4
    male sex work and, 29-30
    as venue for male sex workers,
        220-221
Internet escorts. *See also* Male escorts;
        Male sex workers (MSWs)
    becoming addicted to being,
        235-236
    business basics for, 226-227
    getting started as, 225-226
    health and safety concerns of,
        227-231
    maintaining self worth and, 233-235
    personality and, 231-233
    study of needs of
        analytic strategy for, 224-225
        discussion of results, 236-238
        materials for, 224
        participants for, 222-223
        procedure for, 223-224
        results for, 225-236
Intervention strategies, for sex work, 104

Jackson, Jonathan David, 4
    on reasons people seek services of
        sex workers, 280-282

on use of term "sex work," 287-288
Jeffries, Doug, 191
Jerk-off shows, 287
Jocks, 135
Johnston, Barry, 5
    on status of sex workers, 316

Kaye, Kerwin, 3
    on economic arrangements for
        sexual activity, 293-294
    on use of term "sex work," 286
Kenny, Paula M., 4
    on exploitation in sex transactions,
        304-305
    on paying for sex, 313
Kept boys, 18,20
King, Jon, 178
Knight, Barry, 183
Koken, Juline A., 4

Lap dancing, 114
Larry Flynt Hustler Club, 166
Leary, David, 3
    on economic arrangements for
        sexual activity, 295
    on exploitation in sex transactions,
        303
    on paying for sex, 312
    on payment for "prostitution" *vs.*
        "one-night stands," 307
    on reasons people seek services of
        sex workers, 284
    on status of sex workers, 315
    on stigma of sex workers *vs.* clients,
        298-299
    on use of term "sex work," 290-291
Lee, Gypsy Rose, 131-132
Literature review of research
    of gay porn industry, 175
    on male sex industry, 2
    of male sex work, 10,76-78
    of male sex workers, 8-9,10-11,
        24,221

Live performance, 192,287-288
Lucas, George, 154
Lucas, Michael, 191

Macho types, 20
Male escorts, 4. *See also* Internet
        escorts; Male sex workers
        (MSWs)
    addiction of escorting and, 235-236
    business basics for, 226-227,237
    dealing with clients and, 237-238
    emotional health and, 233-235
    getting started as, 225-226
    health care and, 237
    health/safety concerns of, 227-231
    loneliness and, 234
    peer support and, 231
    personality and, 231-233
    role of, 11
    safe sex practices and, 236
    self-worth and, 233-234
Male physique, admiration of, 139
Male sex industry. *See also* Sex
        industry
    defined, 3
    difficulties doing research on, 1-2
    Internet and, 29-30
    literature review of, 2
    racial politics and, 158-159
Male sex work. *See also* Street-based
        male sex work (SMSW)
    agency and, 41-42
    delinquency paradigm of, 9-10
    early research on, 10
    literature review of, 76-78
    portrayals of, 39-41
    studies of, 38-39
Male sex workers (MSWs). *See also*
        Internet escorts; Male
        escorts; Male strippers
    avocational, 21
    classifications of, according
        self-reported motivations, 21
    condom use and, 29-30

delinquents and, 19
drag, 20
early research on, 8-9,24
effects of working in stigmatized
        industry and, 211-213
evaluating needs of, 221-222
first article on, 18
habitual, 21
heterosexual, 24
Internet and, 220-221
vs. men not paid for sexual services,
        308-310
paradigms for
    future, 29-30
    psychopathological, 11-17
    sex as work, 27-28
    typologic, 18-25
    as vectors of disease, 25-26
perception of stigma about sex
        work and, 203-204,207-211
research on, 10-11,221
situational, 21
study of Canadian, 204-215
    data collection, 206-207
    discussion of results of, 213-215
    participants, 204-206
    results of, 207-213
study of Dominican
    discussion of results for,
        268-271
    methodology for, 245-248
    results for, 248-268
types of, 18,23
as "vectors of HIV transmission,"
        221
vocational, 21
Male street sex workers
    case studies of
        Aaron, 43-45,50
        Don, 63-64
        Ernest, 49-51,55,58,62,65
        Jeremy, 46-47,50,55,63,67
        Kevin, 47-48,50,51-55,56,
            58,60,62
        Stephen, 45-46,50

    Timothy, 48-49,50,56
    class and, 68
    newcomers and, 56-57
    poverty and, 67-68
    role of social service institutions
        and, 68
    self-management of identity and,
        66-67
    space and material underpinnings
        of, 51-55
    street families and, 56-61
    types of, 41
    violence and, 61-65
Male strippers, 4. *See also* Gay strip
        clubs; Stripping
    aesthetic judgment in, 130,137
    "close-up" time and, 119-120
    competition among, 124
    constructing "personality" of, 137
    control and, 125
    customers and, 120
    deviance and, 132
    emotional services and, 131
    gay, 146-147
    literature on, 112-113
    occupation of, 130
    personal boundaries and, 141-143
    as post-porn careers, 191
    "product" of, 137,149
    psychological explanations for
        becoming, 131-133
    resources of, in strip clubs, 117-118
    sociological explanations for
        becoming, 131-133
    speculation of "real" sexuality of,
        140-141
    straight, 146-147
Manshots magazine, 175
Miguel, Dominican *bugarrón*, 248-252
Minichiello, Victor, 3
Miss Oprah, 160
Mitchell, Sharon, 237
Models, 22
Morin, Edgar, 176
Morrison, Todd G., 4

on economic arrangements for
　　sexual activity, 294
on exploitation in sex transactions,
　　300-301
on paying for sex, 310
on payment for "prostitution" *vs.*
　　"one-night stands," 305-306
on payments to men for sexual
　　services *vs.* men who are not,
　　308-309
on reasons people seek services of
　　sex workers, 279-280
on status of sex workers, 314
on stigma of sex workers *vs.* clients,
　　297
on use of term "sex work," 286
MSWs. *See* Male sex workers (MSWs)

Networking, male escorts and, 236-237
Newcomers, male street sex work and,
　　56-57
Nob Hill, San Francisco, 287
Norms, community, enforcement of, 63

Occasionals, 23
One-night stands, payment for, *vs.* sex
　　work, 306-308
Orgasm, gay porn stars and, 185
Overexposure, gay porn stars and,
　　188-190

Padilla, Mark B., 4
　　on economic arrangements for
　　　　sexual activity, 292
　　on exploitation in sex transactions,
　　　　299-300
　　on paying for sex, 310
　　on payment for "prostitution" *vs.*
　　　　"one-night stands," 305
　　on payments to men for sexual
　　　　services *vs.* men who are not,
　　　　308

on reasons people seek services of
　　sex workers, 279
on status of sex workers, 313
on stigma of sex workers *vs.* clients,
　　296
on use of term "sex work," 285-286
Paradigms, of male sex work
　　delinquency, 9-10
　　disease, 10
　　psychopathological, 11-17
　　sex as work, 10,27-28
Parker, Al, 178
Parsons, Jeffrey T., 4
　　on economic arrangements for
　　　　sexual activity, 295
　　on exploitation in sex transactions,
　　　　304
　　on paying for sex, 312
　　on payment for "prostitution" *vs.*
　　　　"one-night stands," 307
　　on reasons people seek services of
　　　　sex workers, 285
　　on status of sex workers, 316
　　on stigma of sex workers *vs.* clients,
　　　　299
　　on use of term "sex work," 291
Payment, for sex work *vs.* one-night
　　stands, 306-308
Peer support, male escorts and, 231
Periodic hustlers, 20-21
Permanent street hustlers, 20
Personality, 136,137
　　male escorts and, 231-233
Phillips, Dino, 180,184,191
Phoenix, Dean, 180
Plato, 154,157,170-171
Porn industry. *See* Sex industry
Porn stars. *See also* Gay porn stars
　　as human capital, 178
　　influence of Hollywood and, 177
　　persona of, 176-177
　　psycho-cultural dynamics of, 176
　　as workers, 177-178
Poverty, male street sex workers and,
　　38,67-68

Power
    of dancers *vs.* customers, 121-124
    defined, 114
    dynamics of, in strip clubs, 113-116
    methods of exercising, 116
    scare resources and, 116-120
Privacy invasion, concept of, 143-145
Produced self
    contextual determinants of, 138
    sexuality and, 138-148
Professional male sex workers, 21,23
Prostitutes. *See* Male sex workers
        (MSWs); Male street sex
        workers; Sex workers
Prostitution, abandonment of term, 9.
        See also Male sex work; Sex
        work
Pseudo-prostitutes, 19,23
Pyschopathological paradigm, of male
        sex workers, 11-17

Racial politics, at Club Atlantis,
        4,157-158
Ray, Aldo, 287
Reed, Logan, 180
Relationships, street-based male sex
        work and, 103-104
Remittances, to Dominican
        Republican, 253,257-258
Rent boys, 23. *See also* Hustlers
Resiliency, 104
Retrogressive dynamic, 4,190-191,195
    gay porn stars and, 186-190
    psychology of fantasy and, 187
Rogelio, Dominican *bugarrón,*
        252-253
Rough trade, 19
Rush, Matthew, 180,191
Ryker, Ken, 179,193

Safer sex practices, male escorts and,
        236

Safety concerns, male escorts and,
        227-231
Sanky panky, 246,248,269
    defined, 247
Schmoke, Kurt, 164
Self, 136. *See also* Produced self
Self-worth, 281
    male escorts and, 233-234
Sex, paying for, 310-313
"Sex as work" paradigm, of male sex
        work, 27-28
Sex educators, sex workers as, 228-229
Sex industry, 174. *See also* Male sex
        industry
    employment in, 175-176
    reasons for small number of studies
        of, 174-175
    revenues of, 175
    use of exclusives in, 181
Sex tourism, 271
    in Dominican Republican, 244-245
Sexual activity, private economic
        arrangements for, 291-295
Sexuality
    performance of, 136
    produced self and, 138-148
Sex work. *See also* Male sex work
    defined, 9,174,202
    fourth wall in, 280-281
    male sex workers and stigma about,
        203-204
    payment for, *vs.* "one-night stands,"
        306-308
    as performance, 281
    stigma of, 203
    vs. stripping, 192
    use of term, 285-291
Sex workers
    reasons people seek services of,
        279-285
    social stigma of, *vs.* clients,
        296-299
    status and, 313-316
Show Palace, New York City, 287
Shulman, Brian, 156

Silver Bullet (strip club), 134-135
  dancers at, 134-135
  patrons at, 135,135t
Situational male sex workers, 21
SMSW. *See* Street-based male sex
    work (SMSW)
Social service institutions, role of,
    male street sex workers and,
    68
Social stigma
  defined, 215n1
  gay and bisexual male social
    workers and, 17
  in heterosexual sex work, 15
  male sex workers and,
    203-204,207-211
  of sex work, 203
  of sex workers, *vs.* clients, 296-299
Solitary hustlers, 21
Sportsman (bar), Baltimore, 165
St. Cyr, Lili, 131-132
Stage dancing, 114
Stars (Morin), 176
*Star Wars Episode I: The Phantom
    Menace*, 154
Steele, Chris, 191
Stefano, Joey, 178
Sterling, Matt, 179,183-184,184
Stigma. *See* Social stigma
Straight male strippers, 146. *See also*
    Heterosexual male sex
    workers
Straight types, 20
Street-based male sex work (SMSW).
    See also Male sex work
  adaptation to adversity and, 104
  capacity for conversation and, 104
  initiation, 85-88
  interventions strategies for, 104
  methodology for studying, 78-79
  pathways out of, 97-103
  relating to scene, 88-97
  relational experiences prior to,
    80-85
  relationships and, 103-104

resiliency and, 104
Street-based prostitution, 3
Street families, 56-61
Street hustlers, 18,20
  permanent, 20
Street life, portrayals of, 39-40,65-66
Strip clubs. *See* Gay strip clubs
Strippers. *See* Male strippers
Stripping. *See also* Gay strip clubs;
    Male strippers
  explanations for entry into, 132-133
  vs. prostitution, 192
Stryker, Jeff, 178,179,180,183-184,
    188-189
Sugar-daddies, 54,60-61
Survival sex, 19,87-88
Syncopation (strip club), 134-135,135t
  dancers at, 134-135

Taxi dancers, retrogressive dynamic
    and, 186
Taylor, Colby, 191
Throwaways, young gay male sex
    workers as, 20
Timaeus (Plato), 154,170
Tipping, 191
  stripping and, 130-131
Top whores, 24
Tourism, search for authenticity and,
    268-269
Transmutation of feelings, 141
Travis, John, 179,183-184

Urban ethnography, sexuality and,
    38-39

Violence, male street sex workers and,
    38,61-65
Virtual self, 136
Vivid Studios, 175,180
Vocational male sex workers, 21
Vulnerability, need to conceal, 66-67

Wade, Travis, 180,189,191,192
Western Union daddies, 252-261
Whitehead, Bruce W., 4
    on exploitation in sex transactions,
        301-302
    on paying for sex, 311
    on payment for "prostitution" *vs.*
        "one-night stands," 306-307
    on payments to men for sexual
        services *vs.* men who are not,
        309

    on reasons people seek services of
        sex workers, 282-283
    on status of sex workers, 315
    on stigma of sex workers *vs.* clients,
        298
    on use of term "sex work," 289
Williams, John, 156
Working Men Project, 237

Young, Kurt, 179-180